international
review of
social history

Special Issue 19

The Joy and Pain of Work:
Global Attitudes and Valuations,
1500–1650

Edited by Karin Hofmeester and Christine Moll-Murata

CAMBRIDGE
UNIVERSITY PRESS

Shaftesbury Road, Cambridge CB2 8EA, United Kingdom

One Liberty Plaza, 20th Floor, New York, NY 10006, USA

477 Williamstown Road, Port Melbourne, VIC 3207, Australia

314–321, 3rd Floor, Plot 3, Splendor Forum, Jasola District Centre, New Delhi – 110025, India

103 Penang Road, #05–06/07, Visioncrest Commercial, Singapore 238467

Cambridge University Press is part of Cambridge University Press & Assessment, a department of the University of Cambridge.

We share the University's mission to contribute to society through the pursuit of education, learning and research at the highest international levels of excellence.

www.cambridge.org
Information on this title: www.cambridge.org/9781107609754

A catalogue record for this publication is available from the British Library

ISBN   978-1-107-60975-4   Paperback

CONTENTS

The Joy and Pain of Work: Global Attitudes and Valuations, 1500–1650

Edited by
Karin Hofmeester and Christine Moll-Murata

NOTES ON CONTRIBUTORS

Tarcisio R. Botelho, Department of History, Universidade Federal de Minas Gerais, Avenida Antônio Carlos, 6627, Belo Horizonte, MG, Brazil; e-mail: tbotelho@fafich.ufmg.br

Andrea Caracausi, Department of History, University of Padua, Via del Vescovado, 30, 35141 Padua, Italy; e-mail: andrea.caracausi@unipd.it

Raquel Gil Montero, Instituto Superior de Estudios Sociales, Consejo Nacional de Investigaciones Cientificas y Tecnologicas (CONICET-UNT), San Lorenzo 429, 4000 San Miguel de Tucumán, Argentina; e-mail: raquelgilmontero@conicet.gov.ar

Najaf Haider, Centre for Historical Studies, Jawaharlal Nehru University, New Delhi 110067, India; e-mail: snajafhaider@yahoo.co.in

Karin Hofmeester, Internationaal Instituut voor Sociale Geschiedenis, Cruquiusweg 31, 1019 AT Amsterdam, The Netherlands; e-mail: kho@iisg.nl

Marcel van der Linden, Internationaal Instituut voor Sociale Geschiedenis, Cruquiusweg 31, 1019 AT Amsterdam, The Netherlands; e-mail: mvl@iisg.nl

Henk Looijesteijn, Internationaal Instituut voor Sociale Geschiedenis, Cruquiusweg 31, 1019 AT Amsterdam, The Netherlands; e-mail: hlo@iisg.nl

Regine Mathias, Faculty of East Asian Studies, Ruhr-Universität Bochum, Universitätsstrasse 150, 44780 Bochum, Germany; e-mail: regine.mathias@rub.de

Luca Mocarelli, Departimento di Economia Politica, Università di Milano Bicocca, Edificio U6, Piazza dell'Ateneo Nuovo, 1, 20126 Milano, Italy; e-mail: luca.mocarelli@unimib.it

Christine Moll-Murata, Faculty of East Asian Studies, Ruhr-Universität Bochum, Universitätsstrasse 150, 44780 Bochum, Germany; e-mail: Christine.Moll-Murata@rub.de

Shireen Moosvi, Centre of Advanced Study in History, Aligarh Muslim University, Aligarh (UP), 202002 India; e-mail: shireen.moosvi@gmail.com

Ariadne Schmidt, Institute for History, Economic and Social History, Leiden University, PO Box 9515, 2300 RA Leiden, The Netherlands; e-mail: a.schmidt@hum.leidenuniv.nl

Arkadiy E. Tarasov, Faculty of History, Lomonosov Moscow State University, Lomonovsky Prospekt 27-4, Moscow 119992, Russia; e-mail: tarasov@histmsu.ru

Harriet T. Zurndorfer, Leiden University Institute for Area Studies (LIAS), Leiden University, PO Box 9515, 2300 RA Leiden, The Netherlands; e-mail: h.t.zurndorfer@hum.leidenuniv.nl

IRSH 56 (2011), Special Issue, pp. 1–23 doi:10.1017/S0020859011000460
© 2011 Internationaal Instituut voor Sociale Geschiedenis

The Joy and Pain of Work: Global Attitudes and Valuations, 1500–1650
Introduction*

KARIN HOFMEESTER

Internationaal Instituut voor Sociale Geschiedenis, Amsterdam

E-mail: kho@iisg.nl

CHRISTINE MOLL-MURATA

Ruhr-Universität Bochum

E-mail: Christine.Moll-Murata@ruhr-uni-bochum.de

We can safely assume that from 1500 to 1650 much of the world's population worked to earn their living. Though we know roughly what kind of tasks people performed, we know surprisingly little about their perception of work. This Special Issue aims to present the first inventory of its kind of prevailing attitudes towards work and of how work was valued in what is termed for some, but not all, parts of the world the early modern period. Our aim is inspired largely by a long-term project being conducted at the IISH: The Global Collaboratory on the History of Labour Relations, 1500–2000. That project endeavours to establish a quantitative overview of labour relations worldwide for the period 1500 to 2000. Within the framework of that

* A workshop on "Work: Ethics, Norms, Valuations, Ideologies, 1500-1650" was held in Düsseldorf in November 2009. The workshop was organized with the generous support of the Gerda Henkel Stiftung, the sponsor of the 1500–1650 segment of the Global Collaboratory. This volume contains the results of our endeavours. In addition to the authors of the contributions included in this collection, the participants in the Collaboratory project and the specialists in the field invited for this occasion were Josef Ehmer, who lectured on the social construction of work in the early modern period, Touraj Atabaki, with a presentation on "Work-Discipline in the Ottoman Empire/Turkey and Persia/Iran, 1800-1950", and Jun Seong-ho, who discussed "A Qualitative Aspect of Work Valuation in Confucian Korea, 1500–1650". Others who presented data were Jan Lucassen, José Miguel Lana Berasain, Jacques van Gerwen, Gijs Kessler, Dmitrij Khitrov, and Peter Förster; Erdem Kabadayı, Aad Blok, and Reza Jafari participated as observers. The editors express their thanks to the English language editor, Chris Gordon, and to the cartographer, Annelieke Vries-Baaijens, for their committed and reliable work on the articles presented here.

project the members of the Collaboratory collect data on labour relations for the years 1500, 1650, 1800, 1900, and 2000, thereby enabling shifts in labour relations to be identified. Those shifts and their interconnectedness will subsequently be analysed and explained.

The early cross-section years – 1500 and 1650 – are part of a crucial period in which a polycentric world became globally interlinked by large-scale circulations of people, ideas, and commodities. Since demographic and occupational statistics for these years are based chiefly on rough estimates, a more qualitative approach to attitudes towards work and the valuation of work in these periods is important for interpreting and understanding the statistical data and estimates collated. These attitudes and valuations differed from region to region and changed over time; such changes point to shifts in labour relations globally.

WORK AND ITS PERCEPTIONS IN HISTORIOGRAPHY

In their recent volume *The Idea of Work in Europe from Antiquity to Modern Times*, the editors Catharina Lis and Josef Ehmer observe that little systematic work has been carried out on the development of work ethics in pre-industrial Europe. As a consequence, a standard narrative – leaning heavily on Max Weber – of a linear development, from a work ethic based on sixteenth-century Christian values to a work ethic rooted in capitalist culture and directed towards success, remains largely undisputed.[1] Such a perspective not only neglects variant views on work in earlier periods, it also lacks a differentiated linear narrative, which, moreover, remains too narrowly focused on the perspective of the "Rise of the West". In a critical overview of the literature on the influence of Christian religion on work ethics, Lis and Ehmer explain that the idea of a distinct shift from the sixteenth century onward is misleading. They stress the continuity of religious attitudes to work in both Catholicism and Protestantism, implying on the one hand that work meant pain and toil in succession to Christ's suffering, and on the other that manual work meant serving God and one's community and was thus to be valued.[2]

Since the late Middle Ages, labour discourse became influenced by political and social theories. The debate was no longer confined to monastic scholars, but was taken up by larger social groups. Lis and Ehmer explain the reasons for this intensification of the discourse and the greater esteem attributed to work largely in terms of socio-economic change.[3] They claim

---

1. Catharina Lis and Josef Ehmer, "Introduction: Historical Studies in Perceptions of Work", in Josef Ehmer and Catharina Lis (eds), *The Idea of Work in Europe from Antiquity to Modern Times* (Farnham, 2009), pp. 1–30, 5–6, 8, and 9.
2. *Ibid.*, p. 16.
3. *Ibid.*, p. 18.

that an increase in wage labour led to an increase in labour discourse.[4] Lis and Ehmer argue that the next major shift occurred in the seventeenth and eighteenth centuries, when the discourse on labour was disseminated even more widely and became influenced by philosophers.[5] Work was now considered "work for the nation", forming the foundation of "national wealth". In central Europe this was understood to mean working for the state.[6]

For the purpose of the Global Collaboratory, the explanation of the connection between shifts in labour relations on the one hand and shifts in perceptions of work on the other is fundamental, and it is for this reason that the authors of this volume owe much in the way of inspiration to the book edited by Ehmer and Lis. Other influential studies on the concept of work in European conceptual history can be traced to the impressive pioneering work of Herbert Applebaum, *The Concept of Work: Ancient, Medieval, and Modern* (Albany, NY, 1992), which described and analysed trends and tendencies from antiquity to the industrial age.

In an earlier publication, the same author had already addressed the subject of work from an anthropological perspective. His edited volume, *Work in Non-Market and Transitional Societies* collected essays on work organization among hunters and gatherers in pastoralist societies, among cultivators and gardeners in villages, and in cultures and societies where non-market and market-oriented work values underwent change and adaptation. These studies discuss mostly contemporary, non-European cases. In his categorization of work in non-market societies, Applebaum defines work as embedded in the total cultural fabric, with strong communal aspects that involve mutuality and reciprocal exchange, aimed mostly at subsistence; furthermore, that work was not highly specialized, and was task-oriented rather than time-oriented.[7] The transition from non-market to market societies is important in this project as well, and many of the qualifications Applebaum made for the present can be found in our contributions, especially the changing role of reciprocity, the shift from task to time orientation, and the changing relationships between women's work and men's work.

While Applebaum treated Europe and many non-European regions and communities separately, other historians have focused on both. Michel Cartier's edited volume *Le Travail et ses représentations* stands in the tradition of Maurice Godelier,[8] which has a strong anthropological and linguistic focus. The case studies in Cartier's volume discuss extra-European communities

---

4. *Ibid.*
5. *Ibid.*, p. 19.
6. *Ibid.*, p. 20.
7. Herbert Applebaum, "Theoretical Introduction", in *idem* (ed.), *Work in Non-Market and Transitional Societies* (Buffalo, NY, 1984), p. 2.
8. Lis and Ehmer, "Introduction", p. 6, give an outline of Godelier's initiative *History Workshop Journal*, founded in 1980.

from the eighteenth century to the present, with the exception of the editor's own field of research, China, for which he offered a perspective on work in antiquity.[9]

More recently, Jürgen Kocka and Manfred Bierwisch have separately edited collections of articles on the history of work.[10] Both share a concern with contemporary changes in work, the decrease in the dominance of wage labour, and the diminished long-term commitment on the part of employers. Both collections link up to periods when dependent wage labour was not the norm, and they also look to extra-European regions for patterns of work organization that diverged from the western European case. They do so for reasons of contrast in a situation where the West is in crisis rather than in the ascendant. As for the European historical experience, both continue to convey the standard narrative. In their introduction, Jürgen Kocka and Claus Offe stress various factors that promoted the rise of capitalism: Christianity, especially Protestant work ethics, the discipline imposed on urban citizens, and the philosophy of the Enlightenment.[11] The non-European cases they present, from India, Japan, Malaya, Africa, and the Islamic world, cover mostly the present and can also be understood as contrasting with the European, or to be more precise, the German case.

The intention of these volumes is to explain the current occupational crisis in Europe and to offer suggestions for "therapy",[12] or to propose a new orientation for the relationship between work and life.[13] Bierwisch's collection does not intend to provide new details, but to offer overviews of work in European antiquity, work organization in twentieth-century industrial Russia and its rural roots, conceptual aspects of work in China from antiquity to the present, work in Islam, and a case study of conceptions of work in a present-day African rural community.[14]

As Lis and Ehmer have remarked, until now there has been no systematic treatment of perceptions of labour,[15] which makes comparison over time and space a complicated and risky undertaking. In view of this state of the field,

9. Michel Cartier, "Travail et idéologie dans la China antique", in *idem* (ed.), *Le Travail et ses représentations* (Paris, 1984), pp. 275–304.

10. Jürgen Kocka and Claus Offe (eds), *Geschichte und Zukunft der Arbeit* (Frankfurt, 2000); Manfred Bierwisch (ed.), *Die Rolle der Arbeit in verschiedenen Epochen und Kulturen* (Berlin, 2003).

11. Jürgen Kocka and Claus Offe, in *idem, Geschichte und Zukunft der Arbeit*, p. 20.

12. *Idem, Geschichte und Zukunft der Arbeit*, section "Beschäftigungskrise in Europa: Konkurrierende Erklärungen und Therapieangebote".

13. Manfred Bierwisch, "Arbeit in verschiedenen Epochen und Kulturen – Einleitende Bemerkungen", in *idem, Die Rolle der Arbeit*, p. 16.

14. Georg Elwert, "Wissen, Freude und Schmerzen. Über Arbeit in einer afrikanischen Gesellschaft", in Bierwisch, *Die Rolle der Arbeit*, pp. 153–172. Elwert presents the same thought-provoking case in "Jede Arbeit hat ihr Alter. Arbeit in einer afrikanischen Gesellschaft", in Kocka and Offe, *Geschichte und Zukunft der Arbeit*, pp. 175–193.

15. Lis and Ehmer, "Introduction", p. 6.

the Global Collaboratory on the History of Labour Relations has aimed at synchronic observation in order to achieve a more coherent approach.

A NEW CONCEPTUALIZATION OF GLOBAL LABOUR RELATIONS

In the past decade a new and global approach to labour history has been developed, stressing the global development of labour and labour relations over a long time span. Global labour history as developed by the IISH is not a theory but a field of research. It concerns the history of all those people who, through their work, have built our modern world – not only wage labourers, but also chattel slaves, sharecroppers, housewives, the self-employed, and many other groups. It focuses on the labour relations of these people, as individuals but also as members of households, networks, and other contexts. Global labour history covers the past five centuries and, in principle, all continents. It compares developments in several parts of the world and attempts to reveal intercontinental connections and interactions.

To capture labour relations worldwide over a period of five centuries, labour needs to be defined broadly. Following Tilly and Tilly's definition,[16] the Global Collaboratory project considers as work "any human activities adding use value to goods and services". This is a far more encompassing concept than the "gainful workers" or "economically active" that appear in the statistics of later eras, mostly starting from the nineteenth century, but compiled mainly for the twentieth. It takes account of the unpaid, mostly household-based labour of more or less all family members, including women and children, who are physically able to work. It also comprises all types of labour relations, from slavery to independent entrepreneurship and everything in between.

To systematize our approach, the members of the Collaboratory have developed a taxonomy of labour relations, based on four large categories: the non-working population and people either performing reciprocal, tributary, or commodified labour. These main categories focus on the target unit for what workers produce (be it goods or services); this can be either the household or community, the state or the market. In principle, we can classify the entire population using these main categories, which are sub-divided into categories based on the level of dependency and degree of freedom, or lack of it. Any classification must of course leave room for intermediary stages and combinations of labour relations. (For our taxonomy of labour relations see Figure 1; for the definitions see Appendix.)

For a number of regions, sources of information are available on the labour relations of at least part of the population in the early period,

---

16. Chris Tilly and Charles Tilly, *Work under Capitalism* (Boulder, CO, 1998), p. 22.

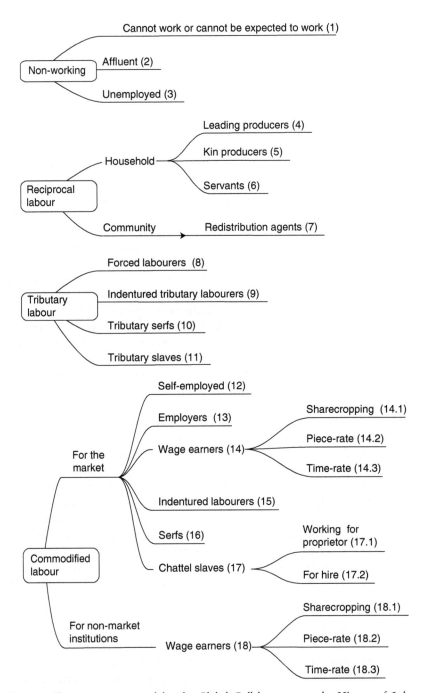

Figure 1. Taxonomy constructed by the Global Collaboratory on the History of Labour Relations. See Appendix for detailed descriptions.

1500–1650. However, our extrapolations and guestimates need to be confirmed by qualitative data. Knowing how people valued different types of work and labour relations helps us to interpret the scarce numeric data. In our search for perceptions of work, we wanted to look specifically at the concepts of work held by the majority of people, most of whom in the period 1500–1650 were working in agriculture, housekeeping, or subsistence labour but who have not left any written traces. This proved to be very difficult, as there are few sources that yield information about the perceptions of the workers themselves, and those that do exist are hard to date. However, the work people actually performed can tell us something about their valuation of work. If images depict working women and children even though normative texts disapprove of such work, we can assume that women worked if it was opportune and necessary to do so.

PERSPECTIVES ON WORK ETHICS, NORMS, VALUATIONS, AND IDEOLOGIES

To further systematize our approach, we introduced a set of seven perspectives to describe and analyse early modern work ethics. First, we asked the authors to identify texts or other expressions and traditions that deal with work ethics, norms, and valuations. Secondly, we wondered whether changes over time in the appreciation or disdain of work could be reflected in socio-linguistic perspectives. What terms and concepts were associated with "work" and "worker"? Thirdly, the authors were asked to ponder the question of the position of work and worker in society. In particular, how was wage labour as a kind of commodified labour perceived in comparison with other labour relations? A fourth set of questions concerns free and unfree labour. It is included in the taxonomy but transcends the four main categories since it occurs in reciprocal household labour, in tributary labour for states and polities, and in market-based, commodified labour. One important perspective is therefore the valuation of free labour and the legitimation of unfree labour. The fifth issue relates to the motives behind the rankings of particular occupations. Criteria on the negative side include the physical strain, or risks to life and health, associated with a specific occupation, or the connection with death and decay. On the positive side are particular skills (in part a social construction) or other qualifications, the income generated by the occupation, and its connection with luxury production. The sixth question relates to who was allowed to do what work. What can we discover about divisions of labour relating to gender and age, to ethnic and religious affiliations, or to belonging to particular families, lineages, or voluntary associations, such as guilds? The seventh and final question concerns ideas about and approaches to realizing a "just" wage or other forms of remuneration.

WORK ETHICS IN THE WORLD, 1500–1650

In the history of norms and perceptions, 150 years may seem a short period, and we have often been asked why a period was chosen for our project's inception in which acute change and expansionist activity can be found in western Europe while other regions might appear to have been more static or passive. Different timeframes might be more meaningful for other world regions. Nevertheless, being based in western Europe, we consider it legitimate to start "digging where we stand", fully aware that different cognitive maps are centred on other parts of the world and the periodicity of their rise to economic prosperity. A consideration of these differing timeframes must, indeed, form an integral part of this globally comparative exercise.

The first contribution to this volume, "Studying Attitudes to Work, Worldwide, 1500–1650: Concepts, Sources, and Problems of Interpretation" by Marcel van der Linden, sets the Global Collaboratory's approach in a broader methodological perspective that transcends the parts of the world and periods covered elsewhere by the other contributors to this volume. It deliberates on concepts of work, work incentives, and work attitudes, explores possible source types and their problems, and identifies problems of interpretation. These may include the researcher's projections of his or her expectations on to the available sources, or in false generalizations. The remedy for such problems is careful source criticism, critical self-reflection, and the contextualization of the observations made.

The subsequent contributions are geographically ordered. We set out from the Netherlands, turning south and east, before finally arriving in Portuguese and Spanish America.

The essay by Ariadne Schmidt, "Labour Ideologies and Women in the Northern Netherlands, c.1500–1800", discusses the meanings of work in Protestant, humanist, mercantilist, and Enlightenment thought as reflected in books on conduct and household management. She concludes that in all of these philosophies, labour was held in high esteem. Paintings and conduct books of the period 1500–1650 present women working in the public sphere, as vendors and artisans for example, as unproblematic, though some of the conduct books emphasized that women should work at home.

Henk Looijesteijn's essay "Between Sin and Salvation: The Seventeenth-Century Dutch Artisan Pieter Plockhoy and his Ethics of Work" analyses the philosophy of one individual seventeenth-century thinker. Plockhoy (c.1620–1664) conceived of a work and life balance in which everybody should work. Idleness was a sin, but work should leave enough free time for spiritual obligations. His ideal was a community engaged in reciprocal labour, producing surplus for the market in the outside world. Wage labour for the market was to be avoided.

In "Attitudes to Work and Commerce in the Late Italian Renaissance" Luca Mocarelli compares two important late sixteenth-century writings that discuss the occupations in Italian cities. Garzoni, an Augustinian monk, presents a scholarly study of urban occupations, in a work presumably intended as a manual of instruction for a prince. Urban aristocrats at that time were contemptuous of merchants, and we find criticism of merchants in Garzoni's work. Fioravanti, the other author, was a gifted physician who led a restless life of travel and adventure and had probably seen with his own eyes much of what he described in his book. His intention, clearly, was to dignify all the various types of craft and trade he had observed, without ranking them as "noble" or "ignoble" as Garzoni does.

About fifty years later, by which time rural and urban proto-industry had spread, merchant-manufacturers emerged and wage labour in the manufacturing sector gained in importance. In "The Just Wage in Early Modern Italy" Andrea Caracausi shows that, at this point, a first systematic attempt was made by Lanfranco Zacchia, a Roman jurist, to establish legal norms on differentiated wage payment and other forms of remuneration. Caracausi then compares the norms with the labour disputes also recorded by Zacchia. The need for codification demonstrated the importance and the frequency of such disputes.

In an essay on Russia, "The Religious Aspect of Labour Ethics in Medieval and Early Modern Russia", Arkadiy Tarasov discusses the impact of Orthodox Christianity on work ethics. As early as the second half of the fourteenth century, a process of monastic colonization commenced. The Russian Empire expanded far to the north and the east as the khanates of the Mongolian Golden Horde and their successors declined and disintegrated. The monasteries played a large role in the dissemination of Russian culture and the Orthodox religion. The author stresses that although the representatives of the Orthodox Church insisted on the importance of work, it was never considered an aim in itself, intended for economic success, as was the case in Catholic monasteries in western Europe. Instead, work was intended to advance spiritual development, and thus had a pedagogical rather than an economic function. This can also be seen in the *Domostroi*, a rule book which intended to set out the principles of household management for prosperous urban families. It was compiled in the fifteenth and sixteenth centuries and continued to enjoy a wide circulation well into the nineteenth century.

Karin Hofmeester's contribution, "Jewish Ethics and Women's Work in the Late Medieval and Early Modern Arab-Islamic World", presents religious ideals as the basis of work norms, a gendered division of labour, and social ranking, with special reference to Cairo between the thirteenth and seventeenth centuries. Paying special attention to the difference between text and social practice, she contrasts normative writings with legal documents for more immediate use, such as marriage contracts, court records on divorce, and wills. The picture that emerges is one in which all women were expected to work and have an income, also – at least in the ideal case – to allow their husbands some free time for contemplation and the study of religious texts. However, female activity had to be reconciled with the concept of *zniut*, or female modesty and restraint, which implied that women should have little contact with men and the outside world, and not leave their homes too often. Hofmeester argues that urbanization and the commercial revolution in the Arab-Islamic world led to the rise of waged work, and work opportunities at homes increased, especially as the textile sector flourished.

Shireen Moosvi's "The World of Labour in Mughal India (c.1500–1750)" first introduces the dominant types of labour relations, stating that commodified labour was fairly common in urban settings. Drawing on a variety of sources, this study stresses the importance of an official account of the Mughal Empire, the *A'in-i Akbari* by Abu'l-Fazl (c.1595). This record, while acknowledging the usefulness of manual workers and peasants, nonetheless transmitted a sense of superiority towards them. The Mughal emperor Akbar (reigned 1556–1605) was a famous exception to that rule, being purported not only to have valued manual labour highly but also to have personally undertaken several kinds of physical labour. In this contribution, we also find an approach to the actual voices of workers. The author presents them in the form of the religious songs composed by a group of manual workers (cloth-dyers, weavers, and peasants) referred to as monotheists. They rejected both Islam and Hinduism and in their lyrics insisted on the dignity of their professions.

Focusing on one occupational group within the Mughal Empire, in his article "Norms of Professional Excellence and Good Conduct in Accountancy Manuals of the Mughal Empire", Najaf Haider analyses one specific type of source. Accountancy manuals were written by practitioners and conveyed a particular set of work ethics. Addressing the question of the division of labour and the entitlement to specific professions, the author explains that the change of language, calendar, and accounting system which the Mughal conquest engendered confronted Hindu clerks with competition from Muslim specialists. With the help of these handbooks, in the course of time Hindus too obtained the knowledge required to serve in the Mughal bureaucracy. This is reflected in the fact that the strict moral norms for this profession incorporated references to both Hindu and Muslim religious rituals and concepts.

Christine Moll-Murata's article, "Work Ethics and Work Valuations in a Period of Commercialization: Ming China, 1500–1644", gives an overview of work ethics and how work was valued in another large centralized empire. The traditional classification of the ruler's subjects referred to scholar-officials, farmers, artisans, and merchants. The attitude of the official elite towards merchants was ambivalent, because merchants were establishing commercial networks that caused a mobility that seemed to threaten the existing social order.

The voices of the great majority who worked in reciprocal and sub-sistence rural labour relations are heard much more rarely, though, and need to be detected using indirect evidence. Lyrics and songs that can be confidently dated to the period under observation are descriptive rather than self-expression. They concern mainly the urban trades and show great diversification.

In her essay "Prostitutes and Courtesans in the Confucian Moral Universe of Late Ming China (1550–1644)", Harriet Zurndorfer demon-strates a shift in the value attached to the work of prostitutes and courtesans during the last 100 years of the Ming dynasty and the transition to the Manchu Qing. This shift affected the high-class courtesans rather than the lower-class prostitutes who worked in cheap brothels and remained in socially and legally more marginal circumstances. The courtesans were more highly esteemed during the late Ming period. As the philosophical ideas of the Confucian philosopher Wang Yangming took root, the idea of individual self-cultivation and free expression of one's emotions spread among the urban literati. The courtesans and their clients could regard themselves as enacting freedom, independence, and bravely overcoming the conventional boundaries between the private and the public. This so-called "cult of the *qing*" (true feeling) gained popularity also among gentry women, who lived a secluded existence in their homes.

Turning to Japan, Regine Mathias portrays a rural society that experienced a change from predominantly reciprocal and tributary labour relations to the beginnings of commodified labour. In "Japan in the Seventeenth Century: Labour Relations and Work Ethics", the author discusses the largely unsuccessful attempts of the new political system to curb mobility and flexibility. Confucian scholars of the "School of the Heart" propagated ideas of the worthiness and equal value of all occupational "callings", even of the merchants. The concept of the "four occupational groups" had been adopted from China, but it was less firmly rooted in Japan. Therefore, and because of the different relationships between the commercial sector and the bureau-cracy, the enhancement of the merchants' role was less problematic. Mathias also evaluates the contribution of women to rural proto-industrial activity. These were most considerable in textile production. Women were not expected to remain at home; they worked in the fields alongside the male members of their families.

The last group of articles in this volume treats labour relations and work ethics in colonial settings in South America and the imposition of unfree labour on Amerindian and Afro-American people. The essay by Tarcisio Botelho, "Labour Ideologies and Labour Relations in Colonial Portuguese America, 1500–1700", discusses the justification for the dominant labour relation in the Brazilian sugar mills, the unfree com-modified labour forced upon the Afro-American slaves. The author sets the ranking of occupations into the context of the medieval three estates

that applied in Portugal in the fifteenth century. The notions of the tripartite European system of "those who pray", "those who fight", and
"those who labour" were at the root of Brazilian slavery, since the masters
of the sugar mills conceived of themselves as belonging to the nobler
classes, who were not expected to do manual work. In their sermons to
the African slaves in Brazil, the Jesuit missionaries argued that the slaves
were being held in captivity in order to save their souls, and their suffering
was likened to the passion of Christ and defined as a punishment for the
original sin of mankind.

The second essay on South America, "Free and Unfree Labour in the
Colonial Andes in the Sixteenth and Seventeenth Centuries" by Raquel
Gil Montero, enquires into the nature of a particular kind of tributary
labour relation inflicted upon the native population living in the vicinity
of Potosí, in present-day Bolivia, where large silver mines were being
operated. It has been argued by historians of Latin America that the
forced-labour obligations, the so-called *mita*, were a kind of voluntary
unfree labour. Closer analysis of colonial statistics and contemporary
reports reveals that some of the labourers were in fact going to the mines
voluntarily, in spite of the harsh working conditions there. While some of
the natives were obliged to render service, others could pay monetary
tribute. The wages for free labour were higher, and hence the tributes
could be paid off sooner by working in the mines voluntarily. The Potosí
mita thus created a kind of dual system, where tributary and commodified
labour relations existed side by side.

GLOBAL CONJUNCTIONS AND DIFFERENCES

Between 1500 and 1650 most of the world's population were unaware of
the existence of other countries, let alone continents; nor could they
comprehend whether, or how, events abroad influenced their own life and
work. For some, however, being linked to a commercial circuit became an
experience that profoundly affected their existence.

In the period 1500–1650, European naval powers expanded eastward
and westward. Dutch and British ships arrived on North American shores
and those lands were settled, while the Portuguese and Spanish mon-
archies declared parts of South and Central America their colonies. The
relationship of those colonies to Europe, from where powerful groups
tried to transpose their values and work ethics on to the South American
territories, becomes clear not only in the essays on Brazil and Potosí but
also in that on Plockhoy, the Dutch practical visionary whose North
American settlement formed a testing ground for ideas on work developed earlier in the Netherlands, England, and Ireland.

Early modern Europe was bound in a multitude of ways to the Mediterranean. Important for our context are the connections between the

Spanish *Reconquista*, the Inquisition, and the exodus of Jews from Spain to other parts of Europe and the southern Mediterranean, including Cairo.

Further east, the conjunctions are also evident. By the thirteenth century, the Mongols had conquered and were ruling an enormous empire. As Mongol rule disintegrated, the Russian Tsars extended their territory in the second half of the sixteenth century to include Siberia. One descendant of the Timurid Mongolians struck out southward and conquered India. Still further east, the Ming dynasty had forced the last emperor of the Mongol Yuan dynasty to flee north, but the Mongol threat persisted throughout the Ming. Japan remained unaffected by direct Mongolian influence, but the circle closes when we consider the eastern expansion of the Portuguese and Dutch East India companies, which reached India, China, and Japan in the sixteenth century. Some of the articles in this volume show how labour systems and work ethics were affected as ideas and commodities travelled along those routes. It is in this global and spatial setting that the articles investigate the layers and perspectives of work ethics and valuation of work.

The sources for our historical enquiries are texts, and to a certain extent images too. The most desirable and straightforward type of text for analysing the voices of those who actually worked, their self-valuations, and their attitude towards their work, would seem to be autobiographical ego documents. However, such documents are completely lacking in our samples. In fact, even for European regions where they do exist, they often do not express attitudes towards work. By way of explanation, James S. Amelang argues that "self-writing was a practice different from, and even alien to work", a contention that accords with James Farr's observation that "early modern artisans were indifferent or even hostile to work".[17] In the samples of workers' voices we have in this volume, the Indian weaver's song and the Indian handbook written by clerks for clerks, the former stands in close relation to the religious elevation of work, and thus "lifts the curse" by likening craftwork with divine creation. The other tells professionals the secrets of the trade, and advises them on how to behave in private life. It is thus normative rather than descriptive.

In sum, for several reasons the voice of workers is difficult to discern for periods when work was not yet an isolated feature for all or most people. The case of the utopian thinker, Plockhoy, is special since he, as an artisan, still tried to set norms rather than describe actual conditions. Yet, implicitly, his work contrasts the situation in his utopian society with actual labour relations, showing how Plockhoy despised the position of wage workers outside his society. The other articles also give us hints.

---

17. James S. Amelang, "Lifting the Curse: or Why Early Modern Worker Autobiographers Did Not Write about Work", in Ehmer and Lis, *The Idea of Work*, pp. 91–100, 97.

Even though work songs from China and Japan are difficult to date, they still tell us something about the valuation of physical labour. The Jewish women in late medieval Cairo who went to the Islamic court to fight for the right to keep their own earnings demonstrate that many Jewish women worked for an income, that they valued this, and regarded it as their property.

This meant that, if possible, people made deliberate choices, and these reflect their valuation of work. The article by Raquel Gil Montero suggests that people sometimes opted for harsh working conditions in the mines, performing free, monetized labour in order to pay off tributes, rather than rendering labour service. The Chinese upper-class ladies who copied the lifestyle of courtesans show how the ladies of high society valued a position of freedom and independence. The Italian men, women, and children who went to court to sue for "just wages" not only prove that wage labour had become a widespread, institutionalized, and accepted form of labour in Renaissance Italy, their litigation also demonstrates that workers regarded their labour as subject to an inviolable contract between worker and employer.

Texts created by secular or clerical authorities are obvious sources of information on work ethics and on how work was valued; thus legal or religious norms and regulations can be found for most of the regions studied. Apart from canonical texts, we find in all societies conduct books for cloisters, households, ideal societies such as Plockhoy's, real societies such as Italian cities, and greater regions and spheres of power, such as empires.

Rather than describing the actual situation, they represent model situations. These texts were often written in periods of change and dictated rules of work that were not, or no longer, in accordance with social practice. Examples include the development of market economies and the role of the merchant class, so detested by Plockhoy, Zacchia, and others, and suspected by Chinese officials such as Zhang Han; the proliferation of free wage labour, which Garzoni would have preferred to ban; and the increase in women's work outside the home, of which different types of Dutch conduct books as well as rabbinical writings did not approve. Sometimes, those texts were intended to provide proper guidelines for the new situation, such as Fioravanti's rules on proper wages, or to inform the public or administrators of new work specializations, such as the Chinese and Japanese agricultural handbooks which also commented on the gendered division of labour. Directly or indirectly, they reflected the actual situation and tried to set norms for achieving an ideal situation.

Since Le Goff, historians of work have paid particular attention to the time factor in changes of work organization. In many of the societies described here, wage labour increased, and it was formalized in contracts, in which time played an important role. However, in the cases presented here, time is not always mentioned in relation to work contracts. Also, Dutch household management books show that reciprocal work and unfree labour within the household continued. The standard contract for the sale of daughters in the Chinese household encyclopaedia does not mention a period of commitment, and the rules in the Russian *Domostroi* suggest that the lady of the house should always be ready to give orders to her servants and be prepared to work herself. Apparently, texts not only described ideal situations in response to changing labour relations, they also signalled continuities, such as the never-ending phenomenon of non-wage labour, which was often performed by women.

Concerning the expression of work and the value attributed to it, in almost all the societies treated in this volume we found texts that valorized "work". Often "work" was esteemed as an abstract concept, as opposed to idleness. Female idleness seemed particularly harmful. The terms *labor/labour/lavoro*, *Arbeit*, *travail/trabalho* in the European context, but also *lao/rō* in China and Japan, were associated with "pain" until the early modern period. In Indo-Persian, this conjunction can also be found in the common designation for labour, the Persian words *mahnat* (literally "pain") and *ranj* (literally "grief, pain, toil").[18] Since Max Weber, the idea that in the sixteenth century work was not only divine retribution for the original sin of mankind, but also a divine "calling", has often been pointed out. Likewise, in Japanese, a seventeenth-century term for work also implies "heavenly calling" (*tenshoku*). However, if work was held in higher esteem from 1500 onward – some scholars stress a continuity that included the period prior to 1500 – did this also imply that it was a "joy", and that the accumulation of recompense for work, which Max Weber ascribed to the "Protestant ethic", was an ultimate goal?[19]

The articles in this volume do not give a consonant answer to this question. Work in the Brazilian sugar mills needed to be justified by reference to the original sin of mankind, and other oppressive work conditions – that stressed the pain rather than the joy of work – are discussed in this volume. The occupational specializations analysed in works such as those by Garzoni and Fioravanti, or in Chen Duo's songs on urban occupations, which might potentially express the joy of work, could have been due to the interest and pride of the elites or middling classes in an affluent and sophisticated environment. The attractive features of the rice-planting women in Japanese fields were praised in an agricultural treatise. This is the onlookers' perspective, which may have been joyful and entertaining. Some of the images of people at work in this volume were designed to satisfy this interest or to suggest joy in the work of others and to convey the message of harmonious labour relations.

Many religions promise metaphysical rewards for a life of hard work and punishment for a life spent in idleness, or, as in the Christian case, claim

18. This was pointed out by Shireen Moosvi in her presentation at the workshop.
19. See the contribution by Marcel van der Linden in this volume, and Lis and Ehmer, "Introduction", p. 16, for a discussion of 1500 as a turning point, and p. 17 for a critique of Max Weber's thesis of the connection between the Protestant work ethic and the "spirit of capitalism".

that the strain of work was the redemption for man's original sin. However, all religious ethical systems also insist on the importance of spiritual engagement, and demand that sufficient time be reserved for contemplation in everyday life. Between 1500 and 1650, activity and contemplation formed an indissoluble bond, as far as the religious authorities studied in this volume – Christian (Protestant, Catholic, Orthodox), Jewish, Muslim, Indian monotheist, Confucian, and Buddhist – are concerned. The time spent on non-working activities (i.e. on not adding use value to goods and services) was, from these religious perspectives, at least as joyful as the time spent on work, though often this was not made explicit.

In many of the regions discussed in this Special Issue, we see the consequences of rapidly developing transcontinental markets, including urbanization and the development of free wage labour. In the Dutch Republic and the cities of Italy and China we see a shift from combined reciprocal and self-employed artisan labour to more commodified labour. The contributions also demonstrate shifts from slave labour (Arab-Islamic north Africa), serfdom, and indentured labour (Japan) to free wage labour. In India commodified labour seems to have already been widespread by the end of the sixteenth century, so here the major shift might have taken place before 1500.

The growing extent of free wage labour in western Europe and Asia coincided with a shift from reciprocal labour to slavery in the Spanish and Portuguese colonial empires. This leads to one of the core questions addressed by this Special Issue. Was commodified labour valued differently from other forms of labour relations, and did the increase in wage labour prompt an increase in the discourse on labour?

The answer is ambiguous. We see in the work of Garzoni and Plockhoy a true distaste for wage labour. Garzoni, writing for aristocrats keen to preserve the social hierarchy, had a special reason for that. Plockhoy despised the position of wage workers as they had to sell their labour to the abject class of merchants. Reciprocal labour was his ideal. In Chinese cities, the freedom and independence of wage labour (as compared with indentured labour) was clearly valued, since we see people moving voluntarily in that direction, just like workers in Japan, where rulers first tried to prevent geographical and occupational mobility.

Once commodified wage labour led to new thinking and conflicts regarding contracts, hours of work, and other aspects of labour relations, it automatically triggered greater discourse on labour. Also, the growing number of women working for wages (sometimes outside the home, and sometimes wanting to keep their own income) led to debates concerning the nature of work. At the same time, we must remember that both in rural areas and within cities reciprocal labour was still very much the norm. In Brazil, the shift from reciprocal or tributary labour to slavery also led to a "labour discourse", if we can term as discourse the justifications adduced by Jesuit missionaries in their sermons.

Many of the studies in this volume show the fluidity of the categories "free" and "unfree" labour. This is clearest in the article on forced labour in Potosí, where free and the unfree workers all ended up working in the same mine. Yet the ability to meet one's labour obligations by payment of a monetary tribute could mean the difference between life and death, which is why local people insisted on the option of paying tribute rather than rendering labour service.

The article on Brazil discusses the shift from first enslaving part of the Indian population, to resorting to Afro-American enslavement for securing a supply of labour in the sugar mills after the demographic decline in the 1560s. The Portuguese also established a different kind of less unfree work organization, which involved organizing those Indians who worked for the Portuguese and were subject to reciprocal labour, into hamlets controlled by religious orders, mainly Jesuits. The shift here occurred from one ethnic group to the other, and saw labour relations among the Indians being transformed from outright slavery to life and work under Portuguese control.

In some cases in China voluntary bonded labour arrangements could be entered into on a temporary basis. In China, as in Japan, the boundary between unfree service to an upper-class landowner or feudal lord and free labour arrangements could be transgressed if a serf proved able to buy his own land and freedom. A less costly status which also involved less freedom for the former serf or bondservant was tenancy, with the tenant leasing from his former master. Finally, the unfree labour undertaken by prostitutes could be transformed into concubinage, thus changing the type of labour relation into that of reciprocal household work.

In all the societies discussed here, whether Protestant, Catholic, Orthodox Christian, Perso-Islamic, Jewish, or Confucian, occupations were ranked according to specific criteria. These were hierarchical systems of orders, estates, or castes in which manual labour was found mostly at the bottom, the exception being the "four occupational groups" of China and Japan, where farmers were allocated to the two upper classes. Intellectuals and clergy were generally found at the top, unless they belonged to orders that were – in theory – viewed with suspicion by the state, such as Daoists and Buddhists in China.

As the articles show, in practice those rankings were not fixed and rigid; they were sometimes reconsidered, and could be revised over time, especially when people, commodities, and ideas began to circulate. The Persian ranking found in Mughal India gave precedence to warriors, followed by artisans and merchants, while men of letters occupied a third category and clerics were not included at all. This contrasted with the previous Hindu orders, which categorized people as priests, rulers and warriors, traders, or manual workers, with a residual category of menial workers and outcastes.

In China, change also occurred within the group of menial labourers. For almost a century the better-off prostitutes achieved a kind of glamorous

and heroic image, as external trade expanded, cities flourished, and a cosmo-
politan lifestyle formed a fertile breeding ground for the development of
theories of individual morals. Another example is the notion of the medieval
European three estates exported from Portugal to Brazil: in the colony,
merchants became nobles, moving from the third to the second estate.
As flexible as these taxonomies might have been, people still defined
themselves and were defined by others in terms of their work, as Tarcisio
Botelho has shown.

In the period between 1500 and 1650, access to work was not free to
everybody. Various criteria for inclusion in or exclusion from particular
sectors of production and services applied. The most important were
gender, ethnicity, hereditary occupation, as with the castes, and region
of origin.

Almost all the essays in this volume show gender to have been
important. In many contexts the main argument was that women should
work in the home, and in emerging proto-industrial or commercializing
settings that they should also work in their homes for the market.
Domesticity was an ideal in normative texts in the Netherlands, Cairo,
and China. For the Dutch Republic, it has already been argued that the
affluence gained through overseas trade enabled Dutch men to work as the
family's sole breadwinner and women to confine themselves to household
work. However, as Ariadne Schmidt shows, this change did not take root
until the eighteenth century. Evidence more empirically valid than conduct
books and philosophical reasoning suggests that, in reality, women did work
outside the home, though to a variable extent. It is interesting to note that
Japanese female farmers were expected to transplant rice seedlings, while this
was not always the case in China; and that Jewish women in Cairo who
originated from the Iberian peninsula had more chances to engage in income-
generating domestic production, and more possibilities to make decisions
concerning their own property, but less opportunity to go out in public.

Indian women worked both in their own homes and outside. Shireen
Moosvi reminds us that even in market economies most women's labour
was reciprocal, and women would assist their male family members
if they worked at home. Women went outside the home, and even
to construction sites, to work as porters. There was little competition
between women and men for most occupations, which again shows that
gender was an important criterion for inclusion in or exclusion from
particular occupations. For India, occupational restrictions largely affected
the castes of Hindu communities, which were endogamous and had particular occupations allocated to them. Although the caste system changed over
time, the scope it allowed for horizontal or vertical mobility remained
limited. Hereditary occupations were also a feature of the Chinese system
of labour obligations. Military, artisan, and salt-producing households
in particular were obliged to serve the state in particular roles. However,

after 1500 this system was replaced largely by monetary tax payments, a tendency which led to greater flexibility on the labour market.

Ethnicity was another important criterion determining who could do what work. This is explained for the unfree labour conditions of Afro-Americans and Indians in Brazil, and the Indian native population of Potosí, the most striking samples in this volume. Yet cases of a more limited range in which people of a particular descent were forced or entitled to work in specific occupations can be found all over the globe. At one end, for instance, we find among China's "official prostitutes" the descendants of Mongols who had remained in China after the defeat of the Mongol Yuan dynasty. At the other, after 1644, Manchus, Mongols, and their bondservants, the so-called "banner people", occupied all the top-level military and administrative offices in the Qing empire following the demise of the Ming dynasty. Within those extremes, descent and networks played key roles in the commercializing and mobile early modern world. From Europe there are examples of porters working in Milan, most of whom were of Swiss origin,[20] and of Scottish mercenaries in the armies of the Netherlands during the Dutch Revolt and in Danish and Swedish armies during the Thirty Years War.[21]

Although some of the source types presented in this volume, such as books of household management, can be found almost everywhere, others were particular to specific regions. Those include Zacchia's codification of wage-related law, and the collection of guild adjudications in labour conflicts. The Italian wage codifications and the role of corporations in labour-related adjudication are paralleled by the guild institutions of the Arab and Ottoman world.[22] Yet the systematic focus on wage jurisdiction is extraordinary and must be attributed both to a specific legal tradition as well as to the importance of wage labour and wage disputes in Renaissance Italy.

TO CONCLUDE

In many countries, the study of early modern labour relations is still in its infancy. For a number of countries then this Special Issue provides a much-needed overview of developments in labour relations, one which also discusses what we know at this point about how labour and labour relations were perceived.

20. Luca Mocarelli, "The Attitude of Milanese Society to Work and Commercial Activities: The Case of the Porters and the Case of the Elites", in Ehmer and Lis, *The Idea of Work*, pp. 101–121, 109–111.

21. James Miller, *Swords for Hire* (Edinburgh, 2007).

22. Information from Nora Lafi, "The Historical Study of Labour Relations in the Ottoman Middle-East: Sources and Questionings: 1500, 1650, 1800, 1900", unpublished conference paper for the Ottoman Workshop of the Global Collaboratory on the History of Labour Relations, March 2009.

Work ethics and the valuation of work in what for some regions is regarded as the "early modern" period, in others, such as Mughal India and the Arab-Islamic world, as "late medieval", do not converge into a single trend. On the basis of this inventory, we can conclude that while peasant self-subsistence was still the rule in most regions, commodified labour increased in the cities of Europe and South and East Asia, and also in the colonial empires of South America, varying from free wage labour to chattel slavery. This was the result of what today is perceived of as the beginning of globalization, which linked previously unrelated world regions through relationships of trade and often also exploitation.

The voice of the elite concerning the change in the lives of those who worked is anxious in some cases, but full of marvel at the diversity of occupations in others. The traces of the opinions of the working non-elites about their lot are faint, but we find self-assertion in some cases, and a struggle (or the conviction that one should struggle) for more control over the labour process and its remuneration in others.

The period 1500–1650 was one where the dichotomy of activity and contemplation, or self-fulfilment, and in some cases redemption through work, played a central role in work ethics. Labour relations and occupations determined social stratification and vice versa. Kings hardly ever engaged in physical work, while housewives always did. Those in between, if their voices can be made audible, would object to the hardships of work, but occasionally find ways to enjoy it. Changes in work and labour relations could imply greater freedom and bargaining options, but at the same time an infringement on personal choices and preferences, engendering joy for some and pain for others in all the world regions represented in this volume.

Appendix

DEFINITIONS OF LABOUR RELATIONS

Non-working

1. *Cannot work or cannot be expected to work:* Those who cannot work, because they are too young (≤ 6 years), too old (≥ 75 years),[1] disabled, or are studying.

2. *Affluent*: Those who are so prosperous that they do not need to work for a living (*rentiers*, etc.).

3. *Unemployed*: Though unemployment is very much a nineteenth- and, especially, twentieth-century concept, we distinguish between those in employment and those wishing to work but who cannot find employment.

Working

RECIPROCAL LABOUR

Within the household:

4. *Leading household producers*: Heads of self-sufficient households (these include family-based and non-kin-based forms, such as monasteries and palaces). In many households after 1500, "self-sufficiency" can no longer have been complete. Basic foodstuffs, such as salt, and materials for tools and weapons, such as iron, were acquired through barter or monetary transactions even in tribal societies that were only marginally exposed to market production.[2] "Self-sufficiency" in our sense, which occurs in labour relations 4, 5, and 6, can include small-scale market transactions that aim at sustaining households rather than accumulating capital by way of profiting from exchange value.[3]

5. *Household kin producers*: Subordinate kin (men, women, and children) contributing to the maintenance of households.

6. *Household servants*: Subordinate kin and non-kin (men, women, and children) contributing to the maintenance of households. This category

---

1. These minimum and maximum ages are very much culturally determined and can differ for certain regions or cross-sections.

2. According to Amalendu Guha, "The Medieval Economy of Assam", in Tapan Raychaudhuri and Irfan Habib (eds), *The Cambridge Economic History of India* (Cambridge, 1982), I, p. 487, "village self-sufficiency in a total sense was a myth", even for the relatively remote sixteenth- and seventeenth-century Assam.

3. Marcel van der Linden, "Global Labour History and 'the Modern World-System'", *International Review of Social History*, 46 (2001), pp. 423–459, 452, referring to G.A. Cohen, *Karl Marx's Theory of History: A Defence* (Oxford, 1978).

does not refer to household servants who earn a salary and are free to leave their employer of their own volition, but rather to servants in feudal autarchic households.

Within the community:

7. *Community-based redistribution agents*: Persons who perform tasks for the local community in exchange for communally provided remuneration in kind, such as food, accommodation, and services, or a plot of land and seed to grow food on their own. Examples of this type of labour include working under the Indian *jajmani* system, hunting and defence by Taiwanese aborigines, or communal work in nomadic and sedentary tribes in the Middle East and North Africa.

TRIBUTARY LABOUR

8. *Forced labourers*: Those who have to work for the polity, and are remunerated mainly in kind. They include *corvée* labourers, conscripted soldiers and sailors, and convicts.

9. *Indentured tributary labourers*: Those contracted to work as unfree labourers for the polity for a specific period of time to pay off a debt. For example, German regiments (the "Hessians") in service with the British Empire which fought against the American colonists during the American Revolutionary War.

10. *Tributary serfs*: Those working for the polity because they are bound to its soil and obliged to provide specified tasks for a specified maximum number of days, for example, state serfs in Russia.

11. *Tributary slaves*: Those who are owned by and work for the polity indefinitely (deprived of the right to leave, to refuse to work, or to receive compensation for their labour). One example is forced labourers in concentration camps.

COMMODIFIED LABOUR

For the market, private employment:

12. *Self-employed*: Those who produce goods or services for market institutions, possibly in cooperation with other household members or no more than three wage labourers, apprentices, serfs, or slaves (for example, peasants, craftsmen, petty traders, transporters, as well as those in a profession).

13. *Employers*: Those who produce goods or services for market institutions by employing more than three wage labourers, indentured labourers, serfs, or slaves.

14. *Market wage earners*: Wage earners who produce commodities or services for the market in exchange mainly for monetary remuneration.
    14.1. Sharecropping wage earners: Remuneration is a fixed share of total output (including the temporarily unemployed).
    14.2. Piece-rate wage earners: Remuneration at piece rates (including the temporarily unemployed).
    14.3. Time-rate wage earners: Remuneration at time rates (including the temporarily unemployed).

15. *Indentured labourers for the market*: Those contracted to work as unfree labourers for an employer for a specific period of time to pay off a debt. They include indentured labourers in the British Empire after the abolition of slavery.

16. *Serfs working for the market*: Those bound to the soil and obliged to provide specified tasks for a specified maximum number of days, for example, serfs working on the estates of the nobility.

17. *Chattel slaves who produce for the market*: Those owned by their employers (masters). They are deprived of the right to leave, to refuse to work, or to receive compensation for their labour.
    17.1. Sharecropping chattel slaves working for their proprietor, for example, plantation slaves working in the Caribbean.
    17.2. Slaves for hire, for example, for agricultural or domestic labour in eighteenth-century Virginia.

For non-market institutions that may produce for the market:

18. *Wage earners employed by non-market institutions*: Such as the state, state-owned companies, the Church, or production cooperatives, who produce or render services for a free or a regulated market.
    18.1. Sharecropping wage earners: Remuneration is a fixed share of total output (including the temporarily unemployed).
    18.2. Piece-rate wage earners: Remuneration at piece rates (including the temporarily unemployed), e.g. hired artisans in Chinese imperial silk weaveries during the Ming and Qing dynasties.
    18.3. Time-rate wage earners: Remuneration at time rates (including the temporarily unemployed), e.g. hired artisans on Chinese imperial construction projects during the Ming and Qing dynasties, but also workers and employees in twentieth-century state enterprises.

IRSH 56 (2011), Special Issue, pp. 25–43 doi:10.1017/S0020859011000368

Studying Attitudes to Work Worldwide, 1500–1650: Concepts, Sources, and Problems of Interpretation*

MARCEL VAN DER LINDEN

Internationaal Instituut voor Sociale Geschiedenis

E-mail: mvl@iisg.nl

SUMMARY: The period 1500–1650 was characterized by huge global transformations. These had a major impact on a wide range of societal forms and cultures. As a result, different work ethics clashed and formed hybrid combinations, and new work ethics came into being during many-sided confrontations. The question of how the labouring poor in different parts of the world experienced these changes in the context of their work is an extremely difficult one. The present essay attempts to define a number of key concepts ("work", "attitude"); it evaluates critically the various sources which might give us an insight into attitudes to work; and it reflects on interpretative difficulties. The essay concludes by presenting a few substantive hypotheses.

The period 1500–1650 was, as we know, characterized by huge transformations. Gradually, the modern world system started to extend across the globe, and the influence of market forces increased. That had a major impact on a wide range of societal forms and cultures and as a result in many cases different work ethics clashed and formed hybrid combinations. In other cases, traditional work ethics remained almost unaffected or new work ethics came into being during many-sided confrontations.

Much has been written about some aspects of those developments, especially the rise of a capitalist *Wirtschaftsethik*, with Max Weber's famous hypothesis regarding the "Protestant ethic" in particular leading to an enormous amount of literature.[1] Seen from the point of view of

---

* I am grateful to Karin Hofmeester and Christine Moll-Murata for their critical remarks on an earlier version of this essay and for alerting me to additional sources. I would also like to thank Josef Ehmer and Alice Mul for their comments on the penultimate draft.

1. See the surveys in Robert W. Green (ed.), *Protestantism and Capitalism: The Weber Thesis and Its Critics* (Boston, MA, 1959); Johannes Winckelmann (ed.), *Max Weber, Die Protestantische Ethik*, II: *Kritiken und Antikritiken* (Gütersloh, 1978).

social history, this immense literature has two important shortcomings. First, much of it deals with the views of certain theologians and religious leaders in the period, without asking what the impact of their views was on the societies of their time. Second, if attention is paid to the social impact of ideas, then that research is generally focused more on entrepreneurs and much less on the lower classes.

In this preliminary contribution I will be reflecting on the scope offered by an alternative mode of interpretation, one that attempts to determine more emphatically the relations experienced by the labouring poor in the context of their work. First though, I will endeavour to describe a number of the key concepts ("work", "attitude") before critically discussing the various sources which might give us an insight into attitudes to work. I will conclude by discussing the interpretative difficulties and present a few substantive hypotheses.

CONCEPTS

The first question we need to ask ourselves is of course what do we mean by "work"? Interestingly, there are linguistic indications to suggest that work was originally associated with womanhood. Evans has pointed to "female associations of the English word *labo[u]r* and the French *travailler*. The Greek *techne* included all manual skills: the verb, *tikto*, means 'to bring forth into the world' and is used of the woman in the sense of 'to bring forth.' Its general sense is to 'create' or 'produce'."[2] In addition, there was probably an association with suffering (a woman's labour pains). From there, the past two or three centuries have seen a demarcation emerging between work and other human activities, for example leisure. Prior to that there was no strict dividing line, and indeed the division between work and non-work remains contested and is subject to continuous change.[3]

2. W.N. Evans, "The Cultural Significance of the Changed Attitude to Work in Great Britain", *Bulletin of the Menninger Clinic*, 13 (1949), pp. 1–8, 6.
3. Lucien Febvre, "Travail: évolution d'un mot et d'une idée", *Journal de psychologie normale et pathologique*, 41 (1948), pp. 19–28; Viktor von Weizsäcker, "Zum Begriffe der Arbeit", in Edgar Salin (ed.), *Synopsis. Festgabe für Alfred Weber* (Heidelberg, 1948), pp. 705–761; Hannah Arendt, *The Human Condition* (Chicago, IL, 1958); Werner Conze, "Arbeit", in Otto Brunner *et al.* (eds), *Geschichtliche Grundbegriffe. Historisches Lexikon zur politisch-sozialen Sprache in Deutschland*, I (Stuttgart, 1972), pp. 154–215; Michel Cartier (ed.), *Le Travail et ses représentations* (Paris, 1984); Jean-Marie Vincent, *Critique du travail: le faire et l'agir* (Paris, 1987); Herbert A. Applebaum, *The Concept of Work: Ancient, Medieval, and Modern* (Albany, NY, 1992); Keith Thomas (ed.), *The Oxford Book of Work* (Oxford, 1999); Gerd Spittler, "Arbeit – Transformation von Objekten oder Interaktion mit Subjekten?", *Peripherie*, 85–86 (2002), pp. 9–31; Madhavan K. Palat, "Rabochii", *Jahrbücher für Geschichte Osteuropas*, 50 (2002), pp. 345–374; Hélène d'Almeida-Topor *et al.* (eds), *Le Travail en Afrique Noire: représentations et pratiques à l'époque contemporaine* (Paris, 2003); Manfred Füllsack, *Arbeit*

Discussions of answers to the question "What is work?" have been raging for decades. Many of the definitions proffered limit themselves to situations in which money plays a role. Nels Anderson, for example, talks about the "time given to a job for which one is paid".[4] Such a description is not particularly helpful for our project, unless we wish to assume that unpaid work is not work. Other scholars have proposed broader definitions. Margaret Mead, for instance, has described work as "activity that is purposeful and directed towards ends that lie outside that activity", in contrast to "play", an "activity which is self-rewarding".[5]

A very simple definition could perhaps be: work is the purposive production of useful objects or services.[6] There are two elements here that should be emphasized. Work is a purposive activity ("premeditated"), and work creates objects or services that are useful to some people.[7] Usefulness is, of course, subjective: some people may find extremely useless what others consider to be very useful. Warfare, for example, is – apart from other things – a kind of labour process, but many people do not regard it as a useful activity – generally depending on the war that is being fought and the side those people are on. Work might also take the form of providing symbolic services: exorcism performed by a shaman is work, as is the hearing of confession done by a Catholic priest.

Work can be distinguished from non-work and from anti-work. Here non-work means recovery from work through, for instance, relaxation

(Vienna, 2009); Josef Ehmer and Catharina Lis (eds), *The Idea of Work in Europe from Antiquity to Modern Times* (Farnham, 2009).

4. Nels Anderson, *Work and Leisure* (London, 1961), p. 1; *idem, Man's Work and Leisure* (Leiden, 1974).

5. Margaret Mead, *Male and Female: A Study of the Sexes in a Changing World* (London, 1950), p. 163.

6. The definition is essentially the same as that of Charles and Chris Tilly: "Work includes any human effort adding use value to goods and services"; Charles Tilly and Chris Tilly, *Work Under Capitalism* (Boulder, CO, 1998), p. 22. I prefer not to use the Marxian concept "use value" in this context, since use values always exist in conjunction with exchange values (prices) and thus that definition is really only applicable to commodified labour. The anthropologist Gerd Spittler has defined work as "a continuous human activity aimed at producing goods and services"; Gerd Spittler, "Work: Anthropological Aspects", *International Encyclopedia of the Social and Behavioral Sciences*, XXIV (Amsterdam, 2001), pp. 16565–16569, 16565. I share his view to a large extent, though I would include discontinuous activity too. My definition is entirely compatible with that of the sociologist Heiner Ganßmann: "Work is human activity that transforms matter/energy and applies information for the purpose ultimately of providing resources to satisfy needs"; Heiner Ganßmann, "Ein Versuch über Arbeit", in Frithjof Hager (ed.), *Geschichte denken. Ein Notizbuch für Leo Löwental* (Leipzig, 1992), pp. 254–293, 263.

7. What consciously directed or purposive action means precisely is in itself a complex question. See, for example, Tim Ingold, "The Architect and the Bee: Reflections on the Work of Animals and Men", *Man*, New Series, 18 (1983), pp. 1–20.

or sleeping. Anti-work covers all playful activities that cost a lot of energy
but are not meant to produce useful objects or services.

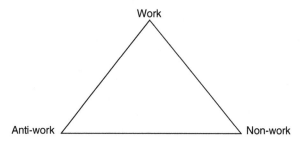

Naturally, those three components cannot always be distinguished neatly as
they overlap to some extent; nor are they clearly separated in time. During
work time workers sometimes do things other than work, such as playing,
sleeping, or relaxing. Cottage labourers, modern teleworkers, and many self-
employed people working from home combine different activities.

The boundaries between those three types of activity are therefore
vague and continue to be contested. That can be seen in the *Eigensinn*
shown by workers during their work.[8] At the same time, there is not
necessarily a sharp distinction between leisure activities and work: "Many
hobbies and leisure pursuits are utilitarian activities which, though in
themselves a source of interest and satisfaction, are undertaken initially
for economic reasons. There is no clear line of demarcation between
gardening or house-painting done from necessity and done from choice."[9]

When we ascribe these categories to reality, it is obviously important to
distinguish between our own classifications and the classifications applied
by the people we are studying. For example, in numerous societies men
(and, often women) believe that many things done by women are not
work at all – while we, basing ourselves on a certain definition of work,
would certainly consider those female activities to be work.

The second question is: "Why do people work?" Here I would distinguish
three kinds of work incentive: coercion; compensation, and commitment.[10]

8. Alf Lüdtke, *Eigensinn. Fabrikalltag, Arbeitererfahrungen und Politik vom Kaiserreich bis in
den Faschismus* (Hamburg, 1993). For an extensive review of this important work, see my
"Keeping Distance: Alf Lüdtke's 'Decentred' Labour History", *International Review of Social
History*, 40 (1995), pp. 285–294. Exemplary studies of *Eigensinn* include Douglas A. Reid, "The
Decline of Saint Monday, 1766–1876", *Past and Present*, 71 (1976), pp. 76–101; and Shankar
Ramaswami, "Masculinity, Respect, and the Tragic: Themes of Proletarian Humor in Con-
temporary Industrial Delhi", in Rana P. Behal and Marcel van der Linden (eds), *India's
Labouring Poor: Historical Studies, c.1600–c.2000* (New Delhi, 2007), pp. 203–227.
9. Sylvia Shimmin, "Concepts of Work", *Occupational Psychology*, 40 (1966), pp. 195–201, 195.
10. Tilly and Tilly, *Work under Capitalism*, pp. 74–75, 87, 259; Johannes Berger, "Warum
arbeiten die Arbeiter? Neomarxistische und neodurkheimianische Erklärungen", *Zeitschrift für
Soziologie*, 24 (1995), pp. 407–421, 416.

Coercion includes threats with or without the application of force, including incarceration, tormenting, mutilation, sale (of slaves), dismissal (of wage workers), or even death. Commitment is based on persuasion and sometimes joy, on workers being convinced that what they are doing is useful, important, and honorific. Compensation encompasses all material and non-material rewards, including wages and food rations.

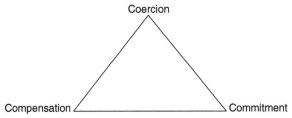

The three work incentives never occur in isolation but always in constantly changing combinations and, again, their mutual boundaries cannot always be drawn sharply. A university professor, for instance, will work because it gives her or him status, but also because the job is paid handsomely.

Furthermore, we should recognize that during the various phases of a work relationship the combination of incentives can change. "The incentive to take up a particular kind of work or even to work at all has a logic distinct from incentives to working *well*."[11]

The third question then is: "What do we mean by attitudes to work?" An attitude could be described as: "a psychological tendency that is expressed by evaluating a particular entity with some degree of favor or disfavor".[12] Incentive structures and attitudes to work are closely related. The core concept here is that of internalization: if at time t_1 an individual must be induced to work by external compensation or coercion and at time t_2 does so on their own initiative, then he or she can be said to have internalized those external incentives. Internalization is thus a psychological process that converts external incentives (coercion, compensation) either entirely or partly into internal incentives (commitment).[13]

Consistent with that, David Landes has made a distinction between "time-discipline" and "time-obedience", or punctuality coming "from within" or "from without".[14] In relation to chattel slaves in the

11. Sandra Wallman, "Introduction", in *idem* (ed.), *Social Anthropology of Work* (London, 1979), pp. 1–24, 6.

12. Alice H. Eagly and Shelly Chaiken, *The Psychology of Attitudes* (Fort Worth, TX, 1993), p. 1. See also the special issue of *Social Cognition*, 25 (2007), on "What Is an Attitude?".

13. See, for example, Kenneth C. Wallis and James L. Poulton, *Internalization* (Buckingham [etc.], 2001), esp. pp. 3–14.

14. David S. Landes, *Revolution in Time: Clocks and the Making of the Modern World* (Cambridge, MA, 1983), p. 7.

antebellum American South, Mark Smith has defined that difference as follows:

> [...] time-obedience refers to a respect for mechanical time among workers that, unlike time-discipline, was not internalized, but was rather enforced by time-conscious planters, either with the threat or the use of violence or with the constant repetition of mechanically defined time through sound, as with the chiming of clock-regulated bells.[15]

How such internalization occurs is an issue that lies beyond the scope of this article.

Attitudes to work relate primarily to the duration, intensity, and quality of the work. The Pakistani sociologist, Shahid Alam, has proposed a slightly more extensive taxonomy, distinguishing three elements that, when combined, characterize an attitude to work (work ethic). First, effort propensity: this dimension covers work–leisure choices. Effort propensity is larger when the time devoted to work is larger too. Second, social efficiency, which covers socially acquired attributes that determine the effectiveness with which work or leisure activities are performed. The aspects involved are dexterity, perfectionism, consistency, and discipline. And third, social rationality: this dimension indicates in what measure labour relations and other social relations are characterized by such factors as trust, honesty, orderliness, discipline, courtesy, and foresight.[16]

Many types of factor can play roles in analysing attitudes to work. First and foremost, we must know, of course, whether we are dealing with an ego-perspective or an alter-perspective. In the case of an ego-perspective, we shall be considering what individuals or groups think about themselves; in the case of an alter-perspective we shall be considering the views of individuals or groups about other individuals or groups. Within the ego-perspective, we can identify two levels, which, following Anthony Giddens, we could term practical consciousness and discursive consciousness. Practical consciousness is what people think when they actually do something, while discursive consciousness is what people say when they talk about what they do. Those two levels are not necessarily congruent. People may, for instance, say that they are orderly and efficient, while their actual behaviour reveals that they are not. Practical consciousness is much more difficult to study than discursive consciousness, since it is easier to find out what people say than what they actually do.

---

15. Mark M. Smith, "Time, Slavery and Plantation Capitalism in the Ante-bellum American South", *Past and Present*, 150 (1996), pp. 142–168, 145.

16. M. Shahid Alam, "Some Notes on Work Ethos and Economic Development", *World Development*, 13 (1985), pp. 251–254; *idem*, "Some European Perceptions of Japan's Work-Ethos in the Tokugawa Era: A Limited Survey of Observations from the West's First Encounters Offers Parallels to Today's", *American Journal of Economics and Sociology*, 46 (1987), pp. 229–243.

Related to that is a second distinction, between general and specific attitudes. People can regard "work" in an abstract sense as meaningful while at the same time loathing certain forms of work. In almost all societies, gender differentiation has resulted in some tasks being carried out principally or exclusively by men, or principally or exclusively by women.[17] Further, many sources create the impression that women have to work harder than men and have less power than men. For instance, Jean Barbot writes about Senegal around 1700 that the men "do not care to exert themselves greatly, either in body or mind", while most women

> [...] work at weaving cloths from cotton, or mats from straw or rushes [...].
> Wives and daughters also look after the house. They pound millet and make
> bread from it. They attend to the cooking. They fetch water from the river
> or the nearest supply. They feed their infants. Finally, they have to be respon-
> sible for keeping going all night a fire which burns near where their husband
> sleeps.[18]

And François Valentijn noted that in Ceylon (Sri Lanka), "the men here are mostly lords and the women generally in the Indies mostly slaves of the men".[19]

Moreover, different specializations within a given social division of labour are perceived differently. In Senegal, Barbot writes, "they occupy themselves either in tilling the fields or sowing them, because this occupation is the most honoured after that of soldiering. Those who make fishing-nets, and the potters, the fishermen, the weavers and the weapon-makers, are considered mere mechanics."[20] In contrast, in Scandinavia, according to Bishop Olaus Magnus, referring to a slightly earlier period, "men generally hold smiths in extraordinary esteem, whether blacksmiths, founders, or metal-turners".[21] A similar differentiation can be found for various other types of labour relation. While today wage labour is pre-ferred by many to other available forms of work, in sixteenth- and

---

17. The discussion of why the gendered division of labour is so persistent has been going on since the nineteenth century. For recent discussion see, *inter alia*, Rayna R. Reiter (ed.), *Toward an Anthropology of Women* (New York [etc.], 1975); Stephanie Coontz and Peta Henderson (eds), *Women's Work, Men's Property: The Origins of Gender and Class* (London, 1986); or Sylvia Walby, *Theorizing Patriarchy* (Oxford [etc.], 1990).
18. P.E.H. Hair *et al.* (eds), *Barbot on Guinea: The Writings of Jean Barbot on West Africa 1678–1712*, I [Works Issued by the Hakluyt Society, Second Series, No. 175] (London, 1992), pp. 89–90.
19. Sinnappah Arasaratnam (ed. and trans.), *François Valentijn's Description of Ceylon*, [Works Issued by the Hakluyt Society, Second Series, No. 149] (London, 1978), p. 165.
20. Hair, *Barbot on Guinea*, p. 89.
21. Olaus Magnus, *Historia de Gentibus Septentrionalibus/Description of the Northern Peoples* (Rome, 1555), II, Peter Foote (ed.) and Peter Fisher and Humphrey Higgens (trans.), [Works Issued by the Hakluyt Society, Second Series, No. 187] (London, 1998), p. 295.

seventeenth-century England it was regarded as very lowly because it was associated with a completely uncertain existence, and entailed no rights.[22]

A third aspect is that attitudes to work may be individual or group-based. Implicitly, contemporary Western researchers are often inclined to assume that relations and behaviours are based broadly on perceptions of individual self-interest. However, in the West as well as in many other societies work is often interpreted as a fundamental social activity which individuals engage in not only for themselves but also for others (compare the English servant/service or the German *Diener/Dienst*). Thomas Smith, a scholar of Japan, has observed that:

> The language of Tokugawa agriculture was rich in vocabulary expressing work in a context of obligation to others. *Suke* was labour given by a dependent to a protector in return and gratitude for benefits such as the loan of land, animals and a house. *Yui* was an equal exchange of like labour such as mutual help in transplanting rice. [...]. It is difficult to find any word that suggests work in a social context without carrying a sense of obligation to others.
>
> After the Meiji Restoration of 1868, this limitation of vocabulary became an inconvenience. None of the words mentioned could properly be used for factory employment, which in both theory and law was held by the new westernizing government to result from a contract freely entered into by autonomous and equal parties. So foreign to social experience was this notion, however, that no satisfactory general term for worker was found until the 1930s.[23]

SOURCES

How can we identify what attitudes to work existed between 1500 and 1650? We can sometimes discover sources through which "the subaltern speaks", to quote Gayatri Chakravorty Spivak, but such sources are not numerous. One example is the traditional songs sung by people performing labour.[24] It is likely that, in many parts of the world, a great deal of singing took place during work. In Shakespeare's *Twelfth Night, or What You Will* (c.1601), Duke Orsino says:

> O, fellow! come, the song we had last night.
> Mark it, Cesario; it is old and plain;

22. Christopher Hill, "Pottage for Freeborn Englishmen: Attitudes to Wage Labour in the Sixteenth and Seventeenth Centuries", in C.H. Feinstein (ed.), *Socialism, Capitalism and Economic Growth: Essays Presented to Maurice Dobb* (Cambridge, 1967), pp. 338–350.

23. Thomas C. Smith, "Peasant Time and Factory Time in Japan", *Past and Present*, 111 (1986), pp. 165–197, 183.

24. Compare Gerald Porter, "'Work the Old Lady Out of the Ditch': Singing at Work by English Lacemakers", *Journal of Folklore Research*, 31:1–3 (1994), pp. 35–55, 39. As early as the 1950s, the author noted, with regard to the Caribbean island of St Lucia: "It is unusual for two or more people working together at the same task not to be singing work songs, and a woman working alone will nearly always be humming or singing to herself"; Daniel J. Crowley, "Song and Dance in St Lucia", *Ethnomusicology*, 1:9 (1957), pp. 4–14, 13.

The spinsters and the knitters in the sun,
And the free maids that weave their threads with bones,
Do use to chant it; (Act 2, Scene 4, 42–46)

Such work songs encouraged not only a willingness to work, they could also facilitate the synchronization of activity, as in construction work, or in hoisting and lowering the sails of a ship, or planting rice in long rows.[25] In the case of Chinese earth-pounding songs, the singing was designed to encourage perseverance, because the longer the workers pounded the earth the stronger the walls would be.[26]

Another potential direct source is the collective fantasies of another, better, life, as expressed in stories about Cockaigne and similar constructs – in all utopias we encounter a society without sorrow. Referring to European narratives of the kind, Piero Camporesi spoke of:

> [...] the idea of eradicating barons and dukes, rejecting the parasitic and suffocating logic of the rich classes, the dream of the naked body carefree in its innocence, the yearning for physical health and the struggle for victory over disease, famine and cold, and freedom from the brutality of forced and inhuman labour.[27]

That kind of utopia is not typically European, however, and we can find it in a tributary society such as China, where the origins of such stories date back even further.[28]

Proverbs passed down through the ages can be used too, though it is particularly difficult to interpret them correctly since they are generally extremely short. Consider, for example, the following traditional proverbs from sub-Saharan Africa:

"You cannot kill game by looking at it."
"Laziness lends assistance to fatigue."

---

25. Marek Korczynski, "Music at Work: Towards a Historical Overview", *Folk Music Journal*, 8 (2003), pp. 314–334, 317; Harold Whates, "The Background of Sea Shanties", *Music and Letters*, 18 (1937), pp. 259–264; Hans-Jürgen Wanner, "Die Hauptformen des Hochseeshantys", *Jahrbuch für Volksliedforschung*, 11 (1966), pp. 26–36; Helge Gerndt, *Kultur als Forschungsfeld. Über volkskundliches Denken und Arbeiten* (Munich, 1981), pp. 98–117.
26. Wolfram Eberhard, "Pekinger Stampferlieder, gesammelt von Hong Fengju", *Zeitschrift für Ethnologie*, 67 (1935), pp. 232–248; Christine Moll-Murata, "Maintenance and Renovation of the Metropolitan City God Temple and the Peking City Wall during the Qing Dynasty", in *idem et al.* (eds), *Chinese Handicraft Regulations of the Qing Dynasty* (Munich, 2005), pp. 233–262, 255.
27. Piero Camporesi, *The Land of Hunger*, Tania Croft-Murray (trans.) (Cambridge, 1996), p. 52.
28. Wolfgang Bauer, *China und die Hoffnung auf Glück. Paradiese, Utopien, Idealvorstellungen in der Geistesgeschichte Chinas* (Munich, 1971), ch. 3/3; Romer Cornejo Bustamante, "On Utopia and Its Limits in China", in David N. Lorenzen (ed.), *Studies on Asia and Africa from Latin America* (Mexico City, 1990), pp. 25–36.

"A lazy man looks for light employment."
"The sieve never sifts meal by itself."[29]

It is not easy to draw conclusions about attitudes to work from such proverbs, other than that work inevitably involves effort. Naturally, this list of possible sources could be expanded.[30] But the difficulty with all these sources, which directly reflect what people thought four centuries ago, is that they are seldom transmitted to us in a pure form; usually "they are narrative in form and go through mutations and interpolations in being handed down through generations".[31] Such sources therefore constitute only "soft evidence" – unlike archaeological material or authentic texts.[32]

The reports of contemporaries from elsewhere, usually written by the elite including travellers and missionaries, form a second type of source. We have a large number of travel narratives for our period, varying from Richard Hakluyt (1589) to Samuel Purchas (1625).[33] Some of the travel narratives are reflective, but by far the most are, as Ter Ellingson has put it, "unphilosophical"; they "describe without reflecting much on the significance of what they see, particularly on the meanings of similarities and differences in the ways of life of human communities".[34] Such sources

29. A.O. Stafford, "The Mind of the African Negro as Reflected in His Proverbs", *Journal of Negro History*, 1 (1916), pp. 42–48, 45–46.
30. See e.g., the contributions of Gerhard Jaritz, Ilja M. Veldman, and Peter Burke in Ehmer and Lis, *Idea of Work*.
31. Vijaya Ramaswamy, "Women and Farm Work in Tamil Folk Songs", *Social Scientist*, 21:9–11 (1993), pp. 113–129, 114. See also, however, Imre Katona, "Reminiscences of Primitive Divisions of Labor Between Sexes and Age Groups in the Peasant Folklore of Modern Times", in Stanley Diamond (ed.), *Toward a Marxist Anthropology: Problems and Perspectives* (The Hague, 1979), pp. 377–383.
32. Jan Vansina, *De la tradition orale. Essai de méthode historique* (Tervuren, 1961). For an example of how labour historians can use mural paintings as a source, see Alec Gordon and Napat Sirisambhand, "Evidence for Thailand's Missing Social History: Thai Women in Old Mural Paintings", *International Review of Social History*, 47 (2002), pp. 261–275. In Europe, countless paintings were made which can serve as a source. For the Low Countries, see Annette de Vries, *Ingelijst werk. De verbeelding van arbeid en beroep in de vroegmoderne Nederlanden* (Zwolle, 2004).
33. For surveys see, for example, J.N.L. Baker, *A History of Geographical Discovery and Exploration* (London, 1931); Percy G. Adams, *Travelers and Travel Liars, 1660–1800* (Berkeley, CA, 1962); Helen Delpar, *The Discoverers: An Encyclopedia of Explorers and Exploration* (New York, 1980); Felipe Fernández-Armesto (ed.), *The Times Atlas of World Exploration* (New York, 1991). Examples of missionary reports chosen more or less at random include: William Campbell, *Formosa under the Dutch, Described from Contemporary Records* (London, 1903); Alfonso de Sandoval, *De instauranda Aethiopum salute. El mundo de la esclavitud negra en América* (Bogota, 1956); C.R. Boxer (ed.), *South China in the Sixteenth Century: Being the Narrative of Galeote Pereira, Fr Gaspar da Cruz, OP, Fr Martín de Rada, OESA. (1550–1575)* (Nendeln, 1967).
34. Ter Ellingson, *The Myth of the Noble Savage* (Berkeley, CA, 2001), p. 47.

may be used only with the utmost caution, because often they are partly projections and sometimes contain imaginative fabrications – a problem to which I will return shortly.

One might expect reports to be more reliable the longer the observer had lived in the society about which he or she was writing – one reason why reports written by captives, diplomats, and missionaries, who stayed for many years, would seem worthy of special attention. In the case of the Scottish missionary Thomas Cullen Young (1880–1955), for example, it has been noted that the "objectivity" of his writings on the Tumbuka-Kamanga peoples "increased the longer he spent in Malawi. Initially he suffered from one strong prejudice: he was affronted by the apparent lack of a work ethic." Later he would change his position and *"refute* the notion that Africans are lazy, stressing hard work within the village context, and showing that laziness is a serious offence in traditional values".[35]

Third, there is a miscellany of official texts, including reports on local relations and on the regulation of work. Naturally, such texts were a feature only of societies with literate bureaucracies. Insofar as it relates to the work process and work relations, legislation offers an initial point of access; it tells us something not only about the economy and culture, but also about what the labouring population was expected to do and what they apparently sometimes or frequently did not do.[36] The descriptive inventories of local relations are another variant. For the Spanish-speaking world we have, for example, Juan López de Valesca's *Geografía y descripción de las Indias* (1574) and Antonio Vázquez de Espinosa, *Compendio y descripción de las Indias Occidentales* (c.1628) – two large-scale surveys, one of which covers

---

35. Peter G. Forster, "Missionaries and Anthropology: The Case of the Scots of Northern Malawi", *Journal of Religion in Africa*, 16:2 (1986), pp. 101–120, 110. A fine exploration of the stories of British captives in North Africa, India, and the Americas is Linda Colley's *Captives: Britain, Empire, and the World, 1600–1850* (New York, 2002); Colley also gives a provisional survey of British captivity narratives on pp. 380–385. For North American narratives see, *inter alia*, Alden T. Vaughan, *Narratives of North American Indian Captivity: A Selective Bibliography* (New York, 1983); Frances Roe Kestler (ed.), *The Indian Captivity Narrative: A Woman's View* (New York, 1990); and Paul Baepler (ed.), *White Slaves, African Masters: An Anthology of American Barbary Captivity Narratives* (Chicago, IL, 1999). For examples of Spanish and German captivity narratives, see, for example, Álvar Núñez Cabeza de Vaca, *The Narrative of Cabeza de Vaca* [1542], Rolena Adorno and Patrick Charles Pautz (trans.) (Lincoln, NE, 2003), and Neil L. Whitehead and Michael Harbsmeier (eds), *Hans Staden's True History: An Account of Cannibal Captivity in Brazil* [1557] (Durham, NC, 2008).
36. See, *inter alia*, Karl Heinz Ludwig and Peter Sika (eds), *Bergbau und Arbeitsrecht. Die Arbeitsverfassung im europäischen Bergbau des Mittelalters und der frühen Neuzeit* (Vienna, 1989); Maya Shatzmiller, "Women and Wage Labour in the Medieval Islamic West: Legal Issues in an Economic Context", *Journal of the Economic and Social History of the Orient*, 40 (1997), pp. 174–206; *The Great Ming Code: Da Ming lü*, trans. Jiang Yonglin (Seattle, WA, 2005), including penal-law clauses on work-related crimes; Kellie Robertson, *The Laborer's Two Bodies: Literary and Legal Productions in Britain, 1350–1500* (Basingstoke, 2006).

not only the entire Spanish-American continent but also the Philippines and the Moluccas.[37]

Fourth, studies from later periods can be used heuristically. In societies in which slave labour was widespread the major slave owners and their families generally looked down on menial labour. Ancient Greece and the American South are classic examples of that, and the same attitude can be found in other societies too. Mary Kingsley, who travelled through the French Congo during the 1890s, wrote, for example, about the Igalwa, who lived on Lambaréné Island:

> The Igalwa is truly great at sitting, the men pursuing a policy of masterly inactivity, broken occasionally by leisurely netting a fishing net, the end of the netting hitched up on the roof thatch, and not held by a stirrup. The ladies are employed in the manufacture of articles pertaining to a higher culture [...] – the most gorgeous bed-quilts and pillow-cases – made of patchwork [...]. On the island they [...] laze their lives away like lotus-eaters. Their slaves work their large plantations, and bring up to them magnificent yams, ready prepared agooma, sweet-potatoes, papaw, &c., not forgetting that delicacy Odeaka cheese.[38]

And about the Californios, the Spanish-speaking inhabitants who dominated California before it was acquired by the United States, observers wrote unanimously that they "were lazy and lacked all semblance of personal enterprise or willingness to work" – that they had all the heavy work done by Native Americans, who received a nominal wage in return for their labour but who were, effectively, a kind of slave.[39] Such a pattern leads one to presume that in other societies too in which unfree labour played an important role the elite shared similar attitudes to labour, though it should be noted that often this negative work ethic in slave societies was much less evident among free groups of poor and the less affluent.[40] Based on other historical experiences, there is every reason

37. Juan López de Valesca, *Geografía y descripción de las Indias*, M. Jiménez de la Espada (ed.) (Madrid, 1971); Antonio Vázquez de Espinosa, *Compendio y descripción de las Indias Occidentales*, B. Velasco Bayón (ed.) (Madrid, 1969); *idem*, *Compendium and Description of the West Indies*, Charles Upson Clark (trans.) (Washington DC, 1942). López de Valesca wrote reports on Brazil, China, Japan, New Guinea, and the Solomon Islands. The two surveys mentioned here form the basis of the study of Spanish America c.1600 written by Bernard Slicher van Bath and published as *Spaans Amerika omstreeks 1600* (Utrecht [etc.], 1979) (available only in Dutch).
38. Mary Kingsley, *Travels in West Africa* (London, 2000 [1897]), pp. 84 and 89.
39. David J. Langum, "Californios and the Image of Indolence", *Western Historical Quarterly*, 9 (1978), pp. 181–196, 181.
40. See, for example, Carl R. Osthaus, "The Work Ethic of the Plain Folk: Labor and Religion in the Old South", *Journal of Southern History*, 70 (2004), pp. 745–782. Osthaus argues that for many smaller farmers in the US South, even those who owned a few slaves, "Manual labor performed at one's own behest and for the benefit of one's own family [...] was admirable"; p. 746.

to suppose therefore that this type of work ethic was prevalent among large slave owners in the period 1500–1650 too.

PROBLEMS OF INTERPRETATION

Work processes are always embedded in wider social relations. Attitudes to work reflect not only labour relations in a narrow sense, but also the society in which those labour relations are situated. The anthropologist Maurice Godelier, who studied this issue thirty years ago, noted rightly that "what we in the West today call 'working,' 'worker,' and 'work' may be expected to have many different representations in other societies".[41] Furthermore, attitudes to work depend on social status and change over time. Shashi Upadhyay has perceptibly observed then that:

> Even within a given society, the meaning of work may change over time, and the various groups or classes too may view work differently. Thus it is possible that capitalists, artisans and the proletariat may have different notions of work. In fact, even within a class, different attitudes towards work are likely to exist. Attitudes regarding work vary depending on whether the country is at war or at peace, whether work is to be found easily or with difficulty, whether the worker is a supervisor or a labourer, whether he is the employer or an employee, and finally depending on the nature and amount of wages. There is no essential and universal meaning attached to "work", nor one that transcends time, space, class or status.[42]

It is precisely because of that variation and fluidity that historians are repeatedly tempted to be led astray by two different types of error. The first is that of projection: we tend to see what we want to see. Often, the images we form of a different society say more about ourselves than about that other society.[43] Europeans in the nineteenth century believed, for example, that East Asians were decadent: "At a time when the industrial nations of the West were strong and social ideologies such as Calvinism and social-Darwinism exuded a sense of direction and determination, the lesser races, it was held, were backward and would remain so because they were indisposed to work." When, after 1868, Japan embarked on a programme of modernization, European observers were therefore sceptical since the Japanese lacked "the requisite powers not only of industry but

---

41. Maurice Godelier, "Aide-Mémoire for a Survey of Work and Its Representations", *Current Anthropology*, 21 (1980), pp. 831Ė835, 832–833.
42. Shashi Bhushan Upadhyay, "Dalits and the Ideology of Work in India", in Marcel van der Linden and Prabhu P. Mohapatra (eds), *Labour Matters: Towards Global Histories. Studies in Honour of Sabyasachi Bhattacharya* (New Delhi, 2009), pp. 152–171, 152.
43. On this see Urs Bitterli, *Die "Wilden" und die "Zivilisierten". Grundzüge einer Geistes- und Kulturgeschichte der europäisch-überseeischen Begegnung* (Munich, 1976), esp. Part IV. Also V.G. Kiernan, *The Lords of Human Kind* (Harmondsworth, 1972), or William Brandon, *New Worlds for Old: Reports from the New World and Their Effect on the Development of Social Thought in Europe, 1500–1800* (Athens, OH [etc.], 1986).

also of perseverance".[44] It is extraordinarily difficult to determine how work was thought of in other societies 500 years ago. Reading the reports written by Europeans, one is quickly struck by the impression that most inhabitants of South America, Africa, or Asia were extraordinarily lazy. Indolence was a complaint made repeatedly against them.

The second type of error is that of false generalization. We often tend to assume that observations we have made in a number of cases apply more generally in time and place, without there actually being a solid empirical basis for that assumption. One good example of such a generalization is E.P. Thompson's theory of "task-orientation". Drawing on the English situation, Thompson argued that the task-orientation of pre-industrial workers (peasants, for example) was characterized by three features: their work rhythm was determined by the "observed necessity" of the natural environment; they made no clear distinction between "work" and "life" (i.e. social intercourse); and their attitude to work was, to modern eyes, "wasteful and lacking in urgency".[45] That generalization has been convincingly refuted, however, based on studies of agricultural producers in late Tokugawa Japan. Owing in part to the pressure of a growing population density, peasants were forced to plan their crops in advance, to coordinate a variety of activities over longer periods, and to keep records.[46]

There would seem to be just three approaches, preferably used in combination, to counteract the dangers of projection and false generalization. First, being extremely critical in how one uses the sources. Second, engaging

44. Jean-Pierre Lehmann, "Old and New Japonisme: The Tokugawa Legacy and Modern European Images of Japan", *Modern Asian Studies*, 18 (1984), pp. 757–768, 761. There is a direct link with racism here. The sinologist Walter Demel has demonstrated how, in the sixteenth century, Europeans regarded the Chinese as "white", and in the eighteenth century as "yellow", a change that probably reflected shifts in the international balance of power. See Walter Demel, "Wie die Chinesen gelb wurden. Ein Beitrag zur Frühgeschichte der Rassentheorien", *Historische Zeitschrift*, 255 (1992), pp. 625–666.
45. E.P. Thompson, "Time, Work-Discipline and Industrial Capitalism", *Past and Present*, 38 (1967), pp. 56–97, 60. Henri Lefebvre, *Critique de la vie quotidienne*, 3 vols (Paris, 1958–1961), II, pp. 52–56, made a similar distinction between the cyclical (seasonally related) time of pre-industrial labour and the linear time of capitalistic accumulation, which in turn provoked fundamental theses concerning "cumulative" and "non-cumulative" processes from Alfred Krovoza, *Produktion und Sozialisation* (Frankfurt am Main, 1976), pp. 67–93.
46. Smith, "Peasant Time and Factory Time". For centuries, a similar decontextualization has tempted European scholars to claim that Muslims were "fatalistic" and unenterprising – the *fatum mahumetanum* about which Leibniz wrote. In doing so, they generally considered just the poor farmers. However, in a study of the Tunisian countryside in the 1950s, Gérard Destanne de Bernis convincingly showed that this "fatalism" was primarily a function not of irrationality nor religion but of an assessment based on experience of the scope to change things. And he added that "Anyone so placed would be fatalistic, at the very least"; Gérard Destanne de Bernis, "Islam et développement économique", *Cahiers de l'Institut de Science Economique Appliquée*, 106 (1960), pp. 105–150, 114ff.; compare Maxime Rodinson, *Islam and Capitalism*, Brian Pearce (trans.) (Harmondsworth, 1977), p. 113.

in critical self-reflection, acknowledging and addressing one's prejudices as much as possible. And third, by considering the contextual explanation of observations made. One example might suffice here to clarify what I mean. In the past it was often said about the Maoris that they had "never been capable of performing consistent labour in one field for any great length of time". The Maoris were said to have a "volatile temperament", which led them "to work in bursts of energy, but is not conductive to life in a steady and settled occupation". That contrasted with the European, "who is able to concentrate on one task and complete it without needing constant change of surroundings".[47]

The New Zealand anthropologist Raymond Firth has rightly pointed out that such claims are decontextualized value judgements. He does not doubt that, by European standards, the Maoris showed a "lack of steady application and failure to concentrate on work", but, he argues, this so-called limitation was related less to "innate mental endowment" than to "definite social circumstances". To support his claim, Firth adduced a number of arguments. First, the standard of comfort among the Maoris differed from that of the Europeans: "The native does not ask for all our civilized products, he is content with the satisfaction of his needs for food, clothing and shelter, with the addition of a few subsidiary pleasures." And thus the Maori "does not feel impelled to put in extra labour to secure articles for which he has no real desire"; his "erratic habits of labour and his periods of inactivity [...] are the result – in part at least – of this lack of conformity to our scheme of civilized wants".

Second, there was a clear reason for the volatility that characterized their work ("a somewhat haphazard succession of employments, never pausing long with one, unable to concentrate but always seeking change"):

> In a society where there was no great division of labour or specialization of employments, where each man carried on work in a number of fields, there was scope for the principle of variety in occupation to come into play. When the craftsman was tired or bored with his job, he turned to another, and so was able to work with renewed zest. The beneficial effects of a diversion of attention when the interest flags are well known in psychology. By following this principle the Maori revealed, not a sheer inability to do consistent work, but an appreciation of the element of flexibility in his economic system.

By so explaining Maori attitudes to work, Firth made it possible on the one hand to avoid essentialistic projections and on the other to recognize the limits of generalizations,[48] since a number of important hypotheses are implicitly concealed in Firth's explanation, for example that volatile

47. Raymond Firth, *Primitive Economics of the New Zealand Maori* (London, 1929), pp. 185–186.
48. All the preceding quotations are taken from *ibid.*, pp. 186–189.

labour patterns are less likely in a society with more complex internal divisions of labour, and that attitudes to labour will change once people become tempted by the appeal of modern consumer society. His analysis also reveals how notions of time can differ so much in different societies. Having grown up, as we have, with concepts of continuous and objective time, we find it difficult to understand other time schemes.[49]

SOME CONCLUDING HYPOTHESES

Mindful of the above, I will conclude by formulating a few extremely tentative ideas regarding attitudes to labour around the world in the sixteenth and seventeenth centuries. In doing so, I will be drawing on a very limited number of sources in just a few languages, and applying a degree of deduction. Here, I will briefly characterize four "types" that prevailed at the same time. Naturally, this list is by no means complete; nor does it describe an evolutionary pattern.

The first type are hunter-gatherers. Nowadays, they are limited to the most desolate and inhospitable areas of the world – the Arctic regions, and deserts; nonetheless, most scholars have argued that they need relatively little time to provide themselves with the things they need. A systematic overview in *The Cambridge Encyclopedia of Hunters and Gatherers* has summarized the results of anthropological research as follows:

> Typically, "immediate return" hunter-gatherers, those with the simplest technology such as the Hadza and !Kung, spend only three or four hours per day occupied with what we could call economic activities. These activities include hunting a large number of animal species and gathering a large variety of plant material. [...] Hunting and gathering is integrated with rituals, socialization, and artistic expression. The idea that earning a living is drudgery whose only purpose is to make it possible for us to live our "real" lives is not present in hunter-gatherer cultures.[50]

49. More extensive reflections can be found in J.T. Fraser, *Of Time, Passion, and Knowledge: Reflections on the Strategy of Existence*, 2nd edn (Princeton, NJ, 1975); and Donald J. Wilcox, *The Measure of Times Past: Pre-Newtonian Chronologies and the Rhetoric of Relative Time* (Chicago, IL [etc.], 1987). For a historical study of a "non-standard" concept of time see Keletso E. Atkins, *The Moon is Dead! Give Us Our Money! The Cultural Origins of an African Work Ethic, Natal, South Africa, 1843–1900* (London, 1993).
50. John Gowdy, "Hunter-Gatherers and the Mythology of the Market", in Richard B. Lee and Richard Daly (eds), *The Cambridge Encyclopedia of Hunters and Gatherers* (Cambridge, 2004), pp. 391–398, 393. In the more modern literature, immediate-return hunter-gatherers (in contrast to delayed-return hunter-gatherers) are taken to mean those who "go out hunting or gathering and eat the food obtained the same day or casually over the days that follow. Food is neither elaborately processed nor stored. They use relatively simple, portable, utilitarian, easily acquired, replaceable tools and weapons made with real skill but not involving a great deal of labour"; James Woodburn, "Egalitarian Societies", *Man*, New Series, 17 (1982), pp. 431–451, 432.

Given that, one can understand why Marshall Sahlins termed the society of immediate-return hunter-gatherers "the original affluent society".[51] If his assessment is correct, we can expect hunter-gatherers who lived 400–500 years ago and who had at that time a much more varied living environment to have been less focused on labour than are their contemporaries today.[52]

A second type can be found among sedentary groups without leaders and hierarchies (so-called acephalous societies) with a low population density. One presumes they work more hours a day, especially the women, but the labour process retains its autonomous character. The Iatmul in Papua New Guinea (East Sepik Province) around 1930 had a subsistence economy dominated by women, who supplied approximately 80 per cent of food products. In addition to catching fish daily, they produced fish traps, nets, bags, and baskets, cared for the younger children, and prepared meals. The men were primarily artisans. They built houses, carved canoes and paddles, and made weapons and some of the work tools. Their woodcarvings were highly artistic. Men and women gardened together. Heteronomy was absent:

> Whether a task is to be done or not, where it is to be done, how long it may take, how large the group is to be, and whether particular persons are to take part are matters to be decided by the individuals concerned in accordance with the situation at the moment. No one is entitled to dictate the tempo at which a job is done, or when the work must be finished; every working individual determines this himself. Communal decisions of short-term validity are reached in loose cooperation with other members of the group and in direct relation to technical necessities or personal needs. Work may be interrupted by intervals of relaxation, joking, or ritual, as desired.[53]

It would seem reasonable to suppose that such relations, with their corresponding attitudes to work, existed several centuries earlier under similar conditions.

Pre-capitalist small peasants in relatively densely populated areas are a third type. They generally lived in constant fear of not having enough to

51. Marshall Sahlins, "La première société d'abondance", *Les Temps Modernes*, 268 (1968), pp. 641–680. See also *idem*, *Stone Age Economics* (Chicago, IL, 1972), ch. 1.
52. There are, however, anthropologists who do not share the optimistic assessment of Sahlins and others. They suspect it is based on too limited a definition of work, since if "we were to define work not only as subsistence activities but more generally as all life-sustaining activities – not only hunting and gathering but also the making and repairing of tools, housekeeping, curing of skins, child care, the migration from one site or waterhole to another, and so on – then the number of hours hunter-gatherers can be said to work each week would increase dramatically"; David Kaplan, "The Darker Side of the 'Original Affluent Society'", *Journal of Anthropological Research*, 563 (2000), pp. 301é324, 313.
53. Milan Stanek, "Social Structure of the Iatmul", in Nancy Lutkehaus *et al.* (eds), *Sepik Heritage: Tradition and Change in Papua New Guinea* (Bathurst, 1990), pp. 266–273, 266.

eat – especially if they were required to pay a tribute to a landowner or lord. They developed what James C. Scott has termed a "subsistence ethic":

> This ethic [...] was a consequence of living so close to the margin. A bad crop would not only mean short rations; the price of eating might be the humiliation of an onerous dependence or the sale of some land or livestock which reduced the odds of achieving an adequate subsistence the following year. The peasant family's problem, put starkly, was to produce enough rice to feed the household, buy a few necessities such as salt and cloth, and meet the irreducible claims of outsiders. The amount of rice a family could produce was partly in the hands of fate, but the local tradition of seed varieties, planting techniques, and timing was designed over centuries of trial and error to produce the most stable and reliable yield possible under the circumstances. These were the *technical arrangements* evolved by the peasantry to iron out the "ripples that might drown a man." Many *social arrangements* served the same purpose. Patterns of reciprocity, forced generosity, communal land, and work-sharing helped to even out the inevitable troughs in a family's resources which might otherwise have thrown them below subsistence.[54]

Based on the principle of safety first, such a subsistence ethic is generally associated with considerable labour input.

> Because labor is often the only factor of production the peasant possesses in relative abundance, he [sic] may have to move into labor-absorbing activities with extremely low returns until subsistence demands are met. This may mean switching crops or techniques of cultivation (for example, switching from broadcasting to transplanting rice) or filling the slack agricultural season with petty crafts, trades, or marketing which return very little but are virtually the only outlets for surplus labor.[55]

The subsistence ethic thus implies a work ethic that is related to the ecological, demographic, and economic relationships in which such farmers live and work.

Finally, I would include commodified labour relations under capitalism, including chattel slavery, share-cropping, and wage labour.[56] All those forms of labour share the same characteristic, namely that they create abstract value. Because output is intended for the market, labour processes are not directly focused on the needs of producers, but on those of

54. James C. Scott, *The Moral Economy of the Peasant: Rebellion and Subsistence in Southeast Asia* (New Haven, CT [etc.], 1976), pp. 2–3. Chayanov had already noted that the overriding principle for such peasants is "To select crops and forms of exploiting them which will give the highest and most stable payment for labor"; A.V. Chayanov, *The Theory of Peasant Economy*, Daniel Thorner *et al.* (eds) (Homewood, IL, 1966), p. 134.
55. Scott, *Moral Economy of the Peasant*, pp. 13–14.
56. For descriptions of the concepts "commodification" and "capitalism" see Marcel van der Linden, *Workers of the World: Essays toward a Global Labor History* (Leiden, 2008), chs 2 and 16.

consumers, who may or may not be anonymous. In that sense, all capitalist labour is alienated.[57] At the same time, I suspect though that Max Weber's "spirit of capitalism" has remained a marginal phenomenon.[58] In practice, alienated attitudes to work can vary considerably, from shirking to excessive zealousness, from deference to recalcitrance – often in combinations, too. The exploration of all these disparate attitudes and the contexts within which they emerged is a fascinating challenge for further research.

57. See, for example, István Mészáros, *Marx's Theory of Alienation*, 5th edn (London, 2005).
58. Weber describes this "spirit" as follows: "In fact, the *summum bonum* of this ethic, the earning of more and more money, combined with the strict avoidance of all spontaneous enjoyment of life, is above all completely devoid of any eudaemonistic, not to say hedonistic, admixture. It is thought of so purely as an end in itself, that from the point of view of the happiness of, or utility to, the single individual, it appears entirely transcendental and absolutely irrational. Man is dominated by the making of money, by acquisition as the ultimate purpose of his life"; Max Weber, *The Protestant Ethic and the Spirit of Capitalism*, Talcott Parsons (trans.) (New York, 1958), p. 53.

IRSH 56 (2011), Special Issue, pp. 45–67 doi:10.1017/S0020859011000538
© 2011 Internationaal Instituut voor Sociale Geschiedenis

Labour Ideologies and Women in the Northern Netherlands, c.1500–1800*

ARIADNE SCHMIDT

*Institute for History, Economic and Social History,
Leiden University*

E-mail: a.schmidt@hum.leidenuniv.nl

SUMMARY: The ideology of domesticity that identified women with a domestic role became more articulated in north-western Europe throughout the early modern period. At the same time, perceptions of work changed and a new appraisal of labour emerged. These seemingly contradictory tendencies prompt the question how women fitted in with the ideology of work. This article discusses common notions of the economic role of women as they emerged from the debates on women, gender relations, and work; how these notions were translated into practical advice in conduct literature; and with what norms women were confronted in everyday life. It appears that work was valued positively for both women and men. Women's involvement in remunerated work was not considered problematic. There was a dividing line, however, and that was drawn between work within the home, which was deemed women's work, and work outside the home, which was deemed men's work. In practice, a differentiation was made between social groups; women who lacked income from capital were supposed to earn their living from work.

INTRODUCTION

The historiography of European women's work has long been dominated by the marginalization thesis. It was widely assumed that the opportunities for women to work were restricted owing to the rise of capitalism, the ideology of the separation of spheres, and the growing cult of domesticity. With production and consumption becoming separated, growing proletarianization, and the concentration of production under one roof, production moved outside the household to factories, depriving women of the opportunity to carry out the economically rewarding,

* The research conducted for this article was carried out as part of the "Women's Work in the Northern Netherlands in the Early Modern Period (c.1500–1815)" project, financed by the Friends of the International Institute of Social History and the Netherlands Organization for Scientific Research (NWO). I am grateful to Manon van der Heijden, Lex Heerma van Voss, and Jan Lucassen for their comments on earlier versions.

skilled, and high-status work they had been involved in when production
had been home-based. The poorer women were condemned to work hard
in factories for low wages. The more well-to-do were confined to the
home, while their husbands, as family breadwinners, went out to earn a
living.[1]

The ideology of the separate spheres that divided the world into a public
domain, for men, and the private domestic sphere, the domain of women,
became more sharply articulated in the eighteenth century. It grew to
become the dominant ideology regarding the proper place of women in the
nineteenth century and became a central element in the creation of middle-
class identity.[2] The paradigm of the separate spheres has been much criticized. Sceptics have argued that the public–private dichotomy is inadequate
as an analytical framework as the distinction between the two spheres was
often unclear and does not capture actual female experiences.[3] Yet many
historians do agree that gender norms narrowed during the early modern
period, and, at least in the prescriptive literature, women were unmistakably
and increasingly identified with a domestic role.[4]

Dutch society is said to have played a pioneering role in the development of the concept of middle-class domesticity.[5] Both the specific social
and economic developments and changes on the religious front were of
influence. As elsewhere in post-Reformation north-western Europe, the
Protestant elevation of marriage emphasized and celebrated the role of
women as mothers and housewives.[6] More exceptional, compared with
other European countries, were its early urbanization, economic specialization, and emergence of a labour market, and the coincidence of those
three factors. Combined with the absence of a strong nobility, the social
dominance of the middle class, and the rise of the bourgeois family in the
seventeenth century, these developments stimulated the emergence of an

1. Alice Clark, *Working Life of Women in the Seventeenth Century* (London, 1992 [1919]),
was influential in this debate. See also Louise Tilly and Joan Scott, *Women, Work and Family*
(New York, 1978); Merry E. Wiesner, *Working Women in Renaissance Germany* (New
Brunswick, NJ, 1986); Bridget Hill, *Women, Work and Sexual Politics in Eighteenth-Century
England* (Oxford, 1989); and Heide Wunder, *Er ist die Sonn, sie ist der Mond. Frauen in der
Frühen Neuzeit* (Munich, 1992).
2. Leonore Davidoff and Catherine Hall, *Family Fortunes: Men and Women of the English
Middle Class, 1780–1850* (Chicago, IL, 1987).
3. Amanda Vickery, "Golden Age to Separate Spheres? A Review of the Categories and
Chronology of English Women's History", *The Historical Journal*, 36 (1993), pp. 383–414;
Dorothee Sturkenboom, *Spectators van Hartstocht: Sekse en Emotionele Cultuur in de Achttiende
Eeuw* (Hilversum, 1998), p. 333.
4. Deborah Simonton, *A History of European Women's Work: 1700 to the Present* (Abingdon
1998), pp. 13–14; Sturkenboom, *Spectators van Hartstocht*, p. 334.
5. Jan de Vries and Ad van der Woude, *The First Modern Economy: Success, Failure, and
Perseverance of the Dutch Economy, 1500–1815* (Cambridge, 1997), p. 605.
6. Merry E. Wiesner, *Women and Gender in Early Modern Europe* (Cambridge, 2000), p. 28.

ideal that divided the public from the private sphere and assigned the task of earning an income to men and household activities to women.

Furthermore, the relatively high standard of living during the Golden Age of the Dutch Republic enabled the early practical realization of this dominant ideology and led to an early withdrawal of women from the labour market.[7] Work inside the home must have occupied women earlier than in other countries. "Standards of domestic comfort rose higher and spread further down the social scale than elsewhere before the nineteenth century", Jan de Vries and Ad van der Woude concluded.[8]

At the same time, the early modern period has been characterized as a turning point in the perception of labour. Traditionally, manual labour was seen as degrading, but in the late Middle Ages attitudes towards work changed and a new appraisal of labour emerged.[9] Again, the northern Netherlands represents an interesting case. Calvinism was said to have encouraged a new work ethic that was characterized by diligence, thrift, and self-discipline.[10] According to economic historians, profound socio-economic changes led to an intensification of labour and to work being highly esteemed.[11] Work became increasingly perceived as beneficial to both the individual and to society as a whole. There was, moreover, a growing awareness of the economic importance of work, and work was also increasingly linked with consumption.[12] The emergence of new industrious behaviour, and especially the increased industriousness of women, forms a key element in De Vries's theory on the economic transformation of the early modern period. To be able to purchase new consumer goods, married women and children especially changed how they allocated their time, devoting less to leisure and household production and more to income-earning work.[13]

---

7. Hettie A. Pott-Buter, *Facts and Fairy Tales about Female Labor, Family and Fertility: A Seven Country Comparison* (Amsterdam, 1997), pp. 66–67, 282–287; De Vries and Van der Woude, *First Modern Economy*, pp. 604–605.

8. De Vries and Van der Woude, *First Modern Economy*, p. 605.

9. Diana Wood, *Medieval Economic Thought* (Cambridge, 2002), pp. 52–53.

10. Catharina Lis and Josef Ehmer, "Introduction: Historical Studies in Perceptions of Work", in Josef Ehmer and Catharina Lis (eds), *The Idea of Work in Europe from Antiquity to Modern Times* (Farnham, 2009), pp. 1–30, 9.

11. *Ibid.*, p. 18.

12. Robert Jütte, *Poverty and Deviance in Early Modern Europe* (Cambridge, 1994), p. 198; James R. Farr, *Artisans in Europe 1300–1914* (Cambridge, 2000), pp. 15–20; Thomas Buchner, "Perceptions of Work in Early Modern Economic Thought: Dutch Mercantilism and Central European Cameralism in Comparative Perspective", in Ehmer and Lis, *The Idea of Work in Europe*, pp. 191–213, 211.

13. Jan de Vries, "Between Purchasing Power and the World of Goods: Understanding the Household Economy in Early Modern Europe", in R. Porter and J. Brewer (eds), *Consumption and the World of Goods* (London, 1993), pp. 177–205; Jan de Vries, *The Industrious Revolution: Consumer Behavior and the Household Economy, 1650 to the Present* (Cambridge, 2008), pp. 82, 108.

There seems to be a discrepancy between the narrowing norms for women and the increasingly positive evaluation of work. How did women fit in with the ideology of work? This article discusses common notions of the economic role of women as they emerged from the sixteenth- and seventeenth-century debates on women, gender relations, and work. It examines how these notions were translated into practical advice in conduct literature, household guides, and marriage manuals. The question to what extent ideology affected the actual labour practices of women lies beyond the scope of our study, though the last section examines the gender norms with which women were confronted in everyday life.

IDEAS ON WOMEN

Work, women, and marriage were the subject of lively debates in the early modern period. Those often intertwined debates shaped the context in which norms about women and work were set and contributed to a growing interest in such matters.[14]

A large body of literature on women and gender differences was published in the context of the *Querelle des femmes*, the international Renaissance literary debate on the question of which sex was superior.[15] Also, in the late fifteenth and sixteenth centuries the pictorial tradition of stories concerning the "power of women", disseminated through the arts and literature, became a popular theme in Dutch art. The women in these stories, of whom Eve, Delilah, and Phyllis, seducing Adam, Samson, and Aristotle respectively, are probably the best known, cunningly discredit men. The stories served an exemplary function, warned about the dangers of women, tried to preserve men from foolish behaviour, and pointed to the importance of self-control as a male virtue.[16] Around the same time, the theme of reversed gender roles also gained popularity. The ridiculing of reversed gender roles in comic literature and visual representations aimed to emphasize male authority. Women and men each had their own tasks and responsibilities, and the popular theme taught them that they should stick to this "natural" allocation of those tasks and responsibilities.[17]

14. Marijke Spies, "Women and Seventeenth-Century Dutch Literature", *Dutch Crossing*, 19 (1995), p. 3; Yvonne Bleyerveld, *Hoe Bedriechlijck dat die Vrouwen zijn: Vrouwenlisten in de Beeldende Kunst van de Nederlanden, circa 1350–1650* (Leiden, 2000), p. 12; Els Kloek, *Vrouw des huizes. Een cultuurgeschiedenis van de Hollandse huisvrouw* (Amsterdam, 2009), pp. 16–19.
15. Wiesner, *Women and Gender in Early Modern Europe*, p. 20; Spies, "Women and Seventeenth-Century Dutch Literature", pp. 8–9; Bleyerveld, *Hoe Bedriechlijck dat die Vrouwen zijn*, p. 215; S. Veld, "Tot lof van vrouwen? Retorica, sekse en macht in paradoxale vrouwenloven in de Nederlandse letterkunde (1578–1662)" (unpublished Ph.D. thesis, Utrecht University, 2005), pp. 10–11, 16, 253.
16. Bleyerveld, *Hoe Bedriechlijck dat die Vrouwen zijn*, pp. 296–297.
17. Lène Dresen-Coenders, *Helse en Hemelse Vrouwenmacht omstreeks 1500* (Nijmegen, 1988), pp. 31–38.

The popularity of the theme of reversed gender roles was part of the growing interest in gender relations, an interest linked to the profound socio-economic changes in this period, and more specifically to the emergence of a new division of labour from the late Middle Ages.[18] With the emergence of labour markets, old production forms and labour relations were replaced by new ones. Tasks had to be redefined and became more strictly divided between women and men; women were assigned the household and men the world of work. The gender hierarchy propagated in books of instruction and in visual representations are said to have supported the tendency of the urban bourgeois to exclude women from the urban labour market.[19]

Changes on the religious front also contributed to the heightened interest in what were deemed proper roles for women. The Reformation rejected the superiority of celibacy and defended matrimony. New norms had to be set, specified, and legitimized. Marriage became the standard, mutual help and companionship the aim, and in wedlock men and women were assigned specific, gendered roles. Reformists emphasized the "natural" differences between women and men, and propagated a gender-specific allocation of tasks.[20]

It is difficult to assess the precise effects of Protestantism on the position of women. New norms cannot simply be qualified as positive or negative, as much depended on whether such norms were actually enforced. Historians have pointed out that there were many similarities between Protestant and Catholics ideals and that the assignment of household tasks to women was a constant factor that transcended religious boundaries.[21] However, even though the Reformation did not engender a completely new gender ideology, the religious changes of the sixteenth century certainly did intensify the debate on gender roles.

IDEAS ON WORK

Obviously, norms concerning women and work were influenced not only by ideas about women, but also by ideologies about work. In the early modern northern Netherlands work was valued positively, and this high

18. *Ibid.*, pp. 34–35; *idem*, "De machtsbalans tussen man en vrouw in het vroegmoderne gezin", in Harry Peeters, Lène Dresen-Coenders, and Ton Brandenbarg (eds), *Vijf eeuwen gezinsleven: Liefde, huwelijk en opvoeding in Nederland* (Nijmegen, 1988), pp. 57–98, 58; Herman Pleij, "Wie wordt er bang voor het Boze Wijf? Vrouwenhaat in de Middeleeuwen", *De revisor*, 4:6 (1977), pp. 38–42, 41. For an overview of this debate see Bleyerveld, *Hoe Bedriechlijck dat die Vrouwen zijn*, pp. 251–252.
19. Dresen-Coenders, "De machtsbalans", p. 58. See also Bleyerveld, *Hoe Bedriechlijck dat die Vrouwen zijn*, p. 253.
20. M.J. Gunning, *Gewaande Rechten: Het Denken over Vrouwen en Gelijkheid van Thomas van Aquino tot de Bataafsche Constitutie* (Zwolle, 1991), pp. 79, 97.
21. Wiesner, *Women and Gender in Early Modern Europe*, pp. 26, 29.

esteem is often related to the spread of Calvinism. Weber asserted that
the Calvinist doctrine of predestination contributed to the development
of a new work ethic that emphasized the necessity for hard work and
ultimately contributed to the development of capitalism.[22] This causality
has become the subject of debate in the historiography on religion and
work ideologies.[23] Many scholars have reversed the theory and claimed
that changing economic and social structures drove ideological changes,
and that the capitalist mentality engendered a new economic mentality,
the Protestant "work ethic".[24] As Lis and Ehmer have shown, there is a
broad consensus that the intensification of labour and the greater esteem
in which work was held were caused in part by profound socio-economic
changes, such as the transformation of agrarian class structures, the
processes of urbanization, proletarianization, and social differentiation
with an ongoing stratification of the population.[25] These factors are also
very plausible explanations for the emergence of a new work ethic in the
Dutch Republic.

Despite the debates, there seems to be agreement about the existence of
a particular work ethic in early modern western Europe.[26] This work
ethic was further strengthened by humanist ideas on work and diligence.[27]
The opposition of diligence to idleness was a central theme in humanist
thought on human virtues and vices. From 1550 onward, labour became a
means to acquire not just prosperity but also self-confidence and self-
esteem, and to distinguish oneself from others. Idleness was considered
the ultimate vice.[28]

In the sixteenth century, the representation of labour and diligence
became extremely popular in Dutch art. According to Ilja Veldman, the
work ethic stemmed from the development of an urban citizenry. The
increasing independency of the individual, the impact of moral precepts to
guide burghers in their everyday lives, and the influence of humanist ideas
were factors that led to the development of the view that labour and diligence

22. Max Weber, *The Protestant Ethic and the Spirit of Capitalism* (New York, 1930). See also
Lis and Ehmer, "Introduction".
23. Wood, *Medieval Economic Thought*, p. 53; Birgit van den Hoven, *Work in Ancient and
Medieval Thought: Ancient Philosophers, Medieval Monks and Theologians and their Concept
of Work, Occupations and Technology* (Amsterdam, 1996).
24. Lis and Ehmer, "Introduction", pp. 13–14; Ilja M. Veldman, "Representations of Labor and
Diligence in Late-Sixteenth-Century Netherlandish Art: The Secularization of the Work
Ethic", in Arthur K. Wheelock, Jr and Adele Seeff (eds), *The Public and Private in Dutch
Culture of the Golden Age* (Newark, NJ, 2000), pp. 123–140, 123–124.
25. Lis and Ehmer, "Introduction", p. 18.
26. De Vries and Van der Woude, *First Modern Economy*, pp. 165–172, 172. See also Veldman,
"Representations of Labor and Diligence", p. 123; Lis and Ehmer, "Introduction", p. 15.
27. Veldman, "Representations of Labor and Diligence", p. 133.
28. *Ibid.*, p. 133; Annette de Vries, *Ingelijst Werk. De verbeelding van arbeid en beroep in de
vroegmoderne Nederlanden* (Zwolle, 2004), p. 23.

were a means of obtaining prosperity.[29] This work ethic remained strong during the Golden Age. Humanists encouraged industriousness as a remedy for poverty, crime, and moral decay. But there was also a growing awareness of the economic importance of work,[30] and it was increasingly perceived as a road to prosperity, as beneficial to both the individual and society as a whole.[31] Seventeenth-century mercantilism emphasized labour as a means to increase productivity.[32] To Dutch mercantilist economists, work was a means to achieve wealth and to enhance one's social position, as Thomas Buchner has shown.[33]

In the eighteenth century, again, new attitudes to work emerged, but work continued to be valued highly. Productivity and the connection between work and economic progress were central in how eighteenth-century economists perceived work.[34] Enlightenment philosophers emphasized work as fundamental to human self-realization.[35] In implementing Enlightenment ideals, the elevating and educational effects of work were stressed.[36]

The meanings attached to "work" in Protestant, humanist, mercantilist, and Enlightenment thought differed, but all held work in high esteem, and in one way or another they all propagated industriousness. This prompts the question of how women fitted in to the ideology of work. After all, the positive evaluation of work, the often high esteem in which gainful employment was held, and the strict norms which required people to provide for their own subsistence by means of work seem to conflict with the narrowing gender roles that increasingly assigned the task of bread-winning to men and the private world and the household to women.

WOMEN AT HOME, MEN ON THE STREET

The association of women with the home was deeply rooted in European culture, but the advice to women to remain at home became a "clamouring chorus" in seventeenth-century Holland, as Elizabeth Honig put it.[37] In Anthonis de Roovere's poem *Van den hinne tastere*, published around 1555,

---

29. Veldman, "Representations of Labor and Diligence", pp. 123, 138.
30. Jütte, *Poverty and Deviance in Early Modern Europe*, p. 198.
31. Veldman, "Representations of Labor and Diligence".
32. Farr, *Artisans in Europe*, p. 16.
33. Buchner, "Perceptions of Work in Early Modern Economic Thought".
34. Farr, *Artisans in Europe*, p. 18; Cynthia J. Koepp and Steven Laurence Kaplan, "Introduction", in *idem* (eds), *Work in France: Representations, Meaning, Organization and Practice* (Ithaca, NY, 1986), pp. 13–53, 15; Lis and Ehmer, "Introduction", p. 20.
35. Lis and Ehmer, "Introduction", p. 8.
36. J.W. Spaans, *Armenzorg in Friesland 1500–1800: Publieke Zorg en Particuliere Liefdadigheid in Zes Friese steden: Leeuwarden, Bolsward, Franeker, Sneek, Dokkum en Harlingen* (Hilversum, 1997), pp. 330, 365–366.
37. Elizabeth Alice Honig, "Desire and Domestic Economy", *Art Bulletin*, 83 (2001), pp. 294–315, 306.

a peasant complains that he has to work so hard while his wife just stays at home, having a quiet and easy life. The couple decide to switch roles for one day. After having spent a day working hard in the field in the open air, the wife returns home, tired but satisfied. For the peasant, the day was less successful. He appeared unable to cope with the household chores and to take care of the animals and the young children at home. De Roovere's message is clear: each sex should stick to its own tasks, and the typical feminine responsibilities of attending to the household should not be underestimated.[38] The caricatures within the tradition of the reversed gender roles also assigned household tasks to women and outside work to men.

Presenting attending to the household as a typical feminine task was combined with the propagation of chastity as a feminine virtue. This ideal implied that women were supposed to remain at home. Desiderus Erasmus prescribed that women should leave their home as little as possible. At home, a woman would not be exposed to any seduction or bad company.[39] Juan Luis Vives shared this opinion and in his influential *De Institutione Feminae Christianae*, a Dutch edition of which appeared in 1554, stated that the advice not to appear too often in public was addressed especially to married women, as they had already found what non-married women were still looking for.[40]

A century later, when the Dutch Republic experienced an economic boom, women were still advised to stay at home as much as possible. Jacob Cats, author of the best-known and most widely disseminated conduct book of the seventeenth century *Houwelick, dat is het gansche beleyt des echten-staets* (1625), was very clear about gender roles: a husband must leave the house and practice his trade, a wife should stay at home and watch the kitchen.[41] For Cats the responsibilities of women lay first and foremost in attending to the household. Petrus Wittewrongel, clergyman and famous representative of the Further Reformation, the movement resembling English Puritanism, which desired to apply Reformation teachings to their day, claimed that it would not suit women to be seen too often in the open field or in public streets. It is not without reason, he argued in his *Oeconomia Christiana* (1655), that a woman is called a "housewife".[42] Johan van Beverwijck had addressed the same issue in his *Van de Wtnementheyt des vrouwelicken geslachts* (1639) [On the Excellence of the Female Sex], one of

38. Bleyerveld, *Hoe Bedriechlijck dat die Vrouwen zijn*, p. 163; Kloek, *Vrouw des huizes*, p. 15.
39. Arend V.N. van Woerden, *Vrouwelijk en mannelijk bij Erasmus. Een onderzoek inzake genus* (Rotterdam, 2004), p. 55.
40. Juan Luis Vives, *Die Institutie en de Leeringe van een Christelijke Vrouwe* (Antwerp, 1554).
41. Jacob Cats, *Houwelick, dat is het gansche beleyt des echten-staets* (Amsterdam, 1625) p. 90.
42. Petrus Wittewrongel, *Oeconomia Christiana ofte christelicke huys-houdinghe* (Amsterdam, 1655), p. 721.

the most famous examples of appraisal literature on Dutch women. He argued that a woman's virtue consists primarily in keeping the household and that this was the very reason why married women "in our language" are called "housewives" (*Huys-vrouwen*).[43] Both Wittewrongel and Van Beverwijck referred to the analogy of a housewife and the tortoise, the traditional emblem of female virtue, as this animal carried its house on its back and was therefore always at home.

Conduct books, works of household management, proverb collections, and moral treatises all urged women to stay at home.[44] Yet these recommendations did not imply that women were not allowed to leave their homes at all. Women had to serve God and thus attend church, keep in contact with neighbours, and visit friends. Moreover, attending to the household would require them to leave home once in a while, and they might be taken out by their husbands. Even so, their prime responsibilities lay in the home, and the household required their continuous attention.

The idea that women were better suited to running the household than men was substantiated by references to the Bible and to women's physical characteristics. Luther claimed, for example, that women have a small chest, broad hips, and a broad seat; broad hips facilitate childbirth; and a broad seat indicates that they should keep seated and not leave the home.[45] Van Beverwijck too referred to the female anatomy. Physically, women were of a more delicate design, their flesh was softer, and their muscles weaker because women would fulfil their duties within the house. Men, on the contrary, could withstand coldness, heat, and travelling and were thus, according to the medical doctor, better equipped for outdoor activities.[46] Therefore, all work outside the house was assigned to men, and work that could be done inside the home was assigned to women.[47]

INDUSTRIOUSNESS AND THRIFT

Sixteenth- and seventeenth-century writers assigned work outside the home to men and inside the home to women. But what tasks were women supposed to fulfil? Women were in charge in the home. A housewife had to ensure that her orders would be acted upon, and, furthermore, she should dedicate her time to cleaning the house, washing clothes, preparing food, raising children, and instructing and managing her servants, if she had any. Spinning, making and mending clothes, and other textile chores

---

43. Johan van Beverwijck, *Van de Wtnementheyt des vrouwelicken geslachts* (Dordrecht, 1639), p. 206.
44. Honig, "Desire and Domestic Economy", p. 306.
45. Gunning, *Gewaande rechten*, p. 88.
46. Van Beverwijck, *Van de Wtnementheyt des vrouwelicken geslachts*, p. 207.
47. *Ibid.*, p. 205.

were also considered household chores.[48] Erasmus advised girls to learn spinning and weaving. The seventeenth-century poet Gillis Jacobs Quintijn instructed mothers to keep their daughters at home and ensure they were kept occupied in spinning, sewing, and lacemaking.[49] Wittewrongel referred to spinning, making clothes, and work with wool and flax when he urged women to be continuously busy.

In the conduct literature of the sixteenth and seventeenth centuries, these activities were presented first and foremost as part of the household chores, as production for subsistence. However, if, Erasmus and Wittewrongel stated, a woman produced more than she needed for her household, the produce could be sold at the market.[50] Dirck Volkertsz. Coornhert also included spinning among the "necessary and useful" means by which women could earn an income.[51] It took until the eighteenth century, however, before these "feminine handworks" were more explicitly presented as honourable income-earning activities.[52]

Even though women acted as producers, for a long time they were associated more with consumption than with production. In his poem "Men behoeft veel die huijs sal houwen" (1524) [One Needs a Lot to Keep up a Home], Jan van Stijevoort emphasized the feminine virtue of thrift by criticizing the squandering behaviour of a housewife who shouts to her husband "Provide or find money in public so that I can buy".[53] If a woman wanted to contribute to the economy of the household – and it was her duty to do so – she was obliged in the first instance to run the household thriftily, as Vives asserted.[54] Seventeenth-century writers also appealed to the role of women as consumers and men as producers. Van Beverwijck referred to Aristotle when he recalled that men should obtain the goods and women preserve them.[55] Wittewrongel urged married women to be economical, as what a man brought in should be used by her thriftily.[56]

---

48. *Ibid.*, p. 207; Van Woerden, *Vrouwelijk en mannelijk bij Erasmus*, p. 55.

49. Cited in E.M. Kloek, "De Vrouw", in H.M. Beliën, A.T. van Deursen, and G.J. van Setten (eds), *Gestalten van de Gouden Eeuw. Een Hollands Groepsportret* (Amsterdam, 1995) pp. 241–279, 254.

50. Van Woerden, *Vrouwelijk en mannelijk bij Erasmus*, p. 56. Wittewrongel, *Oeconomia Christiana*, p. 723.

51. De Vries, *Ingelijst werk*, p. 232.

52. J. le Francq van Berkhey, *Natuurlyke historie van Holland*, 9 vols (Amsterdam, 1769–1811), pp. 1320–1321. See also Danielle van den Heuvel, *Women and Entrepreneurship: Female Traders in the Northern Netherlands, c.1580–1815* (Amsterdam, 2007), pp. 44–45.

53. Frederik Lyna and Willem van Eeghem (eds), *Jan van Stijevoorts Refereinenbundel anno 1524* (Antwerp, n.d.), p. 159, available at http://www.dbnl.org/tekst/stij001refe01/stij001refe01_212.htm#N1450.

54. Vives, *Die Institutie en de Leeringe*, cap IX.

55. Van Beverwijck, *Van de Wtnementheyt des vrouwelicken geslachts*, p. 207.

56. Wittewrongel, *Oeconomia Christiana*, p. 724.

Sixteenth- and seventeenth-century conduct literature was usually addressed to married women and prepared women for their ultimate calling in life: marriage. But what advice was given to women who were not married? Moralists were usually not very explicit about the matter. Unmarried women were usually referred to as women who were not yet married. We have already seen that Vives considered it more important for married women to remain at home than for single women to do so. Nonetheless, this did not imply that unmarried women were permitted to manifest themselves in public too loudly and prominently. Erasmus too argued that single women would be better off staying at home than wandering around. As far as widows were concerned, they were supposed to replace their husband as responsible household heads and dedicate their time to the upbringing of their children.[57] In the debate about the question of whether women were capable of learning, Anna Maria van Schurman had argued as early as 1638 that women who were exempt from household tasks had the right, even the obligation, to develop their intellectual potential and to dedicate their time to intellectual work.[58]

Although moralists did not encourage women to work for profit, it was not presented as problematic in literary or visual representations. As Annette de Vries has pointed out in her essay on the visual representation of labour and diligence, in the anonymous seventeenth-century painting *De strijd om het dagelijks brood* [Struggle for Daily Bread] women were also depicted among the representatives of different crafts and trades struggling to earn their daily bread.[59] In the middle, two women with spindles can be discerned, apparently just as dedicated as the men to winning the struggle.[60] In conduct books that taught women to be good housewives, working women figured too without any further explanation apparently having to be given.

Working women also appear in Cats's work. The depictions of the lacemaking girl and sewing widow that decorate the cover page of *Houwelick* probably represent household tasks.[61] But Cats also wrote poems about milkmaids and fishwives, who obviously worked for pay outside the house.[62] When, in his *Lof der vrouwen* (1711) [In Praise of Women],

57. Van Woerden, *Vrouwelijk en mannelijk bij Erasmus*, p. 132; Ariadne Schmidt, *Overleven na de dood. Weduwen in Leiden in de Gouden Eeuw* (Amsterdam, 2001), pp. 44–45.

58. Mirjam de Baar, "Schurman, Anna Maria van", in *Digitaal Vrouwenlexicon van Nederland*, available at: http://www.inghist.nl/Onderzoek/Projecten/DVN/lemmata/data/Schurman,%20Anna%20Maria%20van; Kloek, *Vrouw des huizes*, p. 76.

59. Annette de Vries, "Toonbeelden van huiselijkheid of arbeidzaamheid? De iconografie van de spinster in relatie tot de verbeelding van arbeid en beroep in de vroegmoderne Nederlanden", *Tijdschrift voor Sociale en Economische Geschiedenis*, 2 (2005), pp. 103–125, 118.

60. De Vries, *Ingelijst werk*, p. 231.

61. *Idem*, "Toonbeelden van huiselijkheid of arbeidzaamheid?", p. 116.

62. Jacob Cats, "Invallende gedachten op voorvallende gelegentheden", in *idem*, *Alle de wercken* (Amsterdam, 1700), pp. 393–394.

Figure 1. Women depicted with spindles.
Printed in Anonymous, The Struggle for Daily Bread, *1600–1650. Amsterdam Museum. Used with permission.*

Jan van Gijsen fiercely defended the hard-working women of Amsterdam in response to an anonymous satirical work on women, he mentioned the female street vendors who walked down the streets and "carried, hauled, and wheeled" wagons full of fruit, vegetables, herring, and haddock, trying to sell their merchandise.[63]

Van Beverwijck, who advised women to stay home and dedicate their time to the household, did not imply that women were capable solely of doing housework. In his *Van de Wtnementheyt*, one of most famous Dutch examples of the tradition of appraisal literature on women, he reminds us that, without neglecting their households, many Dutch women were involved in crafts and trades ("nering ende koopmanschap") and others in arts and sciences.[64] Likewise, in his *Swart register van duysent sonden* (1679) [Blacklist of a Thousand Sins] the clergyman Jacobus Hondius fiercely criticized gadabout women. A virtuous woman ought to stay at home and look after the household, *unless* her occupation required her to leave the house often and she had to earn a living.

Moreover, despite the strict advice to women to dedicate themselves to housework, throughout the book a whole range of female occupations are mentioned without any further comment. Hondius, for example, forbade female mattress-stoppers, female knitters, domestic servants, female soul-sellers, seamstresses of linen, seamstresses of wool, and female knitters of fishing nets to carry out their regular work on Sundays. Implicitly, therefore,

63. Jan van Gijsen, *Lof der vrouwen of weederlegging tegens het Leven van de hedendaagse vrouwen* (Amsterdam, 1711), p. 4.
64. Van Beverwijck, *Van de Wtnementheyt des vrouwelicken geslachts*, p. 211.

it was allowed on the remaining six days of the week. Bosses, masters, *and* mistresses had to do their utmost to teach their apprentices a craft. Midwives were urged to attend to women in childbirth and unborn babies with care and shop girls were told to be loyal to their "Boss or Mistress".[65] Even though in the seventeenth century widows were considered deserving recipients of poor relief, Hondius urged them to first try to find a means of subsistence and maintain themselves before seeking poor relief.[66]

Abundant examples of working women in conduct books urged women to be diligent and industrious. In doing so, these literary works linked up with a theme propagated in the visual arts as well. With her reinterpretation of the depiction of female spinners, who represent the virtue of female diligence rather than of domesticity, Annette de Vries has shown that diligence, and not domesticity as such, was at the core of female virtuousness. Hard work would prevent not only men but also women from all kinds of vice – in the first place the vice of idleness – just as spinning in the spinning houses that mushroomed in the eighteenth century was supposed to be the right remedy to lead "disorderly" women back on the track of a virtuous life.[67]

The theme of the diligence of Dutch women had a long tradition and probably dates back to Tacitus (AD 55–120), who, in his *Germania*, described Batavian men as idle and women as industrious.[68] In the early modern period this theme was taken up and diligence became celebrated as a feminine virtue. The sixteenth-century conduct books by Erasmus and Vives praised the industriousness of Dutch women, many of whom were said to be active in trade and even maintained their husbands as the latter were too idle to work.[69] Wittewrongel urged women to work continuously. Women could work harder than men, he claimed: men go to work after sunrise, as their outdoor activities require sunlight. But as women work inside the house, they could light a candle and thus start work early, as early even as in the night.[70]

The connection of diligence with paid work was also still prevalent in seventeenth-century discourse. But this time, the connection with work inside the home was not made. Cats praised milkmaids and fishwives, who were said to work harder than domestic servants.[71] That they worked outside the home is obvious. Grotius took up the familiar theme in his

---

65. Jacobus Hondius, *Swart register van duysent sonden* (Amsterdam, 1679), nos. 42, 46, 144, 336, 414, 804, 959, 968, and 989.
66. Schmidt, *Overleven na de dood*, pp. 179–180; Hondius, *Swart register van duysent sonden*, no. 983.
67. De Vries, "Toonbeelden van huiselijkheid of arbeidzaamheid?", pp. 103–125.
68. Kloek, *Vrouw des huizes*, pp. 28–30.
69. *Ibid.*
70. Wittewrongel, *Oeconomia Christiana*, p. 722.
71. Cats, "Invallende gedachten op voorvallende gelegentheden".

Vergelijking der gemeenebesten (1603) and attributed the affluence of the Dutch to the involvement in trade of both women and men. Women raised children, cared for the household, and at the same time took part in trade when their husbands were absent: they administered capital, sold goods, kept accounts, and travelled back and forth without putting their dignity and chastity at risk.[72] That the reputation of Dutch women as hard-working entrepreneurs was widely known is shown by the large body of literature written by foreign visitors commenting upon their prominent involvement in commercial activities.[73] And, again, these women must have worked in public places, as their industriousness would otherwise have remained unnoticed by the commentators.

Seventeenth-century Dutch economic theorists either neglected female work or regarded it as of minor importance for the wealth of a society, as Thomas Buchner has shown.[74] Josiah Child, the English merchant and proponent of mercantilism, apparently formed an exception. In his *A New Discourse of Trade*, first published in 1668, he wrote:

> The Education of their Children, as well Daughters as Sons; all which, be they of never so great Quality or Estate, they always take care to bring up to write perfect good Hands, and to have the full knowledge and use of Arithmetick and Merchants Accounts; the well understanding and practice whereof, doth strangely infuse into most that are the owners of that quality, of either Sex, not onely an Ability for Commerce of all kinds, but a strong aptitude, love, and delight in it; and in regard the Women are as knowing therein as the Men, it doth incourage their Husbands to hold on in their Trades to their dying days, knowing the capacity of their Wives to get in their Estates, and carry on their Trades after their Deaths.[75]

Writers of seventeenth-century household manuals acknowledged the importance of the labour of women to the household economy, and both Dutch and foreign observers acknowledged the importance of their efforts for the common good. In the eighteenth century, however, ideas about gender roles changed. Whereas sixteenth-century humanists had told women to stay at home and dedicate their time to the household, the eighteenth-century advice literature taught women that it was their responsibility to create an atmosphere of homeliness in which a father could fulfil his role as breadwinner and where children could be raised. Prescriptive works more explicitly excluded married women from the public sphere. The role of a woman as mother, wife, and homemaker

72. Els Kloek, "De Geschiedenis van een Stereotype: De Bazigheid, Ondernemingszin en Zindelijkheid van Vrouwen in Holland (1500–1800)", *Jaarboek Centraal Bureau voor Genealogie*, 58 (2004), pp. 5–25, 12.
73. *Ibid.*; Van den Heuvel, *Women and Entrepreneurship*, pp. 40–43.
74. Buchner, "Perceptions of Work in Early Modern Economic Thought", p. 212.
75. Josiah Child, *A New Discourse of Trade, Wherein is recommended several weighty Points relating to Companies of Merchants etc.* (London, 1698), p. 4.

became celebrated.[76] That she was supposed to raise the children and manage the household was stressed even more than before – at least in literature.

GENDER NORMS IN DAILY PRACTICE

The humanist message about the virtue of diligence was diffused not just throughout north-western Europe in the arts. It also reached a broad public with its ideas on social welfare. Social and political unrest, economic decline, increased migration, and urbanization all increased concerns about poverty. Humanist views changed the perception of poverty and inspired the reorganization of municipal poor relief in the sixteenth century. The emphasis on diligence was one of the key themes in sixteenth-century projects to reorganize poor relief.[77]

In the most famous treatise on the subject, *De Subventione Pauperum* (1526) [On Assistance to the Poor], Juan Luis Vives distinguished between the idle and the deserving poor, advocated civic supervision of all poor relief, and the employment of those who were fit and healthy.[78] Like other humanists, such as Bucer and Melanchton, Vives also strongly advocated education as a remedy to combat idleness and discipline the poor.[79] In his recommendations for publicly supported schools for children Vives made no exception for girls, as he argued in favour of "a similar school for girls, in which they could be taught the fundamentals of literacy", and even claimed that if a "girl is particularly qualified for studies and is inclined to them, she should be permitted to progress farther, provided that the courses coincide with the development of her character".[80] Dirck Volkertsz. Coornhert too believed that employment was the remedy for beggary and vagabondage and suggested that the poor should be put to work: men could be employed by artisans, women and girls should be put to work spinning and weaving.[81]

The humanist perceptions of poverty that inspired the reorganization of poor-relief systems in several countries also resonated in the programmes to reform public assistance in various Dutch towns: begging was prohibited, the healthy poor were employed, their children were educated, and public assistance for the undeserving poor was restricted.[82]

---

76. Sturkenboom, *Spectators van Hartstocht*, pp. 327–333.
77. S. Groenveld, J.J.H. Dekker, and T.R.M. Willemse, *Wezen en boefjes. Zes eeuwen zorg in wees- en kinderhuizen* (Hilversum, 1997), pp. 21–22; Spaans, *Armenzorg in Friesland*, p. 40.
78. Jütte, *Poverty and Deviance in Early Modern Europe*, pp. 215–216.
79. C. Lis, H. Soly, and D. Van Damme, *Op vrije voeten? Sociale politiek in West-Europa (1450–1914)* (Leuven, 1985), p. 62.
80. Juan Luis Vives, *On Assistance to the Poor* [with an introduction by Alice Tobriner] (Toronto, 1999), p. 43.
81. Spaans, *Armenzorg in Friesland*, pp. 83–85.
82. *Ibid.*, p. 43. Groenveld, *Wezen en boefjes*, pp. 21–24.

In his 1577 treatise on the reorganization of poor relief, the Leiden
secretary Jan van Hout, for example, also distinguished between the idle
and what were considered the "honourable poor", those people who
were not to blame for their poverty. He mentioned women in childbed,
the sick, widows, and "poor people burdened with children" as deserving
recipients of public support. These people were apparently not considered
able to maintain themselves through work. It is significant that women
were not mentioned as a separate category.[83] Apparently, healthy women
who were not pregnant were supposed to work. In practice, public
assistance was considered as an additional source of income for both
women and men, and a request for support was legitimized only if one
was unable to work or if one's earnings were insufficient.[84]

In the Dutch Republic, as in most other countries in north-western
Europe, the intellectual debate on poverty resulted in the employment of
vagabonds and the poor. Inspired by Coornhert, work became a central
element in the punishment of criminals in the houses of correction
established in Dutch cities in the late sixteenth and seventeenth centuries.
By providing work, the authorities tried to stimulate the work ethic and
teach prisoners a trade to facilitate their rehabilitation. In practice, it
appeared difficult to implement these ideals, and punishment became
more important than vocation. But inmates of both sexes were set to
work, as women had to spin and men to rasp in these institutions.[85]

The need to provide work to the poor and vagabonds also resulted in
the establishment of workhouses from the late sixteenth century onward.[86]
The meaning of work in these institutions shifted gradually. In the
seventeenth century workhouses were established to provide employment to combat poverty and beggary; in the eighteenth century humanist
ideals were replaced by enlightened perceptions of work. Workhouses
too came to be seen as instruments for moral discipline, education, and
elevation.[87]

83. J. *Prinsen*, "Armenzorg te Leiden in 1577", *Bijdragen en mededelingen van het Historisch Genootschap*, 26 (1905), pp. 113–160, 154–155.
84. Hilde van Wijngaarden, *Zorg voor de kost. Armenzorg, arbeid en onderlinge hulp in Zwolle 1650–1700* (Amsterdam, 2000), p. 134; Ingrid van de Vlis, *Leven in armoede. bedeelden in de zeventiende eeuw* (Amsterdam, 2001), p. 179.
85. P. Spierenburg, "The Sociogenesis of Confinement and its Development in Early Modern Europe", in *idem* (ed.), *The Emergence of Carceral Institutions: Prisons, Galleys and Lunatic Asylums, 1550–1900* (Rotterdam, 1981), pp. 9–77, 24–42; Spaans, *Armenzorg in Friesland*, pp. 85–86.
86. Farr, *Artisans in Europe*, pp. 14–15; Jütte, *Poverty and Deviance in Early Modern Europe*, p. 169.
87. Spaans, *Armenzorg in Friesland*, pp. 330, 339–340; H.F.J.M. van den Eerenbeemt, *Armoede en Arbeidsdwang: Werkinrichtingen voor "onnutte" Nederlanders in de Republiek, 1760–1795: Een Mentaliteitsgeschiedenis* (The Hague, 1977), p. 33.

Alongside philanthropic and moral intentions, economic motives too came to play a role in the employment of workhouse inmates.[88] The authorities recognized the productive potential of forced labour, and work in workhouses was regarded as a contribution to the development of manufactories.[89] In the eighteenth century, by employing the inmates of workhouses, local authorities and private entrepreneurs hoped to revitalize the industrial sector, which had been so important for the economic prosperity of the Golden Age but which had declined since the late seventeenth century. Production based on the processing of domestic raw materials should furthermore substitute the import of foreign goods.[90] Women were not excluded as a category from these different perceptions of work. Workhouses provided hemp, flax, and wool to poor women so that they would be able to earn something from spinning, and workhouses often chose to employ their inmates in one of the sectors of the textile industry as this was work that was thought to be suitable for women as well.[91]

Practices in court also demonstrate that women were expected to maintain themselves and their children through paid work. Women who were summoned to court and confined because of theft were often introduced as being "strong, young, and brave" enough to "earn a living with their own hands".[92] Their ability to work – their physical strength – made their crime even more serious.

Women were supposed to work for their own subsistence, and this was the norm not just for the poorest among the female population. The issue of responsibility for maintaining a family came to the fore when marriages were dissolved. When marital conflicts became irresolvable, a marriage could be legally dissolved. Lawyers agreed that a wife could be awarded a maintenance allowance after separation from her husband if she was at least unable to maintain herself on income from capital or work. After all, a legal separation still implied that the husband and wife were legally married, in which case, it was argued, the man was obliged to continue to maintain his spouse. Apparently, however, this was a reciprocal obligation, as women could also be forced to pay a maintenance allowance to their former husbands. This happened, for example, when the children were assigned to the father because the mother was to blame for the separation.

---

88. Jütte, *Poverty and Deviance in Early Modern Europe*, p. 198; Farr, *Artisans in Europe*, pp. 15–16.
89. Farr, *Artisans in Europe*, pp. 15–16.
90. Van den Eerenbeemt, *Armoede en Arbeidsdwang*, pp. 33–34; Spaans, *Armenzorg in Friesland*, pp. 354–361; Elise van Nederveen Meerkerk, *De draad in eigen handen. Vrouwen en loonarbeid in de Nederlandse textielnijverheid 1581–1810* (Amsterdam, 2007), pp. 177–179.
91. Spaans, *Armenzorg in Friesland*, p. 340; van den Eerenbeemt, *Armoede en Arbeidsdwang*, p. 33.
92. See for example Rijksarchief Leiden (RAL), Oud Rechterlijk Archief (ORA), 3, 5, *passim*.

This practice illustrates the fact that in the early modern period maintenance allowances were intended in the first instance for the maintenance of children, not as a provision for women. Only 12 per cent of divorced women received a maintenance allowance for themselves. It was not asked for very frequently, not even by women from the upper or middle classes, who might be assumed to have been less likely to perform paid work.[93]

The maintenance allowance, often paid weekly or annually, was usually rather low and insufficient to sustain a family. It is significant that in a very few cases women were even assigned the business the couple had previously run together as a form of maintenance allowance. Moreover, the examination of thousands of cases of separation and divorce by Dini Helmers has revealed that women never supported their request for maintenance by arguing that it would be "indecent" for them to work. Most people could probably not afford to put forward such an argument, and it is highly unlikely that all these working women would have been considered "indecent".[94]

The concept of the male breadwinner is very much associated with the rise of capitalism and often considered an invention of the nineteenth century.[95] The *ideal* of the male breadwinner existed earlier, though. The widow Jannetgen Gillis petitioning Leiden's city council in 1646 for support as she, a "sad widow", had lost "her beloved husband and breadwinner" ["haren welbeminden man ende brootwinner"] is a rather early reference to the notion of the male breadwinner, but not the only one.[96] That a married man had to be able to maintain his family was a frequently used argument in conflicts between parents and children on the choice of marriage partner, as Manon van der Heijden has noted.

Legally, only minor children, those under the age of twenty-five, needed their parents' consent to marry; for those of age, the consent of their parents was desirable nonetheless. In seventeenth-century Holland the most common reason put forward by parents for withholding their consent to the marriage of their daughters was that they were not convinced that the intended spouse would be able to support a family. Girls' parents might object to his lack of experience or skill, and some required that a bridegroom first pass his examinations before they would consent to the marriage. Married women were also expected to contribute to the

93. D. Helmers, *"Gescheurde bedden." Oplossingen voor gestrande huwelijken, Amsterdam 1753–1810* (Hilversum, 2002), pp. 257–262, 264.
94. *Ibid.*, p. 263.
95. Angélique Janssen, "The Rise and Decline of the Male Breadwinner Family? An Overview of the Debate", in *idem* (ed.), *The Rise and Decline of the Male Breadwinner Family?*, International Review of Social History, Supplement, 42 (1997), pp. 1–23.
96. Ariadne Schmidt, "Survival Strategies of Widows and their Families in Early Modern Holland, c.1580–1750", *History of the Family*, 12 (2007), pp. 268–281, 268.

household economy. But the skills of potential brides were never mentioned, and the economic contribution of the prospective wife was rarely questioned by the parents of the bridegroom.

Even so, the inability to maintain a family was not necessarily an insurmountable impediment to marriage. For church councils, which had an important say in matrimonial affairs, financial objections were not accepted as valid reasons to break marriage vows. For magistrates too, who ultimately decided on marital issues, the ability to keep a family was not of decisive importance in the choice of marriage partner.[97]

Due to the growing wage dependency of men in the course of the seventeenth century, many women were confronted with a loss of income after the death of a spouse. Structural solutions in the form of guaranteed benefits provided by guilds or state pensions did not yet exist. In the course of the seventeenth century various social groups began to develop new and specialized forms of support for their widows, and these initiatives might be interpreted as an indication of the growing importance of the ideal of the male breadwinner.

Clergymen were the first group within society to propose comprehensive arrangements for the maintenance of their widows. Provisions for clergymen's widows had been identified as a point of concern at the national synod in 1581. At the end of the sixteenth century, the church authorities tried to find a solution for the loss in income suffered by the widows of clergymen. Local religious communities were advised to establish mutual assistance funds, but owing to lack of finance such local initiatives could not be realized everywhere. Initiatives at provincial level were more successful from the 1590s. In large parts of the province of Holland, widows of clergymen were paid an annual pension of 50 guilders, and later of between 100 and 250 guilders. These payments were inadequate to compensate for the income loss sustained by those widows, as the average clergyman's stipend had increased considerably since the end of the sixteenth century and by the second half of the seventeenth century annual stipends of 600–800 guilders were not uncommon. These initiatives nevertheless demonstrate the awareness of the vulnerability of widows, and underline the fact that men were considered responsible for maintaining their families, even after their deaths.[98]

It is probably no coincidence that the first pensions were established for the widows of clergymen, as they functioned as role models in the period so soon after the Reformation. During the provincial synod of Holland

97. Manon van der Heijden, "Contradictory Interests: Work and Parent–Child Relations in Early Modern Holland", *History of the Family*, 9 (2004), pp. 355–370, 359–361.
98. A. Schmidt, "'Dat oock de Weduwen ende Weesen der Dienaren niet vergethen werden': de Ontwikkeling van de Zorg voor Predikantsweduwen in Leiden in de Zeventiende Eeuw", *Leids Jaarboekje* (Leiden, 2000), pp. 38–53.

in 1574, the church authorities tried to restrict the work options of clergymen's wives to certain occupations: they were forbidden to engage in a
public trade ["openbare- of winkelnering"]. Twenty years later the regulation was relaxed somewhat, although clergymen's wives who wanted
to trade still had to ask permission first as some occupations were considered dishonourable. Church councils were instructed to be aware that
clergymen's wives should not undertake professional activities that would
dishonour them. Moreover, the general opinion of the authorities was that
church councils should ensure that clergymen's stipends were sufficient to
maintain a family. This ideal, however, did not correspond with the reality, as stipends were still rather low relative to the social standing of
clergymen. An increase in stipends remained an important issue for the
Reformed Church well into the seventeenth century.[99]

Arrangements for widows were especially popular in those sectors in
which women's access to work was somehow restricted. After the
Reformation, the informal mutual assistance of guild members developed
into more formalized and regulated assistance in the form of mutual
trade-based funds. Some, though by no means all, of these support funds
used to provide pensions for widows in addition to assistance in meeting
burial costs and support in the event of illness or old age.[100] Bargemen, for
example, used to provide for their widows as early as the beginning of the
seventeenth century. For a limited period, newly appointed bargemen
were required to pay some of their earnings to the widows of their predecessors to compensate them for loss of income. Widows of journeymen
bargemen were recompensed from the journeymen's support fund, as
were the widows of the journeymen brewers, who received modest
weekly allowances.[101] In 1666 bargemen from Leiden to Utrecht even
supported the establishment of widows' funds, stating explicitly that an
honourable father and husband ought to provide for his wife and children,
and in particular for his widow.[102]

The early statutes of transport guilds in Holland mention female
members, and indirect evidence indicates that widows were admitted until
well into the seventeenth century.[103] During the course of the seventeenth
century, however, women in the transport sector lost this privilege.
Widows' pensions were not very common, because their potentially
extended duration made them rather expensive. However, it is significant

99. Schmidt, *Overleven na de dood*, pp. 196–197.
100. Sandra Bos, *"Uyt liefde tot malcander": Onderlinge Hulpverlening binnen de Noord-
Nederlandse Gilden in Internationaal Perspectief (1570–1820)* (Amsterdam, 1998), pp. 344–345.
101. Schmidt, *Overleven na de dood*, pp. 206–207.
102. *Ibid.*, p. 208.
103. Martha Hulshof, "De gilden", in Koen Goudriaan *et al.* (eds), *De gilden in Gouda*
(Zwolle, 1996), pp. 87–148, 100.

that in the transport sector the payment of small allowances to widows seems to have replaced the older practice of widows carrying on the work of their husbands, a practice still widespread among other craftsmen and tradesmen.[104]

From the second quarter of the eighteenth century onward, many voluntary widows' funds were established. The first private general widows' and orphans' fund was founded in Middelburg in 1735, soon followed by similar funds in Leiden and Haarlem. These private initiatives, which were mainly concentrated in the large urban centres of Holland, were established not so much to meet the needs of poor widows as to avoid widows facing a lower standard of living after the deaths of their spouses. The funds were not successful. Most soon went bankrupt as provision for widows was extremely expensive and the actuarial knowledge necessary to ensure their survival was applied improperly.[105]

The social polarization seen in the eighteenth century and the growing social insecurity contributed to an increased concern for one's personal reputation, since this could be threatened by a possible descent into poverty. But it is likely that, combined with the increased dependency on income from wage work, the male breadwinner ideology also contributed to the development of specialized financial provisions for widows among certain groups of urban society. It is important to stress that the establishment of widows' pensions could simply be seen as an indication of the spread of the *ideal* of the male breadwinner. We may assume that its impact on the actual labour-force participation of women was negligible as the twenty-one mutual widowhood insurance schemes that existed in 1800 covered less than 1 per cent of the total population.[106]

CONCLUSION

The ideology of domesticity that identified women with a domestic role became more articulated throughout the early modern period. Dutch society is said to have played a pioneering role in the development of this middle-class concept. The popular genres of conduct books, works of household management, collections of proverbs, and moral treatises all

104. Schmidt, *Overleven na de dood*, pp. 206–208.
105. Sandra Bos and Ida H. Stamhuis, "Begrafenis- en weduwenfondsen, en prebende sociëteiten", in Jacques van Gerwen and Marco van Leeuwen (eds), *Studies over zekerheidsarrangementen. Risico's risicobestrijding en verzekeringen in Nederland vanaf de Middeleeuwen* (Amsterdam, 1998), pp. 175–182.
106. Marco H.D. van Leeuwen, "Historical Welfare Economics from the Old Regime to the Welfare State: Mutual Aid and Private Insurance for Burial, Sickness, Old Age, Widowhood, and Unemployment in the Netherlands during the Nineteenth Century", in B. Harris and P. Bridgen (eds), *Charity and Mutual Aid in European and North America since 1800* (New York, 2007), pp. 89–130, 107.

urged women to remain in the home and indicate a narrowing of gender norms. Yet, at the same time, the early modern period was characterized by profound changes in the perception of work. Protestant, humanist, mercantilist, and Enlightenment thought shared a high esteem for work and propagated industriousness. These seemingly contradictory tendencies of narrowing gender norms and the positive evaluation of work prompt the question of how women fitted in with the early modern ideology of work. How did a society like the Dutch Republic, with its high standard of living and high labour productivity, reconcile the positive evaluation of work and the strict norms that required people to provide for their own subsistence with the restricted gender roles?

A closer examination of the sixteenth- and seventeenth-century debates on the role of women and the ideology of work, the practical advice given to women, and representations of work in literary publications (and the visual arts) reveals that in the early modern northern Netherlands labour was indeed valued positively and that in this respect no exception was made for women's work. The propagation of a work ethic by religious reformers and humanists did not conflict with gender norms that prescribed that women should dedicate their time to household tasks. The abundance of examples in conduct books and paintings of women figuring as crafts-women or merchants, spinners, weavers, lacemakers, knitters of wool or fishing nets, mattress-stoppers, domestic servants, soul-sellers, seamstresses of linen or wool, midwives, shop girls, and mistresses emphasized that women should be diligent. Industriousness was propagated as a virtue for both women and men. Men, but also women, ought to be diligent, and even though women's involvement in remunerated work was not encouraged in the didactic literature, nor – and that is even more remarkable – was it considered problematic.

This paradox can be solved by looking at the perception of work, which is highly gendered. Whereas nowadays we perceive of remunerated work and unpaid household work as being two separate categories, writers of conduct literature made no sharp distinction between work for subsistence (or the household) as women's work and paid work for the market economy as men's. Instead, they drew a dividing line between work within the home, which was regarded as women's work, and work outside the home, which was regarded as men's work. Women were advised to remain inside. Their responsibilities lay primarily in running the household – a rather compre-hensive task in the early modern period, which included not only household chores but also feminine handwork. However, categories were never rigid. When a woman's diligence resulted in a surplus of produce, or if economic need forced her to do so, her work could be extended to include production for the market too.

Industriousness was propagated because, in the first place, it was thought to prevent women from the ultimate vice of idleness. The opposition of diligence to idleness became central in humanist thinking on human virtues: labour was perceived not only as a means of acquiring prosperity but also of self-confidence and self-esteem. In everyday life, however, industriousness also served a more practical purpose. The craftswomen, merchants, spinners, knitters, domestic servants, seamstresses, midwives, and shop girls had to be industrious because they had to earn their own living.

This brings us to the differences between the gender norms as presented in literary works and the norms with which people were confronted in everyday life. The often heard argument that a husband was supposed to be able to maintain his family, seventeenth-century examples of widows referring to the loss of their family's "breadwinner", and the more general search for structural solutions to the financial need of widows in the form of guaranteed benefits provided by guilds or state pensions are three examples indicating the growing popularity of the ideal of the male breadwinner. However, the influence of such norms on the actual lives of working women is another story. In practice, an explicit differentiation between different social groups of women had always been made.

The humanist message on the virtue of diligence directly influenced ideas about social welfare. Work was promoted as an instrument to combat poverty. Only those unable to work were excused and considered the legitimate recipients of public support. The gender norms embedded in and reproduced by institutions were clear: charity boards, criminal courts, local government, and church councils expected women to be able to maintain themselves. This implied that women from those social layers that lacked income from capital should provide for their own subsistence through work.

In literature, gender roles narrowed even more in the eighteenth century. The perception that men ought to maintain their families slowly trickled down to everyday life. References to the notion of the male breadwinner could be found in the seventeenth century and became more widely disseminated during the course of the eighteenth. Yet this ideal was realistic only for a small group of privileged women. In principle, society expected all able-bodied women to provide for their own maintenance by working.

IRSH 56 (2011), Special Issue, pp. 69–88 doi:10.1017/S0020859011000459
© 2011 Internationaal Instituut voor Sociale Geschiedenis

Between Sin and Salvation: The Seventeenth-Century Dutch Artisan Pieter Plockhoy and His Ethics of Work*

HENK LOOIJESTEIJN

Internationaal Instituut voor Sociale Geschiedenis, Amsterdam

E-mail: hlo@iisg.nl

SUMMARY: There have been few attempts systematically to study the ethics of work in the early modern age on the basis of contemporary sources. Such a study should start with case studies of individual thinkers, as stepping stones to a more comprehensive study of the ethics of work. This article provides such a case study, of the seventeenth-century Dutch artisan Pieter Plockhoy (c.1620–1664). As will be shown, work was a central component of Plockhoy's philosophy of true, practical Christianity, and on the basis of his tracts a more or less coherent ethics of work can be reconstructed. Although this article concentrates on Plockhoy's philosophy of labour, his thought fits into a broader context of related contemporary thinkers, many of whom shared his concerns. Thus the article shows that for scholars wishing to study the ethics of work there is still a whole field which, though yielding a potentially rich harvest, lies fallow.

Though generations of scholars have engaged with Weber's famous thesis on the connection between Protestantism and the rise of capitalism, systematic attempts to study the ethics of work in the early modern age on the basis of contemporary sources have been limited. This is not surprising, given that in many ways the history of the idea of work is still uncharted, as Ehmer and Lis have noted.[1] Given this lacuna, a study of early modern work ethics should perhaps begin with studies of individual thinkers, as stepping stones to a more comprehensive study of the ethics of work.

---

* I would like to thank my colleagues Karin Hofmeester, Piet Lourens, Jan Lucassen, and Christine Moll-Murata, and the participants of the Fifth Workshop of the Global Collaboratory on the History of Labour Relations (Düsseldorf, 12–14 November 2009) for their comments on earlier drafts of this article.
1. Catharina Lis and Josef Ehmer, "Introduction: Historical Studies in Perceptions of Work", in Josef Ehmer and Catharina Lis (eds), *The Idea of Work in Europe from Antiquity to Modern Times* (Farnham, 2009), pp. 1–30, 24.

One such individual thinker was the seventeenth-century Dutch artisan Pieter Plockhoy. His stance on the ethics of work can be reconstructed from one of the three short tracts he published in the late 1650s and early 1660s. Plockhoy did not write about work for the sake of it – in this he seems to have been no different from those artisans studied by James Amelang who left autobiographies.[2] What mattered to Plockhoy, and why he wrote his tracts, was the question of how a true Christian should live. Nevertheless, as will be seen, work was a central component of Plockhoy's philosophy of true, practical Christianity. It is therefore possible to extract a more or less coherent ethics of work from his tracts.

Plockhoy's work ethic is all the more interesting in that he was an artisan, not one of "the leisured or the recipients of the state's or a patron's largess", able to devote more time and energy to thinking about work and its ethics. His thought therefore can give a small, written voice to "the humble" who, to quote Herbert Applebaum, "speak [only] through their work and the objects they create".[3]

In this article, Plockhoy's personal ethics of work is reconstructed and contextualized by following the seven-layered structure of investigation developed by the Collaboratory.[4] Given that Plockhoy is hardly a household name even among specialists of seventeenth-century thought, a brief introduction to the life and thought of Pieter Plockhoy is appropriate here.

PIETER PLOCKHOY: AN INTRODUCTION[5]

Pieter Plockhoy was born in the Dutch town of Zierikzee in the southwestern island province of Zeeland, but as a young man he settled in the Zeeland capital, Middelburg, where he married and started a family, made a living as an artisan – presumably either as a carpenter or tinsmith – and played an active role in the local Mennonite congregation. From 1649 until late 1652 he was one of the congregation's unsalaried ministers, but from the start Plockhoy was highly controversial, perhaps because of the heterodox religious opinions he would espouse later in life, but certainly because of his loose sexual morals. His refusal to accept censure led eventually to his expulsion from the congregation in 1654.

A few years afterwards Plockhoy travelled to London, at the time a hotbed of religious heterodoxy, where he seems to have lived between the

2. *Ibid.*, pp. 7, 26; James S. Amelang, "Lifting the Curse: Or Why Early Modern Worker Autobiographers Did Not Write about Work", in Ehmer and Lis, *The Idea of Work*, pp. 91–100, 93.
3. Herbert Applebaum, *The Concept of Work: Ancient, Medieval and Modern* (Albany, NY, 1992), p. xii.
4. See for this the Introduction to the present volume.
5. The following section is based on my thesis, "'Born to the Common Welfare': Pieter Plockhoy's Quest for a Christian Life (c.1620–1664)" (unpublished Ph.D., European University Institute, 2009).

middle of 1657 and late 1660. He wished to discuss the vexed issue of church settlement with the English Lord Protector, Oliver Cromwell. England had been without a settled church since the early 1640s, a situation deplored by virtually everyone but the dissenters – such as Plockhoy, who advised Cromwell not to set up a new state church but to found meeting places where everyone would be at liberty to discuss Scripture. Cromwell happened to be sympathetic to Plockhoy's ideas, but died shortly after. His son and successor had no interest, and Plockhoy eventually published his correspondence with the Cromwells in an attempt to win over parliament to his views on confessional policy. This tract, *The Way to the Peace and Settlement of these Nations*, was published in 1658, and went through two editions. In *The Way*, Plockhoy argued that the government should steer clear of attempts to lord over the conscience of its subjects – which is a sin – and instead set up meeting places all over the country, where everyone should be allowed to speak freely on religious matters. According to Plockhoy, that would be the only way to ensure civil and internal peace.

While trying to influence government policy, Plockhoy also promoted a second project, which he publicized in *A Way Propounded to make the Poor in these and other Nations Happy*, published in 1659. This tract is the main source for reconstructing Plockhoy's ethics of work. Partly a response to the dire poverty he had seen in England, in *A Way* he set out a blueprint for a "society or little commonwealth" in which artisans, farmers, mariners, and scholars might combine and pool their, usually limited, resources. Rather than struggle individually on the brink of poverty, Plockhoy envisioned them as working together for the greater good of all, avoiding sin, and living according to Christ's tenets. The little commonwealth would strive for economic autonomy and the community's combination of cost-saving and diligent labour would result in a profitable enterprise, Plockhoy hoped.

Unlike his attempt to influence government policy, *A Way* became a runaway success of a sort, for it went through at least six different editions between 1659 and the spring of 1660. Plockhoy came close to realizing his "little commonwealth", but in the end this project came to nought too, probably because the monarchy was restored in 1660. Plockhoy returned to the Dutch Republic, to Amsterdam, where he attended the free-speech colleges of heterodox Christians and became notorious for publicly defending polygamy. Taking advantage of Amsterdam's desire to populate its American colony, Plockhoy concluded a contract with the Burgomasters to set up a colonial settlement where he hoped to establish his "little commonwealth". In the summer of 1662 he published his third tract, *Kort en Klaer Ontwerp* ["Short and Clear Design"], which is based largely on the blueprint he outlined in *A Way*.

In July 1663 Plockhoy and his fellow colonists finally disembarked near what is now the town of Lewes, Delaware, and founded a settlement there.

Fourteen months later, however, the Dutch colonies in North America were seized by the English, and Plockhoy's settlement was destroyed in the process. What happened to him is unclear; six years later his widow and children were living in Amsterdam, but where and when exactly Plockhoy died is unknown.

PLOCKHOY'S ETHICS OF WORK: A RECONSTRUCTION

Plockhoy never formulated a coherent world view in his writings, and his ethics of work must be reconstructed on the basis especially of his second tract, *A Way*. His third tract, *Kort en Klaer Ontwerp*, is mainly an abbreviated version of *A Way*, but differs in some details. Plockhoy's tracts had a specific purpose, namely to promote practical solutions to what he perceived to be society's ills,[6] and are therefore limited in their scope and coverage of themes. Furthermore, all three of his tracts served to attract the support of the powerful and the wealthy and will have been written in such a way as to minimize the risk of antagonizing prospective sponsors.

There is thus a real danger that any reconstruction of his ethics of work will remain fragmentary. Nonetheless, the attempt will not be without its rewards, since these tracts show how an artisan, engaged with the problems of his day, thought labour should be conducted and rewarded. As his thought was firmly rooted in the Christian thinking that pervaded his age, Plockhoy's solutions were mandatory rather than optional in as much as they conformed to Christ's tenets. His texts are thus prescriptive, reflecting on what could be and should be rather than what actually was. But they are also, in a lesser sense, descriptive in that Plockhoy occasionally refers to how one should do one's work, and what working practices were unacceptable to him.

THE CENTRALITY OF WORK

To Plockhoy, who like many of his contemporaries aspired to be a "true Christian", work was an integral part of Christianity. His concern with work, however, went further than with most of them: his proposal for a "little commonwealth", or "society" as he called it, was designed in principle for the workers in society, the great part of humanity which had to work to make a living. To Plockhoy, the primary division within society was between those who had to work – either with their hands or with their brains – and those who did not have to, or did not want to. In a truly Christian society everyone should contribute to the common good by spending their time usefully, and Plockhoy clearly disagreed with

---

6. The particular social ills Plockhoy wanted to redress will be discussed in greater detail later in this article.

those who believed that the wealthy need not work. Idleness was a sin. In his view,

> Princes are not born on purpose to reare up stately Palaces, the Learned are not born for the writing of many unprofitable, and for the most part frivolous Books; the rich are not born to boast of their gold, silver, and christal vessels; the rest of the people are not born for so many various unprofitable Handy-crafts.[7]

Princes, scholars, the rich and the poor alike were to use their stations in life to work for the greater good of society, which was part of the Christian duty of working towards the goal of one's salvation.

Work was essential in a Christian's life, and it could hardly be anything else in an age so steeped in biblical lore. Everyone knew Genesis, 3.19: "In the sweat of thy face shalt thou eat bread, till thou return unto the ground." But sweating was one thing, back breaking quite another. To Plockhoy, work should be in proportion to other things in life, especially the time spent on more elevated activities. Normally, one would labour from dawn to dusk, but working until body and spirit were exhausted was not conducive to attending to one's spiritual obligations. Thus, Plockhoy envisioned a working day of only six hours, three in the morning and three in the afternoon, or divided in whatever way it suited the society's members, so that they could bestow "the rest of their time, for the refreshing of their bodies, and profitable excercises of the mind".[8] Like adults, children should not work more than six hours a day so that they could spend their time "in other usefull imployments, that they may be fitted for some what ells beside working".[9]

Plockhoy was less generous to the wage workers employed by the society: they should work the normal average of twelve hours a day, from dawn till dusk, "till any of them be fit and willing to come into us",[10] that is, to become a full member. Plockhoy thus offered an incentive to become a member of the society, but he was also more generous than the average employer by offering the possibility of advancement, and improvement of working conditions. Offering this incentive might have been connected with the opprobrium attached to wage labour in Plockhoy's day. In England at least, artisans and husbandmen greatly disliked being reduced to wage labour and looked down on the landless wage labourer.[11]

---

7. Peter Cornelius van Zurik Zee [pseudonym of Pieter Plockhoy], *A Way Propounded to make the Poor in these and other Nations Happy* (London, 1659), p. 31.
8. *Ibid.*, p. 4.
9. *Ibid.*, p. 12. Though Plockhoy did not elaborate here on what these "other usefull imployments" might be, it is probable that he was referring to a study of the Bible and of the "natural Arts, Sciences and Languages"; *ibid.*, p. 15.
10. *Ibid.*, p. 4.
11. For many examples of this interesting but understudied phenomenon, see Christopher Hill, "Pottage for Freeborn Englishmen: Attitudes to Wage Labour in the Sixteenth and Seventeenth Centuries", in G.H. Feinstein (ed.), *Socialism, Capitalism and Economic Growth: Essays*

Every member of his society should work, preferably, with perhaps the exception of the intellectual workers, with his hands. What was in Plockhoy's eyes perhaps the most sinful occupation – that of merchant – was not to be a separate profession at all: instead, all artisans were to sell their own products, taking turns, the artisans normally residing in the society's rural settlement, with only the temporary "merchants" staying at the urban settlement. What work merchants normally did – the keeping of accounts – Plockhoy hoped to entrust to those young members of the society with a head for figures. They would be instructed in "Ciphering, and keeping Books of accompts", in order to assist the merchant-artisans so "that the merchants also may sometimes work".[12] Plockhoy applied the same principle to the mariners, who in foreign parts were to act as the society's merchants.[13] Plockhoy's dislike of merchants stood in a long tradition of Christian thinkers distrustful of merchants, who were regarded as especially prone to succumb to the capital sin of greed.[14]

Plockhoy was consistent in his insistence on the centrality of work in the life of actual society members. But just as the society's wage workers were expected to work a normal working day, so Plockhoy also kept open the possibility for wealthy and godly supporters of the society, who shared its concern for practical Christianity, to live there without the obligation to work.[15] Instead they were expected to pay their fare and lodgings from their own capital. But if they did do some work for society, Plockhoy would applaud it and they would "hold forth a good Example to all rich time-loosers in the world".[16] For the "Children of rich people",

Presented to Maurice Dobb (Cambridge, 1967), pp. 338–350. He even speaks of "the 'ideological' hostility to the status of wage labourer"; *ibid.*, p. 338. See also Applebaum, *The Concept of Work*, p. 367. It would be interesting to see how widespread this antipathy to wage labour was, and whether it also existed outside England. There is certainly some evidence that it did: in Renaissance Milan, for poor guild masters and workers to become wage labourers meant the loss of dignity, pride, and control over their means of production. See Luca Mocarelli, "The Attitude of Milanese Society to Work and Commercial Activities: The Case of the Porters and the Case of the Elites", in Ehmer and Lis, *The Idea of Work*, pp. 101–121, 108.
12. Plockhoy, *A Way Propounded*, p. 8.
13. *Ibid.*, p. 7.
14. Lis and Ehmer, "Introduction", p. 15. Thomas Aquinas typically rated merchants and shopkeepers lower than farmers and artisans; see Jaume Aurell, "Reading Renaissance Merchants' Handbooks: Confronting Professional Ethics and Social Identity", in Ehmer and Lis, *The Idea of Work*, pp. 71–90, 86–87. Another example of a critic of merchants and their behaviour is the sixteenth-century Italian monk, Tomaso Garzoni; see Luca Mocarelli's contribution to the present volume.
15. I use the term "godly" to refer to all those people who – whatever other differences they might have had – shared a common concern for acting and thinking as a true Christian. What that meant was often debated, as was the question of who exactly was "godly", but that does not detract from the fact that they all shared this concern.
16. Plockhoy, *A Way Propounded*, p. 5. The idea that time needed to be spent usefully was much older: for example, in the sixteenth century the theme of good and bad use of time was popular as the subject of prints in the southern Netherlands; see Ilja M. Veldman,

who, Plockhoy hoped, would attend the society's school for instruction in "Arts, Sciences and languages", there was no escape from labour however. They would be expected to work three hours a day at school, "learning some usefull Trade", so that if they or their parents lost their wealth they might still be able to earn their bread "without being necessitated to fall upon such courses [...] as may prove hurtfull to their souls and bodies".[17] For the members there was no escape from work, but they would enjoy a better balance between work and life. Thus, in Plockhoy's envisioned society the active life and the contemplative life were to be combined, for the greater good of Christian society in general and his little Christian commonwealth in particular.

WORK AND WORKERS IN THE SOCIAL ORDER

In Plockhoy's view, Christ had done away with hierarchy among Christians, "Abollishing amongst his disciples, all preheminency, or domineering, of one over another", and declaring that his followers should regard themselves as equal brothers.[18] For a radical Christian such as Plockhoy, this meant that all human hierarchies were pointless. What mattered to one's salvation was not one's status in life, but one's faith, and acts of faith. Plockhoy reflected that "The world hath her delights in different degrees of Dignities, States, Titles, and offices; exalting themselves above another"; Christ, however, had willed "that everyone shall perform his office as a member of one and the same body". No one should therefore exalt himself or account himself worthier than the other.[19]

Consequently, Plockhoy had no interest in defining a particular social order: all Christians should be one under Christ. His tracts are therefore not explicit about the role of the worker in society, in terms of actual status, place in the hierarchy, or economic position, nor did he make a distinction within his own little society. What hierarchy there was in his society was based on proven skill and individual leadership qualities, not on inherited status or monetary wealth. This in itself was a radical departure from practice in seventeenth-century Dutch and English society, in which even guilds could be largely oligarchic in nature, the wealthier guild brethren dominating the guild leadership. In Plockhoy's society the governor of the society would be chosen not "for his riches or wealth [...] but for his wisdom".[20] All positions of leadership, including the governorship, were

"Representations of Labour in Late Sixteenth-Century Netherlandish Prints: The Secularization of the Work Ethic", in Ehmer and Lis, *The Idea of Work*, pp. 149–175, 158–163.
17. Plockhoy, *A Way Propounded*, p. 4.
18. *Ibid.*, p. 24.
19. *Ibid.*, p. 25.
20. *Ibid.*, p. 9.

for one year only.²¹ Moreover, the governor's leadership was confined to the executive – collectively, all members of the society formed the legislative. Leadership was also accountable: every six or twelve months "an account shall be given". The treasury of the society would be entrusted to three men: the treasury chest would have three locks, and "three of the uppermost in the Government, shall allwayes have the keyes", so that the chest could be opened only if all three were present.²² As the governor was chosen on merit, so were the masters who oversaw their fellow artisans: the best workmen would be appointed to that responsible position.²³

All status within the society thus depended on merit, election, and accountability, and all members were otherwise equal. Plockhoy's society was both egalitarian and democratic, and espoused a work ethic to which all members were to subscribe. It is likely that Plockhoy believed that these principles of organization applied to all organizations of "true Christians". That life in fact rarely conformed to "true Christianity" was of course the main reason for founding his community.

Though Plockhoy did not set out to write a systematic analysis of the position of the workers in society in his time, what he wrote about life outside his proposed community is enough to get an impression of what he believed to be the common lot of the average worker. A whole section of *A Way* is devoted to the ills to which an artisan's life was subject outside Plockhoy's community: sickness, lack of trade or work, loss of customers, poverty, and debt,²⁴ inability to marry and found a family because limited resources could not provide for one, parents struggling to give their children a sound basis for starting out in life, the young struggling to attract and keep customers, mental depression induced by one's economic distress, the breakdown of marriages when material success remained elusive, early death leaving their wives as widows and their children orphans, and the widows often unattractive on the marriage market precisely because they were hindered by the mouths they had to feed.²⁵

In the outside world some artisans with physically demanding occupations, such as smiths and carpenters, had to undergo "allmost intollerable labour" for twenty to thirty years in order to save and invest some money, only to lose the investment or die before reaping the rewards of their hard labour, which then might end up in undeserving hands. Even if they lived long enough to enjoy the results of their hard work, often their bodies were so "spoiled with working" that they "suffer them

---

21. Incumbents could stand for re-election though, since, in Plockhoy's opinion, "he that hath a mind to continue in the Government will have an Inducement to rule well"; *ibid.*
22. *Ibid.*
23. *Ibid.*, p. 11.
24. *Ibid.*, p. 12.
25. *Ibid.*, p. 15.

to take no rest". If they have not been able to save enough money, an old age awaited them in "Hospitalls of old men and women", whose inhabitants "come in out of necessity [...] with their contentions, opposition, and deeply rooted Infirmities, [...] their bodies by hard labour spoiled and made decrepite, and their mindes corrupted by evil manners, being many times, beside a deep stupid ignorance, so ill natured, that no reason can sink into them".[26] There can be no doubt that in Plockhoy's eyes such an end was hardly conducive to attaining salvation. The place of the average worker in society was thus one of constant anxiety and imminent material and spiritual ruin.

Against this bleak image of the average worker's life in the world outside, Plockhoy projected his community as the solution to all of these ills. A member of the society would never "stand singly by himself alone", and "there will be no need [...] to take any care or to make provision for the aged time, or day of sickness, nor for the children", for whomever became unable to work by sickness or old age, or left widows and orphans behind, would be provided for by the rest who, "being united as members of one body", would work for them.[27] In Plockhoy's society the solidarity of its members would ward off all the disastrous consequences of personal misfortune and the accompanying propensity to sin, so that the members would not have just to fret about their material and social position, but could also turn their minds to higher things – not the least of which is their salvation. In fact, the society itself would assist its members to work towards salvation, for it was Christ,

> [...] who by his Doctrine and example, hath instituted a partnership or Society of mutuall love [...] requiring that the gifts, and meanes of subsistence in the world [...] should be Common [...] so that all Christendome ought to be meerly, a certain great fraternity consisting of such as [...] conspire together in

26. *Ibid.*, p. 13. Though there is no evidence that Plockhoy read Classical writers, the detrimental effects of labour on body and mind was also a topos in ancient Greece; Catharina Lis, "Perceptions of Work in Classical Antiquity: A Polyphonic Heritage", in Ehmer and Lis, *The Idea of Work*, pp. 33–68, 40–41, 47. It could also be heard on occasion in, for example, Renaissance Venice; Mocarelli, "The Attitude of Milanese Society to Work", pp. 107–109.

27. Plockhoy, *A Way Propounded*, p. 13. Plockhoy might have been inspired by, but goes much further than, the provisions for mutual assistance offered by many early modern Dutch guilds, which might "insure" their members against the consequences of sickness, temporary lack of work, or even the costs of old age and death; see Sandra Bos, *"Uyt liefde tot malcander".Onderlinge hulpverlening binnen de Noord-Nederlandse gilden in internationaal perspectief (1570–1820)* (Amsterdam, 1998) for a general overview, and the autobiography of the Amsterdam furrier, Hermanus Verbeeck, *Memoriaal ofte mijn levensraijsinghe*, J. Blaak (ed.) (Hilversum, 1999), for one particular example. It should be said, though, that the mutual assistance provided by guilds could be haphazard and dependent on how successful a certain incorporated profession was. In Plockhoy's native Zeeland, for example, this mutual assistance seems to have been meagre; see L.H. Remmerswaal, *Een duurzame alliantie. Gilden en regenten in Zeeland, 1600–1800* (Utrecht, 2006), pp. 117–125.

Christ, the sole head and spring of love; doing well to one another, and for his sake distribute their goodes to those that stand in need.[28]

It is this idea of partnership, or a society of mutual assistance, that is closely intertwined with Plockhoy's ideas on how his society should interact with the world outside. Plockhoy did not believe in a transformation of all human society along the lines of his ideals, but preferred to realize his ideal society as a private enterprise, a community of like-minded people not of the world, but in the world. As we have seen, Plockhoy's society was open to wealthy and godly people and their children, provided they paid for the privilege. Plockhoy also hoped that they would patronize the shops of the society, as the products of the society were to be sold to outside customers.[29] The key to profitable trade, and thus to making the society a success, was collaboration between its members, which would save costs and manpower normally otherwise engaged, thus enabling, for example, three-quarters of the female labour force to be employed for the common good.[30] Thus the society would be able to produce more cheaply, the profitability of the enterprise increase, and its participants assured of their material well-being.

The place of Plockhoy's society is thus rooted firmly within the wider structure of society as a whole, but the role of its constituent members is – materially and spiritually – radically different from that of their counterparts in the world: instead of being isolated and subject to the whims and wiles of affluent customers who are their social betters, united in their little commonwealth they can become a commercial force to be reckoned with. Within the framework of the Collaboratory's taxonomy of labour relations, Plockhoy's ideal was of a community engaged in reciprocal labour, but producing its surplus for the market in the outside world.

FREE AND UNFREE LABOUR

This commercial power of unison also brought with it an aspect which brings us to the fourth layer of investigation: the acquisition of freedom to work where, when, and for whom one wanted. To Plockhoy any form of unfree labour was unacceptable, as it would be irreconcilable with the egalitarian structure of his little commonwealth. Plockhoy used the word "slavery" only in a pejorative sense,[31] as becomes clear from the observation that "evil Governours or Rulers, covetous Merchants and Tradesmen,

---

28. Plockhoy, *A Way Propounded*, p. 24.
29. *Ibid.*, p. 7.
30. For this in greater detail see the first paragraph of "Who May Do What Work?" below.
31. Elsewhere he writes how "unprofitable, and hurtfull handy Crafts" were not just the cause of sin, but also of slavery, though he does not elaborate on this; Plockhoy, *A Way Propounded*, p. 34. He might have believed that those handicrafts which were unprofitable would force people to resort to wage labour, or to be exploited by others.

lazie, idle and negligent Teachers, and others, have brought all under slaverie and thraldom".[32] He used the word also for arrangements in society which were not slavery in a legal sense, but which limited the freedom of employees, such as the system of binding apprentices in England, in which the young could be reduced to unfree labour.[33]

Since the Elizabethan Statute of Artificers and Apprentices was promulgated in 1586 all would-be artisans were forced to undergo an apprenticeship of at least seven years. In practice this meant that employers were offered seven years of cheap labour, and in many cases apprentices were exploited, malnourished, or did not actually learn a trade.[34] In his proposed community by contrast the children would "always [be] chearfull by not being oppressed with bondage and slavery, as common is seen amongst children of the World, especially in England, who must endure [...] to pass through 7 years, as slave under the Turk". That was a strong condemnation, for slavery in a Muslim country was regarded as particularly dangerous to the soul, as it often entailed forced conversion to Islam. It was therefore greatly feared by Dutch sailors, many of whom came from Plockhoy's native Zeeland.[35] Plockhoy was thus highly critical of the English system of apprenticeship.

No wonder then that in Plockhoy's community the apprentice system would not apply, so that the children would always remain with their families.[36] Plockhoy regarded not just apprenticeship but any form of service as nothing short of slavery, writing for example that "many young men and maides being wearied under the slavery and service" of "hard, strict, severe Masters and Mistrisses" would be willing to join his community.[37] In this

---

32. *Ibid.*, p. 3.

33. Children of the poor could be forcibly apprenticed by judges; see David Eltis, "Labour and Coercion in the English Atlantic World from the Seventeenth to the Early Twentieth Century", in Gad Heuman and James Walvin (eds), *The Slavery Reader* (London, 2003), pp. 58–73, 59.

34. Applebaum, *The Concept of Work*, pp. 274–275.

35. For this see in general R.C. Davis, *Christian Slaves, Muslim Masters: White Slavery in the Mediterranean, the Barbary Coast, and Italy, 1500–1800* (New York, 2003). For the specific Dutch fear of forced conversion see Gerard van Krieken, *Kapers en kooplieden. De betrekkingen tussen Algiers en Nederland 1604–1830* (Amsterdam, 1999), pp. 104–108, and P. Boon, *Een Westfriese Zeeman als slaaf in Barbarije, verslag van de belevenissen van Jan Cornelisz Dekker in Marokko, 1715–1743* (Schoorl, 1987), pp. 44, 67–70.

36. Plockhoy, *A Way Propounded*, p. 11. Note that Plockhoy saw nothing wrong in child labour. The children and those who were under age would work half a day "so that they, being freed from slavery, may not decline into laziness or carelessness" [*op datse van slavernije bevrijd sijnde, tot geen luyigheyd ofte on-achtsaemheyd mochten komen te vervallen*]; idem, *Kort & Klaer Ontwerp*, p. 8. That would have been detrimental to their souls. What Plockhoy objected to was child labour that was not conducive to a Christian way of life.

37. *Idem, A Way Propounded*, p. 14. Especially because then there would be no restrictions on marriage and pregnancy, as was normally the case; Eltis, "Labour and Coercion", p. 59. The Dutch Republic was an exception to this rule.

context it is perhaps telling that many early modern Englishmen regarded wage labourers as unfree.[38] Plockhoy may have shared this idea, even if he never says so explicitly.

Slavery in a legal sense was hardly an issue in England or the Dutch Republic, where it was forbidden, but it was a different matter in their colonies.[39] Once Plockhoy had embarked on his colonial venture he needed to take a clearer stance on the issue. In the prospectus for his American colony he explicitly stated that "we do not want to burden our Company" with domination or subjugating slavery".[40] This terse statement meant that Plockhoy would not allow chattel slavery in his colony, nor would there be room for indentured labour, another well-known feature of labour in English colonial society.[41]

In Plockhoy's community labour was also free in other ways. The wage labourers serving the society were not destined to remain wage labourers forever, as often happened in practice in the outside world: if they wanted to, they could join the society. Guests staying temporarily were free to pay for the hospitality they enjoyed with money or labour.[42] The young members of the society would enjoy another labour freedom: they were to be taught two or even three crafts, so that they would always find work even if their main craft were no longer profitable owing to changes in fashion.[43] Implicitly that also allowed them to change occupations if they wanted to. Furthermore, members of the society were free to leave the little commonwealth, with generous farewell bonuses, such as their share of the surplus accumulated during their membership.[44] Therefore, opting for the society did not compromise one's liberty.

Such freedom of choice was unheard of – once one had become a member of a certain guild, it was not so easy to make a career shift to another occupation. To be sure, artisan's sons could choose an occupation different from that of their fathers, and this often happened in both England and the

---

38. As Hill put it: "There is plenty of confirmatory evidence for Professor MacPherson's argument that in the sixteenth and seventeenth centuries those in receipt of wages were regarded as unfree"; Hill, "Pottage for Freeborn Englishmen", p. 342.

39. In fact, labour was normally free in the Dutch Republic, and contract-based; Jan Lucassen, "Labour and Early Modern Economic Development", in Karel Davids and Jan Lucassen (eds), *A Miracle Mirrored: The Dutch Republic in European Perspective* (Cambridge, 1995), pp. 367–409, 386, 395.

40. "Alsoo wy met geen heerschappije ofte knechtische slavernije onse Compagnie en willen belasten"; Plockhoy, *Kort & Klaer Ontwerp*, p. 10.

41. On indentured labour see, for example, David Eltis, "Slavery and Freedom in the Early Modern World", in Stanley L. Engerman (ed.), *Terms of Labor: Slavery, Serfdom and Free Labor* (Stanford, CA, 1999), pp. 25–49, 27, 30, 41.

42. Plockhoy, *A Way Propounded*, p. 8.

43. *Ibid.*, p. 12. A real danger, as the furrier Hermanus Verbeeck experienced; Verbeeck, *Memoriaal*, pp. 12, 69.

44. Plockhoy, *A Way Propounded*, p. 6.

Dutch Republic,[45] but once established in a trade it was not easy to change career paths. Plockhoy's plan ensured that the society's children would be more occupationally mobile and thus more employable.

THE RANKING OF OCCUPATIONS

This brings us to the next layer of investigation. To Plockhoy, all useful trades were equal and perhaps therefore interchangeable, but this did not apply to those occupations deemed useless. The distinction between useful and profitable occupations and those that are not is the only form of ranking Plockhoy makes. For the foundation of his society he needed men from four categories: husbandmen (a generic term for all agricultural labourers), mariners (likewise for all maritime labourers), "Masters of severall Arts and Sciences", and "Usefull Handy Craft-people".[46]

What occupations he considered useful, if not necessary, becomes clear from the lists of necessary occupations, mostly of an artisan nature, he attached to his tracts.[47] These lists contain such artisan evergreens as smiths, masons, carpenters, cobblers, and weavers, but also more specific occupational niches, such as glovers, bleachers, compass-makers, spectacle-makers, and distillers. The lists were clearly not meant to be exhaustive, and they differed slightly.[48] With the exception of that of physicians, only artisanal occupations featured in these lists, though perhaps Plockhoy regarded the work of physicians as an artisanal form of work rather than the intellectual occupation its practitioners considered it to be.

Elsewhere in his tracts Plockhoy divided the agricultural labourers into husbandmen proper and gardeners,[49] and the "Masters of severall Arts and Sciences" into at least four categories: first, "one that can write extraordinary well"; secondly "another that understands arithmetick, Geometry, Astronomy, Navigation, Italian book-keeping or Merchants Accompts"; thirdly "some for Latin, Greek, Hebrew and other Languages"; and, fourthly, as a rest category, also for "Physick, Musick, and other usefull things, referring all to a good and spirituall end".[50] The mariners

---

45. Paul Seaver, "The Puritan Work Ethic Revisited", *The Journal of British Studies*, 19 (1980), pp. 35–53, 52.
46. Plockhoy, *A Way Propounded*, pp. 3, 18; *idem, Kort & Klaer Ontwerp*, pp. 6, 11.
47. Plockhoy, *A Way Propounded*, pp. 18–19 (72 occupations: the number, however, varies between the various editions of this tract); *idem, Kort & Klaer Ontwerp*, p. 11 (63 occupations).
48. The lists are not wholly compatible with each other: thus the list in *A Way* contains occupations which are not listed in *Kort & Klaer Ontwerp*. For example occupations relating to the manufacture of paper and books are mentioned in *A Way*, but not in *Kort & Klaer Ontwerp*, whereas the occupation of bleacher is mentioned only in *Kort & Klaer Ontwerp*.
49. Plockhoy, *A Way Propounded*, p. 7.
50. *Ibid.*, p. 6.

were apparently expected to work simultaneously as fishermen and transporters of goods for the society.[51]

The typically female occupation of managing the household was not specifically mentioned, but housekeeping is referred to throughout the text and clearly of importance. Plockhoy probably regarded its importance as self-evident. There was no question of ranking typically male labour above typically female labour, although, as will be seen in the next layer of investigation, Plockhoy clearly believed that many women would prefer to work in other occupations.

Useless were those parasitic occupations which Plockhoy regarded as held by those "that have sought and found out many inventions to live upon the labour of others".[52] Some of those useless occupations may be identified by the fact Plockhoy is silent about them. Soldiers are never mentioned for example, nor police officers. In the latter case Plockhoy probably hoped that by reserving membership to deserving, truly Christian people there would be much less risk of unsocial behaviour. Otherwise he apparently trusted in military and policing protection by the authorities.[53]

Other "useless" occupations are mentioned explicitly in Plockhoy's tracts. As we have seen, Plockhoy had little time for "evil Governours or Rulers, covetous Merchants and Tradesmen" and "lazie, idle and negligent Teachers" – which is how Plockhoy refers to the clergy.[54] Rulers could not be dispensed with, hence the comparatively detailed description of how and by whom the society should be governed. This indispensability did not, however, apply to merchants and ministers. The covetous merchants have already been dealt with above. Ministers of any kind were another occupational group for which Plockhoy and his society had no use. In Plockhoy's view, "those that are called spirituall persons or Clergy-men" misled the people into believing that they could take care of the people's spiritual needs, so that the people "may the more willingly drudge for them".[55]

Instead, however, the faithful could have direct communion with Christ without any form of intercession or mediation, and did not need to be told how to understand the scriptures. "In spirituall things, we acknowledge none but Christ for head and Master",[56] Plockhoy wrote, and envisioned how his society would facilitate a meeting place where everyone would be free to discuss the scriptures without censure. Ministers were thus as superfluous as

---

51. *Ibid.*, p. 7.
52. *Ibid.*, title page.
53. In his American plan he does take account of the need to defend his colony by arms; *idem*, *Kort & Klaer Ontwerp*, p. 9.
54. *Idem*, *A Way Propounded*, p. 3.
55. *Ibid.*, p. 4.
56. *Ibid.*, p. 16.

merchants, and Plockhoy hoped that those ministers who were "convinced of their persevering and erroneous teaching" but were "not strong enough to bear poverty" and thus, to the detriment of their souls, remained in their ministry would join his society and publicly renounce their teaching[57] – yet another reminder of the importance of the society as a means to salvation.

Finally, not all handicrafts were considered useful by Plockhoy. Children were to learn only "necessary and allwayes usefull trades", so that they might always earn their living.[58] What he then regarded as useless handicrafts he does not state explicitly, but as his society is expected to make all things "without unnecessary trimmings" and that clothes should be made "fitted to the body, and convenient for work, without being tyed to fashion, colour, or stuff", the fact that occupations such as jeweller, goldsmith, and furrier are not listed among the "Usefull Handy Craft-people" implies he had little patience for the more frivolous aspects of the growing consumer market of his day.[59]

Plockhoy thus ranked occupations into only two categories: useful and useless occupations. Given his Christian egalitarianism Plockhoy would have regarded all useful occupations as of equal importance to the society, and made no ranking between them. Nor generally did he distinguish between who could and who could not engage in a particular occupation.

WHO MAY DO WHAT WORK?

As noted above, one way or another every member of Plockhoy's little commonwealth was expected to work. This applied not just to the men, but also to the women and children. Plockhoy clearly believed that women would applaud being freed from the demands of the traditionally female domain of housekeeping, and that his society would give them this freedom: outside his society every woman was obliged to keep house, but in his little commonwealth the resources of women would be used more efficiently since they could combine their efforts. A quarter of the women would therefore suffice to do the housekeeping, such as cooking the communal meals of the society, "the rest [...] being imployed about some work together with men for the common good, which many women will rather do, than to be a whole day troubled with diversities of cares". Three-quarters of womanpower could thus be employed by the

---

57. *Ibid.*, p. 14.
58. *Ibid.*, p. 12.
59. Intriguingly, Plockhoy adds to his censure of "fashion" and "unnecessary trimmings" that they be "forborn, that God's creatures, which he hath made, be not misused"; *ibid.*, p. 11. Here he seems to be a proto-conservationist. It is striking that even his American colony did not require the services of a furrier, even though the export of beaver hides and other furs was an important part of Dutch transatlantic trade. See Jaap Jacobs, *New Netherland: A Dutch Colony in Seventeenth-Century America* (Leiden, 2005); and Janny Venema, *Beverwijck: A Dutch Village on the American Frontier, 1652–1664* (Hilversum, 2003).

society, which would profit greatly from the availability of this extra labour force.[60] The young women of the society should not only "be fitted to do the housewifery" but also be taught "a good Handy-craft Trade", so that if they were minded to leave the society or marry outside it "they may be able to get a livelihood".[61]

Work was thus not necessarily gendered, though some of the required labour was. Housekeeping clearly remained a female domain also in Plockhoy's society, and it seems that decisions about the course to be followed by the society were a male prerogative, since the governor and the masters were spoken of only in male terms.[62] There was one explicit exception: oversight of the society's victuals would be "governed by turns" by a committee consisting of both men and women. Ten to twelve men and women would govern for six months, after which half of them would be replaced by new overseers, while, to ensure continuity, the other half would continue for a further six months to instruct the newcomers.[63] The only domain in which women could attain a position of leadership was thus closely connected with traditional female housekeeping tasks.

Though traditional male labour was thus open to women too, this was not the case with housekeeping tasks. Plockhoy must have regarded housekeeping as essential to the society's well-being, but perhaps not as actively contributing to the society's profitability. It is conceivable that even though he allowed women to work in occupations traditionally reserved for men, he was reluctant to have manpower dissipated in work other than that directly conducive to the productivity of the society.

In giving the women of his community the chance to work in whatever trade they preferred, it is likely that Plockhoy was at least partly influenced by the comparatively strong – and growing – labour participation of

60. Plockhoy's notion that this also encourages growth is supported by recent research into early modern female labour in the Dutch Republic, which connects the higher rates of female labour participation with the economic growth of the Dutch Republic. See Manon van der Heijden *et al.* "Terugkeer van het patriarchaat? Vrije vrouwen in de Republiek", *Tijdschrift voor Sociale en Economische Geschiedenis*, 6 (2009), pp. 26–52, 46, 50–51. See also Elise van Nederveen Meerkerk, *De draad in eigen handen. Vrouwen en loonarbeid in de Nederlandse textielnijverheid, 1581–1810* (Amsterdam, 2007); Danielle van den Heuvel, *Women and Entrepreneurship: Female Traders in the Northern Netherlands, c.1580–1815* (Amsterdam, 2007); and Marjolein van Dekken, *Brouwen, branden en bedienen. Werkende vrouwen in de Nederlandse dranknijverheid, 1500–1800* (Amsterdam, 2010).
61. Plockhoy, *A Way Propounded*, p. 10. Plockhoy does not say explicitly that young women should learn a trade to assist in the society's work, but it would be a logical consequence of freeing the labour of women for them to apply their knowledge also within the society.
62. Unfortunately, Plockhoy is vague in the extreme about whether women had a say in the society's legislative and religious meetings: he does not exclude them explicitly, which might suggest that, like many other dissenters of that period, he was not unfavourably disposed to women speaking in public.
63. Plockhoy, *A Way Propounded*, pp. 9–10.

Dutch women in his day. Women were active in almost all sectors of the Dutch labour market, though there was a strong labour division between the sexes,[64] and there were occupations and guilds in the Republic in which women predominated.[65] Plockhoy may well have based his observation that many women preferred to work with the men rather than be occupied in housekeeping on the fact that many Dutch women worked with their husbands in their trades and shops.[66]

Women outside the Republic often had fewer prospects than Dutch women, and that also applied to England, where Plockhoy first promoted his society.[67] Nevertheless, for Dutch women too Plockhoy's proposed community would have offered even greater freedom of choice as to what work they could engage in. Gender was not an impediment to participating in the market-orientated labour of the society.[68]

There was perhaps a stronger labour division between age groups, between those who had attained majority and those who had not. The young men in his American colony attained majority at twenty,[69] and so apparently did the women.[70] Plockhoy had no qualms in assigning "young people to do the hardest work", while the elder and more experienced workers would supervise them "for it doth suit the aged to give orders, and the young to obey". During the communal meals, the young unmarried people would wait on the table by turns.[71] Also, the younger children were apparently expected to work, though the distinction between education and labour seems not to have been made. The children, and all under-age persons, would

64. For a general overview of the way women's freedom of action increased in the Dutch Republic see Van der Heijden *et al.*, "Terugkeer van het patriarchaat?".

65. See, among others, Bibi Panhuysen, *Maatwerk. Kleermakers, naaisters, oudkleerkopers en de gilden (1500–1800)* (Amsterdam, 2000), for the relationship between men and women in the tailoring business; Van Nederveen Meerkerk, *De draad in eigen handen*, for women active in the Dutch textile industry; Van den Heuvel, *Women and Entrepreneurship*, for female merchants; and Van Dekken, *Brouwen, branden en bedienen*, for women active in the production and trade of beverages in the Netherlands.

66. Van der Heijden *et al.*, "Terugkeer van het patriarchaat?", p. 46.

67. See here, for example, the international comparison drawn by Van Dekken, *Brouwen, branden en bedienen*, pp. 195–248, especially 234–237 and 247–248. It seems that other urban societies also offered greater opportunities: in Cologne, for example, there were three guilds whose membership was restricted to women; Applebaum, *The Concept of Work*, p. 276.

68. Or to participating in the society's administrative and religious meetings for that matter. Plockhoy is very vague about this, and does not explicitly – or implicitly – exclude women. That he was so vague might, however, have to do with the fact that even in his circles it was by no means accepted that women should have an independent voice, and that an explicit avowal of female independence of thought might hinder the establishment of his community.

69. Plockhoy, *Kort & Klaer Ontwerp*, p. 7.

70. Although he does not say so explicitly, this can be deduced from the fact that every person over the age of twenty was to share in the profit of the society; *ibid.*, p. 8.

71. At the table the young men and women sat next to their fathers and mothers, an indication that Plockhoy took parental authority over the young for granted; *idem, A Way Propounded*, p. 10.

not work more than six hours a day, so they could spend their time "in other usefull imployments, that they may be fitted for some what ells beside working".[72] It seems that their other time would be occupied with being taught "the writings of the Saints, and natural Arts, Sciences and Languages".[73] Education seems to have ended only at the age of twenty, after which the young man or woman became a full member of the society.

In general, however, Plockhoy allowed both women and the young greater scope to engage in labouring activities, in which aspect his proposed community would be much more liberal than usual.

INCENTIVES AND REMUNERATION

Plockhoy would have regarded the comparative freedom of labour within his society as a major incentive to join his community, but perhaps as great an incentive was the resulting independence from wage labour. Whereas the "traders in the world" oppressed their workmen with heavy labour and low wages, within Plockhoy's society "the gain of the tradesmen will redound to the benefit and refreshment of the workmen".[74] The members of his society were not dependent on wage labour or the ever uncertain income of the self-employed. They laboured not just for themselves and their immediate family, but united "into one Familie or Houshold-government",[75] for the good of the whole society, "as if they are one family".[76] Instead of earning wages for their labour, they worked in principle to be at least self-sufficient, but, beyond that, were entitled to an equal share in the eventual surplus generated by the society's economic activities. Thus, in Plockhoy's little commonwealth, labour was largely reciprocal, as if his society was indeed a household, though supplemented if necessary by the wage labour of outsiders, and active within the wider framework of a market economy.

As noted earlier, Plockhoy believed his society would become a commercial force to be reckoned with, and that it would not only ensure its members assistance in times of need but also actually make a profit. He clearly believed that this prospect would work as an incentive not just to join his community, but also to work diligently. Profit and the accumulation of wealth were not the primary aim however: the surplus arising from the society's economic activities served both to support all members of the community, but also the poor outside it.[77]

72. *Ibid.*, p. 12; idem, *Kort & Klaer Ontwerp*, p. 8.
73. *Idem, A Way Propounded*, p. 15.
74. *Ibid.*, p. 12. Perhaps Plockhoy is referring here to the practice of subcontracting.
75. *Ibid.*, p. 3.
76. *Idem, Kort & Klaer Ontwerp*, p. 6.
77. This attitude can also be found, for example, in an anonymous tract published in Antwerp in 1552, *Vanden borgheren hoe dat si onder malcanderen leven sullen*; Veldman, "Representations of Labour", p. 154.

PLOCKHOY'S ETHIC OF WORK IN CONTEXT

To summarize, in his tracts Plockhoy displayed a work ethic in which work was central to the life of a true Christian. Apart from physical work, the Christian should also make time available for other pursuits, not the least of which was salvation. Work was everyone's duty, and despite providing few details in general he expected all Christians – men and women – to work, in whatever occupation they saw fit, provided these occupations were useful and profitable to the commonwealth. Moreover, they were to work in unison, none of them having a position of responsibility without the qualifications required for it, and with the aim of being able to provide each other with the mutual assistance Christians should render one another. The workers could thus evade the many temptations of sin awaiting them outside the society, where they were much more on their own and risked succumbing to salvation-impeding poverty. In that way Plockhoy's little commonwealth served to help in attaining salvation. Plockhoy's ethic of work was thus deeply and primarily Christian, even though it contained elements which could be regarded as premonitory of later seventeenth-century writing on commerce.

In this, Plockhoy was not alone, but part of a greater whole, and a distinct minority.[78] His ethic of work may not be applicable to the vast majority of workers in his age, for it was rooted in a vocal subculture, that of the godly. The term "godly" refers here to a wide range of thinkers deeply influenced by Christianity but not necessarily in full conformity with another, especially where it concerns religious doctrine. They are difficult to class, but with regard to work ethics there was more that united than divided them. Underlying their opinions was a widely shared concern with the practice of Christianity, irrespective of whether one was a committed predestinarian Calvinist Puritan or a spiritualist Collegiant espousing freedom of conscience. Despite the theological hostility, all members of the godly minority believed that it was not enough to be Christian in name only: one should also be Christian in practice. Around 1650 they enjoyed a high public profile on both sides of the North Sea, playing a major role in the debates of their time. Their concern was not the ethic of work in itself, but the ethics of Christianity as a whole.

There is certainly much more to be said with regard to the ethics of work if one also takes their writings into account. Space limitations prohibit mentioning more than one case from the other religious extreme, as represented by the committed predestinarian Calvinist Puritan, Nehemiah Wallington (1598–1658), a London turner who was also a punctilious elder of his Presbyterian congregation.[79] Though Plockhoy

---

78. Unless stated otherwise, the following paragraph is based on Looijesteijn, "'Born to the Common Welfare'", ch. 7: "Plockhoy and Practical Christianity in Context".

79. On Wallington, see Seaver, "The Puritan Work Ethic Revisited", and *idem*, *Wallington's World: A Puritan Artisan in Seventeenth-Century London* (Stanford, CA, 1985).

had little patience for the Calvinist church order Wallington espoused, much
of Wallington's ethics would have been approved by him. For Wallington,
and the Puritan divines whose books he read and sermons he heard, work
was a divine blessing, a way to glorify God, and an antidote against sin –
especially the sin of idleness.[80] Its primary purpose was not the acquisition of
wealth – which was the sin of covetousness – but to be useful and profitable
for oneself, one's family, church, and commonwealth.

This concept of the commonwealth in which God was glorified by diligent
labour was a popular one among Puritan divines, and was largely shared by
Plockhoy. And like Plockhoy, the Puritan divines too condemned a parasitic
existence in the strongest terms. Sobriety and honesty in dealing with one's
customers was constantly on the minds of men such as Wallington. In all
this, Plockhoy and Wallington did not differ, although Wallington would
have recoiled in horror from Plockhoy's religious opinions and hotly disputed Plockhoy's claim that the office of minister was parasitic.

Many other examples could be given here, such as Dutch Mennonites
and Collegiants, and English Quakers – often, like Plockhoy, of modest
social status – who all wrote tracts on the fragile balance between wealth
and soul.[81] They shared their concerns with Plockhoy, which is not surprising given that Plockhoy was in turn Mennonite, a sympathizer of the
Quakers, and eventually active as a Collegiant.

The writings of this godly minority form a fertile source for the study, not
just of the concept of practical Christianity as a whole, but also for their
accompanying ethics of work. There are clues that much of their ethics was
shared by others who did not necessarily share their religious enthusiasm,
such as the Levellers and Diggers. The distaste for wage labour among early
modern Englishmen is one example,[82] but perhaps there were other similarities. An artisan such as Wallington greedily imbibed the writings and sermons of Puritan ministers, many of whom were actually from quite humble
backgrounds, and tried to live his life to their ethical standards. It is probable
that the same applied to the artisan Plockhoy. A closer study of the writings
of the godly minority, and an attempt to link those up with a study of their
readership, might therefore shed more light on the general development of
the ethics of work in Europe.

---

80. Lis and Ehmer, "Introduction", p. 16.
81. Idleness and covetousness were in fact already "unforgivable sins" in the thought of such
religious thinkers as Luther, Calvin, and Richard Baxter; see Applebaum, *The Concept of Work*,
pp. 324–325, 330–331.
82. Gerrard Winstanley, for example, regarded wage labour as slavery; Hill, "Pottage for
Freeborn Englishmen", pp. 345–347.

IRSH 56 (2011), Special Issue, pp. 89–106 doi:10.1017/S0020859011000496
© 2011 Internationaal Instituut voor Sociale Geschiedenis

Attitudes to Work and Commerce in the Late Italian Renaissance: A Comparison between Tomaso Garzoni's *La Piazza Universale* and Leonardo Fioravanti's *Dello Specchio Di Scientia Universale*

Luca Mocarelli

Università di Milano Bicocca

E-mail: luca.mocarelli@unimib.it

Summary: This article compares two highly successful treatises written in the second half of the fifteenth century: Tomaso Garzoni's *La piazza universale di tutte le professioni del mondo* [The Universal Workplace of All the Professions in the World], and Leonardo Fioravanti's *Dello specchio di scientia universale* [On the Mirror of Universal Knowledge]. It examines how each of these books presented and considered commercial activities such as the manufacture and trading of silk and wool – which were of great importance to the Italian economy of the day – and other more humble occupations. This is an interesting comparison since Garzoni and Fioravanti personified two very different spirits of the Renaissance. The former was a learned man, anxious to construct a moralistic-literary monument, complete in every detail, while the latter was a great observer, intent on making full use of every kind of knowledge, even that which seemed lowly and contemptible.

Attitudes towards so-called manual skills in Italy during the late Renaissance were not monolithic. In a recently published essay I pointed out how, in the midst of the harsh mainstream condemnation of manual work, differing opinions were also voiced, though they remained minority opinions, in line with a tradition that came from afar, and that was rooted especially in some of St Paul's letters in which he exalted the dignity of work.[1]

---

1. See Luca Mocarelli, "The Attitude of Milanese Society to Work and Commercial Activities: The Case of the Porters and the Case of the Elites", in Josef Ehmer and Catharina Lis (eds), *The Idea of Work in Europe from Antiquity to Modern Times* (Farnham, 2009), pp. 101–124, 105–107. In re-evaluating manual work, Bartolomeo Paganelli, from Prignano, even managed to reverse the very negative connotation of the etymology of the term "mechanic". In his *De imperio Cupidinis* (Modena, 1492), and with few classical references at his disposal, he composed a poetic celebration of technical inventions in which the only distinction he made in

What I intend to do here, developing this line of research, is to compare two highly successful treatises written in the second half of the sixteenth century, a time when the principal manufacturing cities of Italy were still expanding rapidly, with waged work controlled by the merchants becoming more widespread, to the detriment of the independent artisan. I shall examine how each of these books presented and considered commercial activities such as the manufacture and trading of silk and wool – which were of great importance to the Italian economy of the day – and other more humble occupations. This is an interesting comparison because Tomaso Garzoni and Leonardo Fioravanti, the authors of the treatises in question, *La piazza universale di tutte le professioni del mondo* [The Universal Workplace of All the Professions in the World] and *Dello specchio di scientia universale* [On the Mirror of Universal Knowledge],[2] differed widely in terms of their background and beliefs. Consequently, they approach the subject of work and occupations in different ways.

TOMASO GARZONI AND LEONARDO FIORAVANTI

Garzoni was an ecclesiastic, a member of the Augustinian order, who wrote about the world from within the protective walls of his monastery library, inspired by post-Council-of-Trent moral and educational aims, which appear not only in *La piazza universale* but in all his writings. His *L'hospidale de' pazzi incurabili* [The Hospital of Incurable Madness] and *La sinagoga degli ignoranti* [The Synagogue of the Ignorant] contrast sharply with the adverse criticism by many Renaissance writers of the scope for human knowledge. In those studies he derided the idea of the *docta ignorantia* expounded by Cusano in a highly successful book published in 1440.[3]

Leonardo Fioravanti, by contrast, was a well-known physicist and surgeon in his day. He performed the first successful operation in Italy to

mechanical work was between trades that were dirty because of their working conditions and shameful jobs such as those of the moneylender and toll collector, who lived on money earned by others; on Paganelli's work see Giorgio Montecchi, "Bartolomeo Paganelli da Prignano: ossia della nobilità della stampa, arte meccanica e liberale", *Discipline del libro*, 2 (1999), pp. 117–122.

2. In this article I shall refer to the following versions of the two books: Giovanni Battista Bronzini (ed.), *La piazza universale di tutte le professioni del mondo*, 2 vols (Florence, 1996), and *Dello specchio di scientia universale dell'Eccell. Dottore et Cavalier Leonardo Fioravanti Bolognese* (Venice, 1583).

3. For Cusano, the *docta ignorantia* meant a "*visio sine comprehensione, speculatio*". See *De Docta ignorantia* (1440), in Ernst Hoffmann and Raymond Klibansky (eds), *Nicolai de Cusa, Opera Omnia* (Leipzig, 1932), I, p. 26. As mankind cannot grasp the infinity of a deity through rational knowledge, the limits of science need to be surpassed by means of speculation that blur the borders between science and *ignorantia*. In other words, both reason and a supra-rational understanding are needed to understand God.

remove a spleen. He was also known as an inveterate experimenter and globetrotter, who, during his adventurous life, visited most of the Mediterranean world, Spain, and Africa, and worked in Messina, Palermo, Naples, Rome, Pesaro, Genoa, and Venice. He believed that scholastic knowledge was of little use in itself, since true knowledge is none other than the theory of experience. His colourful life has been recreated by the incomparable pen of Piero Camporesi in a book eloquently titled *Camminare il mondo* [Walking the World].[4]

What these two such different personalities shared was an unconditional admiration of the printing press, one of the great innovations of the Renaissance, which they both exploited to the full, producing highly successful books – beginning with the two considered here. *La piazza universale* was indeed a veritable bestseller in its day. Between 1585 and 1665 there were fifteen Italian editions, an adaptation into Spanish, and translations into German and Latin. It then fell into oblivion, but it has been resurrected in recent years in linguistic-cultural studies.[5] *Dello specchio di scientia universale* had similar success. Published for the first time in Venice in 1564, it reached its tenth edition in 1660 and was also translated into French, English, and German. This book is of particular importance because it started the genre of *letteratura dei mestieri* (literature on trades and professions) in Italy. Although the most complete work of this genre is in fact Garzoni's *La piazza*, it owes a great deal to the work of Fioravanti, as we shall see.[6]

TOMASO GARZONI AND *LA PIAZZA UNIVERSALE DI TUTTE LE PROFESSIONI DEL MONDO*

Garzoni's work is more organized, and his system of classification much clearer, than Fioravanti's, since his aim is to provide a comprehensive catalogue. However, it is not merely a rhetorical catalogue, but a conscious attempt to order all social functions, thus presenting the image of a perfectly organized society. Indeed, because of its richness and complexity, *La piazza*, divided as it is into 154 sections dealing with no fewer than 540 professions and trades, can be read in different ways.

---

4. Piero Camporesi, *Camminare il mondo. Vita e avventure di Leonardo Fioravanti medico del Cinquecento* (Milan, 1997).

5. In 1996 two very accurate editions were published, almost contemporaneously: one by Olschki Press, edited by a great anthropologist, Giovanni Battista Bronzini, and the other by Einaudi, edited by the great historian of Italian literature, Paolo Cherchi.

6. There are, in fact, strong links between these two books, as pointed out by Elvina Vidali Giorio, "Una fonte del Garzoni: 'Dello specchio di scienza universale' di Leonardo Fioravanti", *Lingua nostra*, 30 (1969), pp. 39–43. On the other hand, one cannot exclude the possibility that Fioravanti modelled his work on the encyclopaedic *Catalogus gloriae mundi*, the work of the Bourgogne jurist Barthélemy de Chasseneuz, published in Lyon in 1529 and printed in Italian in Venice around 1560.

So whereas Paolo Cherchi recognizes in Garzoni's precise exploration of the world of skills and occupations the desire to be associated with the efforts of the Counter-Reformation to restore the dignity afforded to manual work by the Gospels, Beatrice Collina convincingly proposes that *La piazza* should be read as an instruction manual for a prince. Giovanni Battista Bronzini, however, stresses the author's attempt, which he believes to be successful, to point out the connection between classes, and to engender harmony among the workforce in order to build up a principality in which a man is valued for what he knows and what he can do:[7] a unitarian and harmonious reality in which it would be possible to overcome the bitter observation of Guicciardini that "often between the palace and the town square there is such a thick fog and such a high wall that, since no man can see through them, the populace know as much about what their rulers do and why, as they know about what goes on in India".[8]

Obviously, what we are most interested in is Garzoni's attitude to work and workers, and a significant indicator is the omission of the phrase "noble and ignoble", referring to all the professions of the world, in the title of the book's second edition. This is perfectly consistent with his desire to value work, in opposition to the humanist-Renaissance scepticism seen particularly in the work of Cornelio Agrippa, who had heavily criticized the arts, sciences, and the clergy in *De incertitudine et vanitate scientiarum et artium* (published in Italian in Venice in 1547) while also, in *De occulta philosophia*, exalting magic, considering it the perfection and fulfilment of all natural sciences. This does not mean that Garzoni questioned the superiority of the intellectual, liberal arts, but simply that he wanted us to understand the reciprocal functioning between noble and less noble activities, without in any way reducing the distance between them.

So Garzoni too subscribed to the harmonious and organistic view of society which was so deeply rooted in the aristocratic culture of his day, and he took pains to hide the conflicts, quarrels, and civil strife which, however, were also present. It was a view expressed by many other contemporary writers, such as Silvio Antoniano, who wrote "that the humblest worker wishes to be the equal of the townsman, the townsman of the gentleman, the gentleman of the nobleman, and the latter of the prince; such things are beyond reason and not to be tolerated, they are displeasing to God, and lead to a thousand sins".[9] This was a totally hierarchic concept of society, in which everyone had a role and a well-defined place, in which he had to stay,

7. Compare the essays of Paolo Cherchi and Beatrice Collina in Tomaso Garzoni, *La piazza universale di tutte le professioni del mondo* (Turin, 1996), and that by Giovanni Battista Bronzini in the Olschki edition of *La piazza*.

8. Francesco Guicciardini, *Ricordi, diari, memorie* (Pordenone, 1991), pp. 213–214.

9. Silvio Antoniano, *Tre libri dell'educatione christiana dei figliuoli* (Verona, 1584), p. 296. For Antoniano – humanist, cardinal, and prime mover in the educational changes that followed the

in the order that was assigned to him. Not by chance did sixteenth- and seventeenth-century writers compare this society to the biblical statue of Nebuch, with a head of gold (the prince), breast and arms of silver (the highest ranks of the nobility), other parts of baser metal (the lower-ranking nobles and honoured professions), and feet of mud (the populace).[10]

An example of this thinking is the passage in which Garzoni observes how all the manual (mechanical) arts, from those reputed honourable to those less honourable, are to be taken equally into consideration, because their humble nature sets off "the more noble arts, just as the clouds soften the piercing rays of the sun, which filter through the surrounding haze in spite of them".[11] This passage is taken from the *Discorso universale* [Universal Comments] with which he prefaced *La piazza* and which he entitled, not coincidentally, *In lode delle scienze et dell'arti liberali e mechaniche in commune* [In Praise of All the Sciences and the Intellectual and Manual Skills in Common]. In his all-embracing catalogue of skills and trades he considered necessary to the socio-political scheme of his ideal principality, Garzoni plundered the work of the most disparate authors, often committing outright plagiarism. Fioravanti himself was a victim, although cited in *La piazza*, in a section dedicated to surgeons, as "the glorious miracle-worker Fioravanti".[12]

LEONARDO FIORAVANTI AND *DELLO SPECCHIO DI SCIENTIA UNIVERSALE*

In his *Specchio* Leonardo Fioravanti, who lived by direct observation of and dialogue with a section of humanity eschewed by most, was not a systematic cataloguer like Garzoni. Many trades are missing from his work (suffice it to say that there is practically no mention of domestic service), and there is a strong bias in favour of his own specialism, the preparation of remedies for various illnesses. This is also confirmed by the multiple dedications which preface the book, most of which are to doctors and surgeons practising in Italy's most important cities.[13]

Council of Trent (1545–1563) – see Elisabetta Patrizi, *Silvio Antoniano un umanista ed educatore dell'età del Rinnovamento cattolico (1540–1603)* (Macerata, 2009).

10. An example of this appears in the volume which synthesizes and systematizes this train of thought by Giovanni Battista De Luca, *Il principe cristiano pratico* (Rome, 1680). Of great interest is the essay on these problems by Daniela Frigo, "La 'civile proportion': ceti, principi e composizione degli interessi nella letteratura politica d'antico regime", in Cesare Mozzarelli (ed.), *Economia e corporazioni. Il governo degli interessi nella storia d'Italia dal medioevo all'età contemporanea* (Milan, 1988), pp. 81–108.

11. Bronzini, *La piazza universale*, I, p. 56.

12. *Ibid.*, p. 155.

13. Following the obligatory dedication to an eminent person, in this case the Milanese count Giovanni Anguissola, the most important scholars and physicians of Venice, Padua, Bologna, Naples, and Rome are named and praised (*Dello Specchio*, pp. iii–x).

We need only remember the subject matter of the three books which constitute the *Specchio*, a great deal of which was the fruit of Fioravanti's own studies. The first is dedicated to "all the intellectual and manual skills", the second deals with "various sciences and many fine reflections on ancient philosophies", and the third, "some notable inventions, which it is necessary to know about, and which are most useful". Fioravanti therefore moves through the full circle of human knowledge, strong in the belief expressed in the *Ragionamento importantissimo ai lettori* [Observations of Great Importance to the Readers], with which he opens his work, that interdisciplinarianism is fundamental to knowledge. Indeed, since "no science or art can be perfect without an understanding of the others, it seemed fitting to deal with many arts and sciences in this book".[14] In terms of quantity, however, the result is that Fioravanti dedicated much less space to skills and trades than Garzoni did, roughly 150 pages as opposed to 1,000.

WOOLLEN MANUFACTURING IN THE WRITINGS OF GARZONI AND FIORAVANTI

In spite of this, it is possible to compare these two books by examining what they say about commerce and occupations, and by noting whether observations are based on the perceived importance of the work, and the possible ranking of the professions and trades.[15] Some interesting facts emerge when we consider how Garzoni and Fioravanti examine the textile industry and its most important activities. This was the basis of the economic success of the late Italian Renaissance, starting with the processing of wool, in which cities such as Milan, Florence, and Venice, as well as many smaller centres, still excelled. It should be noted that towards 1570–1580 – that is, when Garzoni was writing *La piazza* and Fioravanti supplementing and reprinting his *Specchio* – around 150,000 bolts of cloth per year were produced in central and northern Italy, much of which was exported.[16]

Fioravanti's comments on this are particularly interesting. After underlining the importance of this activity – a skill which is "noble all over the world, as everyone knows [...] and the masters of this skill are all wealthy and noble men" – and having described in detail the complexity of the production process, from the selection of the wool to the making of the final product, he gives us a realistic glimpse into the organization of this sector, and the unstinting effort that went into the success of Italy's

14. *Ibid.*, pages not numbered.
15. Unfortunately, Garzoni and Fioravanti did not mention gender in their evaluation of the different occupations.
16. See Paolo Malanima, *L'economia italiana dalla crescita medievale alla crescita contemporanea* (Bologna, 2002), p. 192.

wool-manufacturing centres. He observed that the manufacture of wool is "a job that is most lucrative for those who order it to be done: but for the poor workers who actually do it, it is very bad, since they can never earn more than a meagre living, for all the profits go into the pockets of the merchants". He added, however, that "it cannot be said that this is not better for the artisans, even though they live in poverty, than to go begging in the world".[17]

Thus, Fioravanti demonstrated that he was well aware of the change that the sector had undergone since the late Middle Ages, with the gradual disappearance of autonomous artisans and the merchant class taking control of the whole production process as two of the characteristics of the developing market economy. He clearly understood the great importance of the woollen mills as a source of employment. Confirmation that his appraisals were the result of his own observations comes from the fact that he cited some of the most important manufacturers of woollen cloth in Venice at the time, such as Camillo Molgora from Milan and Giovanni Piero Girardoni.

Fioravanti's remarks in the section dedicated to weaving and weavers, which naturally refers to the working of the wool, are also worthy of note. He makes it clear that a job which is considered among the meanest and most humble actually required great skills, which ranged from the ability to recognize "the quality of all the different kinds of yarn" to knowing how to carry out the complex operations involved in weaving. In the production of the best quality goods, this kind of expertise called for skills which could be acquired only after a long apprenticeship.[18]

Fioravanti was well aware of the numerous skills required of weavers, and concluded this section by saying that

> [...] since we are dealing with an art which is extremely intricate, it calls for a much more detailed description; this I do not give, since my knowledge of it is limited. And it is no surprise that I do not know everything about the art of weaving, since among the weavers themselves those doing one job do not know or understand what the others do.[19]

This situation was not surprising given that the wide variety of goods produced by the Italian weaving industry was the fruit of a policy of strict specialization, which meant that "the person doing one type of weaving cannot do another type, nor even understand it".[20]

---

17. *Dello specchio*, p. 58r.
18. Some illuminating ideas on the importance assumed by the guilds in the transmission of these skills were put forward by the late Larry Epstein, as recalled by Maarten Prak, "S.R. Epstein (1960–2007) and the Guilds", *International Review of Social History*, 53 (2008), Supplement, pp. 1–3.
19. *Dello specchio*, p. 26r.
20. *Ibid.*

Garzoni also reconstructed the complex chain of production in this sector, and presented the various and numerous end products in much more detail than Fioravanti, listing dozens of articles, from the finest cloths to the humble beret and mattress. However, it is interesting to note that when writing about the woollen mill, he departed from the mere citation of books only in order to formulate more concrete considerations, when he repeated, almost to the letter, the work of Fioravanti, although he took care not to quote him. In section CII, "De' lanaiuoli o lanefici e mercanti di lana" [On Wool-Workers, Woollen Mills, and Wool Merchants], Garzoni wrote that the activity "yields much more to the merchants than to the poor workers, who, even though they barely manage to earn a living, represent the great number of artisans who would finish badly if it were not for this work".[21] It is significant that the author, consistent with his ideological purpose, did not include in his evident plagiarism the more polemic and less politically correct ideas of Fioravanti – that this art is bad for the workers, and, above all, that the total profits went into the pockets of the merchants.

THE SILK TRADE IN THE WRITINGS OF GARZONI AND FIORAVANTI

The other activity which was experiencing growing success in Italy at that time was the silk trade. There was widespread rearing of silkworms, and an imposing array of spinning and weaving machinery was set up to process the raw silk produced. There were numerous excellent centres of this activity, which provided a steady flow of produce for export, from Milan to Venice to Bologna. Thanks to this development, some 23,000 looms were in operation in the peninsula by the end of the sixteenth century, mostly concentrated in northern and central Italy.[22]

Also in the case of silk, Fioravanti insisted upon the decline in the earning power of the work in "an art which further enriches the rich and helps the poor". In the chain of production which links the countryside, where the silkworms are reared and the silk obtained, to the city, where it is woven, he emphasizes the role of the merchants, who dominated the sector and took charge of the most delicate phases of the process, such as the dyeing. These were people of great standing, not only financial, but also social and political, if what he says is true, namely that "throughout Italy, this art carries great privileges, and in many cities

21. Bronzini, *La piazza universale*, II, p. 898.
22. The number of looms can be calculated from the accurate count by Francesco Battistini, "La tessitura serica italiana durante l'età moderna: dimensioni, specializzazione produttiva, mercati", in Luca Molà, Reinhold C. Mueller, and Claudio Zanier (eds), *La seta in Italia dal Medioevo al Seicento* (Venice, 2000), pp. 335–352, 344–345.

has its own independent court, which administers justice in complete freedom".[23]

Garzoni, on the other hand, besides repeating Fioravanti's detailed description of the whole productive process (without citing the source), dedicated ample space to the variety of products from this sector, and to the changing tastes of purchasers in favour of silk: "is it not obvious that there is as much difference between a lady dressed in silk and one in woollen cloth, as there is between luminous day and dark night?" It is worth noting that in the usual description of the shortcomings of the art, with which he concluded all his commentaries, he directed his criticism not at the workers, accused only of "frequently" stealing the silk given to them to work, but at the merchants who

> [...] underpay them [the workers], avoid paying tax by smuggling out the finished goods, buy the silk from women who have obtained it cut price, so that even the Jews in the bank would have qualms of conscience, and make a thousand deals and contracts among themselves and with others, all illegal.[24]

So Fioravanti alone gave a realistic view of work and workers in these two important sectors. What he looked at, however, is the organizational aspect of the sector, and the logic behind the functioning of the system, created and dominated by merchants and their capital, which was widening and extending market relations. He said nothing about the conditions of workers, or how the work was allocated to the different sexes, aspects which were dealt with, albeit summarily, by other contemporary writers.

One such writer was Count Giovanni Maria Bonardo, whose description of the "miseries of the life" of those engaged in the mechanical arts begins precisely with the woollen mill. "I will not speak again of the toils of transforming wool into cloth, I shall say only that from the middle of the summer when the wool is cut, sometimes until the following summer, without a single day of idleness, the cloth is laboriously formed." Of the utmost importance in this work were the spinners, whose task was "vile and wearisome", and the weavers "who have no sensibility which is not used up in their weaving".[25] His writing shows clearly his awareness of the hard work involved in pre-industrial trades. It was a wearing existence even without factories and assembly lines, because the hours of work could be extended to the bitter end,

---

23. *Dello specchio*, p. 58v.
24. See section CL, "De' setaiuoli ove si comprendono gli accavigliatori, bavellari, agguindilatori, filatori, le maestre, i tessitori e i mercanti da seta" [On Silk Workers, including Thread Crossers, Flossers, Winders, Spinners, Teachers, Wavers and Silk Merchants], in Bronzini, *La piazza universale*, II, p. 1124.
25. Giovanni Maria Bonardo, *Della miseria et eccellenza della vita humana, ragionamenti due dell'ill. s. Gio. Maria Bonardo Frateggiano, conte & caualiere. Nel qual con infiniti essempi, cauati da più famosi scrittori, s'impara quali siano i trauagli, et quali siano le perfettioni di questo mondo. Fatti alla illustriss. signora la sig. Lucrezia Gonzaga marchesana* (Venice, 1586), pp. 17–18.

Figure 1. Silk worker.
Biblioteca Riccardiana Firenze, Ricc. 2580, Libro d'arte di seta, *second half of the fifteenth century, Florentine school. Used with permission.*

without any "day of idleness", and many jobs, such as weaving, required the total involvement and attention of the workers, who were given no rest.

MERCHANTS IN THE WRITINGS OF GARZONI AND
FIORAVANTI

When describing the woollen mill and the silk factory, Garzoni was even less interested in the aspects of the actual work and limited himself, from his strictly hierarchical standpoint, to assigning the most important role to the merchants. However, with reference to the undisputed protagonists of the manufacturing and commercial success of the most important cities in Italy between the Middle Ages and the early modern period, his basic point of view seems very different from Fioravanti's. In his lengthy treatment of merchants, Garzoni, after a fairly technical section (again taken largely from Fioravanti), and some mannered praise for the positive role that merchants played in the economic life of their day, then dedicates much of what follows to a moralistic invective because "looking at it afterwards more closely, and bringing into discussion the strength of this profession, I see it as ragged and ruined, and am aware of the thousand vices and faults contained within it".

According to Garzoni, merchants, as we have seen, already harshly criticized in the section dedicated to the silk factory, were not only fraudulent by nature, but above all

> [...] are the ones who murder the world many times over with their falsified rubbish, with rotten and tainted goods, who bring about famine in the provinces and the cities, hoarding excess food and keeping it hidden, so that the poor gentleman and the miserable populace fall dead from starvation in the streets, they cause their creditors to fail, they ensnare and skin the citizens with documents and bonds of the very devil, they devour the substance of the whole populace through usury and interest, they put up their prices and cause shortages whenever they wish.[26]

Garzoni is very harsh in his criticism, and it is not by chance that section LXV deals not only with merchants, but puts them together with *banchieri, usurai, fondaghieri e merciari* [bankers, usurers, wholesale grocers, and drapers]. Associating merchants with moneylenders, who were "known to be infamous", and with drapers, who, on a smaller scale, used the same incorrect dealings and tricks as the merchants to deceive and harm their fellow men, clearly emphasized the negative connotations of the category.

Here again Garzoni aligned himself with the current of thought, prevalent in his time, which reflected the increasing desire of the urban aristocracy to close ranks against the merchants, who were on the rise and aspiring to nobility themselves. Indeed, in the course of the sixteenth century an ever-widening gap emerged between commerce and the

---

26. Bronzini, *La piazza universale*, I, p. 664.

Figure 2. Jewish Paduan merchant.
Biblioteca Riccardiana Firenze, St. 12886, P. Bertelli, Diversarum nationum habitus, *Patavii, apud Alciatum Alcia et Petrum Bertellium, 1594–1596. Used with permission.*

discharge of public office, attested to by the growing insistence on the idea that the nobility were born with certain qualities and requirements – blood, birth, and honour – which were automatically transposed to political virtue. These "natural" virtues were the prerogative of a single class, and effectively marginalized the members of the merchant class, who could neither possess them nor cultivate them since they were occupied the whole day in "lowly activities and mechanical arts", as Memmo wrote in a volume published in Venice in 1563.[27]

Evidence for this changed attitude to commerce in this period, which in view of its political and social reappraisal led to greater emphasis being laid on its negative aspects, can be found in the most important Italian cities, from Genoa to Milan. In Genoa, the inclusion of the silk industry among the mechanical arts led to a reduction of about 300 in the number of people who could consider themselves noble. In 1575 the College of Jurisprudence in Milan prohibited access to the nobility to "those who, even though only through agents, have been involved in squalid commercial activity", reaffirming, in 1593, that "people, whether they themselves or any of their ancestors, who might be in any way connected with commerce" could not become noble.[28]

It is also significant that in early modern Milan the only pragmatic sanction against luxury, which imposed precise and differentiated modes of behaviour according to sex and social class, was that of 1565. This was in fact a period of great vitality in the local economy, accompanied by remarkable social mobility, and it was consequently deemed necessary to observe the boundaries between the classes, also by safeguarding external symbols such as attire, before eventually cutting off access to the nobility, which, as we have seen, happened quite soon after.[29]

Fioravanti's treatment was much more lucid and devoid of any moralistic tone when dealing with an activity which he regarded as "an art involving great memory and intelligence". He showed the very essence of big business, demonstrating a sound knowledge of the Venetian situation by giving a detailed description of the flow of merchandise to and from the city. His merchant was not a merchant-entrepreneur, but one involved in business on an international scale. He perceived, with great modernity, how the merchant's real capital lies in his knowledge of the market and the

27. Giovanni Maria Memmo, *Dialogo del magn. caualiere m. Gio. Maria Memmo, nel quale dopo alcune filosofiche dispute, si forma un perfetto prencipe, & una perfetta republica, e parimente un senatore, un cittadino, un soldato, & un mercatante, diuiso in tre libri* (Venice, 1564), p. 92.
28. On these topics see Rodolfo Savelli, "Tra Machiavelli e S. Giorgio. Cultura giuspolitica e dibattito istituzionale a Genova nel Cinque-Seicento", in Aldo De Maddalena and Hermann Kellenbenz (eds), *Finanze e ragion di stato in Italia e in Germania nella prima età moderna* (Bologna, 1984), pp. 249–321, 295, and Mocarelli, "The Attitude of Milanese Society to Work and Commercial Activities", pp. 114–115.
29. Luca Mocarelli, "'Lusso dannoso e lusso discreto'. Il lusso nella Milano settecentesca tra prescrizioni legislative e comportamenti", in Antonella Alimento (ed.), *Modelli d'oltre confine. Prospettive economiche e sociali negli antichi Stati italiani* (Rome, 2009), pp. 295–308, 296–297.

product, "knowing the products that are well-received in one place rather than another", and he was equally realistic about the bad business practices that could devour accumulated capital. On the astuteness and trickery so harshly criticized by Garzoni, he had little to say, evidently considering them inherent to the profession, and limited himself to advising that "the merchants should be content to sell their merchandise at a fair price, and not be overcome by greed or tempted by high profits".[30]

A note of criticism was present in Bonardo since the Venetian nobleman limited himself to pointing out, in great detail, the problems and difficulties that made the practice of commerce so complicated, and of uncertain success, "because the selling price of goods bought at a high price so frequently drops, meaning that no profit is made [...] buying dear and selling cheap [...] the increases and falls in business because of the constant changes in the currency, domestic theft, robbery by strangers, taxes". This was an extremely precarious situation, therefore, which led him to conclude that "miserable merchants are not safe at sea, nor on land, neither in the wood nor the city, not even in the town square or their own home".[31]

THE MECHANICAL ARTS IN THE WRITINGS OF GARZONI AND FIORAVANTI

The difference between Garzoni and Fioravanti is even more apparent in their treatment of the trades they considered to be lowly. Here we will consider what Garzoni and Fioravanti had to say about stonemasons and shoemakers. When, after a few mannered praises, Garzoni goes on to consider the meanest occupations such as these, he lays great emphasis on their faults and tricks. So, even though stonemasons carry out work of "strict necessity, since they construct dwelling places", they are not precise and they prolong the work unnecessarily in order to earn more, "thus as a penance they frequently fall from the roof, or the wall or the stairs, and break their necks".[32] Similarly, shoemakers undoubtedly produce useful articles, but they knew little about ancient footwear, and above all they "often cheat you with the stuff they give you [...] difficulties and lies are commonplace with them, as with all such people who serve others".[33]

---

30. *Dello specchio*, pp. 35r–38v.
31. Bonardo, *Della miseria et eccellenza della vita humana*, p. 20.
32. See section XCIIII, "De' muratori o fabricatori et de' biancheggiatori" [On Bricklayers, Builders, and Decorators], in Bronzini, *La piazza universale*, II, pp. 843–844. Bonardo's tone is quite different (*Della miseria et eccellenza della vita humana*, p. 19) when he says "but who is more unfortunate than the bricklayer or the carpenter who when building walls or adjusting beams is in danger, a thousand times a day, of falling from on high and breaking his neck?".
33. See section CXXXI, "De' calzolari, o caligari et ciavattini" [On Shoemakers and Slipper-Makers], in Bronzini, *La piazza universale*, II, p. 1031.

Figure 3. Stonemason.
Biblioteca Casanatese Roma, Rari 212, F. Indovino and A. da Carpentieri, Il mezzo più sicuro per vincere al lotto, o sia nuova lista generale de' Sogni, col Nome di tutte le cose, e numeri corrispondenti all'Estrazioni *(Macerata, 1796). Used with permission.*

The attitude of Fioravanti is totally different; he exalts the art of the stonemason – the most necessary after the provision of food and clothing – to the point where he deals with them before architects. He does not limit himself to the technical abilities and skills required of such workers, but points to the redistributory nature of the building industry, noting how "in no other case will a man so willingly pay others, as when he is having a sumptuous and magnificent house built [...] yet since this is what he wants to do, the art of the stonemason is necessary". He also appreciates the significance of houses as status symbols, remarking that some houses are built with "stupendous facades, which add nothing to the comfort of the owner and serve no purpose other than to be seen by others".[34] Even in the case of shoemakers, whose art he considers the lowliest of all, Fioravanti indicates many positive elements, from the protection of our feet to the aesthetic aspect, reaching the conclusion that "among the other arts this is most necessary and worthy of doing".[35]

CONCLUDING REMARKS

What considerations does this comparison suggest? First, that though dealing with the same subject, the two authors made very different appraisals.

Garzoni built his argument on scholarship and his principal objective was the formation of a humanist prince,

> [...] in this scene and this rich display you will easily understand the good and the bad that all the workers of the world can do; since the prince who governs must take care of so many people and so many things, perhaps there could not be any book more useful than this.[36]

The prince must indeed know the world, since his basic role is to heal the more serious rifts and put the different classes back into their designated places. According to Giovanni Battista Pigna, a writer well-known to Garzoni, the prince had to reduce the nobles and the populace "to their (just) dimensions and mediocrity". That was no easy task since, if it is true that "gentlemen have a preference principally for honour, and plebeians for profit", it is also true that without the intervention of the prince to keep

---

34. *Dello specchio*, p. 78v.
35. *Ibid.*, p. 73r.
36. The quotation is taken from Garzoni's dedication to Alfonso II d'Este in Bronzini, *La piazza universale*, I, p. 6. His desire to include everything was echoed in the preface to *L'autore a' spettatori* [The Author to the Spectators], in which Garzoni recalled the "very lowly skills which I have described" and concluded, not without a certain satisfaction, that he has created a "monstrous" building because of "the great number of people it accommodates all together" (*ibid.*, pp. 47–48). It is certainly not a coincidence that Garzoni's work opened with section I, "De' signori o principi, et de' tiranni" [On Lords or Princes, and Tyrants], and finished with section CLV, "Degli humanisti" [On Humanists].

"these two such different natures within their own confines, one will aspire to be a magistrate, and the other will interest himself in merchandise".[37]

This was Garzoni's perspective in attempting to restore order and sense to the bustling life of trades and professions, and it led him to study the multitude of human activities rather as an entomologist studies insects – calmly and clinically. So he takes particular care to reveal the cunning tricks and faults of the humble, without trying to find any meaning in their work.

Fioravanti on the other hand based his work on direct observation and, beyond praising each activity, he attempted to restore dignity to all types of work. His interest was not that of the cataloguer, but of a professional and a participant, and he offered considerations which would be inconceivable to Garzoni. An example of this can be found in what each of them wrote about tailors. To Garzoni, they were people who offered beauty and dignity to all, especially when they made fine clothes,[38] but to Fioravanti they represented an opportunity to question the social hierarchies of the time. It is worth quoting his reasoning:

> [...] for all honours and robes are but smoke. And the truth is that we are born equal and we die equal, the greatest and the least alike, for we are born naked, and in the end we die and abandon our faculties. So I conclude that when all is said and done, we are all the same.

His criticism of dressing in a certain way to show distinction, an unassailable requirement in the most important cities at the time, inevitably became directed at tailors. For Fioravanti their art did not require the skill and competence one might suppose "since making clothes is nothing more than draping a piece of cloth over someone and cutting away the excess, thus the garment is made".[39]

What clearly differentiated the two authors was also the ranking of the professions, which is evident in their work. Garzoni, besides having no doubt about the superiority of the intellectual arts, offers us a catalogue apparently based on aesthetic criteria and the desire of the curious scholar to compile a history of what is lowly and neglected.[40] The structure of Fioravanti's writing is different: he puts human occupations on a functional scale, ordering them according to how necessary and useful they are. Thus, he begins his treatise with agriculture and animal husbandry, and puts among the first the arts of the blacksmith and the woodworker, since very few skills, if any, can be practised without recourse to these.

37. Giovanni Battista Pigna, *Il principe [...] nel qual si discrive come debba essere il principe heroico, sotto il cui gouerno un felice popolo, possa tranquilla & beatamente vivere* (Venice, 1561), pp. 35–36.
38. See section CXX, "De' sartori" [On Tailors], in Bronzini, *La piazza universale*, II, pp. 999–1000.
39. *Dello specchio*, p. 27r.
40. Bronzini, *Introduzione*, in *idem, La piazza universale*, I, pp. xx–xxiv.

Furthermore Fioravanti does not make the traditional distinction between liberal and mechanical arts, preferring instead to distinguish between using one's hands and pure knowledge (skills and sciences):

[...] so that everything that calls for the use of hands can justly be defined as skills, yet medicine, surgery, and anatomy are all manual: therefore I call them skills, as I do all the others. The sciences are composed of memory and intellect, they can be defined as reasoning, and manual work plays no part in them.

Fioravanti goes even further, maintaining that knowledge alone is of little use in itself, as he confirms when speaking about anatomy: "this knowledge is of very little importance, because when one is unlucky enough to be injured [...] one needs to be treated and cured: which cannot be done by knowing about anatomy, but only by medicating with tried and tested remedies". Indeed he claims that "it is far better to operate well than to know how to speak about it [...] therefore we can rightly affirm that anatomy is nothing more than knowing how our body is made. But the truth is that it cannot be used in medical treatment".[41]

In short, it can be said that Garzoni and Fioravanti incarnate two very different spirits of the Renaissance, although both were driven by the same inexhaustible curiosity and thirst for knowledge. The Augustinian was a contemplative, learned man, anxious to construct a moralistic-literary monument, complete in every detail. The restless physician-surgeon from Bologna, however, was a student of first-hand experience, a great observer intent on making full use of every kind of knowledge, even that which seemed lowly and contemptible: a man who was not in the least scholastic, and who would never have agreed with the distinction between noble and ignoble arts included in the original title of Garzoni's *La piazza universale*.

41. *Dello specchio*, pp. 52v and 51v.

IRSH 56 (2011), Special Issue, pp. 107–124 doi:10.1017/S0020859011000484
© 2011 Internationaal Instituut voor Sociale Geschiedenis

The Just Wage in Early Modern Italy: A Reflection on Zacchia's *De Salario seu Operariorum Mercede*

ANDREA CARACAUSI

Department of History, University of Padua

E-mail: andrea.caracausi@unipd.it

SUMMARY: This article aims to understand norms and values pertaining to the definition of just wages in early modern Italy. The starting point is the treatise by the jurist Lanfranco Zacchia, *De Salario seu Operariorum Mercede*, which appeared in the mid-seventeenth century and represented the first attempt to collate a set of rules on wages based on the traditions of Roman and canon law. After a brief presentation of the treatise, I shall analyse the meanings and concepts of wages, and then consider the elements that determined the just wage. To understand how prescriptions were seen by individuals, I shall also compare them with information about court cases and rulings compiled by Zacchia in another book, the *Centuria decisionum ad materiam Tractatus de Salario*, and with the rest of the existing literature. Evidence from my comparison will allow us to understand the interaction and reciprocal influences between juridical thought and daily work practice, and underline the fact that wages were based on a complex system of norms and values where individuals, their social positions, skills, and experience determined the recognition of the just wage with reference to the local context.

WAGES AND THEIR HISTORY

During the early modern age, wages were at the basis of labour relations, especially in commodified labour. A wide range of workers leased their work to public or private employers, receiving payment in the form of money or goods. An analysis of how wages (i.e. the payment for a particular job) came to be considered "just" at certain times and places seems necessary in order to understand the complex system of norms and values regulating work. Furthermore, the debate is more relevant during periods of economic change, as in the Italian context of the sixteenth and seventeenth centuries when the spread of new forms of production caused a need for the rules concerning labour relations to be redefined.

In recent decades, scholars of the social and economic history of pre-industrial Europe have investigated more deeply the history of wages,

108 *Andrea Caracausi*

previously considered a field of labour or price history.[1] During medieval and early modern times wages depended on many factors, including time, skill, and industriousness, and their amounts were difficult to standardize.[2]

On the other hand, the role of justice with respect to wages is poorly understood, which is regrettable considering the importance of law to early modern labour relations.[3] In general, the focus is on such formal aspects as guild regulations, local statutes, and theological texts.[4] Studies have shown important features, such as high levels of negotiation, but conflicts between groups or organizations have been analysed more frequently, while micro-conflicts between actors have not been investigated.[5] Regarding the debate on the "just wage", more attention has been paid to

1. Henry Phelps Brown and Sheila V. Hopkins, *A Perspective of Wages and Prices* (London [etc.], 1981); Ruggiero Romano (ed.), *I prezzi in Europa dal XIII secolo ad oggi* (Turin, 1966).
2. James Farr, *Artisans in Europe, 1300–1914* (Cambridge, 2000), pp. 151–152; Simon A.C. Penn and Christopher Dyer, "Wages and Earnings in Late Medieval England: Evidence from the Enforcement of the Labour Laws", *The Economic History Review*, 43 (1990), pp. 356–376; Donald Woodward, "The Determination of Wage Rates in the Early Modern North of England", *The Economic History Review*, 47 (1994), pp. 22–43; Jeremy Boulton, "Wage Labour in Seventeenth-Century London", *The Economic History Review*, 49 (1996), pp. 268–290; Francesca Trivellato, "Salaires et justice dans les corporations vénitiennes au 17e siècle. Le cas des manufactures de verre", *Annales HSS*, 54 (1999), pp. 245–273; Luca Mocarelli, "Wages and the Labour Market in the Building Trade in 18th Century Milan", *Jahrbuch für Wirtschafts Geschichte*, 2 (2004), pp. 61–81; Guido Guerzoni, "Assetti organizzativi, tecniche gestionali e impatto occupazionale delle fabbriche ducali estensi nel Cinquecento", in Simonetta Cavaciocchi (ed.), *L'edilizia prima della rivoluzione industriale* (Florence, 2005), pp. 771–802.
3. Michael Sonenscher, *Work and Wages: Natural Law, Politics and the Eighteenth-Century French Trades* (Cambridge, 1989).
4. Raymond De Roover, "The Concept of the Just Price: Theory and Economic Policy", *The Journal of Economic History*, 18 (1958), p. 424; Armando Sapori, "Il giusto prezzo nella dottrina di S. Tommaso e nella pratica del suo tempo", in *idem, Studi di storia economica medievale* (Florence, 1940), pp. 189–227. Different approaches can be found in Penn and Dyer, "Wages and Earnings in Late Medieval England", pp. 356–376; Woodward, "The Determination of Wage Rates", pp. 22–43; Francesca Trivellato, *Fondamenta dei vetrai. Lavoro, tecnologia e mercato a Venezia tra Sei e Settecento* (Rome, 2000); *idem*, "Salaires et justice dans les corporations vénitiennes"; Renata Ago, *Economia barocca. Mercato e istituzioni nella Roma del Seicento* (Rome, 1998).
5. Carlo Poni, "Misura contro misura: come il filo da seta divenne sottile e rotondo", *Quaderni storici*, 47 (1981), pp. 385–423; *idem*, "Norms and Disputes: The Shoemakers' Guild in Eighteenth-Century Bologna", *Past & Present*, 123 (1989), pp. 80–108; Michael Sonenscher, "Journeymen, the Courts and the French Trades 1781–1791", *Past & Present*, 114 (1987), pp. 77–109; Catharina Lis, Jan Lucassen, and Hugo Soly (eds), "Before the Unions: Wage Earners and Collective Action in Europe, 1300–1850", Supplement to the *International Review of Social History*, 39 (1994); Simona Cerutti and Carlo Poni (eds), *Conflitti nel mondo del lavoro* [*Quaderni storici*, 27] (1992), pp. 381–508; Walter Panciera, "Padova, 1704: L'Antica Unione de' Poveri Lanieri contro la ricca Università dell'Arte della Lana", *Quaderni storici*, 29 (1994), pp. 629–653; Alberto Guenzi, Paola Massa, and Fausto Piola Caselli (eds), *Guilds, Markets and Work Regulations in Italy, 16th–19th Centuries* (Aldershot, 1998), Part II, "Profession, Monopoly and Conflict", pp. 211–395.

the medieval period thanks to the prominence of scholastic thought.[6] Authorities such as Thomas Aquinas, Baldo degli Ubaldi, and Bartolo da Sassoferrato are fundamental for the early modern period.

However, between the sixteenth and seventeenth centuries the Italian peninsula experienced many economic transformations in trade and manufacture, including the rise of merchant-manufacturers, which had important consequences for labour relations and wage payments. As rural and urban proto-industry spread, there was a reconversion to luxury production and the growth of wage labour in and around guilds.[7] Furthermore, the development of more organized regional states caused public administration to expand, leading to the rise of a new class of salaried workers. Those transformations probably stimulated the new publications on just wages that began to appear in the mid-seventeenth century.[8]

This article aims to understand how it was possible to determine a just wage in an early modern, segmented society; at the same time, I shall show how juridical thought was relevant to daily practice in workshops. My starting point is the treatise by the Roman jurist Lanfranco Zacchia, *De Salario seu Operariorum Mercede* [Wages or Workers' Wages],[9] which represents the first collection of rules and prescriptions entirely concerning wages. It was first published in Italy in 1658.[10]

After a brief introduction to Zacchia's book, the first section of this article analyses the various concepts and terminology used to define wages. This variety does not imply a specific ranking of labour nor of wage relations, but it is necessary to determine what a just wage was.

6. For the early modern period see Gino Barbieri, "Il giusto salario negli scrittori italiani del Cinque e Seicento", *Annali della Facoltà di Economia e Commercio dell'Università di Bari*, 9 (1949), pp. 238–328 [republished as "La remunerazione del lavoro negli scrittori italiani della Controriforma", in idem, *L'ordine economico nei pensatori ecclesiastici dell'epoca moderna* (Bari, 1961)]; Trivellato, "Salaires et justice dans les corporations vénitiennes"; idem, *Fondamenta dei vetrai*, pp. 51–81; Ago, *Economia barocca*, pp. 102–107, 133–157, 201–202; James Shaw, *The Justice of Venice: Authorities and Liberties in the Urban Economy, 1550–1700* (Oxford, 2006), pp. 147–148.
7. Paolo Malanima, *La fine del primato. Crisi e riconversione nell'Italia del Seicento* (Milan, 1998).
8. Gino Barbieri has argued that those new publications on wages reflected changes in economic mentality (especially the emergence of individualism). See Barbieri, "La remunerazione del lavoro", pp. 81–83.
9. Lanfranci Zacchiae, I.V.D. ET ADVOCATI ROMANI, *De Salario seu Operariorum Mercede*. Tractatus in tres partes distinctus, in quo questiones omnes, tàm ad Theoricam, quàm ad Praxim pertinentes proponuntur, pertractantur, resoluuntur, Opus Iurisperitis omnibus tàm in Foris, quam in Scolis versantibus utile, & necessarium, Cum Duplici Indice. Romaes Ex Typographia Nicolai Tinassi, M.DC.LVIII, Superiorum Permissu & Privilegio.
10. Barbieri, "La remunerazione del lavoro", pp. 93, 97. Francesca Trivellato noted that Gino Barbieri was the first scholar to underline the importance of Zacchia's book for the concept of wages during the early modern period; Trivellato, "Salaires et justice dans les corporations vénitiennes", p. 264, n. 42.

During the second part I will show how Zacchia presents the just wage. The Roman jurist stresses the importance of contractual agreements signed by individuals, and his idea is that "just wages" were first and foremost individually determined. Beyond that, Zacchia underlines the role of law, custom, and, finally, judges. I shall show when and how judges were involved in setting the just wage, normally in the absence of the previous elements. In the last part of this article, I shall highlight some key points concerning the complex system of norms and values that governed the idea of wages in early modern Italy.

In order to understand how the prescriptions offered in Zacchia's book influenced or were taken into consideration by society as a whole, I shall integrate this analysis with rulings from the Sacra Rota Romana also collected by Zacchia in his *Centuria decisionum ad materiam Tractatus de Salario* [One Hundred Judgments on Wages],[11] and the extant literature on wage-related court cases.[12] The aim is not to give more relevance to the culture of the elites than to that of the "lower" classes, nor to underline differences between them. My aim is to understand the reciprocal influences between juridical thought and daily work practice, their interactions, and the consequences for the early modern economy and society. That approach could also allow us to identify some key points in early modern labour relations and work ethics, which will be useful for comparison with other countries and cultures.

DE SALARIO SEU OPERARIORUM MERCEDE: AN OVERVIEW

In the mid-seventeenth century (1658 and 1659), two books appeared written by the Roman jurist Lanfranco Zacchia: the *De Salario seu Operariorum Mercede* and the *Centuria decisionum ad materiam Tractatus de Salario*. Information on Lanfranco Zacchia's own life is scanty,[13] but his *De Salario seu Operariorum Mercede* is a very substantial work (covering over 400 pages) and the book had great resonance in the legislation of the seventeenth and eighteenth centuries. Thanks to the many cases discussed, *De Salario* represents a very rich source for understanding early modern labour relations

11. *Centuria decisionum ad materiam tractatus de salario et operariorum mercede*, d. Lanfranci Zacchiae, Iureconsulti Romani Pertinentium, Venetiis, Apud Turrinum, 1664. Superiorum permissu et privilegium.

12. Barbieri, "La remunerazione del lavoro"; Trivellato, "Salaires et justice dans les corporations vénitiennes"; Ago, *Economia barocca*, pp. 181–182, 201–202; Shaw, *The Justice of Venice*, pp. 147–149; Mocarelli, "Wages and the Labour Market"; Andrea Caracausi, *Dentro la bottega. Culture del lavoro in una città d'età moderna* (Venice, 2008), pp. 45–146; *idem*, "I giusti salari nelle manifatture della lana di Padova e Firenze (s. XVI–XVII)", *Quaderni storici*, 45 (2010), pp. 857–884.

13. Lanfranco Zacchia was probably the son or nephew of the famous doctor Paolo Zacchia (1584–1659); Trivellato, "Salaires et justice dans les corporations vénitiennes", p. 264.

and it allows us to reconstruct the doctrine of salary during the two centuries after the Counter-Reformation.[14]

Zacchia's *De Salario* consists of three parts and 110 *Quaestiones*, i.e. questions on several aspects of wages, and it is impossible to summarize. The first part (*Quaestiones* I–XLIX) is a general introduction which analyses several issues relating to the nature of wages and labour relations. The second part (*Quaestiones* L–XC) deals instead with wages and their relation to each wage earner. The final part (*Quaestiones* XCI–CX) concerns the role of justice with respect to wages.

In the first part, Zacchia investigates the nature of wages: the terminologies and modalities of remuneration, the convenient (i.e. proper) wage, and the ways in which they could be increased or decreased. Starting from those general issues, Zacchia analyses a number of elements of wage relations, such as timing and forms of payment (from money to goods), and the lawfulness of working during holidays. He also considers rights and duties within wage relations.

Zacchia focuses on the importance of observing contractual agreements. In particular, he reminds us that wages must be paid regularly to workers who were brought in for a certain time in a specific place to do a job, and he is careful to discuss exclusive agreements between employers and employees.[15] He addresses several aspects of the rights and obligations arising from labour contracts, such as indemnity for infirmity, the rights and duties of fathers and employers concerning working children, the transmission of wages within the family, and the taxation of wages.[16] Finally, a number of questions are discussed with respect to the ecclesiastical world.

Regarding early modern wage relations, Zacchia underlines the wide range of salaried workers, forms of remuneration, and methods of payments. The second part of his *De Salario* focuses on individual aspects of wage relations, according to the individual professions involved. Quoting them in alphabetical order, he shows the wide diversity of "employees" or "salaried workers": ambassadors and bankers, craftsmen and doctors, but also prostitutes, *famuli* and *familiars* (domestic servants). Everyone has a specific place and character in Zacchia's picture, reflecting the diversity of wage relations and their internal logic, rights, and duties. The aim was probably to present a universal picture of an ideal society in terms of the different groups of wage typologies that he sought to analyse.[17]

The last part of *De Salario* examines the role of justice with respect to wages. Zacchia examines judicial proceedings, focusing on courts that were competent to pass judgments on wages, looking also at the days on

14. Barbieri, "La remunerazione del lavoro", p. 97, n. 40.
15. Zacchia, *De Salario*, Quaestiones XXII–XXIII.
16. *Ibid.*, Quaestiones V–VII, XLII–XLV.
17. *Ibid.*, Quaestiones L–XC.

Figure 1. *Lanfranci Zacchiae*, De Salario seu Operariorum Mercede, *Romae, Ex Typographia Nicolai Tinassi, M.DC.LVIII.*
Biblioteca civica Bertoliana di Vicenza. Used with permission.

which it was possible for cases to be heard, and considering the legal remedies that might be implemented to ensure justice. Nor did Zacchia fail to examine the role of lawyers and witnesses and, finally, the types and hierarchy of proof.

The great jurist also introduced to his exposition specific issues concerning contracts, the election of *capitoli*, witnesses, compensation, claims, and debts.[18] For his purpose, Zacchia preferred a more technical approach, focused on the legal system and juridical aspects. Praxis on wage conflict and judgments are at the core of the *Centuria decisionum ad materiam Tractatus de Salario*, which appeared in 1659. Making extensive use of examples of judgments made in the Papal Courts of the Sacra Rota, Zacchia shows the praxis on wage justice, analysing the setting of a just wage, the repayment of damages, the role of judges, witnesses, and experts (*periti*), and the importance of *aequitas*,[19] estimates and valuations (*aestimationes*), customs, and contracts.

MEANINGS OF WAGE

Zacchia opened *De Salario* with a simple but paradigmatic question: "What are wages?". Because he acknowledged "wage" to have many meanings, he was unable to offer a unique and monolithic definition. Quoting Benvenuto Stracca (the Anconite author of the treatise *De mercatura, seu mercatore*, published in the mid-sixteenth century),[20] Zacchia concluded that wage (*salario*) is an "ambiguous concept" (*aequivoca vox*), whose meaning depends both on *solum* (pension given based on the area of land) and "salt" (a commodity ultimately necessary for every human action). That last concept refers in particular to workers (*operari*) and everyone else who received a wage or any remuneration for work. Beyond those differences, Zacchia defined "wage" as "the remuneration due to recompense work".[21]

Wages are different not only in their meaning, but also in their genre. Zacchia identified four categories. First are the wages due for the effort of science and intellect, applying to judges, doctors, lawyers, assessors, and others. While the second category refers to *familiari* and domestic

18. *Capitoli* were the arguments submitted by the two parties involved in a case. They had to be proved by witnesses.

19. *Aequitas* could be translated as "fairness", while the medieval and early modern concept was quite different from that of the present. On the existence of different forms of justice and tribunal, especially distributive justice, see Giovanni Levi, "*Aequitas* vs *fairness*. Reciprocità ed equità fra età moderna ed età contemporanea", *Rivista di storia economica*, 19 (2003), pp. 195–203.

20. Benvenuti Straccae, *Tractatus de mercatura seu mercatore [...] Primae particulae ultimae partis principalis. Quomodo procedendum sit in causis mercatorum*, Lugduni, apud Sebastianum de Honoratis, 1558.

21. "Salarium est remuneratio debita pro operis retributione"; Zacchia, *De Salario*, pp. 5–6.

servants of the "prince", the third includes wages gained "jointly" for science and intellect and physical labour, such as for captains and soldiers. Zacchia recognized such a division in the classification of waged workers of the scholastic tradition. At that point, however, Zacchia identified a fourth category of wage, one surprisingly not quoted earlier, which included the wages of those engaged only in physical labour in "mercenary occupations".[22]

On the one hand, the Roman jurist argued that the meaning of wages was indeterminate. On the other, he drew clear distinctions between the four categories of wages. The division depended not on labour relations nor on the form of remuneration, but on the faculties that allowed an individual to earn a wage (science and intellect *versus* physical work) and the function of the individual within society (such as the household servants of the "prince" or soldiers in the defence of the state). In his ranking of a wage's category, Zacchia recognized the ideal of early modern society which gave greater dignity to intellectual than to physical work. However, the inclusion of a fourth type of wage, previously absent from scholastic thought, implies that Zacchia recognized the specific position and growing importance of wage labour from the late fifteenth to the seventeenth centuries.[23]

That different use of the term "wage" seems to be present in the second part of the treatise too. There, Zacchia used the term "wage" (*salario*) with respect to thirty-one out of forty professions. Exceptions were craftsmen, bankers, *coadiutori*, *divinatori*, inventors, witnesses, huntsmen (associated with the term *mercede*), and soldiers (with the term *stipendium*).[24]

However, the distinctions employed were not entirely clear. Zacchia was certainly not making positive or negative judgements about the status of workers without any well-defined professional rank. Throughout the treatise, the terms and meanings used change frequently, and it is surprising that such apparent vagueness in the use of the term "wage" was similarly present in the language of ordinary people, including not only judges, but merchants and workers too. The words used to indicate remuneration for work were very different. During court cases, people might refer without making any distinction to "salary and wages" or "salary or wages", previously using the term "price": the "price of his wage" or the "price usually paid for wages". Moreover, the term most frequently used is another: "money" (*denaro*), followed by the particular skill concerned or the more general term "work".

22. "Cose mercenarie". See *ibid.*, p. 7. On this point see also Trivellato, "Salaires et justice dans les corporations vénitiennes", p. 264. "Mercenaries" were people whose labour was for hire, rather than soldiers; Shaw, *The Justice of Venice*, p. 148.

23. Barbieri, "La remunerazione del lavoro", pp. 114–115. The first three were the categories stated in the classification of waged workers compiled by Baldo degli Ubaldi; Trivellato, "Salaires et justice dans les corporations vénitiennes", p. 264, n. 43.

24. Zacchia, *De Salario*, Quaestiones L–XC. The *coadiutores* assisted or deputized for others in public office. The *divinatores* practiced divination.

We read of "money in advance for work", "money for work", "money because of work", and "money for the time when he worked".[25]

Such variety was a consequence of a specific economic system that included a wide range of labour relations and forms of remuneration. Zacchia knew that, of course. During the sixteenth and seventeenth centuries, within much of Italian manufacturing, the widening division of labour and the emergence of merchant-entrepreneurs fostered a wide range of labour relations, including direct payment, subcontracting, non-professional relationships, and family ties, which sometimes coexisted in more than one workplace. Labour relations were very complex and included freely contracted waged work but also forced labour (as in hospitals), apprenticeships, and subcontracting.

Regarding wages, the main element was their timing. Zacchia stressed that point too. For the Roman jurist it was impossible to say "when the wage has to be paid", for that depended on the *quality* of work and people. It was necessary to know the "quality of people".[26] If an *operarius* (someone who made his labour available in return for wages) was unable to work before receiving his wages, he was to be paid in advance. Zacchia gave us the example of tailors and other workers (who were all *operari*) who could not finish their work unless they received payment in advance, thereby justifying the practice. He knew that sometimes wages included not only payment for the work itself but also other "charges" and "costs", which recognized the realities of sub-contracting in the organization of production.[27] That prescription was also well known by workers, as in the 1570s, for example, when the textile weavers of Padua asked for an increase in their wages because of an overall rise in prices. They also wanted to receive "wages in advance, as was usual and customary", in order to support their families and pay their workers.[28] As in the case of the textile weavers, Zacchia introduces us to an aspect of the subject that recurs frequently throughout his book: the need to link wages with the needs of individuals.

OBSERVING THE CONTRACTS

Given the wide range of labour relations, and especially the varieties and needs of the people involved, how is it possible to define a just wage?

25. Caracausi, *Dentro la bottega*, pp. 62–64; Germano Maifreda, *L'economia e la scienza. Il rinnovamento della cultura economica fra Cinque e Seicento* (Rome, 2010), pp. 145–148. See also Archivio di Stato, Florence [hereafter, ASF], Arte della lana [hereafter, AL], Register 285, fo. 106v; Archivio di Stato, Padua [hereafter, ASP], Università dell'arte della lana [hereafter, UL], Register 70, fo. 219v. For eighteenth-century France see Sonenscher, *Work and Wages*, ch. 6.
26. Zacchia, *De salario*, Quaestio XIIII, ch. 1.
27. *Ibid.*
28. ASP, UL, Register 79, fo. 431r–v.

Zacchia answers that point in his *Quaestio* IX, which was concerned with the *competens* wage, meaning the "convenient", "legitimate", or "just" wage.[29] How can that amount be determined? For Zacchia, the first determinant was the "law of the prince". That prescription, however, was immediately limited. The jurist recognized that an agreement between parties had an inescapable value and was to be observed absolutely.[30] In fact, Zacchia says, the convenient wages are the wages "agreed between the parties". Agreement must be observed both by those who have promised wages and those who have accepted them. Following that prescription, wages had to be paid following a contract: the tenant, who had *leased* his work, could not ask for more, and the employer, who had *rented* the work of others, could not pay less.[31]

The importance of agreements is confirmed by legal judgments. Courts rarely changed the wages stated in contracts. They preferred to legitimate the agreements. The judgments of the Sacra Rota Romana noted that contracts should not be terminated, and in the civil court of Murano (Venice), which had responsibility for cases involving glass workers, judges rarely changed original agreements.[32] On 15 October 1544, in a dispute on the payment of wages which was heard in the wool guild courts of Padua, a dyer demanded that a merchant pay him the wages agreed for his having dyed some clothes. The judge said that he should be paid "according to their exchange", without reference to wage levels. If individuals had agreed upon wages, those wages had to be paid "according to their agreement".[33] The juridical prescription ascribes an important role to the original promise, which was not to be violated. Wages had to be paid "according to their contract" for the time agreed "without any difference". In fact "it was not lawful to go against the promise", and workers should be paid "in accordance with the contract".[34]

The aim of such legal judgments was to encourage people to respect their contracts. Failing to pay wages according to what had been agreed was bad for the reputation of merchants and masters. They would be called "poor merchants", of "bad quality", and "vagabonds".[35] Those elements – Zacchia also tells us[36] – would constitute a breach of contract. A child was not obliged to work for his master if the man was a "vagabond".

---

29. Zacchia, *De Salario*, Quaestio IX, p. 34.
30. *Ibid.*
31. *Ibid.*, chs 17–18.
32. Trivellato, "Salaires et justice dans les corporations vénitiennes", p. 266.
33. Caracausi, "I giusti salari", p. 870.
34. *Ibid.*
35. Caracausi, *Dentro la bottega*, p. 242.
36. Zacchia, *De Salario*, Quaestio XXIII, ch. 17.

However, "because of his agreement" a father was obliged to put his sons into the workshop of his masters, despite its "poverty and disease".[37]

Contracts were also important as evidence for judges when they had to evaluate "just wages" (*iuxtam summam*). A confession by either of the parties was the highest proof, exceeding anything else. Confession was widely accepted in legal proceedings, having an important role because of its implied legal liability before God.[38] In the absence of such confession, however, evidence could be submitted in the form of public and private instruments. Convenient wages were those stated in "written texts", such as merchant books, legal records, but private, informal agreements too (the *chirografi*).[39] The use of that type of evidence meant that just wages were decided primarily by interested parties.

LAW AND CUSTOM

Further to the importance of contracts, there remains a question: What about the law?. For Zacchia, the just wage could not exceed "the right" (*il giusto*) and the amount stated by law. If wages exceeded the limits outlined by tax law (*taxam legis*), then they should not be paid.[40] However, Zacchia was somewhat ambiguous on the point, recognizing that a judge had the power to set a just wage.[41] On the other hand, judges in court cases also frequently evaluated as just such wages as had been agreed by the parties, without reference to civic or guild statutes.[42] Higher wages could also appear in other forms, such as gifts (*donativi*) or premiums (*premi*) if the employers judged the finished work to be worth more than the amount fixed by law.

In the early seventeenth century, Padua's wool merchant-manufacturers imposed a salary cap on master weavers. However, those amounts could be exceeded depending on the quality of work (*merito*) and the ability of the worker. In fact, once the merchant had received the clothes from the weaver, if he acknowledged that the master weaver deserved a higher

---

37. See Caracausi, *Dentro la bottega*, pp. 114–122 on these types of conflict.

38. Giovanni Battista De Luca, *Il dottor volgare. Libro ottavo. Del credito e del debito. Del creditore e del debitore; e del concorso de' creditori e dell'altre cose sopra questa materia di dare, ed avere* (Venice, 1740 [1st edn 1640]).

39. Maura Fortunati, *Scrittura e prova. I libri di commercio nel diritto medievale e moderno* (Rome, 1996); Simona Cerutti, *Giustizia sommaria. Pratiche ed ideali di giustizia in una società di Ancien Régime (Torino, sec. XVII)* (Turin, 2003), pp. 49–68; Andrea Caracausi, "Procedure di giustizia in età moderna. I tribunali corporativi", *Studi storici*, 49 (2008), pp. 323–360.

40. Zacchia, *De Salario*, Quaestio IX, ch. 21, p. 35.

41. *Ibid.*, Quaestio II, p. 14, chs 51–52.

42. Caracausi, *Dentro la bottega*, pp. 114–122.

wage he could give him a donation, if he saw fit.[43] Merchants and judges
recognized that personal agreements were more important than the laws
of the prince. Moreover, just wages depended first and foremost on
individual workers and their skills: an idea often posited by Zacchia.

Returning to the constitution of a convenient wage, after the laws of the
prince and agreements, Zacchia introduced a third element: "custom",
meaning wage that to "a certain extent is established by custom".[44]
"Customary" wages were "just".[45] Custom included two aspects: the role
of witnesses (*testes deponents*) and the locality of wages. The fact of "just
wages following customs" could not be proved "beyond the place where
the work had been provided". Customary wages reflected the local context, including civic and guild statutes.[46]

"Witnesses" meant people known locally. According to Zacchia, and other
jurists for that matter too such as Giovanni Battista De Luca,[47] witnesses
were to be "worthy and honest" and at least two in number. The consequences are obvious: only a "citizen", well-known locally, could bring a
larger number of witnesses to court.[48] Some examples may be helpful here.

On 20 August 1621, in the wool guild court of Padua, during an action
between a merchant and a beater, judges asked witnesses to assess the
"present common use usually paid" for beating wool. Custom was proved
by several witnesses, heard in court after a week, who stated that at the
time they used to "solve and receive six pence for any quantity of waste
wool".[49] On 1 July 1644, in the Sacra Rota Romana the merchants de
Peculis asked to be allowed to pay a just wage of only 100 *scudi* per year
to their *giovine* (assistant) Giuseppe Camerata from Bergamo. That
amount represented the "customary" wage at Teramo where they lived.
Giuseppe's witnesses had argued for higher wages, since those sums were
"customary" for other cities such as Rome, Ancona, Pesaro, and
Foligno.[50] The *communis aestimatio* changed depending on local market
trends, but it depended on the ability to produce a large number of
witnesses in court in order to prove *local* customs.[51] Sometimes it was also
necessary to link local customs to the private agreement. Giovanni Maria
Meggiorino proved through witnesses that "usually wages to the workers

43. *Idem*, "I giusti salari". On the role of gifts (*donativi*) in Murano glass manufacture,
see Trivellato, "Salaires et justice dans les corporations vénitiennes", pp. 254–255.
44. Zacchia, *De salario*, Quaestio IX, pp. 35–36, chs 29–33.
45. *Centuria decisionum*, n. 4, dec. 18.
46. *Ibid.*, n. 2, dec. 14.
47. De Luca, *Il dottor volgare*, p. 345.
48. On the role of witnesses, see Cerutti, *Giustizia sommaria*.
49. Caracausi, "I giusti salari".
50. *Centuria decisionum*, dec. 13, p. 28.
51. On the role of the *communis aestimatio* (common estimation) in the local community in
seventeenth-century Rome, see Ago, *Economia barocca*, p. 194.

were one *lira* and four *soldi* for 100 *libbra* of wool", but he had to prove
also that the merchant Domenico Morello had promised that sum to him
and other workers.[52]

THE CONSTRUCTION OF THE JUST WAGE

In the absence of laws, private agreements, and custom, how can just
wages be assessed? How might damages be rewarded? Only at that point
did Zacchia – following Giacomo Menochio – introduce the subject of the
judge's discretion.[53] In canon and Roman law, the role of the judge in
defining just wages was marginal compared with the force of contractual
agreement and local custom. Though marginal, that role sometimes
required them to set a just wage. How could they establish that "just
amount"? Judges had to consider many factors, such as the "quality of
the person" (especially whether he was educated or uneducated), along
with the quality of work and the time it took, as well as such factors
as industriousness, skill, and expertise (*industria, abilità e perizia*).[54]
Leonardo Ravena had worked with the Genoese merchant Adamo
Centurione, but he had no specific agreement concerning wages. The
Genoese court of Sacra Rota stated that Ravena's salary was to be based
first and foremost on the customs of the place, and then according to the
quality of his person, industriousness, and expertise.[55]

What were the consequences of such prescriptions? First, just wages
had to be higher or lower depending on the amount of work. Wages could
not be the same for those who worked less and for those who put in a
great deal more effort and care.[56] If a public officer had to administer
more than one city, then compared with earlier agreements wages must
increase proportionally.[57] Workers understood too that their "work"
merited its "reward", following the dictates of natural and civil law. On
23 May 1623, in the Venetian court of *Giustizia vecchia* ["Old Justice"]
the apprentice caulker Pasqualino argued that "it is right that everyone's
work brings its reward and that nobody is cheated of his just wage".[58]

---

52. Caracausi, "I giusti salari". *Lira* and *soldi* were units of account; *libbra* was the unit of
measurement for weight.
53. Zacchia, *De Salario*, Quaestio IX, p. 37, ch. 39. See also Iacobi Menochii, *De arbitrariis
iudicum quaestionibus et causis* (Lugduni, 1606). This prescription continued to be observed
even at the end of the eighteenth century. On Venetian law, see Marco Ferro, *Dizionario del
diritto comune e veneto* (Venice, 1778–1781), X; and Trivellato, "Salaires et justice dans les
corporations vénitiennes", p. 264, n. 42.
54. Zacchia, *De Salario*, Quaestio IX, p. 37, ch. 44.
55. Quoted by Barbieri, "La remunerazione del lavoro", p. 99, n. 42.
56. Zacchia, *De Salario*, Quaestio IX, p. 37, chs 45–49.
57. Barbieri, "La remunerazione del lavoro", p. 100.
58. Cited by Shaw, *The Justice of Venice*, p. 147, n. 59.

On 6 June 1625 the blacksmith Andrea Mazzon emphasized his "great sweat and labour", insisting on his "due wage, which cannot be denied him by divine and human law".[59]

Wages had also to follow economic trends, especially during famines, linking wages and subsistence.[60] Workers referred to those ideals too. In 1577 the weavers of Padua asked for an increase in wages, claiming:

> It is known to everyone how hard it is to live today, and also to dress, so that all the artisans of this city and also the workers (in the face of these calamitous times) are needy, so if they want themselves and their families to survive, their wages and goods and labour must be increased [...]. Therefore, having experienced that we cannot support ourselves and our families with the poor income and little reward in doing clothes, since it is so little that we can [...] resist and we need to leave the art of weaving and rely on other exercises [...].[61]

On the one hand wages depended also on objective criteria such as time, work, and economic trends. However, referring to the quality of the people and their abilities, Zacchia recognized a subjective meaning of wages, based on the individual skills and the social position of a worker (the *qualitas personae*). Zacchia recalls the long tradition of canon law, such as that indicated by scholastic thought: paying a just wage – and the just recompense of damage – was an action of both commutative justice (equality between payment and service) and distributive justice, depending on individual status. As for Thomas Aquinas, wages were *"quasi quoddam pretium"* [like a price], where it was impossible to provide a remedy if the damage exceeded half the cost and the estimate made by workers "does not have a uniform value but depends more or less on the expertise, industry, and skills of the same workers".[62]

The prescriptions invited judges, experts, and witnesses to evaluate the skills and expertise (*abilità* and *perizia*) of individual workers. On 30 May 1608, the judges of the Sacra Rota Romana set an amount greater than the ordinary for the work of Dominus Quinones, based on its "quality, industriousness, and skill". That wage (100 *scudi*) was not excessive, but "highly convenient".[63]

59. *Ibid.*, p. 147, n. 58.
60. Zacchia, *De Salario*, Quaestio IX, p. 38, ch. 48. Here Zacchia quotes Menochio, a jurist of the late sixteenth century: Iacobi Menochii, *De arbitrariis*, cas. 514. num. 11.
61. ASP, UL, Register 79, folio 431r-v.
62. Zacchia, *De Salario*, Quaestio XCVIII, chs 1–6. See also Sapori, *Il giusto prezzo*, pp. 198–204; Giacomo Todeschini, "'Ecclesia' e mercato nei linguaggi dottrinali di Tommaso d'Aquino", *Quaderni storici*, 105 (2000), pp. 585–622; De Roover, "The Concept of the Just Price", p. 424; Trivellato, "Salaires et justice dans les corporations vénitiennes", pp. 265–266.
63. Zacchia, *Centuria decisionum*, p. 24, dec. IX (also quoted by Trivellato, "Salaires et justice dans les corporations vénitiennes", p. 265, n. 45).

Assessments were based both on professional experience within the community and on the knowledge of people.[64] In the Florentine wool court at the end of the sixteenth century, to assess the level of damage to a master arising from the absence of his apprentice, the master weaver Biagio, son of Nicola, said he did not know if the apprentice Gerolamo "was able to stay as journeyman" because "he had not had him as journeyman in his workshop".[65] Instead Prospero, son of Bartolomeo, said that the boy was not "able to stay as journeyman" because he "had had him in his house for three to four days and [...] he would not agree with him". Another witness said that Gerolamo "could stay as every other apprentice", and that "he deserved four *scudi* every year". Weavers evaluated the skills, merits, and expertise of Gerolamo, basing their opinions on their knowledge of him. To assess how the young knitter Taddea could "be merited for her wages", Camilla, the wife of Piero, said that she could earn twenty pence every week. She arrived at that amount because of her knowledge of Taddea and her work, because "when she lived in her house she could do the stockings with a needle". That wage "was deserved by every well-learned person". People who "want to pay convenient [...] pay these wages".[66]

Masters and merchants, journeymen, and apprentices quoted the ideals as stated in Zacchia's *De Salario* (merit and skills, industriousness, and expertise). It is not surprising that the word "work" (an objective concept)[67] was strictly related to "industriousness", "ability", or "skills" (subjective). On 21 July 1565 Tommaso, son of Bernardo Alberigi from Florence, said that he was "for one year as apprentice with the wool merchant Niccolò, son of Matteo Cavalcanti", and that he "has done that work as a good minister". He attempted many times to ensure his "wage was convenient to his work and industriousness".[68]

Judgements of skill could be based on general considerations, such as the time spent with a master, but they also depended on individual workers. Wages were very difficult to standardize within general categories, and it was always necessary to know the apprentices or workers individually, as well as their qualities, such as their age, skills, and expertise.

---

64. On the experts charged with recording the current price in a specific place see Ago, *Economia barocca*, pp. 196–197.
65. Caracausi, "I giusti salari", p. 870.
66. *Ibid.*, p. 872.
67. "Work" (for which the same workers used the Italian term *fatica*) referred generally to the number of days, months, or years during which a worker had been employed, related to his efforts. However, the quantity of work in terms of time spent and occupation was not always easily assessed, especially in the case of piecework. During a case to determine the just wage of an apprentice, witnesses said that they could not precisely estimate the amount of work because "sometimes we work so much, sometimes less". See Caracausi, "I giusti salari".
68. ASF, AL, Register 371, fo. 221.

LOCAL KNOWLEDGE AND THE STATUS OF CONTRACT:
TOWARDS AN EARLY MODERN ETHIC OF WAGES

Combining legal doctrine and court cases allows us to identify some important points about the concept of wages, and just wages in particular, in early modern Italy. Zacchia offers a priori no prescriptions nor evaluations of wages. Beyond differences in their genre, the jurist was careful to show the variety of salaried workers, the absence of wage standards, and the complex world of rights and duties within labour relations. Regarding just wages, judges had to take great care. Abstract evaluations seem to have been very difficult, given the importance of individual knowledge, local practice, and contractual agreements.

Opening his work, Zacchia says that wages "are the aim of every human action" and that "each job deserves one price".[69] He thereby dignifies wages and the human activity devoted to earning them. In evaluating wages, law and custom were important, but contractual agreements were more significant and judgments depended on them above all. It was possible to dispute levels of damages or rights and obligations, but it was impossible to change the idea of legally binding wages agreed on by contract. Only without proof concerning agreements, or in the event of damage, could judges assess wages.

Because of the specific, necessarily incomplete, contractual context, Zacchia considers in detail the rights and obligations of employers and employees. Workers hired for a certain time for a given wage would have to receive payment, even if they had not done the work. If the patron did not respect the wage agreement, workers could go to court to seek the entire amount as compensation.[70] Furthermore, merchants and masters had to pay their workers at the right time,[71] to avoid damaging their own reputations.[72]

Everyone knew well the prescriptions. On 21 November 1565, a number of weavers from Cremona who had gone to Florence with a five-year agreement to work asked for settlement of their agreement. They also said that they had gone "far away from their houses" and were not "able to maintain their families". The weavers asked the court to oblige the merchants to observe their contracts, in fact "to give for five years [...] every year eight ducats for their provision to come to Florence for

---

69. Zacchia, *De Salario*, Quaestio I, ch. 2. On claims for rewarding work see Shaw, *The Justice of Venice*, p. 147; Caracausi, *Dentro la bottega*, pp. 76–78.

70. Zacchia, *De Salario*, Quaestio XXII, p. 77, chs 4, 8, 10–11. On the importance of contracts, mainly for the obligations they impose on labourers, see also Robert J. Steinfeld, *The Invention of Free Labor* (Chapel Hill, NC [etc.], 1991).

71. Barbieri, "La remunerazione del lavoro", p. 96, n. 37 (who cites also the prescription of St Carlo Borromeo, one of the major figures of the Counter-Reformation), p. 100, n. 50.

72. Caracausi, *Dentro la bottega*, pp. 101–114, 242–244.

work [...] to provide houses for five years where they would be able to work with their families and workers without paying other provisions".[73]

Respect for contracts was fundamental, and wages effectively placed individuals in a dialogue about the rights and obligations contained in the contract.[74] The consequence was strict interdependence between workers and employers. Zacchia assigns a key role to contracts, allowing a limiting of differences resulting from social status. In disputes about wages, children too could take their cases to court, and this did indeed occur.[75]

Contracts were required for just wages. In his book Zacchia offers some material on good contracts and for assessing wages in cases of damage or in the absence of proof of agreement. The remuneration of work was surely a value depending on objective criteria, such as time taken, the work itself, and economic trends. But Zacchia also tells us that judges had to evaluate the quality of people, their social condition, skills, and expertise. He applies a strong subjective meaning to the concept of the just wage. Even the status of the proof meant that just wages were difficult for judges to evaluate in the abstract, and had to be linked to individuals (to their industriousness, skills, and expertise) because it was necessary to know the workers, their ages, and their professional skill.[76] That point was common to many early modern Italian and European cities and explains how wages differed with respect to the duration, quantity, and quality of work.[77]

The idea of an individual concept of wages was well known among employers and employees. The Florentine Damiano, son of Antonio, asked only to earn a salary "competent and convenient to his person and to this exercise" of apprenticeship. Without a written contract, Damiano said only that he was sixteen years old and had been an apprentice for five years. On the other hand, the master weaver Bartolomeo, son of Francesco from Pontassieve, said that when the young girl Bartolomea stayed with him in his workshop "for her work [...] not only does she learn and deserve the cost of food and clothing but she also deserves a convenient salary and wage".[78]

Convenient wages depended on both individual merits and pains. The local voice proved that. Witnesses and experts estimated damages or wages because they were both knowledgeable about skills and knew a

73. ASF, AL, Register 371, case no. 106. On this type of judgment see also Trivellato, "Salaires et justice dans les corporations vénitiennes", pp. 268–269.
74. As argued especially by Sonenscher, *Work and Wages*, p. 192.
75. Zacchia, *De Salario*; Caracausi, *Dentro la bottega*, ch. 2.
76. Caracausi, "I giusti salari".
77. Trivellato, "Salaires et justice dans les corporations vénitiennes", pp. 245–273; Mocarelli, "Wages and the Labour Market", pp. 61–81; Penn and Dyer, "Wages and Earnings in Late Medieval England", pp. 356–376; Woodward, "The Determination of Wage Rates", pp. 22–43; Boulton, "Wage Labour", pp. 268–290.
78. ASF, AL, Register 372, case no. 272: Bartolomeo claimed "fatica et opera sua".

worker and his work. Quoting Zacchia, their assessment was based not "outside the place where work was done", but within the community.[79] Following that prescription, wages were not simply a "price for the work" but a *quasi quoddam pretium*, linked to the community, the worker's personal quality, and local customs, as enshrined in an enduring medieval tradition.

An ideology of wages was based on a complex range of norms and values which put at their centre the individual action of actors, their social position, their skills, and their abilities. All those elements were strictly related to the local context (the community, the town, or the country), where customs were consolidated and practices legitimated, and where the ties between individuals and local environment determined – as the young fuller apprentice Giovanni from Padua claimed – the full recognition of their "just wages".[80]

79. See also ASF, AL, Register 372, case no. 352. The Florentine master weaver Francesco, son of Jacopo from Ascoli, said he could estimate the wage of an apprentice because "I have been a master weaver for thirty years; I have had apprentices and have judged on wages many times".
80. ASP, UL, Register 77, fo. 527v.

IRSH 56 (2011), Special Issue, pp. 125–140 doi:10.1017/S002085901100054X
© 2011 Internationaal Instituut voor Sociale Geschiedenis

The Religious Aspect of Labour Ethics in Medieval and Early Modern Russia*

Arkadiy E. Tarasov

Faculty of History, Lomonosov Moscow State University

E-mail: tarasov@histmsu.ru

Summary: This article analyses the basic feature that defined Russian labour ethics in medieval and early modern times – its religious aspect. There are two main elements to the subject. First, the role of Eastern Christianity and Church tradition in labour regulations, and second, the realities of everyday life in Russia and the historical peculiarities of the Russian locale, its natural conditions and climatic features, which had an influence on working activity. Until the time of Peter the Great, the labour ethics of the Russian Orthodox Church saw no significant change, and their main content could be defined as an educational process.

In the late medieval and early modern period, acute change and expansionist activity can be found in western Europe, while other regions appear to have been more static or perhaps passive. The period was marked in western Europe by certain characteristic features: the Renaissance, with its humanist ideology, a great upsurge in art and a stirring of scientific enquiry; the Age of Discovery, or the Age of Exploration; the Protestant Reformation; and the rise of a new economic system – capitalism. The Russian state was removed from most of those developments. Certainly, some trends from western Europe reached Russia during those times, but Russia as a whole continued to live according to its existing traditions, based in social and economic terms on feudalism, and in spiritual and ideological terms on Russian Orthodoxy, with its characteristic system of values. Those traditions were not entirely rigid, and there were changes at the margin, but such powerful upheavals as occurred in western Europe never took place in Russia.

Generally speaking, the issue of Russian labour ethics remains poorly studied, as generations of Russian scholars from the eighteenth to the beginning of twentieth centuries had no sense of it being an inherently worthwhile subject. In spite of a basic orientation towards social and economic problems, Soviet historiography always concentrated on the

* I am grateful to Svetlana Ryabova for her assistance in preparing this article.

study of other questions concerning the history of labour relations, and above all on the class struggle. It is only recently that historians have gradually begun to apply themselves to questions of labour ethics, and no definitive conclusions can therefore yet be drawn.

In view of that, this article will concentrate on the basic theme which has defined Russian labour ethics in medieval and early modern times – its religious aspect. To do so it has been necessary to set out certain basic requirements. First, we must explain the general characteristics of Orthodox attitudes to work and compare those with the attitudes of the Church's Western Christian counterpart. Second, we must identify Russian texts containing thoughts on work ethics and trace through them the path of the influence of religious aspects of labour ethics in medieval and early modern Russia. Chief importance among such texts will be ascribed to the *Domostroi* – a key source of information on the Russian household. Third, it is necessary to show the role of monastic tradition in the formation of labour ethics. The fourth and final task is to identify the position of work and the worker in wider society.

THE RUSSIAN ORTHODOX CONTEXT

Religion had a very strong influence on human consciousness in medieval and early modern Russia, just as it had in the entire Christian world during the same period. Because people everywhere were indoctrinated with the idea that a Superior Being directed the energy of men on the route towards salvation,[1] a thorough examination of representations of work and labour relations in the period is possible only if we take the religious sphere into consideration.

In Russia [in medieval times: Rus'] the articles of faith and canons of Eastern Christianity were guarded by the Russian Orthodox Church, which was founded at the end of the tenth century. The Church played a significant role in the life of medieval Russian men and women, being seen as a representation of the divine presence. At the same time, there were large differences between the rules as contained in the articles of faith on the one hand and social practices on the other. Still, high-ranking Church officials – bishops and abbots – exerted a strong influence on social life. Those who lived in accordance with Christian ideals were highly revered by ordinary people. They included, first and foremost, hermits, and especially fools for Christ.[2]

1. There are many publications devoted to this matter. See, for example, E. Starbuck, *The Psychology of Religion: An Empirical Study of the Growth of Religious Consciousness* (New York, 1911); Johan Huizinga, *The Waning of the Middle Ages* (London, 1924); D. Weinstein and R.M. Bell, *Saints and Society: The Two Worlds of Western Christendom* (Chicago, IL, 1982).
2. M.B. Petrovich, "The Social and Political Role of the Muscovite Fools-in-Christ: Reality and Image", *Forschungen zur osteuropaeischen Geschichte*, 25 (1978), pp. 283–296. See also G.P. Fedotov, *Svjatye Drevnej Rusi* (Moscow, 1990), pp. 198–209.

They helped to determine perceptions by medieval Russian men and women of the clergy and everything connected with them.

A number of remarks should be made about the specific context of the Russian Orthodox Church. First, in comparison with Catholicism and Protestantism, Orthodoxy was far less closely connected to the economic sphere of life, and never created a political economy as scholars in Catholic Europe did. There, Catholic scholars defined the norms of respectability and labour, and pondered the question of "fair" and "legitimate" prices, what was a justifiable amount of profit, how trade norms should be regulated, and so on.[3] In medieval Russia, by contrast, it proved hardly possible to create a doctrine of labour comparable with that written by Thomas Aquinas, in which he stated that the main criterion of labour is its public benefit.

During many centuries, Russian theology had "kept silent", not only on questions of the ethics of labour but also on many other practical aspects of religious life. The Protestant idea that a man demonstrates his love of God in his professional life, and that only through professional perfection might a man obtain his reward in the next life, so that a man's professional calling is the real expression of the Celestial will, are alien to Orthodoxy. The famous Russian religious philosopher Nicolas Berdyaev is quite adamant in stating that "[e]conomically productive virtues are by no means characteristic of Russian ethics".[4]

So, labour ethics were expressed in a completely different way from the west European Christian tradition, because of the differences in how labour ethics were conceived of by Orthodoxy and other Christian confessions. The main difference was in the antithetical approach taken to the priority of labour. In Orthodoxy, labour was regarded not in functional terms but in terms of human development; the intention was not to bring about an environmental change, but to bring man closer to God. Furthermore, in Orthodoxy absolute enslavement of any person by labour was widely criticized.[5]

Second, a detailed and profound historical exploration of the way the ideas of Eastern Christianity were implemented in Russia in practice is complicated by the lack of primary sources that could tell us more about the daily lives of people in medieval and early modern Russia. As a forest country, Russia steadily lost the majority of its primary sources, which were burnt in the frequent conflagrations that broke out. Apart from that,

3. T.B. Koval', "Jetika truda pravoslavija", *Obshestvennye nauki i sovremennost'*, 6 (1994), p. 56. See also the article elsewhere in this volume by Andrea Caracausi, who discusses agreement concerning "legitimate" wages in labour ideologies in early modern Italy, as well as the contribution by Luca Mocarelli.

4. N.A. Berdyaev, *O russkoj filosofii*, 2 vols (Sverdlovsk, 1991), II, pp. 26–27.

5. E.A. Tjugashev, "Pravoslavnoe otnoshenie k trudu v zerkale nravstvennogo bogoslovija", *Chelovek. Trud. Zanjatost': Nauchno-prakticheskoe periodicheskoe izdanie*, 2 (1999), p. 50.

there are hardly any sources in Russia similar to those in Europe primarily describing working life. In addition, because of the less developed legal role of the Church, there are no documents comparable with the *Concordia discordantium canonum* [*Decretum Gratiani*][6] or the papal decrees that can be so helpful to researchers.

RUSSIAN MONASTERIES: *ORA ET LABORA*

Like the German sociologist Max Weber, who stated that Protestant labour ethics influenced the economic development of Europe, the well-known Russian religious philosopher Sergei Bulgakov[7] underlined the importance of religion as a factor determining the value of labour, wealth, and the accumulation of capital. Regarding Christian perspectives on labour, Bulgakov claimed that "[l]abour is invaluable to man as a means of training the will and fighting wicked inclinations and, finally, as an opportunity to serve one's neighbours".[8]

That definition of labour can be considered common to all Christian confessions, but on the historical role of Christianity, "which escalated the awareness of the worth of labour", Bulgakov stressed the great importance of the monasteries as places where economic culture was shaped.[9] What is more, addressing the specific material on Russian history, he demonstrated that in Russian monasteries attitudes to labour were formed as an educational process, the main goal of which was salvation. Furthermore, although the constructive side of labour seemed very important, the everyday economic side of it was believed to be secondary.

In Russia the following verse from Jeremiah is quite well known: "A curse on him who is lax in doing the Lord's work!" (Jeremiah, 48.10). The concept of "the Lord's work" was understood in a broad sense, as it was possible for all work in general to be pious, including physical labour. Indeed, a specially reverential attitude to labour can be found in early Russian literature, and in his many works St Theodosius (d. 1074), of the Kievan Cave Monastery and as one of its first preachers the father of the Russian clergy, as well as a founder of Russian monastic traditions, stated that Russian monks should work and not be lazy.

6. *Concordia discordantium canonum* [*Decretum Gratiani*] [Concord of Discordant Canons] was a collection of Church law compiled and written in the twelfth century as a legal textbook by the jurist known as Gratian. It retained legal force in the Catholic Church until 1918.
7. Sergei Bulgakov (1871–1944), religious philosopher and Russian Orthodox priest; he emigrated in 1923. He was the author of a number of well-known publications, including *Philosophy of Economy* (1912), *Unfading Light* (1917), *On the Feast of the Gods* (1918), and *Tragedy of Philosophy* (1920).
8. *Idem, Pravoslavie* (Kiev, 1991), p. 212.
9. Ol'ga Sidjakina, "Pravoslavnaja jetika truda", http://www.polemics.ru/articles/?articleID=1921&hideText=0&itemPage=1, last accessed 6 September 2011.

For instance, in his *Word about Love and Humility*, referring to Paul the Apostle (2 Thessalonians, 3.7–10), St Theodosius states: "Now I, an unworthy man recalling the commandment of the good Lord, say to you: it is good for us to feed paupers and wayfarers with the fruits of our labour, and not to be idle, going from one cell to another."[10] That is one of the first examples, or perhaps even the very oldest example, in Old Russian literature of a religious text connected with labour ethics and used as a practical guide for daily life in the Russian Orthodox Church. Moreover, St Theodosius elaborated on the theme and developed the first monastic rules of the Kievan Cave Monastery, based on the monastic rules of Theodor Studit,[11] a copy of which was sent from Constantinople to Kiev in 1068. Theodor Studit's monastic rules saw labour as an integral part of the life of a monk.

Although St Theodosius's works [*Words*] were originally addressed to the monks of the Kievan Cave Monastery, they eventually became a guide for all Russian Orthodox believers for a long time. However, at the same time there was another popular view that saw monks as spongers and idlers. A life story of St Theodosius gives a good example of the layman's attitude to a monk. According to that story, once upon a time a prince asked a man to convey St Theodosius to the monastery; the man had no idea who St Theodosius was. On the way to the monastery, the man said: "Listen! You are a monk, you never work, while I am too exhausted to drive a horse. So, let us do it this way: I will have a nap in the cart and you will drive the horse."[12] That attitude might have been caused by a lack of understanding of what monks actually did, because their real work and activity was hidden from laymen. The story is revealing, for it reflects the negligible participation of Russian monks in everyday labour relations.

In comparison with the situation in Europe where, according to a quite popular view among many historians, from the twelfth century onward a new ideal of labour ethics was formulated after changes in social structure,[13] old beliefs were preserved in medieval Russia for a long time. For example, Jacques Le Goff noted that side by side with economic growth in western Europe the relationship to trade was reconsidered, and the two-way influence changed in both the secular and religious fields. Thus, to lay blame on a merchant, a preacher or theologian would have been required to prove that the merchant was operating maliciously.

---

10. *Biblioteka literatury Drevnej Rusi*, 20 vols (St Petersburg, 1997–), I, pp. 434–435.
11. Theodor Studit (also called Theodore the Studite or St Theodore of Stoudios, 759–826), a Byzantine monk and abbot of the Stoudios monastery in Constantinople. He played a major role in the revivals both of Byzantine monasticism and of classical literary genres in Byzantium.
12. *Biblioteka literatury Drevnej Rusi*, I, pp. 392–393.
13. Catharina Lis and Joseph Ehmer, "Introduction: Historical Studies in Perceptions of Work", in Josef Ehmer and Catharina Lis (eds), *The Idea of Work in Europe from Antiquity to Modern Times* (Farnham, 2009), pp. 9–11.

Under the influence of those changes in social structure, the relationship with time changed, as expressed in the arrival of the public clock mounted in a tower. A reliable clock mechanism had been invented by the end of the thirteenth century, but it had begun to replace the church bell only from the mid-fourteenth century. Thenceforward, human life was no longer measured by the times for prayer as if completely belonging to God, but by the natural hours reflected by a mechanism devised by human hands.[14] Neither man's relationship to trade nor his relationship to time changed in Russia. Although the first clock tower in Russia appeared a little later, at the beginning of the fifteenth century, time was determined as before, by liturgical tradition. That can be explained on the one hand by the economic conditions peculiar to Russia, and on the other by the unified traditions of the monasteries, which continued to live by the monastic rules of Theodor Studit throughout the thirteenth and fourteenth centuries.[15]

The fact that the Church was not very actively involved in economic life might also explain why the traditional ethics of medieval Russia survived for so long, and we should not forget that Russia underwent a general economic decline after the Mongol invasion.[16] However, the most important reason is still principally the different view taken by the Russian Orthodox Church in relation to labour. St Joseph of Volotsk (d. 1515) explained the necessity for a monk's labour in the same way as St Theodosius had. In the monastic rules of St Joseph's monastery he required the monks to work constantly, praying at the same time: "a monk can never be idle". St Joseph believed that labour, as a "common deed", was an essential of faith, realized in generous actions, and was a prayer materialized. Moreover, the principle of mandatory labour, proclaimed in all Russian friaries, influenced the layman's attitude to labour, and the monastic way of life contributed nothing to the growth of capitalism nor to any other economic system. The head of the Russian Orthodox Church, Metropolitan Daniel (d. 1547), taught his parish in accordance with classical Orthodox views on labour. In one of his sermons he stated:

> [This] does not mean that Christians should not work, plough, buy and sell, manage slaves, and build homes. We can do all this, but we must not grow too attached to anything or worry too much about anything, putting our hope in God, who alone can bless our labour with success and help us against all enemies.

14. Jacques Le Goff, *Time, Work and Culture in the Middle Ages* (Chicago, IL, 1980), pp. 35–52.
15. Arhimandrit Avgustin, "Studijskij Monastyr' i Drevnjaja Rus' (Iz Istorii Russko-Vizantijskih Cerkovnyh Svjazej)", *Al'fa i Omega*, 3 (2008), pp. 332–345.
16. D. Miller, "Monumental Building as an Indicator of Economic Trends in Northern Rus' in the Late Kievan and Mongol Periods, 1138–1462", *American Historical Review*, 94 (1989), pp. 360–390.

While tilling the soil we must reflect and also look after spiritual fruit; in buying and selling we must be guided by truth and honesty; [...] we must build homes and property in order to help the poor.[17]

In connection with the facts considered above it is interesting to observe also the history of monastic colonization. The second half of the fourteenth century was the time when a very important process known as "the monastic colonization of the north" began in Russia. Monks went to sparsely populated and isolated areas in the north and north-east of Russia and founded monasteries there. The process continued throughout the fifteenth, sixteenth, and seventeenth centuries. In fact, in seventeenth-century Russia, the hermit's life was a widespread practice among monks, and more and more small monasteries [*pustyn'*] and hermitages [*skit*] appeared as monastery subsidiaries that had stricter rules and regulations governing the everyday life of the monks.[18] Such small monasteries, led by hermits, produced no commercial goods and never undertook the task of creating large-scale enterprises or estates. Instead they relied for their existence on charitable donations. Certainly, the monks in *pustyns* and *skits* worked constantly, providing themselves with the bare necessities, but the idea of work – its educational purpose – remained unchanged.

It is also necessary to consider that in the conditions of the severe Russian climate, the country's huge wooded areas and the scarcity of natural resources, the constant arduous toil of the monks yielded an insignificant return. For them it was a question of survival, not of life in abundance. All of that strongly supports the idea of a minor role for the monasteries in the economic life of Old Russia. In each of the places where monasteries were found, there was also a colony of peasant households surrounding the monasteries. The Russian nineteenth-century historian, Vasilii Klyuchevsky, who studied the mechanism of the colonization process, concluded that "sometimes monks were followed by peasants and sometimes it was the other way around, but the connection between one and the other is clear". Furthermore, "a desert monastery served both the religious and economic needs of migrants, and along with it they used their labour and increased the number of brothers with them".[19]

However, scholars today view the question of the influence of monastic colonization on the opening up of new lands in the north in a different way. They emphasize that monastic colonization contributed to the opening up of the northern lands, but culturally and politically rather than economically.

---

17. Mitropolit Makarij (Bulgakov), *Istorija Russkoj Cerkvi*, 7 vols (Moscow, 1996), IV (I), pp. 385–386.
18. I.K. Smolich, *Russkoe monashestvo, 988–1917* (Moscow, 1997), p. 13.
19. V.O. Klyuchevsky, *Sochinenija*, 9 vols (Moscow, 1987), II, p. 453.

For instance, at the turn of the fifteenth century Russian princes distinctively admired the *eparchy* [church diocese] of Perm, a region to the north-west of the Ural mountains. From the late fourteenth century, when the eparchy was founded there, the bishops of Perm had unconditionally supported the princes in Moscow and helped them in civilizing the north-eastern regions of Russia. It is suggested that in the fifteenth century the Perm eparchy existed as a semi-independent state, and that its bishops were vassals of the Moscow prince.[20]

The monastery of St Trifon of the Pechenga, founded in 1520–1530 at a latitude of 70 degrees North, was the most northerly Orthodox monastery and is a brilliant illustration of the fact that monastic colonization had only a secondary economic function. The monastery was traditionally regarded as very significant and influential in its northern situation. Its founder, St Trifon, had been an active merchant, who made connections with Russian traders, local inhabitants, and Scandinavian merchants. His trading activity seemed not to be an end in itself, but rather a tool for collecting money for the foundation of the future monastery, and, what is more, the involvement in trade of the local inhabitants contributed to the dissemination of Christianity among them too. The historian V.L. Derzhavin has emphasized that, although monastic colonization developed simultaneously with industrial colonization, the second obviously prevailed, for it provided a material basis for St Trifon's monastery, and the fact that this economic activity preceded the foundation of the Pechenga monastery is itself proof of that argument.[21]

Nevertheless, the laws of economic life during an era of feudalism and the general religiosity of society meant that, as spiritual corporations, monasteries received all kinds of donations and contributions, and possessions of land were the pivotal form of them. The growth of monastic land tenure contributed to strengthening the economic role of monasteries in public life, not only in territorial colonization but also in the organization of manufacturing. One such aspect of the economic activity of monasteries which began to develop was that of affording credit to peasants, while I.K. Smolich underlines the fact that, due to the constant growth of monastic possessions and the development of a monastic economy, Russian monasteries frequently handled many different products, in quantities surpassing the monastery's own requirements, and that forced them to become involved in trade.[22] Indeed, a number of

20.   G.N. Chagin, "Hristianizacija Permi Velikoj Cherdyni i ejo rol' v razvitii gosudarstvennosti i kul'tury v XV–XVII v.", in *Vehi hristianskoj istorii Prikam'ja: Materialy chtenij, posvjawjonnyh 540-letiju krewenija Permi Velikoj* (Perm, 2003), pp. 5–18.
21.   V.L. Derzhavin, *Severnyj Murman v XVI–XVII vv. (K istorii russko-evropejskih svjazej na Kol'skom poluostrove)* (Moscow, 2006), p. 132.
22.   Smolich, *Russkoe monashestvo*, p. 148.

studies have noted that some of the major monasteries and episcopal cathedrals became economically prosperous during the fifteenth century.

A monastic economy differed much more in terms of stability compared with a secular economy; it was more involved in commodity–money relations, with considerable sums of money being accumulated in monasteries.[23] The largest monasteries of the time played a notable role in social organization, were strong economic organisms, and made a significant impact on the economic life of their neighbourhoods. One particular example was the Solovetsky monastery, founded in 1429, which extended its production and commercial activity until it became an economic and political centre of the White Sea region. The Solovetsky monastery's business activities included salt works (in the 1660s it owned fifty-four of them), seafood production, trapping, fishery, mica works, ironworks, and pearl works, which made many people dependent on the monastery. An outstanding role in the development of such a powerful centre, created in the extremely difficult conditions of the north of the country, was played by the famous saint, Abbot Philip Kolychev (1507–1569), a future Russian metropolitan who dared to oppose openly Ivan the Terrible's authority and was murdered.[24]

Nevertheless monasteries such as that at Solovetsky were exceptions, for, as noted above, Russian monasteries generally existed in adverse conditions, and the majority of them merely managed to survive. The back-breaking work performed by the monks and others provided a small surplus sufficient for them to live on but insufficient to allow much growth. In such conditions, economic mechanisms were insufficient to allow capitalism to emerge.

RUSSIAN SOCIAL ORDER: SOCIALLY USEFUL LABOUR BY EVERYONE

In his book on medieval Moscow monasteries L.A. Beliaev, a historian and archaeologist, concludes, justifiably, that most modern ideals of Russian culture can be traced back to the monastic perception of the world, and those ideals include that of constant labour, especially that which is socially useful.[25] Monastic influence on these traditions could be found in early medieval times.

Another interesting and remarkable fact is that the Russian Orthodox call for labour, addressed to monks in the eleventh century, became

23. N.V. Sinicyna, "Russkoe monashestvo i monastyri. X–XVII vv.", in *Pravoslavnaja enciklopedija. Russkaja Pravoslavnaja Cerkov'* (Moscow, 2000), pp. 305–324.

24. E.V. Romanenko, *Povsednevnaja zhizn' russkogo srednevekovogo monastyrja* (Moscow, 2002), pp. 64–65.

25. L.A. Beliaev, *Drevnie monastyri Moskvy (kon. XIII–nach. XV vv.) po dannym arheologii* (Moscow, 1994), p. 7.

popular among the nobility too. Grand Duke Vladimir Monomakh (d. 1125) left a curious set of instructions to his sons, dated 1117, in which he gave them a great deal of practical advice, reinforced with examples from his own experience. In his well-known *Pouchenie* [Lecture] a precept to work is already mentioned in the introduction and anticipates all other admonitions of the Grand Duke: "My children, or anyone else reading this document, do not laugh, and those of my children who find it pleasing, l et them take it to heart and not be lazy, but work."[26] This claim formed a vector of the attitude to labour of later nobles: in medieval Russian society it was unnatural for the nobility to do hard physical work, but it was possible in difficult circumstances. For example, a remarkable governor of the medieval period, Ivan III, creator of the unified Russian state, participated personally in extinguishing fires in Moscow. The historian Nikolaj Borisov carefully collected such cases: sometimes in extinguishing the fires the great prince was assisted by other nobles [*deti boyarskie*], and once even by his son.[27]

In the mid-sixteenth century the *Velikie Minei Chetii* [The Great Menaion Reader] was compiled. This fundamental book is a collection of biblical books with interpretations of exordiums, originals or translations of hagiographies of Russian saints, and works by the Church fathers and Russian ecclesiastical writers. It was put together in the 1530s to 1540s under the supervision of Metropolitan Macarius, the head of the Russian Orthodox Church. Macarius decided to compile *The Great Menaion Reader* in order to centralize the cult of the Russian saints and to consolidate Church ideology.

For 8 May it includes the *Slovo* [Story] from the Lives of the Holy Fathers to show how beneficial it is to work. The *Slovo* relates a parable in which an old man declares: "If we strive to work and we do not become lazy, we will be saved." He then tells the story of a rich landowner who wanted to teach his sons to work. The landowner said that there is a certain day in the year and those who are found to be working on that day will become rich. "But in my old age I have forgotten which day it is exactly", he said. "Therefore do not be lazy on any day. Work so that you are not caught idle on this blessed day, otherwise you will work in vain the whole year." The old man then concluded with these words: "And so it is with us – if we will work we will always find the path to salvation."[28]

Although *The Great Menaion Reader* addressed a limited number of readers, its compilation amounted to the design of a special programme and a guide for the Russian Orthodox Church, proclaiming concrete ideas. Obviously, labour was one ideal, and that was addressed to the whole of society, from peasants to clergy and the nobility. It is interesting that

26. *Biblioteka literatury Drevnej Rusi*, I, pp. 456–457.
27. N.S. Borisov, *Povsednevnaja zhizn' srednevekovoj Rusi nakanune konca sveta* (Moscow, 2004), pp. 138–142.
28. *Biblioteka literatury Drevnej Rusi*, XII, pp. 236–237.

on 8 May the Russian Orthodox Church celebrates the life of St Arsenij Pecherskij, who lived in the fourteenth century and was very diligent in his work. Indeed, the nickname "Hard-Working" was appended to his name. I believe that the inclusion of *Slovo* on 8 May could be connected with the feast day of St Arsenij Pecherskij the Hard-Working. The practice of combining such events was at least usual in medieval and early modern society.

A formidable presage of the destruction of the world was the most important cultural phenomenon characterizing the era of the Russian autumn of the Middle Ages. Alarming tensions in everyday life in the fourteenth and early fifteenth centuries turned into a constant feeling of doom as the year 7000 of the Byzantine calendar approached (it equates to AD 1492 in the Western calendar). However, it was not believed that all life would cease to exist on the eve of the Last Judgement because the Orthodox eschatology had exalted and enlightened features. Nevertheless, a confident faith that the final days of human existence were at hand was shared by the majority of people living then, and was what mainly determined their attitudes and actions. Thus, the Church calendar showing the dates of Easter [*paschalija*], which was usually worked out in advance, was constructed only for the years prior to 1492. Even after the Day of Doom failed to materialize, people still thought it would. According to widespread representations at that time, expectations were transferred to other septenary dates: the years 7070 (AD 1562) or 7077 (AD 1569). It is interesting to note that at the end of the fifteenth century new *paschalija* were calculated for a period of only seventy years.[29]

Under those circumstances the Church did not encourage its spiritual sons to leave their labour and concentrate only on repentance and ascetic life; on the contrary, the Church insisted that constant labour was necessary and extremely important. For instance, in the first half of the sixteenth century Dositheus Toporkov, the author of *Volokolamsk: Lives of the Holy Fathers*, stated that in contemporary times, before the end of the world should come, it was more than important than ever "to be obedient, to work, to pray and keep the fast to the best of our ability, and also to be humble, considering oneself beneath all others because this is the principal virtue".[30]

The Russian Church not only urged its flock to work, it also protected the interests of those who did. In relation to that, it is worth mentioning the famous apocryphal story *The Wanderings of Our Lady through Hell*, about which Ivan Karamazov speaks in Dostoevsky's novel, *The Brothers Karamazov*. This apocryphal story, which was of Greek origin, had been known in Russia since the twelfth century and was one

29. A.V. Karavashkin and A.L. Jurganov, *Opyt istoricheskoj fenomenologii. Trudnyj put' k ochevidnosti* (Moscow, 2003), pp. 68–115.
30. *Biblioteka literatury Drevnej Rusi*, IX, pp. 32–33.

of the most popular tales in Russian literature. In the seventeenth and eighteenth centuries, the story was rewritten and recast several times by the Old Believers.[31] In the story, the archangel Michael accompanies the Virgin on her walk through hell and shows her the torments of the sinners. Among the sinners shipped in along the fiery river, there are those who – as the archangel says – "reaped another's fields and picked another's fruit, those who eat at the expense of another's work".[32] In addition, in his writings Metropolitan Daniel emphasized that servants must be managed with humility and gentleness, they must be forgiven as one would forgive one's own children, but those who misbehave ought to be kept in fear, although in his heart their master must secretly forgive them.

THE RUSSIAN HOUSEHOLD: THE *DOMOSTROI*

The *Domostroi*[33] is one of the most important primary sources, containing a large quantity of useful information about work ethics in late medieval and early modern Russia.[34] Even in the mid-nineteenth century the *Domostroi* was still in force, being widespread among peasants, who tended to follow its rules because they felt them to be true examples of Orthodoxy and pure wisdom.[35]

It is hard to determine the exact date on which the *Domostroi* was created, although historians believe the material was written at some time between 1475 and 1560. Nowadays, the most widely held point of view states that the *Domostroi* was written in the mid-sixteenth century, but no later than the 1550s.[36] The text is preserved in two versions,[37] of one of

---

31. Old Believers [Russian: *starovery* or *staroobriadtsy*] were participants in the movement for Russian spiritual culture, which started in the 1650s, The Old Believers split from the official Russian Orthodox Church in protest at Church reforms introduced by Patriarch Nikon. Old Believers continue liturgical practices which the Russian Orthodox Church maintained before those reforms were implemented.

32. *Biblioteka literatury Drevnej Rusi*, III, pp. 314–315.

33. The word *Domostroi* consists of two Russian words: *dom* (house) and *stroitel'stvo* (management). It can be translated as "domestic order" or "household management". Originally it was a loan translation of the Greek *oikonomia*. See T.V. Chumakova, *V chelovecheskom zhitel'stve mnozi obrazy zrjatsja: Obraz cheloveka v kul'ture Drevnej Rusi* (St Petersburg, 2001), p. 134.

34. Carolyn Johnston Pouncy (ed. and transl.), *The* Domostroi: *Rules for Russian Households in the Time of Ivan the Terrible* (Ithaca, NY, 1994); Klaus Müller, *Altrussisches Hausbuch "Domostroi"* (Leipzig, 1987).

35. A.S. Orlov, "Domostroi", in *Istorija russkoj literatury*, 10 vols (Moscow, 1945), II, p. 445.

36. L.P. Najdenova, "Svoi i chuzhie v Domostroe. Vnutrisemejnye otnoshenija v Moskve XVI veka", in *Chelovek v krugu sem'i. Ocherki po istorii chastnoj zhizni v Evrope do nachala novogo vremeni* (Moscow, 1996), pp. 290–295.

37. Some historians have identified a third version of the *Domostroi*, of which we have three copies, created as the result of unskilful mechanical copying. See V.V. Kolesov, "Domostroi: Kommentarii", in *Biblioteka literatury Drevnej Rusi*, X, p. 581.

which we have forty-four copies and of the other forty-five, the majority of them made in the seventeenth century. Although the question of the origins of the *Domostroi* has not been completely resolved, we have some clear evidence about them.[38] First, the sources that inspired the authors of the *Domostroi* include the collections of moralizing texts, written on the basis of the teachings [*pouchenie*] of a number of clerics: *Izmaragd*, *Zlatoust* [teachings of John Chrysostom], *Zolotaya Tsep'*, and other moralizing doctrines which appeared in Russia at some time later than the eleventh century.

In the mid-seventeenth century 67 per cent of the *Domostroi* manuscripts signed by their owners belonged to office employees, 22 per cent to clergy, and 11 per cent to private citizens, including artisans and merchants.[39]

Archpriest G.V. Florovskij (1893–1979), a Russian religious philosopher and historian, states that the *Domostroi* "hardly depicts everyday life, a realistic picture [...]. This book is didactic, not descriptive. It outlines a theoretical ideal; it does not portray everyday reality."[40] That argument implies that we should compare the *Domostroi* with traditional Russian Orthodox didactic literature.

The historian L.P. Najdenova stresses that the main feature of the *Domostroi* is its desire to Christianize all spheres of the daily life of medieval Russians. She considers the *Domostroi* a peak in religious understanding of the world, after which the influence of the religious perspective and world view declined, something reflected too in the secularization of Russian culture which had started in the seventeenth century. So it cannot be a mere coincidence that most copies of the *Domostroi* originated in the seventeenth century, when strong religious traditions co-existed with cultural secularization. The real author of the *Domostroi* is unknown, but the most widespread version was edited by Archpriest Sylvester, who lived during the reign of Ivan the Terrible, and was well known as Ivan's tutor. More specifically, Sylvester created the final edition of it as a great literary monument and historical source. The *Domostroi* is the product of secular literature and is addressed to life in the secular world, but it is based on a religious system of values.[41] The idea of a truly ethical working life is central to the *Domostroi*.

38. R. Jagoditsch, "Zu den Quellen des altrussischen 'Domostroi'", in *Österreichische Beiträge zum V. Internationalen Slavisten Kongress* (Graz, 1963), pp. 40–48.
39. C.J. Pouncy, "The Origins of the *Domostroi*: A Study in Manuscript History", *The Russian Review*, 46 (1987), pp. 357–373.
40. G.V. Florovskij, *Puti russkogo bogoslovija* (Parizh, 1983), p. 26.
41. In this respect the *Domostroi* is similar to German household literature. See Torsten Meyer, "Cultivating the Landscape: The Perception and Description of Work in 16th- to 18th-Century German 'Household Literature' (Hausväterliteratur)", in Ehmer and Lis, *The Idea of Work in Europe*, p. 244.

According to the *Domostroi*, any rich burgher owed his status not to his noble birth, but rather to his labour and personal initiative. All work should be done "with prayer and with kind conversation or in silence", and "without procrastination". If "during any labour there sounds a word that is idle, indecent, or blasphemous, or said with a grumble or snicker, or there is nasty and wanton talk, God's grace will shrink from such labour, angels will depart in grief, and wicked demons will rejoice".[42] The *Domostroi* emphasizes that one of the major duties of an owner was not to withhold payment to the worker. The *Domostroi* dictates remarkable rules regarding work clothes: "And a word to all servants: always work in old clothes, but in a clean everyday dress when before the master or in public and in your best dress on holidays and among gentlefolk, or if going out with the master or mistress".[43]

There is a separate article about female work in the *Domostroi* which is almost exclusively to do with housekeeping, the main argument of the article being that the mistress of the house should never be without work to do. She should always be able to give orders to the servants and she herself should always be busy. Illness was the only valid reason to stop working. The image described in the *Domostroi* of a hard-working wife who is religious, not talkative, cares for the poor, and is entirely devoted to her husband might have originated in The Book of Proverbs.[44]

The *Domostroi* contains explicit advice for masters, but none for wage workers. It is a guide for people "free by God", so it is a collection of the rules that are addressed to a sufficiently prosperous family who live in the city.[45] Problems of how to hire workers, how to produce goods one could sell, or how to regulate the commercial affairs of household life were not discussed in its pages. The *Domostroi* did not instruct its readers in how to sell, but it did advise them how to buy. According to the text, a husband was responsible for the wholesale stocking of the products from his fields, meadows, fruit and vegetable gardens, for beekeeping, fisheries, and his seasonal bargainings with Russian and foreign merchants, and for purchasing such goods as spices, lemons, grapes, melons, and watermelons; the book touched too on the storage of all such products.

The main goal of the *Domostroi* was to create an ideal internal household environment within the family. An ideal family's house was compared to heaven, quite a common feature of medieval consciousness and literature. For example, the Russian academic Dmitrii Likhatchyov has noted that:

> [...] this ideal acts as a regulator of real life, and if it is put into practice at home,
> if it becomes a part of all the details of daily life, of behaviour within the family

---

42. *Biblioteka literatury Drevnej Rusi*, X, pp. 136–137.
43. *Ibid.*, pp. 140–141.
44. Kolesov, "Domostroi: Kommentarii", p. 585.
45. A. Bogdanov, "Nravy Domostroevoj ulicy", *Nauka i religija*, 5 (1993), p. 51.

and home, and if there is in everything the moderation it demands – then the ideal almost becomes reality.[46]

It is interesting that in the *Domostroi* a clear distinction was made between the words "labour" and "work". "Work" is defined as forced hard labour, while "labour" means godly virtuous activity for the welfare of a man and his intimates, such as his family, rather than people in general. For example, the word "labour" is used when the author of the *Domostroi* refers to children: "Do not forget the labour of your father and mother, who cared for and worried about you. Give them a peaceful old age and look after them, as they looked after you."[47]

As we can see, the term "labour" closely approximates to the definition of "pious labour". According to the *Domostroi*, labour is the greatest virtue, both physical and moral. The term "pious labour" is very significant in the document. Apart from the common idea that "nobody will be recompensed without labour", "pious labour" underlines honest service to the state, care for a wife and family, and a servant's care about the master's interest. The raising of children is also referred to as "pious labour".

According to the *Domostroi*, labour is not a goal in itself. It is a tool to stand as prayer and to serve God on earth. Everyone's duty is to pray to God at home and in the church, and to serve God by building his life and household according to divine rules. The *Domostroi* is not an actual normative document, because it establishes no juridical norms, only moral ones, basing them on practicalities, seeking to show that by living correctly a man lives virtuously and profitably.[48] In connection with that, Najdenova draws attention to the fact that Archpriest Sylvester, in a letter to his son Anfim, not only instructs him in how to live but also gives him advice on how to become a successful businessman. The secret is to be honest and benevolent with business partners.

In the Orthodox tradition, God gives wealth to people for temporary usage and places additional obligations of charity and goodness on its guardians. It is worth noting that from the Orthodox point of view, material wealth is not harmful in itself, for poverty cannot elevate one's soul. Wealth and poverty are quite neutral. However, a strong desire for wealth, a cult of it, is private and social poison. In the *Domostroi* the same attitude is presented with regard to labour, which it is said can bring no wealth, but only "possessions" [*imenie*], and "wealth" is depicted as a temptation. As a result, the book confirms the principle of temperance as

46. V.V. Shaposhnik, "Sem'ja kak model' gosudarstvennogo ustrojstva v Moskovskoj Rusi XVI v. (po pamjatnikam pis'mennosti)", *Trudy kafedry istorii Rossii s drevnejshih vremen do XX veka* (St Petersburg, 2006), pp. 538–556.

47. *Biblioteka literatury Drevnej Rusi*, X, pp. 134–135.

48. L.P. Najdenova, "Svoi i chuzhie v Domostroe", *Rodina*, 6 (1997), p. 27.

a basis of ascetics – salvation can be reached not only through an ascetic life but also in a righteous, tempered life in a secular world.

To conclude our discourse about the *Domostroi*, it is necessary to emphasize that it is impossible to answer definitively the question of whether the *Domostroi* adds something new or whether it is a collation of everything previously thought about labour in Russian Orthodoxy. Unfortunately, no historical sources similar to the *Domostroi* and which might have illuminated labour ethics in great detail have survived from earlier periods. However, one thing is absolutely clear. Even if the *Domostroi* contained some private innovations, on the whole, in its major ideological component, it remained firmly rooted in earlier traditions. Furthermore, it is just as clear that the ideas of the clergy about the ethics of work spread to the nobility and then to the average sixteenth- and seventeenth-century household, such as those addressed in the *Domostroi*. During those years Russian culture continued to retain its most powerful religious component.

CONCLUSION

The religious aspect of labour ethics in medieval and early modern Russia, defined at first exclusively by the clergy and above all by monks, was based on traditional Orthodox representations, which in turn stated that the main purpose of work was to attain salvation. In the monasteries of Russia attitudes to labour were formed as an educational process. Further, work should certainly have some creative value, although the economic aspect of work was clearly thought of as secondary. Owing to such views, and because of the natural conditions and climate of the country, the monastic way of life did not contribute to the growth of capitalism, nor to other economic systems. Russia's economic base was in any case weak. There is one further important remark to be made: Russia's social order decreed that everybody must work, although not necessarily physically, and that work should be socially useful.

IRSH 56 (2011), Special Issue, pp. 141–164 doi:10.1017/S0020859011000423

Jewish Ethics and Women's Work in the Late Medieval and Early Modern Arab-Islamic World

KARIN HOFMEESTER

Internationaal Instituut voor Sociale Geschiedenis

E-mail: kho@iisg.nl

SUMMARY: In this article, Moses Maimonides' *interpretation* of Jewish law on women and work – as reflected in his *Mishneh Torah* – is contrasted with the daily lives of Jewish working women as portrayed in the documents of the Cairo Geniza. Later rabbinic writings and European travel accounts are analysed to show how Jewish ethics of women and work were translated into social practice in the late medieval and early modern Arab-Islamic world, where Islamic law and the existence of separate worlds for men and women rather than the contrast between public and private spheres seem to have informed general ideas about women and work.

INTRODUCTION

There is no shortage of Jewish texts containing laws and rules on women and work, but finding sources that tell us how those theoretical ethics were applied in practice is more difficult. For the late medieval and the early modern world, however, we have a number of sources that can be contrasted: Maimonides' *Mishneh Torah*, a central text of Jewish ethics, and the documents found in the Cairo Geniza give a wonderful insight into the daily lives of Jews in the Arab-Islamic world. This article intends to show how Maimonides interpreted Jewish law and how his inter-pretation affected – and contrasted with – the working lives of Jewish women in the late medieval and early modern Arab-Islamic world.[1] Since the Cairo Geniza documents cover the period up to the sixteenth century, we shall look at other sources, such as rabbinic writings and European travel accounts, to show how Jewish ethical thinking on women and work was translated into social practice in an Islamic environment.

---

1. S.D. Goitein, who analysed many of the Geniza documents in his seminal six-volume work, *A Mediterranean Society: The Jewish Communities of the Arab World as Portrayed in the Documents of the Cairo Geniza* (Berkeley, CA [etc.], 1967–1993), speaks of the Arab world. Though this article will also discuss Jews in the Ottoman Empire – which included parts of Europe – we shall use the term "Arab-Islamic world".

THE WORLD OF MOSES MAIMONIDES AND HIS WORKS

Moses Maimonides was born in 1135 in Cordoba, the main centre of Jewish culture, which flourished in Islamic Spain, especially in the tenth and eleventh centuries. He studied the Torah, philosophy, law, and the exact sciences, reading the works of Greek philosophers as well as of Muslim scholars. Maimonides and his family left Cordoba when the Almohades, a strict orthodox Berber Muslim dynasty, conquered the city in 1148 and threatened the Jewish community with the choice of conversion to Islam, death, or exile. The family subsequently settled in different places in Spain, ending up in Fez, Morocco, in about 1160. In 1166 they settled in Fustat (Old Cairo), where Moses would become *nagid*, the official leader of the Jewish community recognized by the caliphate.[2] After the Fatimid conquest of Egypt and the foundation of Cairo as the caliph's seat of government in 972, the city had become the political, economic, and cultural centre of the Islamic world.[3] By about the time of Maimonides's arrival in Egypt the less tolerant Sunni Ayyubid dynasty had taken over, although the position of Jews in the city was left largely untouched. Estimates of the number of Jews in Cairo in that period vary from 1,500 to 4,000, at the most making up less than 1 per cent of the total population.[4]

Other important Jewish communities in the Arab-Islamic world at the time were Alexandria and Rosetta (Rashid), Gaza, Jerusalem, Safed, Damascus, Aleppo, Baghdad, and Basra, as well as Tripoli, Fez, and Tunis. Members of the rather small upper layer of the mostly urban Jewish communities worked as government officials, doctors, judges, and leading businessmen, the next layer being smaller businessmen, professionals, including master artisans, followed by urban craftsmen and labourers, and finally the peasants.[5] Like other religious and ethnic communities,

2. For biographical information on Moses Maimonides, see Joel L. Kraemer, "Moses Maimonides: An Intellectual Portrait", in Kenneth Seeskin (ed.), *The Cambridge Companion to Maimonides* (Cambridge, 2005), pp. 10–57; idem, *Maimonides: The Life and World of One of Civilization's Greatest Minds* (New York, 2008); and Mark R. Cohen, "Maimonides' Egypt", in Eric L. Ormsby (ed.), *Moses Maimonides and His Time* (Washington DC, 1989), pp. 21–34.
3. The Fatimid caliphate was an Arab Shi'a caliphate that ruled over varying areas of the Maghreb, Sicily, Malta, and the Levant from 909 to 1171. The caliphate was characterized by a relative degree of tolerance of Jews and Christians. For the position of Jews in Egypt in the period, see Norman A. Stillman, "The Non-Muslim Communities: The Jewish Community", in Carl F. Petry (ed.), *The Cambridge History of Egypt*, I: *Islamic Egypt, 640–1517* (Cambridge, 1998), pp. 198–210.
4. Cohen, "Maimonides' Egypt", p. 24, for the Jewish population. See also E. Ashtor, *The Jews and the Mediterranean Economy 10th–15th Centuries* (London, 1983), p. 20. For the total population of Cairo, see Kevin Shillington, *Encyclopedia of African History* (New York, 2005), p. 199.
5. Goitein, *A Mediterranean Society: The Jewish Communities of the Arab World*, I: *Economic Foundations* (Berkeley, CA [etc.], 1967), pp. 75–79.

Jews specialized in certain professions: they were prominent in the textile industry, above all in silks and dyeing, while the production of glass and metalwork, especially silversmithing, were Jewish specializations. Finally, many Jews were engaged in the food industry and the production of chemicals for medicinal purposes.[6]

Next to his work as physician and community leader – though partly in sabbatical periods from the latter function – Maimonides wrote extensive medical texts and works on Jewish philosophy and law. His most famous philosophical work is the *Guide for the Perplexed*, in which he tried to reconcile Aristotelian ideas about reason and knowledge with the teachings of the Torah. His most important work on Jewish law is the code *Mishneh Torah*, literally meaning "The Second Law", intended to be a summary of the entire body of Jewish religious law.[7] Whereas earlier codes had followed the Talmud's sometimes haphazard arrangement, with only very few attempts to improve on that order, Maimonides classified by topic scattered statements into groups of laws.[8] The main goal of the codification was to facilitate and simplify the law to make it accessible and comprehensible.[9] Also, Maimonides felt that, in comparison with the level of intellectual life in Spain, Jews in the Arab world had left themselves with too little knowledge of Jewish law: "in our days, severe vicissitudes prevail, and all feel the pressure of hard times. The wisdom of our wise men has disappeared; the understanding of our prudent men is hidden."[10]

Maimonides considered *Mishneh Torah* his life's work and spent almost ten years (1168–1177) writing and revising it. Though *Mishneh Torah* was not the final codification, it was very influential among the Jewish communities in the Arab-Islamic world and it became a benchmark for subsequent writing on Jewish law. The *Shulchan Aruch*, a codification written in the sixteenth century by Rabbi Joseph Caro, is a more or less widely accepted codification of practical Jewish law, and his rules are in part based upon Maimonides' rules as formulated in the *Mishneh Torah*.[11]

---

6. *Idem*, "The Main Industries of the Mediterranean Area as Reflected in the Records of the Cairo Geniza", *Journal of the Economic and Social History of the Orient*, 4:2 (1961), pp. 167–197, 171.

7. Jewish law, *halakha*, constitutes the practical application of the 613 *mitzvot* (commandments) in the Torah (the five books of Moses, the "Written Law"), and as developed through discussion and debate in the classical rabbinic literature, especially the Mishnah ("Oral Law") and the Talmud.

8. Kraemer, "Moses Maimonides: An Intellectual Portrait", p. 36. See also Isadore Twersky, *Introduction to the Code of Maimonides (Mishneh Torah)* (New Haven, CT [etc.], 1980).

9. Kraemer, "Moses Maimonides: An Intellectual Portrait", p. 27.

10. Cohen, "Maimonides' Egypt", p. 29.

11. *Jewish Encyclopedia*, available at: http://www.jewishencyclopedia.com/view.jsp?artid= 188&letter=C#668; last accessed 5 December 2010.

To illustrate Maimonides' authority, one of his translators stated "From Moses to Moses, none arose like Moses".[12]

MISHNEH TORAH ON WOMEN AND WORK

The *Mishneh Torah* consists of fourteen books, subdivided into sections, chapters, and paragraphs. One of the books is entitled *On Women* (*Nashim*), which deals with laws mainly of marriage, divorce, and conduct between men and women. In *Nashim*, Maimonides follows the Talmud on women and work, which says "her food against the work of her hands". That sentence, which in essence means that a husband should provide his wife with food and clothing, and in return she should give him her earnings, plays a very important role in the perception of paid work done by married women within Jewish work ethics.[13] Maimonides more or less repeats the sentence, stating: "a wife's earnings are chargeable against her maintenance",[14] which means that women were expected to work, to earn an income, and to hand that income over to their husbands.

Rabbinic literature, written roughly between the second and fifth centuries, gives us some insight into the ideas behind the rule. It teaches that study of the Torah is perceived as the primary means of understanding God's will for the world, and therefore it is the highest spiritual activity in which a man can participate. Preferably, men should study the Torah full-time and it was regarded as unseemly that they should at the same time be engaged in mundane occupations. In the "rabbinically imagined family income", as Gail Labovitz describes that utopian situation, the wives of Torah-studying men provided them with a livelihood.[15] According to Labovitz, the rule that women should earn an income had all kinds of practical advantages for men. If men stayed in the study house all day, they could avoid undesirable contact with women on the shopfloor. Working for an income would protect women from idleness, which could lead either to lustfulness or to dull-mindedness, or – perhaps even worse – the wish to study the Torah themselves.[16]

---

12. Norman Roth, "The Jews in Spain", in Ormsby, *Moses Maimonides and His Time*, pp. 1–20, 3.
13. Babylonian Talmud, *ketubot* 47b, quoted and explained in Goitein, *A Mediterranean Society: The Jewish Communities of the Arab World*, III: *The Family* (Berkeley, CA [etc.], 1978), p. 132.
14. *The Code of Maimonides*, Book IV, *The Book of Women*, translated from the Hebrew by Isaac Klein (New Haven, CT [etc.], 1972), p. 74.
15. For an elaborate analysis of these and other rabbinic texts see Gail Labovitz, "The Scholarly Life – The Labouring Wife: Gender, Torah and the Family Economy in Rabbinic Culture", *NASHIM: A Journal of Jewish Women's Studies and Gender Issues*, 13 (2007), pp. 8–48. See also Miriam B. Peskowitz, *Spinning Fantasies, Rabbis, Gender, History* (Berkeley, CA [etc.], 1997).
16. Labovitz, "The Scholarly Life – The Labouring Wife", pp. 10–11, 19–20. Though Maimonides himself stated that women were exempted from Torah study, some rabbis felt that

That argument could, of course, be turned on its head: who would generate a family's income if women were to start studying the Torah?

Returning to Maimonides' *Mishneh Torah*, we should stress that although several paragraphs in his work indicate that men should study the Torah as much as possible and should not pay too much attention to worldly affairs such as earning an income, he does not explicitly expect wives to provide a man's income. "Even if he is a poor person supported by charity and begging, and even if he had a wife and children, he still has to set aside time during the day and by night for Torah study". If men had to work for an income, they could still study the Torah: "Of the great Sages of Israel, some were woodcutters, others were water-fetchers [...]. Even so, they learnt Torah by day and by night". A man who had to work for an income should divide his time, and to give an example of Maimonides' ideals about the division: "If one had a profession at which one worked for three hours a day, and one learnt Torah for nine hours".[17] Where the extra income would come from is not explained in *Mishneh Torah*, but probably the income of female family members played an important role in Maimonides' "imagined family income".

The idleness argument is a large part of Maimonides's motivation for allowing women to work. Even when a man was rich, a woman should do some gainful work: "she should not sit idle, without work, because idleness leads to immorality".[18] However, there were some exceptions to that rule: "if the wife says: 'I want neither your maintenance nor work', her wish must be respected and she may not be coerced".[19]

Apart from the work women performed to earn an income, there was also the unpaid work women had to do to serve their husbands and families. There were fixed tasks a woman had to perform, no matter how wealthy her husband nor how many maidservants they had. No maidservant could perform the intimate tasks of washing her husband's face, hands, and feet, pouring his cup for him, spreading his couch, and waiting on him. If the family was not wealthy enough for maidservants, a wife should "bake bread in the oven, cook food, wash clothes, nurse her child, put fodder before her husband's mount – but not before his cattle – and attend to the grinding of corn".[20] Maimonides stated that a man was

---

women should be forbidden to study the Torah. For discussions of this question see *ibid.*, pp. 30–31, and Kraemer, *Maimonides*, pp. 335–336.

17. The Yale Judaica series edition of the Mishneh Torah provides an excellent translation of all but one of the fourteen works. The first book "On Knowledge" has not yet appeared in this series, so we have used an English translation available at http://www.panix.com/ ~ jjbaker/ MadaTT.html; last accessed 5 December 2010.

18. *Code of Maimonides: The Book of Women*, p. 131.

19. *Ibid.*, p. 74.

20. *Ibid.*, p. 131.

expected to demand such unpaid work of his wife: "If a man makes his wife vow to do no work at all, he must divorce her and pay her her *kettubah*, because idleness leads to immorality".[21] Here, we can see that the idleness argument applied equally to her paid and unpaid work. Maimonides even added that if a wife refused "to perform any kind of work that she is obliged to do, [she] may be compelled to perform it, even by scourging her with a rod".[22]

Returning to the work women ought to perform to earn an income, an important question to be asked is: What type of work was considered appropriate for women according to Maimonides? Here, his answer is a typically Jewish one: it all depends on the custom of the country.[23]

> Where the custom is for wives to weave, she must weave; to embroider, she must embroider; to spin wool or flax, she must spin. If it is not the custom of the women of that town to do all these kinds of work, he cannot compel her to do any of them, except spinning wool only – because flax injures the mouth and the lips – for spinning is a kind of work that is characteristic of women, as it is said, "And all women that were wise-hearted did spin with their hands". (Exodus, 35.25)[24]

The next important question to be answered is: Where was a woman supposed to work, in private or public space? For that, the *halakhic* rules of *zniut*, modesty, were very influential. They determined the way a woman – especially a married woman – should dress and behave in public. One of the rules was that contact between a woman and a man other than her own husband or close relatives should be restricted to the minimum. In the application of that law, Maimonides once again points to local customs:

> In a place where it is the custom for a woman to go out into the street wearing upon her head not only a cap, but to wear also a veil that covers her whole body like a cloak, he must include in the garments given to her a veil [...] in order that she might wear it to her father's house, to a house of mourning, or to a wedding feast. For every woman is entitled to go to her father's house to visit him, or to a house of mourning or a wedding feast as an act of kindness to her friends and relatives, in order that they in turn might visit her on similar occasions, for she is not in a prison where she cannot come and go. On the other hand, it is unseemly for a woman to be constantly going out abroad and into the streets, and the husband should prevent his wife from doing this and should not let her go out,

21. *Ibid.*
22. *Ibid.*, p. 133. This rule, which seems to be at odds with Jewish ethics in general and Maimonides in particular, has led to an enormous amount of discussion. See Isaac Klein's introduction to his translation of *The Book of Women*, pp. xxxv–xxxvi, and Kraemer, *Maimonides*, pp. 343–346.
23. After the Babylonian conquest, the *halakhic* rule "dina de-malkhuta dina", meaning the law of the kingdom is the law (and is binding), was adopted; see Aryeh Shmuelevitz, *The Jews of the Ottoman Empire in the Late Fifteenth and the Sixteenth Centuries* (Leiden, 1984), pp. 42–43.
24. *Code of Maimonides: The Book of Women*, p. 130.

Figure 1. Jewish woman from Edirne, c.1500.
Nicolas de Nicolay, Discours et histoire véritable des navigations, pérégrinations et voyages, faicts en la Turquie *(Antwerp, 1586). Volume in the collection of the Library of Congress.*

except for once or twice a month, as the need may arise. Rather, the seemly thing for a woman is to sit in the corner of her house, for so it is written "All glorious is the king's daughter within the palace" (Psalms, 45.14).[25]

SOCIAL PRACTICE AS REFLECTED IN MARRIAGE CONTRACTS

Maimonides's judgments should be seen against the background of his position as a Jew in a Muslim society. Having *dhimmi* status, Jews, like all other non-Muslims who adhered to a monotheistic faith while living in Muslim countries, enjoyed relative protection and safety in return for the payment of a capital tax and obedience to certain rules concerning behaviour and dress. Apart from that legal arrangement, Jews in the medieval Arab-Islamic world were very much integrated into the surrounding culture, speaking the same language, reading the same philosophers, sharing intellectual discourse, Islamic codification, and poetry.[26]

For Jewish women, that meant a greater restriction on their freedom to move about than was experienced by their co-religionists in Christian Europe. There, women were active in a number of crafts, sold their products on the open market, and sometimes could even become members of a guild.[27] One searches in vain in the Talmud for rules on the maximum number of times a woman can leave the house.[28] According to Avraham Grossman, it is clear that Maimonides was led to his position by the influence of Muslim society,[29] but there was a difference between rules and social practice. The *Mishnah* states that a woman may be divorced and will not receive her delayed instalment (see below): "if she goes out with her hair flowing loose; or if she spins in the market place; or if she talks with just anybody".[30] That phrase shows that even the sages knew

25. *Ibid.*, p. 83.
26. For this integration, see Mark R. Cohen, "Medieval Jewry in the World of Islam", in Martin Goodman (ed.), *The Oxford Handbook of Jewish Studies* (Oxford, 2002), pp. 193–218, 202ff.
27. Avraham Grossman, *Pious and Rebellious: Jewish Women in Medieval Europe* (Lebanon, NH, 2004), pp. 114–117; Shulamith Shahar, *The Fourth Estate: A History of Women in the Middle Ages* (London [etc.], 1996), pp. 171–177. In the Arab-Islamic world women were listed from time to time in certain guilds, such as the Istanbul slave dealers in 1640 and flower-planters in 1778 and Edirne rosewater producers in c.1650, but these are exceptions; Fariba Zarinebaf-Shahr, "The Role of Women in the Urban Economy of Istanbul, 1700–1850", *International Labor and Working-Class History*, 60 (2001), pp. 141–152, 142.
28. Mordechai A. Friedman, "The Ethics of Medieval Jewish Marriage", in S.D. Goitein (ed.), *Religion in a Religious Age: Proceedings of Regional Conferences Held at the University of California, Los Angeles and Brandeis University in April, 1973* (Cambridge, MA, 1974), pp. 83–102, 92.
29. Grossman, *Pious and Rebellious*, p. 105.
30. Jacob Neusner, *The Mishnah: A New Translation* (New Haven, CT [etc.], 1988), p. 392: Mishnah Ketubot 7.6.

that practice was not always in accordance with theory, and even Maimonides himself admitted that it was sometimes wise not to follow the rules too strictly: "Pay regard to God by disregarding his law".[31]

For the history of the daily lives of Jewish communities in the Arab-Islamic world, including the practical application of the laws, we have a wonderful, unprecedented source: the Cairo Geniza. According to Jewish law, pieces of sacred texts, such as fragments of the Torah containing God's name, should not be thrown away after use but should be buried in a Geniza (burial place). Normally, such a Geniza would be located in a cemetery; however, in Fustat the Geniza was located inside the synagogue. Called the Ben Ezra Synagogue, it was originally built as a Coptic church but at some time during the ninth century it was transformed into a synagogue. It still stands today, although it was heavily reconstructed in the late nineteenth century when the Geniza was discovered. Not only did it contain fragmented pages of religious texts adding up to three-quarters of a million pages, it also comprised a variety of documents, written in Judeo-Arabic (Arabic in Hebrew characters) from everyday life, dating from the eleventh to the thirteenth centuries mostly. The documents vary from letters (business as well as private correspondence), court records, marriage contracts, deeds of divorce, wills, business documents, account books, to lists of people receiving charity, and so on.[32]

Marriage contracts, called *ketuboth*, are an important source for our purpose here. A *ketubah* is a pre-nuptial agreement, drawn up with the consent of bride and bridegroom, which outlines the rights and responsibilities of the groom in relation to the bride and very often also her obligations to him. It also contains the financial agreements they made.[33] The *ketubah* mentions the gifts the bridegroom had to give to the bride, consisting of three parts: the traditional obligatory marriage gift, being a certain number of silver pieces or its equivalent in value; the additional gift, which was seen as the actual gift; as well as a delayed instalment the husband had to pay in the case of divorce, or which his heirs had to pay in case of his death.[34] The *ketubah* includes the dowry the bride received from her parents and which was brought to the marriage. Often the dowry included a detailed list of items, but sometimes only the value was mentioned, and would typically consist of jewellery, clothing, and items

31. Goitein, *A Mediterranean Society: The Jewish Communities of the Arab World*, I: *Economic Foundations*, p. 137.
32. For a short description of the Geniza see Cohen, "Medieval Jewry in the World of Islam", pp. 196–197.
33. For more information on the marriage contracts see Mordechai Akiva Friedman, *Jewish Marriage in Palestine: A Cairo Geniza Study* (Tel Aviv [etc.], 1980).
34. Goitein, *A Mediterranean Society: The Jewish Communities of the Arab World*, III: *The Family*, pp. 188ff.

for the household such as bedding and copper utensils, but might also include entire houses or parts of them or other landed property. The dowry was usually many times greater than a husband's marriage gift.[35]

The rules on a husband's financial obligation were part of *halakha*; the dowry, however, was a matter of practical wisdom and local custom. Therefore, statements about it found in the Geniza *ketuboth* are not influenced by ancient law but reflect the real situation at the time. They are also changeable over time and space.[36] Many hundreds of *ketuboth* were found in the Cairo Geniza. It is worth remembering that they ended up in the Geniza because the marriage was at least "discussed", otherwise the *ketubah*, often accompanied by court documents, would not have been kept there. The *ketuboth* cover the period from the tenth to the beginning of the sixteenth century. Many of them concern couples living in Fustat, but there are also *ketuboth* from other parts of Egypt, Syria (Damascus, Aleppo), Palestine (Jerusalem), Lebanon (Tyre), Algeria (Tinis), Libya (Barqa), and Tunisia (Qayrawan), so we may safely assume that the conclusions that can be drawn from the *ketuboth* are valid for a large proportion of the Jewish communities living in the Arab-Islamic world. The *ketuboth* are evenly spread over seven social classes, as defined by Goitein, varying from destitute to wealthy couples.[37]

For the economic position of women, it is important to consider the control over the possessions each of the partners brought to the marriage. Marriage gifts and dowries were potentially income-producing possessions: money could be lent against interest and houses could be let, or sold. For a woman, the disposal of her properties could enlarge her economic activities and independence if she could use the capital or real estate to earn money as a moneylender or estate agent. Maimonides states: "And the four things he is entitled to are all of Scribal origin, namely the following: he is entitled to her earnings, to anything she finds, and to the usufruct of her estate during her lifetime. And should she die in his lifetime, he is her heir."[38]

That meant that the economic power of a husband included his wife's dowry, since he had the right to any usufruct on it, but that power was limited by the obligation – extended to his heirs – to restore every penny of it in the case of divorce or his death.[39] A wife could dispose of both the original and the additional portions of her marriage gift but not the

---

35. *Ibid.*, p. 139.
36. *Ibid.*, p. 124.
37. *Ibid.*, pp. 95ff., and the appendix, p. 419.
38. *Code of Maimonides: The Book of Women*, p. 74.
39. Goitein, *A Mediterranean Society: The Jewish Communities of the Arab World*, III: *The Family*, pp. 180–181. In practice, it was often hard for widows to collect the debts owed them pursuant to their marriage contracts. See Mark R. Cohen, *Poverty and Charity in the Jewish Community of Medieval Egypt* (Princeton, NJ [etc.], 2005), pp. 140–141.

delayed instalment, and of any gifts or inheritances that she received during her married life from her family. Such personal properties could be explicitly excluded from her husband's jurisdiction,[40] but he retained full jurisdiction over her dowry, which was worth many times more. Also, a wife's transactions, such as the purchase or sale of a house, had to be endorsed by her husband, thus limiting the economic freedom of women.

FINDING WAYS OUT

In practice, women found ways out of their restricted economic position. For the fifteenth and sixteenth centuries we have *responsa* literature that tells us more about social practice. *Responsa* were written "answers" from rabbis and other "decisors of Jewish law" on questions concerning specific *halakhic* matters. After their expulsion from Spain at the end of the fifteenth century, many Jewish exiles found their way to various countries, but chiefly to North Africa, the Balkans, and Palestine, where they met existing Jewish communities which observed different practices. As a result, disputes arose about a number of topics: the power a community could exercise over its members for example, but also about the way contracts and business dealings were handled. All such disputes had to be resolved in accordance with the principles of the *halakha*; therefore we see a lot of *responsa* from that period, written especially by rabbis from Spain.

From fifteenth-century *responsa* we know that women concealed commercial transactions from their husbands.[41] We know too that Jewish women appealed regularly to Muslim courts, especially on matters concerning legacies and inheritance. According to Islamic law a woman could keep her property and was allowed to manage it, and a separation of funds between husband and wife persisted throughout communal life.[42] A woman's property rights included her dowry, gifts, and inheritances.[43] According to one author, "sometimes a threat from a woman or her family to go to the kadi [a judge ruling in accordance with Islamic religious law] was all it took to make a husband change his behaviour and the rabbinic judges adopt a more flexible position on financial and personal matters".[44] A common cause of marital dispute was a husband's management of the dowry. In practice, if conflicts

40. Goitein, *A Mediterranean Society: The Jewish Communities of the Arab World*, III: *The Family*, p. 179.

41. Maya Shatzmiller, *Labour in the Medieval Islamic World* (Leiden [etc.], 1994), p. 364.

42. *Ibid.*

43. *Idem, Her Day in Court: Women's Property Rights in Fifteenth-Century Granada* (Cambridge, MA, 2007), p. 3.

44. Ruth Lamdan, "Levant: Women in the Jewish Communities after the Ottoman Conquest of 1517", in *Jewish Women: A Comprehensive Historical Encyclopedia*. Available at Jewish Women's Archive: http://jwa.org/encyclopedia/article/levant-women-in-jewish-communities-after-ottoman-conquest-of-1517; last accessed 5 December 2010.

really got out of hand, a husband usually gave up control of and responsibility for his wife's dowry, handing it all over to her.[45] If a widow or divorcee remarried, she often stipulated in her *ketubah* that she could keep control of her possessions, "even if she threw them into the Dead Sea".[46] Women not only disputed control of their potentially income-yielding properties, they also tried to circumvent the rule that a woman must hand over her own income, as we can see from changes in the rules relating to women's income as reflected in the *ketuboth*.

Remarks on working women with an income are very rare in tenth- and eleventh-century *ketuboth* but become more frequent in twelfth- and thirteenth-century contracts.[47] Twelfth-century requests have been found addressed to the leader of the Jewish community to the effect that the *ketubah* should include the sentences "that he should under no circumstances demand from his spouse her earnings, and, if she worked, they belonged to her", and "the husband has no right to his wife's earnings, but she has to buy her own clothing from her earnings".[48] In the thirteenth century such remarks about the earnings of women had become a regular feature. Fixed formulas such as "the work of her hands against her clothing" appear frequently in contracts, and there are surviving statements from husbands renouncing the right to their brides' earnings.[49] According to Goitein,

> Most marriage documents from the Mamluk period (1250–1517) contain a reference to the wife's work. Not only widows and divorcées, or poor women, but also brides with a large trousseau would stipulate the retention of their earnings and free their spouses from the obligation of providing them with clothing.[50]

How can we explain the tendency towards more income-earning women, and in which professions did they work?

WOMEN'S WORK AND LABOUR RELATIONS: 1500 AND 1650

During the first centuries of the Islamic era, far-reaching political, social, and economic changes had taken place in the Arab world which had changed the lives of its inhabitants, including the Jews. The changes transformed the inhabitants into a primarily urban people who began to

---

45. Goitein, *A Mediterranean Society: The Jewish Communities of the Arab World*, III: *The Family*, pp. 181–182.
46. Ruth Lamdan, *A Separate People: Jewish Women in Palestine, Syria and Egypt in the Sixteenth Century* (Leiden, 2000), pp. 114–115.
47. Goitein, *A Mediterranean Society: The Jewish Communities of the Arab World*, III: *The Family*, p. 132.
48. *Ibid.*, pp. 132–133.
49. *Ibid.*, pp. 133–134.
50. *Ibid.*, p. 134.

Figure 2. Woman spinning, detail from the Sarajevo Haggadah. A Haggadah is a religious text that sets out the order of the Passover Seder. The Sarajevo Haggadah was commissioned and created in Barcelona, Spain, around 1350.
National Museum of Bosnia and Herzegovina, Sarajevo. Haggadah, folio 3 verso (lower register, detail). Used with permission.

take part in the commercial revolution, spurred by laissez-faire Fatimid politics.[51] In Egypt, land formerly owned by the state was leased to peasants and wage labourers, while slave labour was not only no longer the core of the agricultural labour force, through urbanization and the reorganization of labour in urban centres its importance to manufacturing too was diminished. Productivity in rural areas rose because of the transition, which led to increased availability of raw materials for use by manufacturing industry in the cities, especially for the textile industry, which boomed. As a consequence, more female wage labour entered the textile industry, and evidence from the late medieval period indicates that from the tenth century to the fifteenth century women's participation in the labour force increased in towns, where it came to dominate the textile industry by monopolizing certain tasks such as spinning, dyeing, and embroidery.

The textile industry subsequently became the largest, most specialized, and most market-oriented industry in Muslim cities.[52] Goitein cautiously suggests that the increasing number of remarks about female wage labour in the *ketuboth* of the thirteenth century might be explained by a deterioration in the economic situation and the impoverishment of the population, something which did indeed occur during the Ayyubid and subsequent Mamluk rule.[53] One might also suggest that as women's wage labour increased, ethical debates about it expanded and finally found their way into the *ketuboth*. Maya Shatzmiller adds another argument to this and suggests that the formulas referred to above found their way into Jewish marriage contracts as a result of the increasing influence of Islamic law, where a woman's wage labour was seen as one of her property rights, to which she was entitled absolutely.[54] What we can state safely is that with the transition from slave labour to free wage labour the number of women performing free waged labour increased. For them, that meant a shift from reciprocal work for the household to commodified labour, and the income they earned from their wage labour was often kept by the women themselves. We should, however, stress that although many women worked, the income they generated was in many cases not enough to maintain themselves and their children in the event of divorce or widowhood.[55]

At the end of the fifteenth century and the beginning of the sixteenth century, two major changes took place: the arrival of large groups of

51. Stillman, "The Non-Muslim Communities", pp. 199–202.

52. Shatzmiller, *Her Day in Court*, pp. 150–151.

53. For Goitein's explanation see *A Mediterranean Society: The Jewish Communities of the Arab World*, III: *The Family*, p. 135. For the economic position see Stillman, "The Non-Muslim Communities", pp. 208–209.

54. Shatzmiller, *Her Day in Court*, pp. 169–170.

55. Ruth Lamdan, "Jewish Women as Providers in the Generations following the Expulsion from Spain", *NASHIM: A Journal of Jewish Women's Studies and Gender Issues*, 13 (2007), pp. 49–67, 55; Cohen, *Poverty and Charity*, pp. 139–143.

Sephardic immigrants from Spain and Portugal who had fled the Iberian peninsula in the face of the Inquisition, and integration – in the Egyptian case in 1517 – into the Ottoman Empire. Did those two developments influence women's work and the way it was perceived? They did bring economic advantages to the existing Jewish communities. The Sephardic migrants brought with them knowledge of banking, commerce, tax-farming, management of ports and custom houses, as well as trading networks and sometimes even capital.[56] The expansion of the Ottoman Empire generated administrative state functions for Jews and strength-ened their position in international trade, thereby also increasing the number of "job opportunities" for women.

The newcomers had their own specific views on women and work, however. Rabbis formed part of the Sephardic immigrant group that came to Egypt and some of them expressed their bewilderment at the rules and practices they encountered concerning women's work. Radbaz (an acro-nym of Rabbi David ben Solomon ibn (Abi) Zimra) was born in Spain in 1488 and settled in Egypt, becoming Chief Rabbi there in 1517. He was the author of more than 3,000 *responsa* as well as of several scholarly works, and in one of his *responsa* he stated:

> Concerning the custom in Egypt, whereby the husband stipulates that the wife's handiwork belongs to her, and that he is responsible to pay her a yearly clothing allowance: Let us suppose that the wife is a good worker, and does not use up all her clothing allowance, but puts money aside, and becomes a money-lender, lending money to gentiles for interest, can the husband claim the usufruct thereof? [Answer:] The husband has no grounds for such a claim since [...] he has already waived any claim to her handiwork. Therefore he is not entitled to her handiwork or the usufruct thereof [...]. Moreover, since it is the custom here for a woman to use her earnings to help relatives or marry off daughters, or in any other way she see fit, and since the *ketubah* stipulates that her handiwork is hers, the husband, by marrying her, automatically endorses this custom. For when a man gets married, he takes on the local custom, even if it contravenes *halakha*.[57]

Joseph Caro (Toledo, 1488–Safed, 1575), author of the famous great codification of Jewish law *Shulchan Aruch*, left Toledo for Istanbul and subsequently lived in Adrianople, Nikopol, and Salonika, to settle in Safed in 1536. Observing the position of the Musta'rab men (native Jews from Arab countries), he wrote indignantly: "that they are not entitled to their wives' property. Even if he [the husband] is in dire poverty, or languishing in jail, his wife does not let him use her property."[58]

56. Avigdor Levy, "Introduction", in *idem* (ed.), *The Jews in the Ottoman Empire* (Princeton, NJ, 1994), pp. 1–150, 24–28.
57. Radbaz, quoted in Lamdan, *Separate People*, p. 124.
58. Caro, quoted in *ibid*.

For Radbaz and Caro, social customs concerning women, work, income, and possessions differed from the situation they were used to in Europe, although in their time Spain was still ruled by Islamic adminis-trators. Their ideal consisted of women handing over their income to their husbands, who would have proprietorship of their wives' possessions. That state of affairs is comparable to the situation in medieval and early modern Christian Europe, where the ideal was still that men studied the Torah and women provided a large part of their family's income, although poverty often forced both men and women to work.[59] The *responsa* show us that in the sixteenth-century Arab-Islamic world it was still the custom for Jewish women to keep their own income.

The second development at the beginning of the sixteenth century, the integration of several countries with considerable Jewish communities into the Ottoman Empire, at first brought economic prosperity and increased job opportunities. After the expansions in the fifteenth and sixteenth centuries, however, the economic situation in the Ottoman Empire began to stagnate and went into decline in the first half of the seventeenth century; according to some, this was a natural and expected stage of adjustment after accelerated and widespread expansions in all spheres.[60] The stagnation affected the economic position of the Jews in the Ottoman Empire and in some cases specifically. European traders had discovered trading routes to the Americas, Asia, and Africa, and began overtaking traders in the Ottoman Empire. As a consequence of growing revenues from overseas trade, investment in new industries increased and European industries, such as the English textile industry, became serious competitors to Ottoman industries. Jewish traders in the Ottoman Empire who made their money from overseas trade lost much of their income, Jewish bankers lost clients, and Jewish government officials, such as tax-farmers, lost their jobs.[61] Monetary problems made the economic and social situation even more tense, and although the crisis was not felt evenly throughout the Empire, we know that the wool trade in Salonika and Safed, which gave many Jews an income, collapsed.[62] Did the crisis affect the economic position of women too?

59. Moshe Rosman, "The History of Jewish Women in Early Modern Poland: An Assessment", in ChaeRan Freeze *et al.* (eds), *Polin, 18: Jewish Women in Eastern Europe* (Oxford, 2005), pp. 25–56.
60. Yaron Ben-Naeh, *Jews in the Realm of the Sultans: Ottoman Jewish Society in the Seventeenth Century* (Tübingen, 2008), p. 28.
61. Levy, "Introduction", *The Jews in the Ottoman Empire*, pp. 72–80, and Ben-Naeh, *Jews in the Realm of the Sultans*, pp. 28–32.
62. Ben-Naeh, *Jews in the Realm of the Sultans*, pp. 28–30; Levy, "Introduction", *The Jews in the Ottoman Empire*, pp. 74–84. Levy notes that the Jewish community in Bursa was affected very much by the economic crisis, whereas the communities of Istanbul, Salonika, Edirne, Damascus, and Cairo still had a considerable number of wealthy members; p. 83.

For the seventeenth century we do not have a large set of analysed *ketuboth* – though we do find some that state that "her handiwork belongs to her". There is no large corpus of *responsa* which mention women and work explicitly, although there are texts which mention "her handiwork". There is the work of Rabbi Yehiel Bassan (1602–1625), who mentions a woman who earned a sizeable sum of money and kept her income for herself, causing the community to wonder whether her husband should pay more tax, considering that only heads of households paid tax.[63] We know that during the Ottoman period women in general were legally and socially quite independent, certainly more so in practice than in legal theory.[64] We know too that members of the Jewish communities in the Ottoman Empire continued to go to Muslim courts, for marital issues including divorce, as well as for cases involving inheritance, and that in spite of the sometimes stern disapproval of the rabbis.[65] We may therefore conclude that in 1650 Jewish women still worked for wages and kept their income, and, although we have no information on their numbers, we know that they stayed more or less in the same professions throughout the late medieval, early modern period.

WITH WHAT TYPES OF WORK DID JEWISH WOMEN EARN THEIR MONEY?

The Cairo Geniza and later sources provide an insight into women's paid employment. The most important jobs were in manufacturing, especially textiles: spinning, silk weaving, textile dyeing, as well as embroidery,[66] work for which they were trained on the job by other women.[67]

---

63. Lamdan, "Jewish Women as Providers". For the sixteenth-century *ketuboth* see p. 56; for the tax issue see p. 55.
64. Joel L. Kraemer, "Spanish Ladies from the Cairo Geniza", in: Alisa Meyuhas Ginio (ed.), *Jews, Christians and Muslims in the Mediterranean World after 1492* (London [etc.], 2002), pp. 237–267, 263–264.
65. Joseph R. Hacker, "Jewish Autonomy in the Ottoman Empire: Its Scope and Limits. Jewish Courts from the Sixteenth to the Eighteenth Centuries", in Levy, *The Jews in the Ottoman Empire*, pp. 153–202, 181–187; Aryeh Shmuelevitz, *The Jews of the Ottoman Empire in the late Fifteenth and Sixteenth Centuries: Administrative, Economic, Legal and Social Relations as Reflected in the Responsa* (Leiden, 1984), ch. 2. Najwa Al-Qattan, "Dhimmis in the Muslim Court: Legal Autonomy and Religious Discrimination", *International Journal of Middle East Studies*, 31 (1999), pp. 429–444, shows that Christian Copts too went to Muslim courts, especially to arrange marriage issues, and that Jewish and Christian women still went to Muslim courts to settle marital issues in eighteenth- and nineteenth-century Damascus.
66. Goitein, *A Mediterranean Society: The Jewish Communities of the Arab World*, I: *Economic Foundations*, p. 128.
67. Shatzmiller, *Labour in the Medieval Islamic World*, p. 360. See also Kraemer, "Spanish Ladies from the Cairo Geniza", who cites a woman who thanked her mother-in-law for the artisanship she learned, p. 259.

Figure 3. Midwife helping a woman to give birth, detail from the Sarajevo Haggadah (see Figure 2). *National Museum of Bosnia and Herzegovina, Sarajevo. Haggadah, folio 9 verso (upper register, detail). Used with permission.*

Only a small number worked in food preparation.[68] According to Shatz-miller, this might be explained by the prejudicial belief that menstruating women had a negative influence on the quality of food.[69] Women worked in trade too: they sold their products, either directly or via brokers, and sold commodities such as perfumes or comestibles including wine, olive oil, and spices.[70] They worked as pedlars and in small-scale commerce, although some women were described as "shrewd businesswomen".[71]

A third sector where women worked was what we would now call the service sector: they might be doctors, practitioners who applied traditional medical knowledge and skills and who most likely learned the trade from their fathers or brothers.[72] We find occultists, midwives, wet nurses, "bride combers", who not only combed brides' hair but also dressed them and organized part of the ceremony. There are references to women who washed the dead and earned money wailing as professional mourners,[73] and there were *mikveh* (ritual bath) supervisors, astrologers, and fortune-tellers.

Women worked as teachers also. Domestic work, a source of income for many women in other parts of the world, was done by slaves in Arab society and so was not a remunerative occupation.[74] The economic top layer was formed by women who worked as estate agents, selling properties or renting rooms in houses they owned, acting as moneylenders.[75] In terms of status, that top layer would be followed by women working in trade and services, followed by women who earned their money in the textile industry, and finally by the pedlars.

In general, those trades as well as labour relations within the various economic branches remained unchanged between 1500 and 1650. Ben-Naeh tells us, for the seventeenth century: "Female labor was a vital element in the chain of production, and women formed an integral part of the labor force in the textile industry, where they were paid lower wages than men."[76]

Women worked in all stages of what remained to a large extent a household industry: weaving, dyeing, and the final preparation of luxury fabrics and clothes. Women's work in trade from property dealing to peddling and services remained more or less unchanged. We do not know

---

68. Goitein, *A Mediterranean Society: The Jewish Communities of the Arab World*, I: *Economic Foundations*, p. 129.
69. Shatzmiller, *Labour in the Medieval Islamic World*, p. 352.
70. Lamdan, *Separate People*, pp. 118–119.
71. *Ibid.*, p. 119.
72. Shatzmiller, *Labour in the Medieval Islamic World*, p. 360.
73. Goitein, *A Mediterranean Society: The Jewish Communities of the Arab World*, I: *Economic Foundations*, pp. 127–129; Lamdan, *Separate People*, p. 122.
74. Goitein, *A Mediterranean Society: The Jewish Communities of the Arab World*, I: *Economic Foundations*, p. 129.
75. Lamdan, *Separate People*, pp. 118–119.
76. Ben-Naeh, *Jews in the Realm of the Sultans*, p. 348.

if the ratio of Jewish women who contributed to family income was greater than among other groups, but we do know that their presence in public places and their industriousness and skill were frequently mentioned by European travellers.[77] That then brings us to another important question: Where did Jewish women work?

WHERE DID JEWISH WOMEN WORK?

According to Maimonides, Jewish women in Islamic countries were not supposed to leave the house more often than once or twice a month. How could they earn a living if they were confined to the four walls of their dwelling? One answer lies in their main trade of textile manufacture. Goitein states that it is not clear from the Geniza whether textile manufacturing took place in workshops employing groups of women or whether all the work was done individually and at home.[78] Shatzmiller found no evidence for workshops for women, and therefore suggests that spinning, weaving, and embroidery were done at home. She found one reference to women congregating at one woman's home to spin flax and wool.[79] We know that, although some women owned storehouses, workshops, and flour mills, they probably would not have worked in them themselves.[80] Work was commissioned to the women in the textile industry by traders, brokers, or tax-farmers. Women workers most probably sold their finished products via brokers, who might be either Jewish or Muslim.[81] A solution for women going out to sell their products might have been the existence of special markets attended only by women.[82] Commercial activity too was carried on from the home: there are several references to women doing their property dealing and moneylending from their residences, and even peddling seems to have been done from home.[83]

Unmarried women, widows, and divorcees had far more freedom to move about in public than married women did. Two famous documents, one court case and one will, illustrate that. The court case is either a late-eleventh or early twelfth-century one, dealing with a married woman whose husband went away on a journey for four years, leaving her with no means of supporting herself and their children. To earn a living the wife started teaching the Torah in the school of her brother, but when her husband came home he

---

77. *Ibid.*, p. 349.
78. Goitein, *A Mediterranean Society: The Jewish Communities of the Arab World*, I: *Economic Foundations*, p. 128.
79. Shatzmiller, *Labour in the Medieval Islamic World*, p. 358; idem, *Her Day in Court*, p. 163.
80. Goitein, *A Mediterranean Society: The Jewish Communities of the Arab World*, III: *The Family*, p. 326.
81. Shatzmiller, *Her Day in Court*, p. 163.
82. *Idem, Labour in the Medieval Islamic World*, p. 359.
83. *Ibid.*, p. 189.

complained about the inappropriateness of the situation. His wife had been accustomed to meet the fathers of her pupils and that was not in accordance with *zniut* rules. Furthermore, she was neglecting her duties as a wife since she had no time to cook and clean for him. Therefore he wanted to marry a second wife, which she forbade. Moses Maimonides, acting as the *nagid* of the Jewish community to whom this problem was presented, at first agreed with the husband: he could prevent his wife from teaching the children, but he could not take a second wife if his first one objected. After the man's wife had presented her side of the story, Maimonides's final decision was that he agreed wholeheartedly with her. Her husband should have provided his wife with money to maintain her and the children, although the husband was also entitled to prevent her from teaching, so the best thing for her to do was to "rebel", leave without the delayed instalment, and then he would be forced to divorce her: "She will be her own woman, [free to] teach whomever she pleases and do whatever she pleases."[84] The other famous case concerns the will of Wusha, an unmarried woman banker and broker who had a child born out of wedlock. Her will shows that the economic freedom she enjoyed had made it possible for her to make a fortune during her lifetime.[85]

To return to our female traders: not all of them were unmarried, divorced, or widowed; we know some of them were married,[86] so we must conclude that at least some violations of the social barriers must have taken place. The same goes for a number of the women who worked in the service sector: midwives, bride-combers, women washing the dead, and wailing women could hardly have worked from home. They must often have found themselves in all-female companies, but not always; for example, European travellers in the Ottoman Empire noticed Jewish women in Istanbul, Salonika, Cairo, Jerusalem, and Safed trading both indoors and in public markets. They worked trading mainly in silk, wool, and linen fabrics, jewellery, needlework, spices, olive oil, wine, vegetables, and various other items.

An early example of such a traveller is Rabbi Obadiah of Bertinoro, born in Italy in the second half of the fifteenth century. In 1486 he went to Jerusalem, and he wrote travel letters, from Egypt and Palestine among other places.About Cairo he writes that the Jewish families cooked at home only for the Sabbath, because men and women were busy the whole week and fuel (wood) was very expensive so they bought ready-made food in the bazaars.[87] Unfortunately the rabbi does not mention what

84. Renée Levine Melammed, "He Said, She Said: A Woman Teacher in Twelfth-Century Cairo", *AJS Review*, 22 (1997), pp. 19–35, 27.
85. S.D. Goitein, "A Jewish Business Woman of the Eleventh Century", *The Jewish Quarterly Review, New Series*, 75 (1967), pp. 225–242, 239.
86. Lamdan, *Separate People*, pp. 125–126.
87. "Zwei Briefe Obadjahs aus Bartenuro aus dem Jahre 5258 und 5249, [1487–1488]", *Jahrbuch für die Geschichte der Juden und der Judenthums* (Leipzig, 1863), pp. 193–270, 244. Many

exactly kept both men and women so busy, but it was obvious that they were busy outside their homes or he would not have noticed it.

The mid-sixteenth century traveller Pierre Belon wrote that Jewish women acted as brokers for Muslim women and traded their products on the market, whereas George Sandys, travelling at the beginning of the seventeenth century, observed: "They are good workwomen, and can and will doe any thing for profit that is to be done by the art of a woman, and which sutes with the fashion of these countries."[88] For the Ottoman Empire in the seventeenth century, Ben-Naeh concludes that Jewish women did sell their goods in markets and streets, even if that contravened behavioural norms "despite repeated denunciations by preachers and teachers of ethical behaviour of any activity that entailed baring women's faces and hands and the fear they expressed of possible loss of innocence by female peddlers who made the rounds of the streets and the homes of Jewish and Gentile customers".[89]

The moral argument of opponents was supplemented by complaints from Jewish guilds about unfair competition from women pedlars.[90] Still, we must conclude with Ben-Naeh that "Both the general public and Islamic law exhibited a certain flexibility vis-à-vis the system of strict segregation".[91]

TO CONCLUDE

Ideas about Jewish women's work in the late medieval and early modern Arab-Islamic world were shaped by various laws and traditions as well as by socio-economic realities and necessities. One of those traditions was the ideal of the Jewish man studying his Torah, who through his study could understand God's will for the world and thereby would be performing the task valued the highest in Judaism – he did not have to bother too much about the family income because his wife would earn at least part of it. As a consequence of that ideal, which was in most cases no more than utopian dreaming, a Jewish woman could earn her wages and if necessary do so in the public sphere as long as the rules of *zniut* were respected. According to Jewish law, the wages a Jewish woman earned had to be surrendered to her husband, and a husband also had control of her dowry, which might very well have the potential to yield an income.

documents in the Cairo Geniza show us that food was indeed often bought ready to eat from the bazaars; Goitein, *A Mediterranean Society: The Jewish Communities of the Arab World*, I: *Economic Foundations*, p. 130, and III: *The Family*, p. 341.
88. Both cited in Lamdan, "Jewish Women as Providers", p. 57.
89. Ben-Naeh, *Jews in the Realm of the Sultans*, p. 349.
90. *Ibid.*
91. *Ibid.*, p. 369.

The Jewish women Maimonides described in his *Mishneh Torah* lived in a Muslim society and so were of course influenced by Muslim ideas about women's work. Under Islamic law, a woman could keep her wages as they were seen as one of her property rights, and she kept full control of her own possessions, a rule that was upheld by Islamic courts. Women had more economic freedom under Islamic law, but Islamic ideals separated women's and men's worlds more than Jewish *zniut* rules did, making it hard for women to earn their money in the public domain.

From the *ketuboth* found in the Cairo Geniza we learn that after the twelfth century more and more Jewish women began to demand that they be allowed to keep their income, most probably as a consequence of the influence of Islamic law. That women could actually find paid work is explained by a previous transition in society from a predominantly slave labour market to a free wage labour market. In the textile industry, women took over the positions of slaves and the industry became partly, but not entirely, a "Jewish" industry. For a long time it was a booming industry, with many job opportunities for women. Work in the textile industry appealed to women because many of the tasks could be performed in their homes. Trading and services offered job opportunities for women, and a woman's social position might determine her occupation: the larger her dowry, the bigger the chance that she could become a successful property dealer or moneylender, although we also know of women who earned money from wage labour and saved up until they could establish themselves as moneylenders.

Legal restrictions on women working in the public domain were bypassed in several ways. Business transactions were done from the home and even peddling sometimes seems to have been done from the house. Some women used brokers to sell their products for them. We should keep in mind that in this particular Islamic environment it is important not just to see working women in relation to the contrast between the public and private spheres, but also in the context of the separate worlds of men and women. There were public spaces specifically designed for women's sole use, such as women's markets where traders and customers were female.

The tradition of women working for wages and keeping them continued throughout the late medieval, early modern period. When exiled rabbis from Spain settled in the Arab-Islamic world in the sixteenth century, they were somewhat unpleasantly surprised to see Jewish women keeping their incomes and taking control of their own possessions. Still, the rabbis had to accept those rules since the law of the kingdom was the law, and their power to prevent Jewish women (and men) from going to Muslim courts was at best limited.

As large parts of the Arab-Islamic world became integrated into the Ottoman Empire in the sixteenth century, Jewish women and men alike profited from the booming economy and state expansion. When that growth stagnated in the seventeenth century, economic opportunities diminished, but women continued to earn their money from the textile industry, trade, and services. We should conclude that there were differences between Jewish and Islamic rules and norms on the one hand and social practices in a quickly developing society on the other, leaving room for gainfully working women.

IRSH 56 (2011), Special Issue, pp. 165–195 doi:10.1017/S0020859011000514
© 2011 Internationaal Instituut voor Sociale Geschiedenis

Work Ethics and Work Valuations in a Period of Commercialization: Ming China, 1500–1644*

C H R I S T I N E M O L L - M U R A T A

Faculty of East Asian Studies, Ruhr-Universität Bochum

E-mail: Christine.Moll-Murata@rub.de

SUMMARY: In global terms, Ming China was one of the largest of the economies and political entities that saw increasing integration. Between 1500 and 1650 it experienced a phase of commercialization that influenced perceptions and valuations of work in various ways. Taking a multi-layered approach, this study explores Confucian tenets that made a distinction between mental and physical work, and between four main occupational groups. It discusses earlier Buddhist perspectives on work which were still valid during the Ming period. Further, the legal regulations concerning work in the Ming penal code and the valuations of work and particular occupations in a contemporary literary source, a carpenter's handbook, and an agricultural guide are probed for direct and indirect evidence of the commodification of work in cities and in the countryside, and of gendered division of labour. A consideration of the usefulness of work songs for studying the self-expression of workers concludes the essay.

Among the empires in existence between 1500 and 1650, China stands out for its centralized administration, its large population, and its great historical depth of memory and record, with a particular focus on political philosophy. The period considered in this essay corresponds to the middle and late Ming dynasty (1368–1644), and the rise of the Manchu Qing dynasty (1644–1911). During that era, a commercial market system emerged, evidenced by a rise in the number of recorded markets. The influx of silver from the Spanish colonial empire via the Philippines lubricated these expanding market activities. Human labour formed an important element in this nexus of commercialization. Cash-cropping and artisan production became more common for rural households, often involving all family members. Skilled urban professionals were able to concentrate on production for local, regional, and interregional markets.

---

* In this article east Asian names are given in the sequence family name – personal name. Exceptions are made in cases where the authors have adopted Western personal names.

From the perspective of the state, commercialization and the greater liquidity of the economy entailed the *corvée* duties of the agrarian population being partly transformed into monetary taxation.[1] In a similar process, after 1485 professional artisan households which had been registered for periodic service to the state were given the option to pay taxes rather than render labour obligations.

The size of the Ming Empire's population is still being debated. Estimates range from 97 million to 155 million in 1500, and from 100 million to anything between 152, 230, and even 290 million in 1644.[2] One unresolved issue is the impact of climate cooling on living conditions and population size. According to recent estimates, throughout the period 1500–1650 the climate was cooler than at present. The so-called "Little Ice Age" is said to have started in 1618, when snow fell in subtropical Guangdong province. Droughts, epidemics, and floods occurred frequently in northern China in the 1630s and 1640s.[3] In writings that are concerned with work and occupations, reference is seldom made to such hardships, which must have been compounded by the unstable, warlike political situation at the end of the Ming Dynasty. Nevertheless, they should be borne in mind when discussing the human condition at the end of a period of great change and incremental growth.

Exploring the perspectives explained in the Introduction to this volume, this essay focuses on the sources and issues that marked the late Ming period and the transition to the Qing. These layered questions included the identification of texts and traditions referring to work. The question was raised whether the terms for "work" and "worker" reflected appreciation or disdain. The position of work and the worker in society and the valuation of waged labour, also in comparison with other, non-commodified types of labour, was another focal point. Did both free and unfree labour exist? Moreover, we asked according to which criteria particular occupations were ranked. An ethnic or gendered division of labour was a further concern. Finally, were there theories about what constituted "just" remuneration? For a large empire, and a great body of writings that might contain scattered evidence of work-related thinking,

---

1. Ray Huang, *Taxation and Governmental Finance in Sixteenth-Century Ming China* (Cambridge, 1974), pp. 112–131, 118.
2. The lower estimates are from Cao Shuji, *Zhongguo renkou shi. Di si juan: Ming shiqi* [Chinese Historical Demography, IV: The Ming Period] (Shanghai, 2000), pp. 34 and 452, and the higher figures are from Martin Heijdra, "The Socio-Economic Development of Rural China during the Ming", in Denis Twitchett and Frederick W. Mote (eds), The Cambridge History of China, VIII: *The Ming Dynasty*, Part II (Cambridge, 1998), pp. 417–578, 440. For a critique of the higher figures, see Robert B. Marks, "China's Population Size during the Ming and Qing: A Comment on the Mote Revision"; remarks given at the 2002 Annual Meeting of the Association for Asian Studies, Washington DC, at http://web.whittier.edu/people/webpages/personalwebpages/rmarks/PDF/Env._panel_remarks.pdf; last accessed 1 July 2011.
3. Heijdra, "Socio-Economic Development of Rural China", pp. 425–427.

this was a complex task. The aim of this present contribution is to show the variety of approaches to human work in mid- and late-Ming China.

TEXTS AND TERMINOLOGY

As in many other regions of the world in the sixteenth and seventeenth centuries, descriptive and normative formulations of work and work organizations by urban or rural elites, often those in the service of the state or polity, are the most easily available sources, while written indications of self-perception by working people are rare. Strikes and work riots are reported from the official point of view rather than from the point of view of those actually engaged in labour unrest. "Labour" or "work" is discussed in various contexts.

The texts created by the government which concern work and labour are legislation and administrative regulations. Those were codified in the Great Ming Code, *Da Ming lü*, of 1389, as well as in legal commentaries, in the collected statutes of all administrative branches and ministries of the Ming government (*Da Ming huiyao*), the more detailed statutes and precedents (*zeli*) of individual ministries, and in handbooks for local officials. A prominent example are the regulations *Gongbu changku xu zhi* [What Should Be Known about the Working Sites and Storehouses of the Ministry of Public Works],[4] compiled in 1615, which constituted the Ministry's supervision and accounting guidelines for its work and maintenance projects.

The sources written by rural and urban elites that refer to work in the private sector also consist of more hands-on compendia concerning agricultural techniques and agricultural home industries, such as agricultural handbooks or encyclopaedias. The purpose of those works is to inform landowners and officials about the most efficient use of material resources and labour and thus, ultimately, to maintain the social order. They are neither "classics of labour", nor exclusively technical compendia in their own right.[5] One rare extant sample of a handbook written for craftspeople, namely carpenters and joiners, is the fifteenth-century "Classic of [the patron saint of construction artisans] Lu Ban".

Family precepts (*jiaxun*) are another type of source that can be of special use in identifying which professions were the most desirable within particular families or lineages.

---

4. He Shijin (comp.), *Gongbu changku xu zhi* [What Should be Known about the Working Sites and Storehouses of the Ministry of Public Works], edition *Xuanlan tang congshu xubian*, CCXXIII–CCXXV (Taipei, 1985).
5. Compare, for instance, Dagmar Schäfer's characterization of the concerns of Song Yingxing, the author of *Tiangong kaiwu*, as being directed towards the socio-political rather than the scientific or technical field: "The Congruence of Knowledge and Action: The *Tiangong kaiwu* and its Author Song Yingxing", in Christine Moll-Murata *et al.* (eds), *Chinese Handicraft Regulations of the Qing Dynasty* (Munich, 2005), pp. 35–60, 55–56.

The rise of commercialization during the mid-Ming also found its expression in the genre of merchant route books and manuals, which contain information – interspersed here and there – on ethical maxims in commerce.[6] In the middle- to late-Ming era, guild houses were founded as hostels and institutions for developing merchant networks based on the principle of a common region of origin. It was only in the eighteenth century that self-characterizations by merchants and also by artisan corporations became more frequent.

"Labour" is expressed by the term *lao* 勞, which has the connotation of "toil", "pain", and "exhaustion", or *qin* 勤, which implies diligent or industrious work. Both refer mainly to physical work, especially in agriculture. Another designation for work is *gong* 工. Since this character is derived from a tool-like object, probably a carpenter's square, it is predominantly associated with craft or proto-industrial production. In contrast to *lao* it can designate the worker as well, and, in addition, in public accounting it is a measure of one day's workload, the average workday. Finally, work in the sense of "making a living", *shenghuo* 生活, occurs in many instances in a contemporary agricultural handbook with reference to farmers and farmhands.

In China's political economy since the first millennium BC, the ruler's subjects were obliged to render service to the state in the form of *corvée* labour. The general term for *corvée* is *yi* 役. This was initially associated with military service, but in the Ming dynasty it also referred to service in civilian tasks, mostly in construction and water conservation. Sometimes *yi* was also combined with *lao* or *gong*. In the course of the Ming dynasty, the relatively strict system of artisan registration and work service as a form of tax in kind was gradually replaced by monetary tax payments. For the later developments, especially in the eighteenth and nineteenth centuries, it is interesting to study the change from the concept of *yi* as "unpaid *corvée* labour" to "wage labour in the service of the state", which, though it did not exactly imply "free" wage labour, was more emancipated than the restrictive system at the beginning of the Ming dynasty.

A fourth term, *zhi* 職, which is associated with service for the state, designates both administrative work and the position held by a government official. In comparison with *yi*, this term stands out more constantly during the course of the second millennium.

Further designations of interest for the period in question are "hired labour", *guyong* 雇傭, or the "hired labourer", *gugongren* 雇工人, as well as *dian* 佃, tenancy/bond service, with its extensions *diannu* 佃僕 "'nearly free'

6. Timothy Brook, *Geographical Sources of Ming-Qing History* (Ann Arbor, MI, 2002), and *idem*, "The Merchant Network in 16th Century China: A Discussion and Translation of Zhang Han's 'On Merchants'", *Journal of the Economic and Social History of the Orient*, 24 (1981), pp. 165–214.

tenants",[7] *nupu* 奴僕, "bondservants", or *dianpu* 佃奴,[8] "agricultural bondservants", and *nu* 奴, "a person who does service for a particular master and/or manages his land",[9] a term often rendered as "slave".

WORK VALUATIONS: THE POSITIONS AND USEFULNESS OF WORKERS IN SOCIETY

As a rule, moralist considerations of labour from the Confucian point of view take as their point of departure the statement on the complementary fields of human action: the administrative work of the mind as opposed to subservient physical labour. This can be traced back to the Confucian exegete Mencius (372–281 BC):

> Great men have their proper business, and little men have their proper business. Moreover, in the case of any single individual, whatever articles he can require are ready to his hand, being produced by the various handicraftsmen: – if he must first make them for his own use, this way of doing would keep all the people running about upon the roads. Hence, there is the saying, "Some labour with their minds, and some labour with their bodies. Those who labour with their minds govern the others; those who labour with their bodies are governed by the others."[10]

The other important model is that of the "four occupational groups" (*simin*), consisting of scholar/officials, farmers, artisans, and merchants. This can be found in the *Guanzi* [Master Guan] (third century BC):

> They [the people] should not be allowed to dwell together in confusion. If they do so, their speech will become distorted and their work disorganized. For this reason, the sage kings, in situating the gentry, were certain to send them to places of leisure. In situating the farmers, they were certain to send them to the fields. In situating the artisans they were certain to send them to the bureaus responsible for them. In situating the merchants they were certain to send them to the marketplaces.[11]

Political thought reflecting on these two basic concepts is also interspersed in the works of many Ming thinkers. Recent Chinese historiography emphasizes the fact that a number of Ming philosophers, even if they were

7.   Harriet Zurndorfer, *Change and Continuity in Chinese Local History: The Development of Hui-chou Prefecture 800 to 1800* (Leiden, 1989), p. 199.
8.   Joseph P. McDermott, "Bondservants in the T'ai-hu Basin during the Late Ming: A Case of Mistaken Identities", *Journal of Asian Studies*, 40 (1981), pp. 675–701, 677.
9.   Zurndorfer, *Change and Continuity in Chinese Local History*, p. 199.
10.   *The Chinese Classics*, II, *The Works of Mencius*, James Legge (transl.) (Oxford, 1895), 2nd rev. edn, "Tang Wan Kung", pp. 249–250.
11.   *Guanzi* [Master Guan], Sun Bo (ed. and comm.) (Beijing, 2002), ch. 20, p. 135; "Xiao kuang" [Little Basket], in Allyn W. Rickett's translation, *Guanzi: Political, Economic, and Philosophical Essays from Early China* (Princeton, NJ, 1985), p. 185.

not part of the mainstream, no longer believed that the first two of those groups, the scholars and farmers, were the foundation or "roots" of society and that merchants and artisans mere derivatives or "branches" which needed to be kept under control. Such ideas were formulated in collections of essays or works on political practice and statecraft.[12]

For instance, Zhao Nanxing (1550–1627) claimed that all four groups were "fundamental";[13] Wang Daokun (1525–1593) argued that, although in earlier periods taxation had been light for peasants and heavy for artisans and merchants, this should be adjusted, so that the valuation for all groups would be identical in practical and financial terms.[14] Feng Yingjing (1555–1606) maintained that merchants were even more important than farmers and shouldered a greater responsibility for securing the subsistence of the people than the other groups.[15] Finally, Huang Zongxi (1610–1695) declared that artisans and merchants were already cherished by the ultimate Confucian models of morality, the legendary sage kings of antiquity, and should by all means be considered fundamental.[16] However, such views remained exceptions to the norm. The dominant view was the conviction that agriculture in combination with subsidiary production, mainly textiles, was of the greatest importance to the state and that specialization in manufacture and commerce was undesired and suspect.

This was the case even though official attitudes towards merchants were often ambiguous. Officials were aware of the important role of merchants, and still seemed very critical of their dealings. One example is given in Zhang Han's (1511–1593) essay on the four occupational groups.[17] Timothy Brook has perceptively analysed the section on merchants. Brook's essay shows that despite the traditional view that merchant activities were "secondary" or "derivative", an opinion Zhang Han traced back to the "sage kings" of antiquity, Zhang Han described the merchant networks of his times in detail, and pleaded for taxes on merchants to be reduced on the grounds that this would enhance commerce and thereby

---

12. Zhou Shengchun *et al.*, "Zhongguo lishi shang de nongben gong shang mo sixiang yu zhengfu zhengce de shanbian" [Changes in Chinese Historical Thought on Agriculture as Fundamental and Crafts and Commerce as Secondary Occupations and Corresponding Government Policies], *Zhejiang daxue xuebao (Renwen shehui kexue ban)* [Journal of Zhejiang University: Humanities and Social Sciences], 34:2 (2004), pp. 13–22, 18–19.

13. *Ibid.*, p. 18.

14. *Ibid.*

15. *Ibid.*, p. 19.

16. Huang Zongxi, *Mingyi daifang lu* [Waiting for the Dawn, 1662], Chongxin shushe (ed.) (1898), "Caiji" [Financial Administration], 3, fo. 42b.

17. Zhang Han, *Songzhuang mengyu* [Dream Talk from the Pine Window] (Beijing, 1985), ch. 4, "Shiren ji" [Record of the Scholar-Officials], "Baigong ji" [Record of the Hundred Artisans], "Sannong ji" [Record of the Three Farmers], "Shanggu ji" [Record of the Merchants]. For biographical information on Zhang Han, see Brook, "Merchant Network in 16th Century China", pp. 173–175.

actually increase state revenue.[18] The existence of a profit motive was fully realized and taken for granted. Zhang Han was more critical of artisans and argued strongly that they should return to "fundamental" agriculture, even if that seemed very unlikely. In comparing the profit made from artisanal luxury production and agriculture or home industries, he says that:

> This means that a vessel as tiny as a nutshell equals in value a year's farming, or a pattern of thumb's length is equivalent to one year's weaving. It will be extremely difficult to make people do away with luxury and return to frugality. Therefore the intricate carving hurts the farmer, the complex textile patterns harms the weaver.[19]

To the Confucian scholars in the sophisticated urban society of the high and late Ming, the nostalgic notion of merely four occupational groups must have seemed at least ideologically desirable, even though most people were aware of how antiquated it was. In order to drive home the message that scholars and farmers (or scholars, farmers, artisans, and merchants) were the "good", that is fundamental, groups, some writers developed an extensive list of fourteen and even twenty-four groups. For instance, Yao Lü (fl.1597) explained that in addition to the four respectable and the two tolerable categories (Buddhist monks and soldiers), the following classification applied: "Daoist priests, doctors, soothsayers, astrologers, physiognomists, geomancers, sedan chair carriers, horse dealers, coachmen, shippers, hair-dressers, pedicure masters, beauticians, courtesans and prostitutes, actors, acrobats, and bandits".[20] The author reprimands all those except the first six as being unproductive and vulgar, but also acknowledges that their services were highly cherished by their clients.

There may be an element of irony in this fine categorization of various service trades. Huang Zongxi, the eminent Ming-loyalist historian and political philosopher, more sweepingly blames the "unproductive and parasitic" groups beyond the first four in a typical condemnation of what he thought of as really non-fundamental trades such as those serving for amusement and for religious needs.[21]

BUDDHIST WORK ETHICS: A VARIANT BELIEF SYSTEM

Time and again, Confucians professed profound contempt for Buddhist and Daoist clergy, whom they considered unproductive. Since education in the Confucian orthodoxy was indispensable for a successful career as an official, and thus for attaining positions esteemed most highly, such dismissive

18. Brook, "Merchant Network in 16th Century China", pp. 187, 208.
19. Zhang Han, "Baigong ji", p. 79.
20. Yao Lü, *Lushu* [Disclosed Writings], ch. 9, an encyclopaedia from c.1611, cited in Xie Guozhen, *Mingdai shehui jingji shiliao* [Materials for a Socio-economic History of the Ming Dynasty] (Fuzhou, 1981), III, p. 385.
21. Huang, *Mingyi daifang lu*, fos 41b–42a.

reflections on the representatives of the competing belief systems carried particular weight. Needless to say, Buddhist and Daoist clergy saw things quite differently. Moreover, the impact of lay Buddhism became greater during the Song Dynasty (960–1279), and the influence of Buddhism on syncretistic popular beliefs was considerable. In simplified form, Buddhist tenets on work ethics from the eighth to the twelfth centuries can also be found in contemporary family precepts of the mid-Ming.

The monastic population was basically not supposed to work for a living, but instead to achieve spiritual liberation through meditation and religious exercises. The Vinaya (Lü/Ritsu) school of East Asian Buddhism devised elaborate regulations for the behaviour of monks and, on principle, forbade any other way of maintaining one's subsistence than by living on donations or begging. Other schools, especially meditational Buddhism (Chan), emphasized the usefulness of work as a means of regeneration after strenuous meditation practice, but also for the upkeep of the monastic community. The classical adage "one day without work [means] one day without eating" is attributed to one of the founders of Chinese Chan, Baizhang Huaihai (720–814). According to his recorded sayings, even as a venerated teacher Baizhang insisted on working physically with the other monks.[22] This text may represent hagiography, but the general tendency is well attested that Chan monastic communities not only relied on donations but also performed physical labour.

It is traditionally assumed that Baizhang Huaihai established the first rules for the Chan monasteries,[23] which were adapted and expanded over time. The last great recompilation was made at the command of the Emperor in 1335 and reprinted in 1424.[24] By then it had become a standard set of guidelines. These rules state, for instance, that if monks are called to work together (*pu qing*), they should all comply, with the exception of the elderly and the ill. This rule refers explicitly to Baizhang Huaihai's adage by admonishing the monks that "a day without work is a day without eating".[25]

22. It is said that when the prior of the monastery was unable to bear seeing master Baizhang toiling, he took his tools away from him and asked him to rest. As a result, Baizhang refused to eat; *Baizhang Huaihai chanshi yulu* [Recorded Sayings of Meditation Master Baizhang Huaihai], alternative title *Hongzhou Baizhang shan Dazhi chanshi yulu* [Recorded Sayings of Meditation Master Dazhi (Great Wisdom) of the Baizhang Monastery in Hongzhou], p. 7b, in *Sijia yulu* [Recorded Sayings of the Four Schools], ch. 2, collection *Xinzuan xuzangjing* [New Edition of Continued Buddhist Scriptures], 69, 1322, electronic database of Chinese Buddhist Electronic Text Association, *Chinese Electronic Tripitaka* V1.2, released 2009/04/22; last accessed 1 July 2011, http://www.cbeta.org/result/normal/X69/1322_001.htm.
23. Charles Muller, entries "Baizhang qinggui" and "Chixiu Baizhang qinggui", in *idem* (ed.), *Digital Dictionary of Buddhism*, http://www.buddhism-dict.net/cgi-bin/xpr-ddb.pl?76.xml+id%28%27b767e-4e08-61f7-6d77%27%29; last accessed 1 July 2011.
24. *Idem*, "Chixiu Baizhang qinggui".
25. *Chixiu Baizhang qinggui* [Imperially Commissioned Clear Rules by Baizhang], Dehui (comp.), in *Taishō Tripitaka* 2025, 48, p. 1144a/b, edition *The SAT Taizōkyō Text Database*

This could be any type of work which monks might wish to shun, not only work in the fields; Buddhist ceremonies can also be very strenuous and physically demanding.

Buddhist occupational ethics from the Song dynasty are most clearly formulated in two texts from the second half of the twelfth century that were written by lay Buddhists and expressly address all believers, not only the clergy.[26] They belong to the school of Pure Land or Amidist Buddhism. This school, which was also active during the Ming dynasty, does not strive for gradual or sudden awakening to the truth of Buddhist teachings through meditation during one's lifetime, but hopes that the individual will be reborn into the so-called "Pure Land", or paradise in the West. If that proves impossible, accumulation of karmic merit is the next best option for attaining a position of higher karmic status in the next reincarnation. Work is valued in terms of its usefulness for acquiring better karma, and for helping others to do so. Moreover, work is judged according to the extent to which it allows the worker to maintain the five basic precepts of Buddhism, which are binding for both lay people and the ordained clergy: no killing of sentient beings, stealing, sexual licentiousness, lying, and alcohol.[27] The "Admonishments for Particular [Types of People]" by Wang Rixiu from 1160 discusses thirty-six walks of life, varying according to occupation, gender and age group, and personal destiny.[28] Among these, eighteen groups are distinctly professional.

Seen from the perspective of work ethics, this fascinating sequence contains the message that high and low social positions are predestined by the karmic merit acquired in previous existences, but are by no means unchangeable. The karma of the present and the subsequent existence can and must be shaped and improved by conscious effort. What is specifically bad about butchers, cooks, fishermen, and bird catchers is that they

---

(1998–2008), http://21dzk.l.u-tokyo.ac.jp/SAT/ddb-sat2.php?mode=search&key=%E5%A4%A7 %E8%A1%86&uop=1&uof=264&ktn=&ai=&np=&nm=; last accessed 1 July 2011.

26. Wang Rixiu (d. 1173), "Tewei quanyu" [Admonishments for Particular [Types of People]], in his *Longshu zengguang jingtu wen* [Expanded Pure Land Tracts of Longshu], dated 1160; and Yan Bing (d. 1212), "Xuxiu fangbian men" [Skilful Preaching on [the Topic of] Cultivation]. For bibliographical details, a translation of Yan's text, and a discussion of the differences between both, see Alan G. Wagner, "Practice and Emptiness in the *Discourse Record of Ruru Jushi*, Yan Bing (d. 1212), a Chan Buddhist Layman of the Southern Song" (unpublished Ph.D. thesis, Harvard University, 2008); available on the author's website at http://rurujushi.com/ Wagner_thesis_Ruru_Jushi_2008-10-07.pdf; pp. 26, 278, 305ff, last accessed 1 July 2011.

27. W.E. Soothill and Lewis Hodous, *A Dictionary of Chinese Buddhist Terms* (Hartford, CT, 1937), p. 118, *wu jie*/pañca-veramaṇī.

28. Wang Rixiu, *Longshu zengguang jingtu wen* [Expanded Pure Land Tracts of Longshu], *Taishō Tripitaka* 1970, 47, pp. 269c–275a, edition *The SAT Taizōkyō Text Database* (1998–2008), http://21dzk.l.u-tokyo.ac.jp/SAT/ddb-sat2.php?mode=detail&nonum=&kaeri= &mode2=2&useid=1970_,47,0258a01; last accessed 1 July 2011.

kill sentient beings deliberately in order to make a living. The same is true of sericulturalists, and by extension merchants, who might deal in silk. Those responsible for killing were obliged to appeal frequently to Amitabha and to vow that all the sentient beings killed by their direct or indirect action should be reborn in the paradise of the Pure Land. The prostitute and the wine seller are called upon to vow that all those led astray by their doings should likewise be reborn in paradise. Maids and servants should succumb to the destiny that theirs was a subaltern position, but work to improve their positions in this or the next life. The position of the artisan, especially the carpenter, is ambivalent. He is doing good for others by providing them with housing or material objects, but he cannot gain riches through his profession, nor can he afford to live in the houses he has built. Yet working with utmost diligence will also lay the foundations for his karmic improvement. Unexpectedly, the soldier is not condemned for killing living beings.[29] For this group, service to the state is deemed to be both important and desirable. The text stresses that this class is nourished by the tax payments of the commoners and admonishes soldiers to be aware of that fact. They should be mindful of their task of maintaining peace and of working for the security of the state and the people.[30]

As can be seen from family precepts, such convictions of what was a desirable profession and what was not did not remain confined to the religious realm; they also pervaded the secular sphere to a certain extent. Ideas about enhancing one's karma on more general terms, expressed in so-called "ledgers of merit and demerit" in morality books, but without the direct relationship to professional occupations, originate from the Song,[31] such as those of Wang and Yan. In the late Ming and early Qing, they were taken up again as ideas about individual self-cultivation took on greater importance and certainty about one's place in society gave way in the course of continued commercialization and growing political and social ambiguity.[32]

LEGAL PROVISIONS ON FREE AND UNFREE LABOUR

The Great Ming Code was established in several stages soon after the Ming dynasty was founded; it was finalized in 1397, and applied in

29. *Ibid.*, p. 272a.
30. *Ibid.*, p. 274a/b.
31. Cynthia Brokaw, *The Ledgers of Merit and Demerit: Social Change and Moral Order in Late Imperial China* (Princeton, NJ, 1991).
32. Kenneth Kuan Sheng Chen, *Buddhism in China: A Historical Survey* (Princeton, NJ, 1964), pp. 436–438, refers to works such as Yüan Liao-fan's (1533–1606) *Yinzhi lu* [Record of Silent Recompense], or the Buddhist monk Zhuhong's (1535–1615) *Zizhi lu* [Record of Self-Knowledge].

adjudication together with an increasing corpus of sub-statutes. It defined crimes and punishments, and the general principles for the application of the law.[33] Labour-related legislation concerned administrative tasks executed by officials and sub-officials, military discipline, standards of security, the obligations of hired artisans in government workshops or those that fulfilled *corvée* duties, particular groups in the household registration system, such as salt producers, and finally convict labour, which was also exploited in salt and iron production.[34] The disciplinary intention of this codification is very clear, and it extended from minor to capital crimes. Obedience, diligence, and punctuality were instilled in over a million people working in tributary labour relations.

Legislation on labour issues between civilians was not codified into specialized categories. The Ming penal code did specify general classes of crime to which labour conflicts could also lead, such as cursing, physical violence, and homicide.[35] Philip C.C. Huang has suggested that the Qing code perceived subsistence agriculture on independent family farms as the standard pattern of economic organization.[36] Accordingly, neither the Qing nor the Ming codes showed much concern with hired wage labour, although its existence is attested to.

To conceptualize the difference between free and unfree labour in Ming China, it is necessary to consider the status of "good" commoners (*liangmin*) and that of the debased class (*jianmin*). These concepts are not clearly defined in the Ming penal code. In Qing law, mean people included "slaves or bondservants (*nupu*), entertainers, including prostitutes and actors (*changyou*), and those employees of government offices who were usually referred to as 'yamen runners' (*lizu*)".[37] In Ming penal law, the "servants" or "slaves" (*nubi, nupu*) formed the lowest stratum in society, and an intermediate class of tenant farmers and hired labourers also emerged in that society. The status of the debased class was abolished by government decree between 1723 and 1735.[38] This explicitly referred to particular regionally confined groups in the empire, such as "musician households" in Shanxi and Shaanxi provinces, "beggar households" or "fallen/lazy people"

---

33. Jiang Yonglin, "Introduction", in *idem* (transl.), *The Great Ming Code: Da Ming lü*, (Seattle, WA [etc.], 2005), p. lv.
34. *The Great Ming Code*, ch. 2, "Laws on Personnel"; Articles 182–201, "Laws on Military Affairs"; ch. 7, "Laws on Public Works"; ch. 3, "Laws on Revenue", Section 1, "Households and Corvée Services".
35. *Ibid.*, ch. 6, Section 1, Articles 277–304, "Violence and Robbery"; Section 2, Articles 305–324, "Homicide"; Section 3, Articles 325–346, "Affrays and Batteries"; Section 4, Article 347–366, "Cursing".
36. Philip C.C. Huang, *Code, Custom, and Legal Practice in China: The Qing and the Republic Compared* (Stanford, CA, 2001), p. 2.
37. Anders Hansson, *Chinese Outcasts: Discrimination and Emancipation in Late Imperial China* (Leiden, 1996), p. 1.
38. *Ibid.*, p. 2.

(*duomin*) in the Yangzi Delta, and people living on boats (Dan households) in South China,[39] as well as to hereditary retainers in Huizhou prefecture.[40]

The group of bondservants is the most difficult to define, as has been shown by Joseph McDermott and Harriet Zurndorfer. Their status varied between the extremely unfree and the almost free. The fact that "they could own, inherit, sell, and rent land and moreover, exploit other [bondservants]" complicates the situation.[41] As a rule, the bondservants and their families were recorded on the household register of the master; they no longer existed as independent households and often took on the family name of their masters.[42] Their status could be hereditary or non-hereditary,[43] and was not in all cases permanent. When people commended themselves to the patronage of powerful households, a phenomenon that increased during the very late Ming years, there were cases where they were not even dispossessed of their property.[44]

The tasks of bonded labourers included services for the landlord, such as security, entertainment, assisting at family rituals, and carrying sedan chairs.[45] Article 272 of the Great Ming Code specifically forbade the habit of powerful or wealthy households demanding that their tenants carry the master's sedan chairs at no charge as part of their obligations. Instead, the sedan chair carriers had to be reimbursed.[46] However, from the perspective of the lawgiver this humiliation of the tenants was the lesser offence. Nobody was entitled to be carried in a sedan chair unless with official authorization. Consequently, the breach of the statutory law was a more serious crime, which was sanctioned with corporal punishment of sixty strokes with the heavy stick.[47] That tenants were randomly used for the purposes of landlords is also remarked on and criticized in a mid-sixteenth century agricultural handbook which lists transport of rice and weighing flour as typical tasks unreasonably demanded of bondservants or tenants.[48]

In the context of labour relations, an important issue is the transition from bonded labour to the freer arrangements of hired labour and tenancy.

39. *Ibid.*
40. Cheng Pei-kai *et al.* (eds), *The Search for Modern China: A Documentary Collection* (New York [etc.], 1999), pp. 69–70: "Yongzheng's Edict on Changing the Status of the Mean People".
41. Zurndorfer, *Change and Continuity in Chinese Local History*, p. 198.
42. McDermott, "Bondservants in the T'ai-hu Basin", p. 679.
43. *Ibid.*, p. 680.
44. *Ibid.*, p. 684.
45. Zurndorfer, *Change and Continuity in Chinese Local History*, p. 199.
46. *The Great Ming Code*, Article 272, p. 151, "Making Commoners Carry Sedan Chairs without Authorization". The paragraph states that sedan chair carriers had to be reimbursed at a rate of 60 cash per day.
47. *Ibid.*
48. *Shenshi nongshu* [Mr Shen's Book on Agriculture], alternative title: *Bu nong shu*, [The Farmer's Help], compiled by Zhang Lüxiang (Beijing, 1956), p. 44.

The transition occurred at a time corresponding roughly to the late Ming and early Qing. From the 1580s, workers hired for one year or longer were considered legally inferior to their employers. In consequence, crimes committed by hired labourers were sanctioned more harshly than those of their masters or other commoners. For instance, Article 336 of the Great Ming Code, which concerns "Honourable and Mean Persons Striking Each Other", stipulates (§3) that striking hired labourers was not punishable if no bone fractures were caused; if fractures occurred, the penalty was to be reduced by one degree from that for ordinary civilians.[49] The code spells out more crimes that were to be punished with different severity according to the status (slave, hired worker, ordinary civilian) of the person who committed it. It was only in the course of the eighteenth century that the status of the hired labourers was improved.[50]

During the Qing dynasty, which had already established its rule in Manchuria by 1636, a particular group of bondservants rose to importance. They were specifically subject to the service of the government and military establishment, which was registered in the so-called Eight Banners. Individuals having the hereditary status of bondservant could nevertheless attain official positions of great influence and receive substantial emoluments, as did Cao Yin (1658–1712), Director of the Imperial Weaveries and Salt Commissioner.

In sum, the Ming Code is explicit about crimes committed while on duty in the service of the state, and crimes involving corporal violence that occurred between private employers and employees. Yet legislative rules for litigation between civilians that concerned wage issues or other labour-related conflicts not leading to assault and battery were still beyond the focus of mid- and late-Ming legislation. There is sound evidence of such litigation only from the late eighteenth century onward.[51]

THE RANKING OF INDIVIDUAL OCCUPATIONS

The Ming Code specifies a variety of occupations directly linked to particularly low status. Generally speaking, "mean people" were legally discriminated against and suffered higher penalties than commoners or officials for the same crime. Marriage between those social outcasts and

---

49. *The Great Ming Code*, Article 336.
50. Kang Chao, *Man and Land in Chinese History: An Economic Analysis* (Stanford, CA, 1986), pp. 157, 145; Èmilija Pavlovna Stuzhina, "The Economic Meaning of Some Terms in Chinese Feudal Handicrafts", *Archiv Orientální*, 35 (1967), pp. 232–243.
51. See Christine Moll-Murata, "Legal Conflicts Concerning Wage Payments in Eighteenth- and Nineteenth-Century China: The Baxian Cases", in Jane Kate Leonard and Ulrich Theobald (eds), *Small Currencies Matter: Trade and Transactions in Early Modern East Asian Economies* (Leiden, forthcoming).

commoners was also forbidden.[52] Musicians and actors were particularly singled out as partners not suitable to marry.[53]

An idea of how particular occupations were ranked can be demonstrated using family precepts, a common genre in the Ming that became even more widespread during the Qing. This was also closely linked to the perception of the four occupational groups and those not covered by these four great categories. The family precepts of the Huo clan in Foshan from 1481, for instance, explain which occupations are to be avoided: gunpowder production, because it is too dangerous and many people die from it – sulphur is bad for one's health; entering kilns and laying bricks (i.e. kiln building) – the kiln might collapse; gelding animals and selling beef – those who slaughter pigs should also change their trade; learning martial arts and soldiery; counterfeiting cash and making false silver ingots; catching wild birds or snakes; iron smelting and producing cooking pans, copper gongs, or other metal implements – the danger of fires should not be underestimated; work relating to funerals – only carpentry is acceptable (presumably for coffins); repairing umbrellas, because of the smell; and collecting rags, which is a demeaning job.[54]

From these prescriptions, with their restrictions on occupations that involve the killing of living beings and human death, the fear of high-risk occupations and a certain affinity with Buddhist and Daoist principles can be understood. Such notions certainly prevailed in the greater part of the population. This is not to say that everybody shared the values of the Huos of Foshan, one of the thriving industrial and commercial centres in the vicinity of Canton.

There is a dark side to one of the trades considered respectable in the family precepts of the Huos: carpentry. According to studies by Klaas Ruitenbeek, the reason why it was respected but also feared was that carpenters were thought to be able to influence the fates of those living in the houses they constructed by means of building magic.[55] The manual for carpenters, *Lu Ban jing*, a rare example of an architectural guidebook written by a practitioner for the practitioner, includes a large variety of protective and harmful charms which can be incorporated into parts of newly built or renovated houses. It also points out which positions are auspicious or ill-fated for any type of construction. The charms described in the book were thought to be able to influence the lives of all humans

52. *The Great Ming Code*, Articles 119, 121.
53. *Ibid.*, Article 119.
54. *Ming Qing Foshan beike wenxian jingji ziliao* [Economic Materials in Ming and Qing Foshan Epigraphy], Guangdong sheng shehui kexueyuan lishi yanjiusuo Zhongguo gudaishi yanjiushi *et al.* (eds) (Guangzhou, 1987), p. 476.
55. Klaas Ruitenbeek, *Carpentry and Building in Late Imperial China: A Study of the Fifteenth-Century Carpenter's Manual* Lu Ban jing (Leiden, 1993), pp. 83–84.

and animals dwelling in the respective houses or stables. A protective charm might be:

> If two coins are put on the ridge-pole, one left and one right, long life, wealth and happiness will prevail. The husband will win fame, the son will obtain a noble rank, and titles of honour will be bestowed on the wife. Sons and grandsons will wear robes of office for generations to come.[56]

A negative charm would be: "A broken rice bowl and a single chopstick cause sons and grandsons to end up as beggars. Lacking food and clothing, they will be always cold and hungry, after having sold their house, they will live under bridges or in temples."[57] Both objects were meant to be hidden in the door frame.

The rationality behind the warning to beware of the wrath of carpenters has already been analysed by contemporary observers. Some of them were convinced that this sorcery was justified by the stinginess and maltreatment of carpenters by employers or customers.[58] Yet, keeping the carpenters contented was not only a matter of fair wages or prices for the labour they performed. As Ruitenbeek explains, the social position of carpenters was very lowly relative to the importance of their technical skills in everyday life.[59] According to Shi Tianji (1659–after 1737), the author of a household encyclopaedia from Yangzhou, the best way to prevent harmful building magic was to acknowledge the skills of the carpenters and treat them fairly:

> In general, sorcery is suggested to carpenters by the clients' exaggerated stinginess and preoccupation with trivialities. In my opinion it is absolutely necessary to serve meat once every four or five days. If in addition to that you put on a friendly face and speak kind words, if you treat them leniently when you know that they are suffering from hunger and cold, then the carpenters will no doubt produce their best efforts for you.[60]

It is thus very likely that carpenters adopted a menacing image which would cause customers to pay the prices and wages demanded in return for a high quality of construction and the security of their homes and families.

One of the most famous characterizations of urban occupations originates from Chen Duo (c.1488–c.1521). Chen held a hereditary office as a guard commander in the large metropolis, Nanjing, but he was also an

---

56. *Ibid.*, p. 303.
57. *Ibid.*, p. 301.
58. *Ibid.*, p. 89.
59. *Ibid.*, p. 83.
60. *Ibid.*, p. 115, citing the chapter on building in Shi Tianji (i.e. Shi Chengjin), *Jiabao quanji* [Complete Collection of Household Treasures], published in 1707 and reprinted in 1737.

accomplished composer, scenario writer, musician, poet, and painter.[61] In realistic descriptions this author captured what was typical about people from all walks of life in this large city.[62] Chen did not explicitly rank the occupations, as in family prescriptions or Buddhist exhortations. Rather, his collection of 136 songs, "Huaji yuyun" [The Entertainer's Abundant Rhymes], covers a wide variety of occupations and professions in manufacture and in the private and public service sectors, as well as in branches of trade, with one song dedicated to each occupation or shop.[63] The songs were combined in the Chinese conventional order, according to the particular melodies and rhythmic patterns on which they were sung. They are formulated in simple language and enjoyed great popularity. They were first published in a collection of 1611 and reprinted several times.

What strikes the reader about these couplets is the ironic tone of many of them, as well as the hint of social critique, and the sympathy expressed especially with the lowbrows of Nanjing city. In some of the poems, the author takes the perspective of the workers, asserting their importance. The scaffolder says "The scaffold dangles dangerously in the air; if it wasn't for me, who could do this job?",[64] and the worker who bows cotton to fluff it up, "If you want it warm and cosy, you can't do without me".[65] The connection between the mechanism of supply and demand and the value of goods and services is expressed in many of the verses. The firewood and charcoal dealers are chided for selling their goods at high prices in the cold season, thereby taking advantage of the hungry and poor.[66] In contrast, the lantern dealers, who sell decorative articles for festivals, should store their goods until next year if customers are "too lazy to buy".[67]

61. William H. Nienhauser, Jr (ed.), *The Indiana Companion to Traditional Chinese Literature* (Bloomington, IN, 1986), p. 235.
62. Liang Fangzhong, *Zhongguo lidai hukou, tiandi, tianfu tongji* [Statistics on Chinese Historical Demography, Land, and Land Tax] (Shanghai, 1993), p. 203. Data quoted from official sources are given for Yingtian fu, the prefecture which included Nanjing and its rural hinterland. The population in 1491 is given as 711,000, in 1578 as 790,500.
63. A variant reading of the title is "Guji yuyun". The edition used here is a slightly shortened compilation: Chen Duo, "Huaji yuyun", in Lu Gong (ed.), *Mingdai gequ xuan* [Selected Songs of the Ming Dynasty] (Beijing, 1959), pp. 1–21, which includes 113 songs. Some of the occupations and businesses included in the original text are omitted from the 1959 compilation, such as Confucian scholars, doctors, elementary school teachers, veterinarians, prostitutes, and shops for coffins and funerary clothes. The complete compilation is available online under the title *Zuoyin xiansheng jingding Huaji yuyun* [Carefully Edited Abundant Rhymes of the Entertainer by Mr Zuoyin] on the website of the China-America Digital Academic Library at http://ia700507.us.archive.org/10/items/02110818.cn/02110818.cn.pdf; last accessed 13 July 2011.
64. Chen Duo, "Huaji yuyun", p. 10.
65. *Ibid.*
66. *Ibid.*, p. 17, *chaitan hang* [Firewood and Charcoal Dealers].
67. *Ibid.*, p. 11, *deng shi* [The Lantern Market].

Chen Duo bestows the most praise on those artisans whose fortunes were based on their skill and industriousness rather than good luck or nobility. For instance, the bricklayer is described as follows:

> He handles the plaster until his old age,
> He exhausts all his energy over decennia,
> And yet, the deer may wander through the [scattered] mansions of the Jins and Zhangs,
> Wild grass may grow over the residences of the Wangs and Xies,
> Yet there's nothing as durable as the trowel for plastering in his hand.[68]

Honour is likewise accorded to other artisans who are continuously and industriously engaged in production, even though their crafts do not earn them wealth, and even though they sleep little and work until late at night. This includes the wood turners – always sitting with their backs bent – and the felt makers – who have to withstand the stench of their materials.[69] Greed and acquisitiveness are often commented on ironically. Thus Chen Duo criticizes the midwife who, immediately upon the birth of the child, says that she expects an honorarium for "washing the child on the third day".[70]

Others less fortunate than those who could learn a craft or profession also appear in these verses, and sympathy is expressed for the lot of beggars, peddlers, load carriers, and donkey drivers.[71] Sarcasm is heaped on service trades that are shown to be superfluous and useless, such as marriage matchmakers, who do not always find perfect matches,[72] or Daoist and Buddhist clergy, who think more about worldly matters such as food and money than about giving spiritual guidance, or whose reason for turning to Buddha was lost love rather than spiritual awakening, as in the case of the Buddhist nun. Soothsayers, geomantic advisers, who were consulted about the right position for siting graves, and quack doctors also belonged to this category.[73] Moreover, the author criticizes cheating and fraudulent practices, such as those of building contractors who sold used and rotten materials pretending they were new, and the wasteful

---

68. *Ibid.*, p. 6, *wajiang* [The Bricklayer]. The Jins and Zhangs held hereditary high office in the second and first centuries BC. The Wangs and Xies were famous noble families of the third to the sixth centuries AD.
69. *Ibid.*, p. 8, *xuanjiang* [The Wood Turner], *mujiang* [The Carpenter], *jijiang* [The Weaver]; p. 9, *zhanjiang* [The Felt Maker].
70. *Ibid.*, p. 14, *yinpo* [The Midwife].
71. *Ibid.*, p. 15, *qi'er* [The Beggar Boy]; p. 16, *tiao dan* [Carrying Loads on the Bamboo Pole], *gan jiao* [Driving the Donkey], *tui che* [Pushing the Cart].
72. *Ibid.*, p. 9, *meiren* [The Matchmaker].
73. *Ibid.*, p. 5, *daoshi* [The Daoist Priest], *heshang* [The Buddhist Monk], *nigu* [The Buddhist Nun], *miaozhu* [The Temple Precept]; p. 6, *mingshi* [The Fortune Teller]; p. 14, *xiang mian* [The Physiognomist], *wushi* [The Shaman], *daoren* [The Daoist], *zangshi* [The Funeral Master]; p. 10, *mai zhang* [The Quack Doctor].

lifestyles of those who made excessive profits, such as the salt merchants in charge of the government monopoly on salt, and business brokers in general.[74] The last group of professions in the collection are those in menial public security service, such as guardsmen at gates, archers, prison wardens, escorts for convicts, and the informants of officials. Quite obviously, the author was well acquainted with these, and considers their services useful, though in some cases gruesome.[75]

In sum, this set of skilled and unskilled occupations in crafts and services and trade establishments of all types conveys a nuanced image of a complex socio-economic structure. Here human labour was highly commodified and commercial transactions were carefully monitored by the municipal authorities. Fairness was valued highly in these verses. It is symbolized in the subsequent poems on shops that sell scales and shops that sell dry measures for grains delivered as tax payment at public granaries. Not all the poems are ironic. Some, such as the latter two, insist on the importance of honesty in producing and selling scales and measures. Behaviour of this type, in addition to skilled work in either trade, as, for example, of the butcher, whose dexterous handling of his knives earned him approval,[76] is clearly the ideal expressed here. This type of work ethics can be characterized as merchant and artisan ethics.

GENDERED DIVISION OF LABOUR

As can be seen from the previous source, although not represented to the same extent as male workers, women were all but absent from the streets of Nanjing. Specific poems are dedicated to the Buddhist nun, the prostitute, the female peddler, and the midwife. The fisherman's wife, who mends the nets, is mentioned in the entry on the fisherman's household.[77]

Estimates of the extent of urbanization during the Ming suggest rough figures of between 9 and 10 per cent, with great variance among China's macro-regions.[78] Life in rural settings could imply various degrees of production for self-subsistence and for the market. Between 1500 and 1650 commercialization had also reached the countryside, where the number of

74. *Ibid.*, p. 18, *jiahu* [The Building Contractor]; p. 17, *yanshang* [The Salt Merchant]; p. 15, *yaren* [The Broker].
75. *Ibid.*, p. 20, *menzi* [The Guardian at the Gate], *qianzi* [The Policeman], *jinzi* [The Prison Escort], *kuzi* [The Bailiff]; p. 21, *xun lan* [The Street Gate Patrolman], *gong bing* [The Arrow Shooter], *zaoli* [The Police Runner], *fangfu* [The Guardsman in the Prison], *laoren* [The Old Man who Informs the Officers].
76. *Ibid.*, p. 18, *tuhu* [The Butcher's Household].
77. *Ibid.*, *yuhu* [The Fisherman's Household].
78. Cao, *Zhongguo renkou shi*, IV, p. 368. After the capital had been moved from Nanjing to Beijing, the rate of urbanization in the north increased; Cao (p. 219) estimated it at between 17 and 18 per cent.

market towns increased. This trend occurred earlier in the north. In the Yangzi Delta it was later, though stronger and more sustained.[79] For the latter region, Li Bozhong assumes that about 10 per cent of the rural population did not depend on agriculture for a living.[80]

Since the foundation of Imperial China in the third century BC, taxation in kind for farming households included grains and textiles. The theoretical gender division of labour implied that men did the agricultural work and women wove fabrics. This principle was expressed as *"nangeng nüzhi"* [men plough, women weave]. In her studies on gender and labour in China, Francesca Bray has pointed out that although this norm was maintained as an ideological guideline by all dynasties, in reality it was gradually eroded.[81]

In the Ming dynasty Confucian elites tried to reverse this trend in order to correct conditions towards what seemed to be proper relationships within households. Their efforts, which included reintroducing sericulture and silk weaving in regions where it had long since been abandoned owing to lack of profitability, were also implemented with enthusiasm by the Qing emperors until the eighteenth century.[82] According to Bray, to Confucian intellectuals and officials "the economic significance of work was at best secondary".[83] Orthopraxy, doing the right thing at the right time, was at stake when men wove and women worked in the fields or took up other economically profitable occupations such as growing or processing cash crops.[84] If gender roles in the division of labour were changed, that might endanger social stability and the hierarchical structure of society, with its basic differentiation between those who wielded power in the state and those who were ruled, between the elder and the younger generations, and between the sexes.

Bray demonstrates that the social reality was quite different from what conservatives considered to be the correct order. Some activist local administrators would promote female silk making in districts where it had died out. Among them were the sixteenth-century governor Lü Kun, who tried to reintroduce silk making in the northern province of Shanxi, and the mid-eighteenth century governor Chen Hongmou in neighbouring Shaanxi province. For Lü Kun, women who did not work in sericulture, silk reeling, or silk weaving seemed to be "without occupation", no matter

79. Heijdra, "The Socio-Economic Development", pp. 508–509.
80. Li Bozhong, *Agricultural Development in Jiangnan, 1620–1850* (Houndmills, 1998), p. 23.
81. Francesca Bray, "Towards a Critical History of Non-Western Technology", in Timothy Brook and Gregory Blue (eds), *China and Historical Capitalism: Genealogies of Sinological Knowledge* (Cambridge, 1999), pp. 158–209; Francesca Bray, *Technology and Gender: Fabrics of Power in Late Imperial China* (Berkeley, CA, 1997), pp. 226–237.
82. Bray, "Critical History of Non-Western Technology", p. 197.
83. *Ibid.*, p. 191.
84. *Ibid.*

what other work they actually did.[85] Meanwhile, especially in the Yangzi Delta, men had long since taken over work in textile production. In the cities they worked as professional high-class silk weavers, and some made a living by calendering, a finishing process in which cotton cloth is pressed by heavy stone rollers. In the course of time, in the rural proto-industry in the Yangzi Delta, entire families would often work either in silk weaving or in cotton production and processing, and no longer produce their own food.[86]

On the other hand, evidence that women did continuously work in the fields, and thus, from the point of view of conservative circles, assumed the role of the men, is not very firm. Li Bozhong observed an actual increase in specialization in agricultural work for men and textile work for women, at least in the Yangzi Delta, with a peak in the mid-eighteenth century.[87] Li asserts that there are many indications in mid-Qing sources that women participated in farm work, but this was mostly weeding, harvesting, or pumping water, which, he argues, was not continuous physical labour carried out under great time pressure, unlike preparing the soil or transplanting rice seedlings.[88] According to this view, women abandoned any previous agricultural occupations for the more profitable textile work of sericulture, silk reeling, and cotton spinning and weaving in those regions where this was possible.

Depending on the respective food crops and textiles, such activities could be even more profitable. From evidence for the nineteenth-century Yangzi Delta, we know that a woman spinning and weaving cotton for 200 working days would earn 83 per cent of what a hired labourer would receive for working 180 days, and if she were engaged throughout the whole year she could feed herself and 1.5 other people.[89]

This suggests that in the economically most advanced regions, gender roles in the division of labour were not inverted, and that the general tendency was for both men and women – and children – to take up or be made to participate in the more profitable occupations, if circumstances permitted. An important source for the situation in the heart of the Yangzi Delta, entitled *Bu nong shu* [Farmers' Help] or *Shenshi nongshu* [Mr Shen's Book on Agriculture], was written and circulated in Huzhou prefecture. Its author made suggestions to landowners for the efficient management of estates. In its initial form it can be dated to the last years of the Ming dynasty, in the 1640s; additions from later compilers bear the dates 1658 and 1662.

Next to technical information on the timing of agricultural processes, plant protection, and raising silkworms, the book includes advice on personnel administration, such as wage payments, provisions in kind,

---

85. *Ibid.*, pp. 186, 197.
86. *Ibid.*, p. 190.
87. Li, *Agricultural Development in Jiangnan*, p. 147.
88. *Ibid.*, p. 146.
89. *Ibid.*, p. 150.

especially food and drink, and the general treatment of farmhands, hired textile workers, and tenants. It also comments on the gendered division of labour and makes observations on smaller family farms. While affirming the tenet that "men plough, women weave", it reported that in this particular region every family was weaving. Advice is given on how to calculate the costs and the gains of hiring two women to weave silk for one year, including their wages and provisions.[90] About food provisions, the author holds that "although women and girl servants cannot do really hard physical work, they should still get a taste [of good food and drink], because how could someone who never gets a bite of meat for a long time not stretch out their hand and steal it?"[91] As for the rations of rice, served in soup and as plain, cooked rice, "women receive half of the male rations".[92]

The section devoted to female employees and female work (*nü gong*) states that as a rule, in the western villages of Huzhou, they mostly wove cotton cloth, reeled silk, and spun and produced linen, while in the eastern villages they either raised mulberry trees and carried out miscellaneous agricultural tasks or they wove.[93] Comparing the contribution to household income from female labour and male labour respectively, the author asserts that the fortunes of the family depended on the industriousness of the wife. "Even though she concerns herself only with silkworms and hemp, which does not seem to make much difference for the economic fate of the household, her diligence will cause all other activities to flourish, and her laziness will make them fail."[94] The author does not expressly mention household work and child rearing.

Returning to the question of whether women were engaged in any agricultural labour at all, this handbook, which treats the cultivation of rice, other grains and vegetables, mulberry trees, and cattle raising, does not mention any gendered division of labour for those activities. Women are explicitly mentioned only at one point, where it admonishes the farmer that "wheat should be sown very evenly. Don't save on labour on this or let women or servants be remiss [with this assignment]".[95]

As opposed to India and Japan,[96] where transplanting rice was one of the prominent tasks of women, there is less evidence in Chinese sources. In a large encyclopaedia, one reference to a rice-transplanting song ("Cha yang ge"), by the author Yang Wanli, has the verses, "The farmers throw the rice seedlings, the farmer women catch them, the small children

90. *Shenshi nongshu*, p. 20.
91. *Ibid.*, pp. 15–16.
92. *Ibid.*, p. 16.
93. *Ibid.*, p. 45.
94. *Ibid.*
95. *Ibid.*, p. 9.
96. For Japan see the contribution by Regine Mathias in this volume. I am indebted to Shireen Moosvi for pointing out that rice transplanting was a female task in Mughal India, and that women rather than men controlled the timing of transplantation.

pull up the seedlings, the big children insert them."[97] Two more entries are
more specific to one particular region. The section on the local customs of
the prefecture in the gazetteer for Yunyang in present-day Hubei province[98]
says that "men and women both transplant rice seedlings, they play the drum
and sing with it".[99] This is even more explicit for Jingzhou prefecture, in the
same province. "For transplanting rice seedlings, they often employ women,
the men beat the drum to show the rhythm, or they transport the food.
When asked, they reply: '[Our] hands and feet are clumsy and slow, not as
nimble as those of the girls'."[100]

That the other forty-three references in this encyclopaedia are not gender-specific cannot entirely answer the question, but, as the last one cited
shows, the fact that women transplanted rice was so unusual for some
observers that they had to inquire about it. Possibly the various risicultural
regions of China were characterized by different habits. One sample given
in Francesca Bray's work refers to yet another region in Hubei province
where women, who might not have belonged to the ethnic Han, worked
the earth with a hoe.[101] To the Confucian ideal of decorum, which saw
the home as the proper place of female labour, this was a breach in the
behavioural code, which might disrupt the social order.[102]

For promoting the traditional social hierarchy, including the gendered
division of labour, Confucian elites and the ruling Manchu emperors provided the public with positive illustrative images of a harmonious agricultural
work setting. This can best be seen in the *Gengzhi tu* [Illustrations of
Ploughing and Weaving], an album of illustrations with poems on risiculture
and sericulture. It was first published between 1137 and 1145,[103] and was
subsequently reprinted and expanded, especially to include poems by Qing
dynasty emperors. It was also adapted in Japan and Korea.[104] Despite its

---

97. Chen Menglei *et al.* (compilers), *Gu jin tushu jicheng* [Collected Charts and Writings Old and
New], compiled 1726–1728, photo-mechanical reproduction of the Shanghai edition (1934), ch. 23.
98. In the Ming dynasty, present-day Hubei and Hunan formed Huguang province.
99. Chen, *Gu jin tushu jicheng*, ch. 1160, vol. 152, p. 9/2.
100. *Ibid.*
101. Bray, "Critical History of Non-Western Technology", p. 197.
102. Note, however, that for northern Jiangsu there is evidence of this type in the work songs
that were collected in the twentieth century. "[In the fourth month of the lunar year] Eighteen
girls step into the planting rows, but if they're in their planting rows and have no seedlings to
transplant, they scold the long-term worker [who did not bring them with enough speed from
the seedbed]"; Shi Lin *et al.* (eds), *Zhongguo minjian gequ jicheng. Jiangsu juan* [Collection of
Chinese Folk Songs. Jiangsu Section] (Beijing, 1998), I, pp. 135–136, "Shi'er yue changgong ku"
[The Toil of the Long-Contract Worker in Twelve Months].
103. *Keng-tschi t'u, Ackerbau und Seidengewinnung in China; ein kaiserliches Lehr- und
Mahnbuch* (Hamburg, 1913), p. 70.
104. *Ibid.*, p. 74; Francesca Bray, "Agricultural Illustrations: Blueprint or Icons?", in *idem
et al.* (eds), *Graphics and Text in the Production of Technical Knowledge in China: The Warp
and the Weft* (Leiden, 2007), pp. 521–568, 531.

Figure 1. The print shows that transplanting rice seedlings was a male task; an onlooker is present, in this case a woman with food containers.
Keng-tschi t'u, Ackerbau und Seidengewinnung in China; ein kaiserliches Lehr- und Mahnbuch *(Hamburg, 1913), plate 28, ill. I.9. Japanese reprint, dated 1676, of a Chinese woodblock print edition of 1462.*[105] *Reproduced courtesy of Walter de Gruyter publishers, Berlin/Munich. Used with permission.*

increasing distance from reality, this was the work that exemplified what, since the twelfth century, had been deemed the proper division of labour: that between men and women, the elder and the younger, the landowning and the employed, and between industrious rice farmers, silkworm raisers, and weavers.

LABOUR CONFLICTS AND WAGES

Labour conflicts apparently increased in the late Ming dynasty. Some of them were indirectly related to remuneration, but these were no simple wage conflicts such as those that can be found in the legal records of the eighteenth century. Theoretical debates on the concept of a just wage, depending on skill and the specific contracts between employers and

---

105. A digital version can be found on the website "Digitale Texte der Bibliothek des Seminars für Wirtschafts- und Sozialgeschichte, Universität Köln", http://www.digitalis.uni-koeln.de/digitaletexte.html; last accessed 2 July 2011.

employees, such as the treatise by Zacchia,[106] were rare in sixteenth- and seventeenth-century China. However, the duration of the working day, as well as details concerning non-monetary remuneration in the form of food and drink played a considerable role in the practical planning and accounting of landlords who employed hired labourers. This is evident from "Mr Shen's Book on Agriculture".

According to the book's author, the exact amount of meat, wine, and rice gruel to be served, and the appropriate timings for the meals, in summer and in winter, greatly influenced worker motivation in a period when the price of labour had increased.[107] He gives the following advice:

> The old regulations foresaw that as to ploughing, on every man-day one *mu* [1/6 of a hectare] could be achieved, while as for hoeing, transplanting, and weeding, two *mu* could be worked per day. In days of old, people were used to hard work, they went out and came back when the stars were shining, their habits were obedient and they would listen to the master's orders. Nowadays, people put on haughty and lazy airs; you can't set them to work without wine and food. This is quite different from one hundred years ago. However, if they only perform their jobs well, and if they are supervised according to the right methods, then it is acceptable if they work less, but diligently, than if they work more, but do it coarsely. As for what is offered to them, it is better to be generous. In the hot season, when the days are long, they will be hungry in the afternoon. On winter days in the severe cold, it is difficult to rise with an empty belly. Therefore, in summer, give them additional foods, and in winter, provide them with hot rice soup in the morning.[108]

The text goes on to explain in detail the usual provisions for workers according to the "old rules", and what was necessary at present. For instance, whereas the previous arrangements envisaged workers in summer and autumn being served meat the first day and vegetables on the two subsequent days, it was now necessary to serve meat every other day.[109] As for rice wine, the old regulations indiscriminately envisaged one measure for three persons. Now, workers were to be given one measure per person if they performed hard physical labour, a half measure if the tasks were of medium difficulty, and no wine if they performed light work or remained indoors on rainy days.[110]

All of this shows that labour had become scarcer, putting agrarian workers in a better bargaining position; that it was wages in kind, and food and drink in particular, which could make the difference in terms of

---

106. See Andrea Caracausi's article in the present volume.
107. *Shenshi nongshu*, p. 13: "Both the prices for (human) manure and for labour have become expensive."
108. *Ibid.*, p. 15.
109. *Ibid.*, p. 16.
110. *Ibid.*

work motivation; and that an element of efficiency had been integrated compared with the century prior to "Mr Shen's Book on Agriculture". What was at stake here were market conditions, even if this is not directly addressed in the handbook.

Famous cases of labour unrest included those among silk weavers in Suzhou in 1601, who protested against an extra tax imposed on them by a eunuch tax commissioner. They were to pay a fee for every bolt of silk before it was marketed.[111] With the tacit support of local elites, a relatively small group of silk weavers protested openly and killed several tax collectors in the town.[112]

A similar situation occurred in the Imperial Porcelain Manufactories in Jingdezhen in the same year, when potters protested, in much greater number than the weavers, against another eunuch director who had tried to extort an impossible number of first-grade porcelain wares from them. A few years earlier, Tong Bin, a kiln worker, had thrown himself into the kiln in despair at the excessive demands being made by the same director. Tong became the patron saint of the Jingdezhen potters. Those potters burned down part of the Imperial Manufactory in 1601, and production for the state ceased until the end of the Ming dynasty.[113]

A third field of conflict was mining. This was more latent and less focused on one place or one series of events. During the latter half of the Ming dynasty, coal and mineral miners periodically rose up in protest at the manifold state prohibitions on mining operations that were other than very small scale. The government generally suspected miners of unruliness and of having a high criminal potential because they were migrants and difficult to control.[114]

In all three cases or scenarios, the conflicts were reported by the authorities. No texts recording the thoughts or words of the workers themselves have been transmitted down to us. In the first two situations, later historiography sets the issues into the greater context of discontent with the oppressive administration of eunuch officials. The Qing dynasty, which followed the Ming, often used this feature of the late Ming to legitimize its own rule, and was careful especially to lighten taxation and reduce its dependence on eunuchs for administrative purposes.

111. Cheng, *The Search for Modern China*, p. 2.
112. Tsing Yuan, "Urban Riots and Disturbances", in Jonathan D. Spence and John E. Wills (eds), *From Ming to Ch'ing: Conquest, Region, and Continuity in Seventeenth-Century China* (New Haven, CT [etc.], 1979), pp. 279–320, 287.
113. Michael Dillon, "The Porcelain Industry at Ching-te-chen 1550–1700", *Ming Studies*, 6 (1978), pp. 45–53, 50–51.
114. Bernd Eberstein, *Bergbau und Bergarbeiter zur Ming-Zeit (1368–1644)* (Hamburg, 1974), pp. 137–162.

THE VOICE OF THE WORKERS: SELF-EXPRESSION
IN WORK SONGS

For the period 1500 to 1650 it is difficult to discern the voice of the
workers. Turning to the folk songs collected by nineteenth- and twentieth-
century ethnographers can yield faint echoes of those voices, though.
They cannot be dated with certainty, but it is probable that they originated from after 1650. Since the early twentieth century, systematic
collection projects have been dedicated to Chinese folk songs and stories.
The most recent results of such efforts are two multi-volume series on
Chinese folk songs, one edited in Taiwan and the other in the People's
Republic of China.[115]
Important categories within such collections of Chinese folk songs
include children's songs, love songs, and work songs (*haozi*). That work
was accompanied by singing in order to keep up the rhythm required for
continued repetition of particular procedures can be proven from at least
the Han dynasty (206 BC to AD 220).[116] The term *haozi* for work songs
is more recent and can be dated to the sixteenth century.[117] Some of the
songs in the two collections mentioned refer explicitly to events or objects
in the Republic of China or People's Republic of China, and thus reflect
the changing situation in the twentieth century. Nevertheless, the collections also contain some features that connect to the sixteenth and
seventeenth centuries. One is the typology of work songs, which is related
to work procedures already in existence in the late Ming period; another is
the protagonists of the songs, who worked in labour relationships which
also characterized the period 1500–1650.
Large categories of work songs are the songs for earth pounding and
rice transplanting, the songs of the sailors and fishermen, songs for
guiding oxen and other animals, for carrying loads, and the songs of the
street sellers. These occur, in varying number, in all the provinces in a
sample taken here covering Sichuan in the central west, Shanxi in the

---

115. Shu Lan (ed.) *Zhongguo difang geyao jicheng* [Collection of Chinese Regional Folk
Songs], 65 vols (Taipei, 1989–), which includes historical sources such as the folk songs found
in eighth- and ninth-century Dunhuang documents, and *Zhongguo minjian gequ jicheng*
[Collection of Chinese Folk Songs], 30 vols (Beijing, 1990–2004), which includes over 40,000
songs in a text-critical edition that also offers the music scores. The latter was compiled in a
joint project involving several institutions, under the auspices of the Ministry of Culture of the
People's Republic of China. Both record folk songs in geographical sequence, by province and
smaller administrative units.
116. Chen Zi'ai, "Minjian shige gailun" [An Overview of Popular Songs and Poems], *Xinjiang
Shiyou jiaoyu xueyuan xuebao* [Journal of the Xinjiang Petroleum Institute], 4:4 (1997),
pp. 90–102, 90.
117. Luo Zhufeng *et al.* (eds), *Hanyu da cidian* [Great Chinese Dictionary] (Shanghai, 1991),
VIII, p. 841, traces the first reference to Wu Cheng'en's novel *Xiyou ji* [Journey to the West],
first published in c.1592.

north-west, Shandong, Jiangsu,[118] and Fujian on the east coast, and Guangdong in the south. The categories of labour relations most prominently represented were reciprocal, thus the subsistence farming and household work of the farmers' wives, and commodified labour in the form of long-term or short-term contract workers. One might reasonably surmise that the concentration of explicit social accusation which can be found in the song collections is of a more recent date.[119]

Social accusation occurred in all provinces; it is inherent in the texts as well as in the titles of the songs, such as those from Sichuan province sung by hired labourers: "The conscience of the boss is black", "The heart of the boss is as vicious as a nail board rake".[120] A similar case is that of the farmer's child bride (*tongyang qi* or *xiao xifu*). The system of minor marriage, evident from the tenth century onward, provided for girls to be adopted at a very tender age and raised in the household of their future husband, where they were expected to work for his family.[121] Songs about the plight of both the hired worker and the child bride, whose husband was often younger than herself, could be heard only faintly, if at all, in the sixteenth and seventeenth centuries, but they became more important as the respective labour regimes disappeared or were formally abolished in the twentieth century.

Two examples from Jiangdu in Jiangsu province north of the Yangzi River, thus not the wealthy part of the Yangzi Delta, contain information worthwhile citing here, even though they probably originated after the seventeenth century. Both are structured in a twelve-month sequence, detailing the hardships for the respective times of the year. The narrative in both cases begins in gloom and ends in downright despair.[122] The hired worker starts out in the first month seeing wealthy people celebrating the New Year, but he himself wears poor clothing and cannot get his fill with the meagre meals served at his master's house. The young girl is sent, in the first month, to cut reed and wood for fuel in thorny shrubs, which causes injuries and bleeding. She is given heavy chores, the master and his family scold her continuously, the food and clothing are bad. When she becomes ill, nobody troubles to look after her. After demanding that

118. During the Ming dynasty, the province bore the name of its capital, Nanjing.
119. This assumption is also supported by an observation in the text-critical remarks in the volume on the Jiangsu folksongs, which point to 1840 (the period of the First Opium War) as a starting point for more articulate expression of worker complaints. See Wu Junda, "Jiangsu min'ge gaishu" [An Overview of Jiangsu Folk Songs], in Shi, *Zhongguo minjian gequ jicheng. Jiangsu juan*, I, p. 8.
120. Shu, *Zhongguo difang geyao jicheng*, XLII; *idem* (ed.), *Sichuan min'ge, qingge* [Sichuan Folk Songs and Love Songs] (Taipei, 1989), pp. 61, 63.
121. Hill Gates, *China's Motor: A Thousand Years of Petty Capitalism* (Ithaca, NY, 1996), p. 127.
122. Shi, *Zhongguo minjian gequ jicheng. Jiangsu juan*, I, pp. 134–135, "Xiao xifu ku'nan ai" [The Child Bride Suffers Hardships], and pp. 135–136, "Shi'er yue changgong ku" [The Toil of the Long-Contract Worker in Twelve Months].

wood be acquired for her coffin, she sends for her mother, urging "if mother will arrive one step earlier, we will meet, if she arrives one step slower, she will only be able to cry for me". The editors remark that this song was sung during the rice transplanting process, just as the young shoots were being pulled from the seedbed or "mother field" (*mutian*).

The great variety of tasks carried out by the long-term worker is outlined for each month of the year. During the year, except for bad food and clothing, continuous reprimands for alleged inefficiency oppress him most. Despite the worker weeding, harvesting, and harrowing thirteen *mu* every day, and scooping river mud for fertilizing five to six *mu* per day (compare the two *mu* per day which Mr Shen thought sufficient), the master still scolds him. However, the worst is at the end: in the twelfth month, after the master has calculated his wages, he learns that he has toiled in vain for a whole year. This *topos*, which can be attributed to the fact that certain sums for food or debts incurred could be deducted from the worker's wages, also occurs in other songs of long-term workers, for instance in Sichuan.[123] Yet this is not the entire picture.

Even though labour conditions were oppressive for many of the agricultural population, not all folk songs are work songs, nor do all work songs contain social accusation. In fact, songs of love and courtship prevail in the collections referred to above. Moreover, even though work songs that narrate the position of employers are much rarer, one sample from Shanxi province, again drawing on the twelve-month structure, laments the fact that in the third month workers had to be hired, but that it was very hard to feed them three meals a day, and goes on to enumerate, in the manner of Mr Shen's handbook, all the dishes that needed to be provided.[124] Finally, there are also songs that express the "Joy of the Farmer":

> The joy of the farmer at the end of a prosperous year,
> With mild wind and favourable rain,
> The sprouts came out well. After weeding several times,
> The harvest was good, and he can delight in calmness and leisure.[125]

Though one must be cautious about retrospectively attaching meaning from later to earlier situations, the comparison of the clearly datable textual evidence for the mid- and late-Ming period with more recent folk songs highlights issues that can be understood as continuities spanning the centuries: that the incentives to work among all those who were not actual

123. Shu, *Zhongguo difang geyao jicheng*, XLII; idem, *Sichuan min'ge, qingge*, p. 35, "Changgong ge" [The Song of the Long-Contract Worker].

124. Shu, *Zhongguo difang geyao jicheng*, LIII, *Shanxi*, pp. 217–232, "Nongmin shi'er yue" [The Twelve Months of the Farmer], p. 220.

125. *Ibid.*, p. 177, "Nongfu le" [Joy of the Farmer].

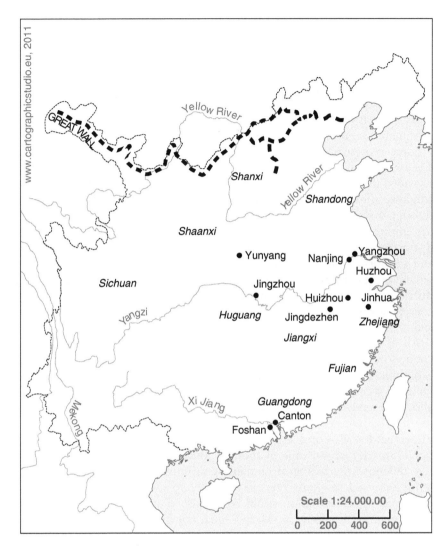

Figure 2. Ming Dynasty China.

family members depended on the investments employers made in terms of monetary remuneration, but much more so on remuneration in kind, and on the social valuation of the workers. Juxtaposing Mr Shen's handbook with the songs of hired workers gives the impression that the bargaining positions of the parties concerned differed markedly over time. However, looking at the small-scale employer of Shanxi province and the Sichuan worker's complaints, the contradiction between employers and employees appears synchronously too.

CONCLUSION

The process of commercialization brought about an increase in markets, which entailed a greater volume of marketable products, business opportunities in distribution, and an expansion in workplace production of both basic materials and processed goods. Farms in economic core areas diversified. In the cities, the service sector expanded, meeting every imaginable need of their residents and visitors.

Some representatives of the Ming state lamented these developments. The system whereby a stable, land-based, self-supplying population provided the revenue necessary for the court and state, and whereby a state administration controlled security, justice, and the livelihood of the people through a sophisticated apparatus of public officials deployed throughout the empire seemed to be at stake. For almost 2,000 years, there had been a distinction between physical (subordinate) work and mental (leadership and administration) work. Moreover, occupations were divided into those which served the basic needs of the state, and those in production and distribution which were perceived of as secondary. A third long-held concept was the gendered division of work, with women working in textiles and men working the land.

All of these tenets seemed threatened to some extent as people left the countryside for the cities, merchants and artisans increasingly took on economically prominent roles, men moved into textile work, and entire families, while remaining in their rural settings, left farming and sericulture altogether and turned to more profitable activities. This situation engendered a literature, sometimes beautifully illustrated, on the norms to be preserved, but also on the need to reconsider those norms.

A distinctly variant line of thought linked human activity to precepts that defended the killing of sentient beings, intoxicating the mind, sexual seduction, and religious exercise in order to attain a state from which the chain of reincarnation could be broken. This was not a mainstream conviction in mid- and late-Ming China, but in weaker forms it could be traced back to family rules on which occupations should be avoided. Moreover, there were points where this type of Buddhist belief and the convictions of state Confucianism coincided. Both argued that, because they served the interests of security and state, warriors should not be reproached for killing sentient beings. Moreover, both shared a critique of the profit motive and human acquisitiveness. Yet in other respects related to occupations, they diverged widely, for instance as to the activities of farmers, silkworm raisers, and butchers.

Looking at one particular field of occupation, the building trade, and carpenters in particular, stand out. For reasons also related to commercialization, carpenters had a mixed reputation because they were suspected of magical practices. Beyond the normative formulations from the realms of political economy and religion, one famous literary source shows a complete set of all urban occupations in Nanjing city. It gives no explicit ranking, but it also values the occupations in question. This is the perspective of the entertainer. On the one hand it displays sarcasm and exaggeration; on the other it reprimands many of those occupations that the Confucians would also chide, especially the clergy. It professes sympathy with the most destitute, a trait familiar also in Confucian thinking. The importance of professionally maintaining public security is affirmed in the portraits of prison wardens, policemen, and guardsmen of various kinds. Most commendable from this perspective are the skills of the craftsman and the honesty of the merchant in using weights and measures. This specific expression was cherished, in its time and ever since, because of the witty characterization of urban professionalism.

In a much more austere and normative sense, the penal legislation of the Ming conveyed a particular work valuation which basically distinguished between the ordinary commoners, officials, and debased groups for which particular occupations were reserved. Among these, bond service was a changing category which evolved, from the sixteenth to the eighteenth centuries, into arrangements involving tenancy and hired labour.

The intention of this article was to come to a view about the variety of perceptions of labour within the empire of the Ming dynasty, and to show the dynamism and longer continuities in thought about work. Was work becoming a commodified category that could be conceived of as distinctly isolated from "non-work" and "anti-work"? The answer must be in the affirmative. Especially in agriculture, monetary value was expressly attached to the time spent in performing labour. The landlord Mr Shen formulated the patriarchal attitude that the livelihood of the farmhands should be well provided for, while at the same time the landlord's economic and social status should be maintained. As we see in some of the work songs, workers believed that the treatment by their employers was not benevolent, but exploitative, and that their efforts were not appreciated. In this perspective, work was something to be endured rather than enjoyed, and the only motive for performing it lay in the urge to survive. In the case of skilled craftspeople or independent farmers, and of the large group who worked in the subsistence and household economy, if more autonomous decisions about its organization and production processes were possible, there was also the prospect that work could generate satisfaction and fulfilment.

IRSH 56 (2011), Special Issue, pp. 197–216 doi:10.1017/S0020859011000411
© 2011 Internationaal Instituut voor Sociale Geschiedenis

Prostitutes and Courtesans in the Confucian Moral Universe of Late Ming China (1550–1644)*

HARRIET T. ZURNDORFER

Leiden University

E-mail: h.t.zurndorfer@hum.leidenuniv.nl

SUMMARY: This study pursues three goals: to unravel the socio-economic conditions which pushed women into prostitution and courtesanship, to analyse their position in Chinese society, and to relate what changes occurred at the end of the Ming dynasty that affected their status. According to contemporary judicial regulations, both prostitutes and courtesans were classified as "entertainers", and therefore had the status of *jianmin* [mean people], which made them "outcasts" and pariahs. But there were great differences, beyond the bestowal of sexual favours, in the kind of work these women performed. That courtesans operated at the elite level of society, and that they were often indistinguishable from women born into the upper or gentry class, is indicative of this era's blurry social strata, which has prompted scholars and writers to elevate the place of the educated courtesan in Ming society.

INTRODUCTION

At some time after 1644, the celebrated literatus Zhang Dai (1597–1689) recorded in his diary *Taoan mengyi* [The Dream Collection of Taoan] the conditions under which both prostitutes and courtesans flourished during the last decades of the Ming dynasty (1368–1644). In a short essay entitled "Yangzhou *shouma*" ["The 'Lean Horses' of Yangzhou"], he wrote:

> In the house of "thin horses" customers were treated to tea and seated to wait for the women. A matchmaker led out all the women, one by one, and gave them instructions; each woman then performed a series of movements for the customer, first bowing, then walking several steps, turning to face toward the light, drawing back her sleeves to show her hands, glancing shyly at the customer to show her eyes, reporting her age, and finally revealing her bound feet. An experienced customer could determine the size of the feet by listening to the noise she made when

* I would like to thank Christine Moll-Murata for all her help with this essay. She obtained a number of texts that were unavailable to me, and also made many valuable suggestions that I have incorporated into this study. In this article east Asian names are given in the sequence family name – personal name. Exceptions are made in cases where authors have adopted Western personal names.

she walked around; the louder the noise from her skirt, the bigger her feet because, if she lifted her skirt to walk around without rustling the fabric, her feet would be revealed. The customer, if not satisfied with any woman, was expected to reward the matchmaker and each servant several *wen* before he left. If he decided to select one of the women, he would put a golden hairpin in her hair near the temple […].[1]

And so it might go on, day after day, inspecting woman after woman, tipping match-maker after matchmaker, until the girls with their powdered faces and their red dresses faded into an indistinguishable blur in which discrimination became impossible.[2]

Yangzhou was not the only location in late Ming China where prostitution and the female entertainment industry thrived – in municipalities all along China's littoral, from Guangzhou to the magnificent cities of the "Lower Yangzi region" (which include Suzhou, Hangzhou, and nearby Nanjing) to the capital Beijing, as well as in inland towns and commercial trading posts, there was a vibrant and highly profitable trade in human beings. As Xie Zhaozhe (1567–1624), a well-known observer of Ming life, wrote about the ubiquity of prostitutes: "In the big cities they run to the tens of thousands, but they can be found in every poor district and remote place as well, leaning by doorways all day long, bestowing their smiles, selling sex for a living."[3]

Given the ambiguity of Ming population figures, it is extremely difficult even to approximate how many persons were involved one way or another in prostitution and the entertainment industry during the Ming dynasty. With a general population figure by the early seventeenth century of c.175 million, as estimated by Timothy Brook,[4] we may assume, using Xie Zhaozhe's quo-tation, that some 1–1.5 million persons would have laboured in this sector. According to the taxonomy of the Global Collaboratory on the History of Labour Relations, this figure includes "labour relation 6" – servants within the household, i.e. those persons who worked within houses of prostitution, as service personnel (cooking, cleaning, fetching, and other domestic tasks) – and "labour relation 14" – wage earners who engaged in sexual relations for a salary. But within this latter category there is a tremendous variation with regard to status and income, from lowly street

1. Hsieh Bao Hua, "The Market in Concubines in Jiangnan during Ming-Qing China", *Journal of Family History*, 33 (2008), pp. 262–290, 272.
2. Jonathan Spence, *Return to Dragon Mountain: Memories of a Late Ming Man* (New York, 2007), p. 33. Spence's translation here is a synopsis based on other sources, including David Pollard, *The Chinese Essay* (London, 2000), pp. 90–92; Victor Mair (ed.), *The Columbia Anthology of Traditional Chinese Literature* (New York, 1994), pp. 597–598; Philip A. Kafalas, "Nostalgia and the Reading of the Late Ming Essay" (unpublished Ph.D. thesis, Stanford University, CA, 1995), pp. 137–138; and idem, *In Limpid Dream: Nostalgia and Zhang Dai's Reminiscences of the Ming* (Norwalk, CT, 2007), p. 95.
3. Xie Zhaozhe, *Wu za zu* [Five Miscellanies], p. 196, cited by Antonia Finnane in, *Speaking of Yangzhou: A Chinese City, 1550–1850* (Cambridge, MA, 2004), pp. 215–216.
4. Timothy Brook, *The Confusions of Pleasure: Commerce and Culture in Ming China* (Berkeley, CA, 1998), p. 162.

walkers to "high-class" courtesans, who could be extremely wealthy, living off their patrons as well as off the rent from the properties they owned.

Yangzhou, of all places, seemed to exemplify all that was reprehensible about commercial sex – by the second half of the Ming era Yangzhou had become the "national centre for the procurement of beautiful girls".[5] The phrase "lean horses" originated in a poem by the Tang dynasty poet Bo Juyi (772–846) in which he lamented the speed at which the ownership of Yangzhou young prostitutes changed hands, and by the Ming era the expression had become a term reserved for girls sold on the Yangzhou market. Among Ming contemporaries, Yangzhou was known for its "production of women" (in the sense of producing apples or other commodities) – literally, *yang shouma* [raising young girls for sale into concubinage or prostitution] – in contrast to the reputation of other locales, with their "secluded and virtuous wives and daughters".[6]

Elite women, i.e. the wives and daughters of men who staffed the imperial bureaucracy or served as leaders in local communities, did not show themselves in public, but this does not mean that they were immune to the rapid economic and social changes occurring during the second half of the sixteenth century. This was a time of extensive economic development and intense commercialization, manifested in an increased degree of local and regional agricultural and manufactured product specialization, the expansion of textile and porcelain industries, growing overseas exchange, large inflows of bullion, an improved transport and communications infrastructure, and, not least, a vibrant publishing industry.[7] Cities flourished as never before: urban prosperity stimulated the promotion of cosmopolitanism, anonymity, and relative freedom in the attendant pleasure districts, which attracted a wide range of clientele, from literati and students seeking relief from the pressures of studying for (and failing) the civil service examinations, to sojourning merchants requiring lavish, conspicuous entertainment for doing business and for their own gratification.[8]

The burgeoning economy also spurred a printing boom which produced a wealth of new reading materials, from fiction and drama to handy "daily" encyclopedias that reached a wide reading public, including

5. Dorothy Ko, *Teachers of the Inner Chambers: Women and Culture in Seventeenth Century China* (Stanford, CA, 1994), p. 261. For more information about Yangzhou, in particular during the Qing dynasty (1644–1911), see the essays in Lucie Olivová and Vibeke Børdahl (eds), *Lifestyle and Entertainment in Yangzhou* (Copenhagen, 2009).

6. Finnane, *Speaking of Yangzhou*, p. 214.

7. Brook, *The Confusions of Pleasure*; Harriet T. Zurndorfer, "Old and New Visions of Ming Society and Culture", *T'oung Pao*, 88 (2002), pp. 151–169. On the role of the publishing industry in the Ming era, see Kai-wing Chow, *Publishing, Culture, and Power in Early Modern China* (Stanford, CA, 2004).

8. For an overview of Ming urban development, see Fei Si-yen, "Introduction: A New Approach to Chinese Urbanism", in *idem, Negotiating Urban Space: Urbanization and Late Ming Nanjing* (Cambridge, MA, 2009), pp. 1–27.

women. Courtesans who were schooled from a young age in reading and
writing poetry, as well as in singing and dancing, assimilated this growing
appreciation of print culture into their work. Also, in upper-class circles,
it was now not uncommon for families to provide female kin with the
opportunity to acquire literacy and to allow them to engage in literary
activities.[9] Thus, by 1600 women from privileged backgrounds as well as
courtesans formed part of a new reading public, "took up the red brush",
and demonstrated their literary acumen and artistic skills.

While upper-class female writers confined themselves to family, and local
networks of other women in private quarters, courtesans showed themselves
in the public domain, which meant, in the long run, that their lives and their
status in society took on an entirely different hue – one that would criss-
cross the values and norms of numbers of male writers and officials, and
eventually their wives and daughters.[10] The late Ming witnessed widespread
anxiety about how the tremendous material growth and monetization of the
economy were damaging the moral fabric of society, a situation which led
some Confucian scholars to seek ways and means to correct and improve the
ethos of the social order. Within this concerned elite were those who came to
link contemporary political and intellectual controversies and themes with
the marginal status of courtesans: ultimately, they steered these women into
the Confucian moral universe, a phenomenon unprecedented in Chinese
history. Prostitutes, on the other hand, unless they were lucky enough to gain
literacy via their "foster homes", would remain outside this intersection of
ethics and changing values among the elite literati.

It is against such a background that we consider prostitutes and courtesans in late Ming society – their legal and societal position, their shifting
roles vis-à-vis the male scholar-elite and female upper-class writers, and
what changes occurred at the end of the Ming that affected their status.

DEFINITIONS, INSTITUTIONS, AND LEGAL NORMS

According to contemporary Chinese judicial regulations, both prostitutes and
courtesans were classified as "entertainers", and, therefore, they had the status
of *jianmin* [mean people], which formally made them "outcasts" in Chinese
society.[11] In the Ming era, the law recognized only two kinds of person –
"mean", or commoner (*liang*), who was considered "good" or "virtuous".
Mean people were outside the four commoner status groups: gentlemen
(scholars), farmers, artisans, and merchants. The chief bias against mean

---

9. Wilt Idema and Beata Grant, *The Red Brush: Writing Women of Imperial China* (Cambridge, MA, 2004), p. 348.
10. See Ko, *Teachers of the Inner Chambers*, pp. 251–293.
11. Anders Hansson, *Chinese Outcasts: Discrimination and Emancipation in Late Imperial
China* (Leiden, 1996), pp. 1–2.

people was that the work they performed was humiliating or polluting, or both, or of little or no value to society – such as entertainment.[12] This meant that not only women working either as performers at the imperial court or on the street as prostitutes but also men who were musicians were not immune from this label.[13]

While the Ming code did not prevent ordinary male commoners from marrying either courtesans or prostitutes, the top group within the four status ranks, i.e. scholar-official, was forbidden from doing so, though this did not stop them from taking attractive women (either courtesans or lowly prostitutes) as concubines to live in their marital homes.[14] Since the law dictated that a Chinese man could have only one wife, it was not uncommon for rich men to acquire a series of concubines to mark their status and boost their prestige. A married man who still had no heir at the age of forty was actually encouraged to take a concubine.[15] Given these conditions, one may conclude that neither prostitutes nor courtesans formed an endogamous group in late Ming society, and they cannot be termed pariahs.

Nevertheless, despite the relatively low formal status that these two types of women shared, there were certain obvious differences between them. The top-class courtesan, known by the expression *mingji* [famous courtesan], usually had a cultured upbringing to prepare her for serving clients.[16] Besides her bestowal of sexual favours, she was also expected to indulge with her patrons in the fine arts – playing the zither or chess, or engaging in calligraphy or painting.[17] While prized for her beauty and sexual charms,

12. *Ibid.*, p. 21.

13. *Ibid.*, p. 55.

14. The Ming legal code was explicit about this matter. See *The Great Ming Code: Da Ming lü*, transl. by Jiang Yonglin (Seattle, WA, 2005), p. 87, Art. 119, "Marrying Musicians as Wives or Concubines", where is written: "In all cases where officials or functionaries marry musicians as wives or concubines, they shall be punished by 60 strokes of beating with the heavy stick". See also p. 217, Art. 397, "Honorable and Mean Persons Committing Fornication"; Art. 398, "Officials and Functionaries Sleeping with Entertainers"; and Art. 399, "Purchasing Honorable Persons to be Entertainers". Given the evidence, however, it would seem scholar-officials for the most part ignored these laws.

15. Francesca Bray, *Technology and Gender: Fabrics of Power in Late Imperial China* (Berkeley, CA, 1997), pp. 352–355; Harriet Zurndorfer, "Concubinage", in Fedwa Malti-Douglas (ed.), *Encyclopedia of Sex and Gender*, 4 vols (Farmington Hills, MI, 2007), I, pp. 328–331. While the sons of concubines were equal to those of the wife in matters of inheritance, the status of their mothers remained "mean". Moreover, a concubine was expected to obey her master's wife.

16. For a study of how a young peasant girl, sold by her parents to work in a high-class brothel (during the early nineteenth century), was educated to become a courtesan and then "married off" by her "madame" to one of her most important clients, see Li Xiaorong, "Woman Writing about Women: Li Shuyi's (1817–?) Project on 'One Hundred Beauties'", *Nan Nü: Men, Women and Gender in China*, 13 (2011), pp. 52–110. Within upper-class homes, it was also not unknown for maid servants to learn to read and even compose poetry, thanks to mentoring by their female employers. See Ko, *Teachers of the Inner Chambers*, p. 205.

17. See Ko, *Teachers of the Inner Chambers*, pp. 253–255; Paul Ropp, "Ambiguous Images of Courtesan Culture in Late Imperial China", in Ellen Widmer and Kang-i Sun Chang (eds),

the true function of a courtesan (as opposed to a prostitute) was that of a "professional hostess" who was educated and cultivated in skills such as conversation, knowledge of classical literature, recitation of poetry, dancing, and musical performance.[18]

Her ability to write poetry was a key tool in her trade because literary exchanges were fundamental in the communication between her and her clients. The most talented courtesans also functioned as counsellors on matters of refinement, as the "resident experts on the elaborate esoterica of a romanticized affective life".[19] They were responsible for creating an aesthetically pleasing atmosphere, whether within a brothel or in private apartments where elite men would hold poetry parties or drinking contests. One of the most important locations where courtesans made their mark as talented and amusing companions was in the setting of gardens; in these beautiful, rustic, and artistic sites people congregated to enjoy leisure pursuits in the open air. Here courtesans met their patrons to enjoy intense cultural exchanges on poetry and singing. In some cases, courtesans actually owned gardens and used them as a form of financial investment.[20] Thus, one may say the late Ming courtesan enjoyed a certain "fluidity": she moved between the nether world of the high-class brothel and the exquisite surroundings of scholar gardens.

The courtesan's rich-looking appearance also distinguished her from the prostitute. By the late Ming, the once strict dress code forbidding certain forms of dress and adornment to particular status groups of the population was fading, and sartorial regulations were becoming a thing of the past.[21] Thus, depending on their personal wealth, courtesans were known to display themselves in the most opulent of fabrics and with the grandest accessories, including jewelled headdresses. Silk, a textile traditionally worn only by those of the privileged highest social status, now became integral to the courtesan's wardrobe. The wearing of embroidery, damasks, brocades, and

Writing Women in Late Imperial China (Stanford, CA, 1997), pp. 17–45, 18; Jean Wetzel, "Hidden Connections: Courtesans in the Art World of the Ming Dynasty", *Women's Studies*, 31 (2002), pp. 645–669, 648; Judith Zeitlin, "'Notes of Flesh' and the Courtesan's Song in Seventeenth-Century China", in Martha Feldman and Bonnie Gordon (eds), *The Courtesan's Arts: Cross-Cultural Perspectives* (Oxford, 2006), pp. 75–99, 75–78.
18. On the rise of courtesans' status in late Ming literati society, see Xu Sufeng, "Lotus Flowers Rising from the Dark Mud: Late Ming Courtesans and Their Poetry" (unpublished Ph.D. thesis, McGill University, Montreal, 2007).
19. Victoria Cass, *Dangerous Women: Warriors, Grannies, and Geishas of the Ming* (Lanham, MD, 1999), p. 26.
20. Alison Hardie, "Washing the *Wutong* Tree: Garden Culture as an Expression of Women's Gentility in the Late Ming", in Daria Berg and Chloë Starr (eds), *The Quest for Gentility in China: Negotiations beyond Gender and Class* (London, 2007), pp. 45–57, 52–54.
21. Sarah Dauncey, "Illusions of Grandeur: Perceptions of Status and Wealth in Late-Ming Clothing and Ornamentation", *East Asian History*, 25/26 (2003), pp. 43–68, 67.

other patterned silks in dark colours such as dark blue, green, and scarlet, once the exclusive right of upper-class women, became negotiable by the second half of the sixteenth century. In illustrated novels, such as *Jin Ping Mei* [The Plum in the Golden Vase], the female characters who are the wives and concubines of a merchant are attired in clothing and jewellery that was once considered entirely inappropriate to their class.[22]

While elite courtesans generally confined their public appearances to within the entertainment quarters, prostitutes were truly "women of the street". As *waiji* [common whores], they plied their trade openly in the public domain. In the early evening hours, prostitutes emerged from their living quarters and hung around the doorways of tea houses and drinking places in search of business.[23] In the capital Beijing during the Wanli era (1573–1620), a customer could pay some seven *wen* to get an hour in bed with a woman who would parade nude before copulation.[24] There was also a category of "official prostitutes" (*guanji*), the descendants either of Mongols who had remained in China after the defeat of the Yuan dynasty in 1368, or of condemned Chinese officials.[25] These women often had the surname Dun or Tuo, indicative of their Mongol heritage. They belonged to the bottom rung of the "mean people", and had relatively little chance to liberate themselves from their economic bondage and to change their lifestyles.

Notwithstanding these clear differences between prostitutes and courtesans, both groups faced a certain ambiguity about the permanence of their social station. Courtesans could, and did, marry their patrons or clients (even among the upper-class elite, despite the legal interdict) while common prostitutes could be bought as concubines and function in well-to-do households as second wives. Fathers sold daughters, and even husbands sold wives (with the excuse that they had misbehaved).[26] Such transactions were

22. *Ibid.*
23. Finnane, *Speaking of Yangzhou*, p. 216.
24. Willard Peterson, *Bitter Gourd: Fang I-chih and the Impetus for Intellectual Change* (New Haven, CT, 1979), p. 143, citing Xie's *Wu za zu*. Seven *wen* was the equivalent of 0.007 tael of silver. We may compare the prostitute's earnings here with those of other labourers. According to Chow, *Publishing, Culture, and Power*, p. 53, the daily wage of a silk worker in the period was 0.04 tael. If the prostitute entertained 6 clients per day (at 7 *wen* each), then her remuneration would not have been all that different from that of the silk worker.
25. Wang Shunu, *Zhongguo changji shi* [History of Chinese Sing-Song Girls] (Shanghai, 1988), p. 262; Cass, *Dangerous Women*, p. 25.
26. For an analysis of the legal and illegal conditions of wife-selling during the Ming era and later, see Kishimoto Mio, "Qi ke mai fou? Ming Qing shidai de maiqi dianqi xisu" [Wives for Sale? On the Customs of Wife-Selling and Wife Pawning during the Ming Qing Era], in Chen Qiukun and Hong Liwan (eds), *Qiyue wenshu yu shehui shenghuo, 1600–1900* [Contractual Behaviour and Social Life, 1600–1900] (Taipei, 2001), pp. 225–264. See also *The Great Ming Code*, pp. 164–165, Art. 298, "Kidnapping Persons or Kidnapping and Selling People"; p. 200, Art. 360, (section 5); p. 214, Art. 390, "Committing Fornication" (section 6); p. 217, Art. 399, "Purchasing Honorable Persons to Be Entertainers".

Figure 1. Courtesan in Ming "patchwork" (*shuitian*) coat with dress.
Source: Hua Mei, Chinese Clothing *(Beijing, 2004), p. 56. Used with permission.*

formalized by a contract, like the one recorded in the 1596 household encyclopedia *Wanbao quanshu* [Encyclopedia of Myriad Treasures]:

> In [name blank] village, I [name blank] had a daughter, [name blank]. When she reached adulthood, I arranged her to be the concubine of [name blank]. The engagement price was received today at the moment when this contract is completed. In the auspicious day and time, she will be sent to her husband's household. With heavenly blessing, she will produce many children. The daughter, as my biological child raised in the family, was never engaged before. There is no cheating in this sale. As soon as she is taken into [name blank's] family, she belongs to [name blank]. In case she runs away, I will chase her and return her to you. We will have no complaint even if she dies. Her death is not the owner's responsibility, but her destiny. This contract is the evidence of marriage.[27]

Given that this encyclopedic source served as a guide to the lower classes anxious to acquire practical information in a rapidly changing commercial world, the publication in it of this contract may be evidence of the need to formalize the trade in human beings at this time, as well as of the increasing frequency of this practice.[28]

In any event, moral confusion permeates this kind of human trafficking: in a society that highly prized the Confucian values of filiality and obeisance, a daughter who was sold to become a maid or prostitute in the entertainment quarters to help her family escape poverty was worthy of praise.[29] Moreover, she herself might see her new surroundings as an opportunity to improve her own material circumstances in a location where beauty, talent, and accomplishment were valued. On the other hand, the Confucian condemnation of lower-class families for selling their daughters should not distract one from the fact that upper-class families frequently bought such women, as well as concubines and servants. As prices for food and cloth rose during the late Ming, many ordinary families had difficulties meeting their expenses and the sale of a daughter became a solution. Price indicators show that during

---

27. Hsieh, "The Market in Concubines", p. 276.
28. This same encyclopedia offered instructions for increasing sexual pleasure both in the home and in the brothel. See Wang Ermin, *Ming Qing shidai shumin wenhua shenghuo* [Common People's Cultural Life during the Ming and Qing Eras] (Taipei, 1999). Another Ming-era daily encyclopedia, *Santai wanyang zhengzong* [Santai's Orthodox Instructions for Myriad Uses] by Yu Xiangdou (15?–1609), contained specific instructions for merchants visiting the entertainment quarters, from etiquette to guidance about the dangers of financial exploitation. On the use of "daily encyclopedias" during the late Ming, see Harriet Zurndorfer, "The Passion to Collect, Select, and Protect: Fifteen Hundred Years of the Chinese Encyclopedia", in Jason König (ed.), *Encyclopedias before the Enlightenment* (Cambridge, forthcoming).
29. One should not underestimate the monetary value of this kind of exchange. According to Ko, *Teachers of the Inner Chambers*, p. 342, n. 18, a preliminary investigation of Ming novels shows that selling a daughter as a maid generated more cash than a shop assistant earned in six months. With the money from the daughter's sale, a family could buy enough rice for a year.

the Zhengde reign (1506–1521) in Nanjing, for example, an ordinary family of average size (around five people) could have enough meat and vegetables with about 20–30 *wen* a day (with pork costing around 8 *wen* per *jin*).[30] But around 100 years later, with the costs of food rocketing (pork, for instance, cost 40 *wen* per *jin*), people found it increasingly difficult to provide for themselves, and thus the sale of a female relative for 100–200 taels of silver could bring relief to the remaining family members.[31]

Despite its cultural brilliance and economic growth, the late Ming also saw increasingly sharp economic and social differences between rich and poor, merchant and farmer, and official and commoner, which did not go unobserved by scholar-officials and intellectuals. How they dealt with the disparities between these groups varied considerably, however.[32] A recent study of charity at that time challenges any facile explanation that institutions of benevolence and goodwill, such as soup kitchens and medical dispensaries, were simply a response to poverty and social unrest.[33] Instead one may look at how the social and economic changes themselves stimulated new ways of thinking about the ethos of Ming society, and the capacity of individuals to approach and absorb Confucian ideals. Literati writings dating from the late Ming exhibit a mixed intellectual agenda, revealing the tensions between these men's academic tenets, moral convictions, and personal feelings. Conventional pity for the oppressed courtesan (or even the condemned prostitute) did exist, but this period also saw the development of another vision of this woman that altered both their status and their place in the Confucian moral universe.

THE TRANSFORMATION OF THE COURTESAN IDEAL IN LATE MING CHINA

Late Ming intellectuals did not consider the plight of courtesans (or prostitutes) as sinful or wicked, but rather as something unfortunate.[34] That rich and famous courtesans or poor and obscure prostitutes sold their services and their bodies in exchange for money was pitiful, and maybe even fatalistic, but not really a matter for reform. While some men of letters pursued the *grandeur et misère* of courtesan life as the subject matter for plays and novellas,[35] few of them "conceived, much less

---

30. Huang Miantang *Ming shi guanjian* [Observations on Ming History] (Jinan, 1985), pp. 346–372.
31. See Hsieh, "The Market in Concubines", p. 273, for estimates of the costs of buying a maid or concubine in the eighteenth century.
32. On late Ming economic and social change, see Brook, *Confusions of Pleasure*, pp. 153–237.
33. Joanna Handlin Smith, *The Art of Doing Good: Charity in Late Imperial China* (Berkeley, CA, 2009).
34. Ropp, "Ambiguous Images of Courtesan Culture", p. 43.
35. Idema and Grant, *The Red Brush*, pp. 353, 355.

proposed, the abolition of these women's bonds to servitude".[36] An air of misfortune was attached even to the stars of the profession.

Such attitudes differed from earlier views of this category of woman some 500 years before when, during the Southern Song dynasty (1127–1279), debates raged among literati and officials about the proper place of courtesans in "polite society". As Song government reformers tried to revitalize Confucianism, they regarded the courtesan as a troubling and contestable figure who was a threat to the stability of the regime. They believed her very existence was a menace "to the social and moral purity of the upper-class male literatus".[37] And as for officials who commingled with her, they were considered "debauched, and emblematic of evil and irresponsibility".[38] Such attitudes were derivative of an altering Chinese cultural tradition that emerged at the start of the Song era. As Peter Bol has argued, while Song neo-Confucians shifted the focus of learning away from literary-historical traditions to the cultivation of ethical behaviour, they created a new body of texts, doctrines, and practices that came to define "This [Chinese] Culture", which lay great emphasis on ethical-philosophical ideas and principles.[39]

Over time, the negative attitude towards courtesans hardened, and both the Yuan (1279–1368) and early Ming regimes tried to discourage their presence in government-sponsored entertainment, such as banquets. The first Ming emperor, Zhu Yuanzhang (r.1368–1398), issued a decree threatening severe penalties for officials caught having sexual relations with female entertainers.[40] But during the course of the Ming era, and especially by the mid-sixteenth century, courtesans were no longer thought about in this way, and towards the end of this period they became "a cultural ideal".

The story of how these women became powerful symbols of morality and virtue is complex, and compels us to turn once again to intellectual developments during the Southern Song. The Confucian revival of that era was dominated by the ideology of *lixue* [study of principle], which put great emphasis on the moral perfection of the individual, an ideal that was achievable through the study of a number of prescribed ancient Confucian texts. One of the leading neo-Confucian *lixue* proponents was the philosopher Zhu Xi (1130–1200), who claimed that an individual could understand the Way (or *dao*) through the study of principle, and in particular the

36. Ropp, "Ambiguous Images of Courtesan Culture", p. 43.
37. Beverly Bossler, "Shifting Identities: Courtesans and Literati in Song China", *Harvard Journal of Asiatic Studies*, 62 (2002), pp. 5–37, 32.
38. *Ibid.*, p. 31.
39. Peter Bol, *"This Culture of Ours": Intellectual Transitions in T'ang and Sung China* (Stanford, CA, 1992), p. 3.
40. Howard Levy, *A Feast of Mist and Flowers: The Gay Quarters of Nanking at the End of the Ming* (Yokohama, 1966), p. 19.

moral principle operative in history.[41] By the beginning of the Ming period, Zhu Xi's interpretation of Confucianism became the backbone of the orthodoxy in which the state examination candidates had to train themselves. But from the sixteenth century a new school of thought represented by the statesman and philosopher Wang Yangming (1472–1529) challenged the idea that *li* [principle] could be found only in the Confucian classics. Wang, with reference to a saying of the fourth-third century BC Confucian exegete Mencius,[42] taught that all human beings were born with an innate "knowledge of the good" that would enable them to understand the Way directly, by trusting their own authentic or "genuine" feelings. According to Wang, "innate knowledge of the good" (*liangzhi*) could be tapped in each individual's mind, regardless of the person's social standing.[43]

As numbers of late Ming intellectuals grew increasingly critical of the Zhu Xi version of neo-Confucian orthodoxy, they considered the relevance of Wang Yangming's teaching to contemporary tensions and problems. Wang's belief that the individual's own moral sense was the basis of ethics and social life inspired thinkers to critique everyday mores, and to search for ways to revitalize Confucian values.[44] They attempted to redefine neo-Confucian values in more human terms, and to invoke the concept of *qing*. *Qing* is a difficult term to translate in one simple word: it means feeling, emotion, sentiment, sensitivity, or passion, and can refer to "human emotional responses to particular circumstances".[45] In contrast to the *li* of orthodoxy, which "represented stale didacticism, rigid dogmatism, and artificial regulation, *qing* signified the plain expression of fresh, natural, romantic and unsophisticated emotions".[46]

These efforts to recast Confucian values first became obvious in the work of Ming writers and playwrights, who fashioned a "cult of *qing*" that they communicated in vernacular literature and popular dramas which the printing industry churned out in great quantities, and about which readers and theatre audiences raved. In the plays of Xu Wei (1521–1593),

---

41. Idema and Grant, *The Red Brush*, p. 349.

42. Mencius, Chapter *Jin Xin I* ("Exhausting the Heart"), p. 15, as translated by James Legge. See the Chinese Text Project website, maintained by Donald Sturgeon, http://chinese.dsturgeon.net/text.pl?node=1791&if=en, last accessed 29 November 2010.

43. Lu Weijing, *True to Her Word: The Faithful Maiden Cult in Late Imperial China* (Stanford, CA, 2008), p. 37.

44. Maram Epstein, *Competing Discourses: Orthodoxy, Authenticity, and Engendered Meanings in Late Imperial Chinese Fiction* (Cambridge, MA, 2001), pp. 62–74; Halvor Eifring, "Introduction: Emotions and Conceptual History of 'Qing'", in *idem* (ed.), *Love and Emotions in Traditional Chinese Literature* (Leiden, 2004), pp. 1–36, 11–13.

45. Hsü Pi-ching, "Courtesans and Scholars in the Writings of Feng Menglong: Transcending Status and Gender", *Nan Nü: Men, Women and Gender in Early and Imperial China*, 2 (2000), pp. 40–77, 51–52. Cf. Kidder Smith, Jr, *et al.* (eds), *Uses of the I Ching* (Princeton, NJ, 1990).

46. Hsü, "Courtesans and Scholars", p. 52.

for example, both the feelings and the physical bodies of the characters were unashamedly revealed – in one of the best-known scenes in his drama *Kuang gulong* [The Mad Drummer] the character Mi Heng reveals his "true moral mettle" to the well-known dictator Cao Cao (155–200) by shedding his clothes and appearing before him stark naked.[47] Attempts to accommodate *qing* to Confucian morality abound in short stories and plays that communicate the importance of sincerity and depth of human feeling in human interaction.[48]

During the late Ming the "cult of *qing*" became immensely popular, and a means for men and women to explore the interplay of ethics and culture. The courtesan became a focal point of this examination. The sensuous side of her existence came to be perceived as the embodiment of *qing*, variously expressed as freedom and independence of spirit, courage and heroic action, detachment and understanding, true feeling and magnanimous spirit, and the overcoming of the boundaries between private and public spheres.[49] The connection between the marginality and dubious social station of the late Ming courtesan and her elevation as the symbol of refinement, high culture, freedom, and the possibility of action[50] was observed by male admirers, who regarded her as the embodiment of *qing*. Courtesans appear in literature as models of loyalty, virtue, and courage, and often more so than the male characters.[51]

Perhaps, the most eloquent spokesman of the late Ming discourse on courtesans and *qing* was the author Feng Menglong (1574–1646), whose writings brought the legally marginal courtesan to the "centre" of the Confucian moral universe. As someone critical of the polarities between high and low culture set by "respectable society", Feng conveyed the "social underdogs" (petty vendors, fallen women, poor farmers) to the middle point of the literary world. He was an astute observer, and true to himself and his readers about what he thought morally right and truthful. Thus, he did not always idealize courtesans: his own honesty and sincerity also led him to write about manipulative ones who fooled their infatuated lovers with empty promises, as well as inconsistent ones who could not

47. Wilt Idema, "'Blasé Literati': Lü T'ien-ch'eng and the Lifestyle of the Chiangnan Elite in the Final Decades of the Wan-li Period", in R.H. van Gulik (ed.), *Erotic Colour Prints of the Ming Period* (Leiden, 2004), pp. xxxi–lix; xxxix. For more information on the historical foundations and literary implications of *qing* in Ming and Qing literature, see Martin Huang, "Sentiments of Desire: Thoughts on the Cult of *Qing* in Ming-Qing Literature", *Chinese Literature: Essays, Articles, Reviews*, 20 (1998), pp. 153–184.
48. Patrick Hanan, *The Chinese Vernacular Story* (Cambridge, MA, 1981), pp. 79, 96–97.
49. Li Waiyee, "The Late Ming Courtesan: Invention of a Cultural Ideal", in Widmer and Sun Chang, *Writing Women in Late Imperial China*, pp. 46–73, 72.
50. *Ibid.*, pp. 46–47.
51. Allan Barr, "The Wanli Context of the Du Shiniang Story", *Harvard Journal of Asiatic Studies*, 57 (1997), pp. 107–141.

remain true to their vows of love.[52] In ideal (and allegorical terms), Feng perceived the devoted courtesan as a symbol of the unrecognized (male) talent who was denied entry into late Ming politics and forced to make a living in the cultural market, but whose authentic talents and *qing* would not be compromised or corrupted by the materialistic demands of the environment.[53]

Feng Menglong's anthology of classical love stories, *Qingshi leilue* [A Classified Outline of the History of Love], interprets all phenomena in the human, supra-human, and sub-human territories from the perspective of *qing*, especially *qing* in the form of sexual love. In this compilation he treated courtesans as the ultimate challenge to orthodox norms of modesty and honesty. For example, in one of the stories in this collection he tells about men who tried every desperate means, including jumping over a wall, to avoid contact with the courtesans their friends had arranged for them to meet. Feng comments on this tale: "These were all people who were richest in emotions. They were earnestly worried that they might all of a sudden fail to control themselves; therefore, they took precautions and shunned the courtesans beforehand."[54] At the end of this collection, Feng proposes the incorporation of virtuous courtesans into the pantheon of Confucian paradigms. He writes:

> According to the teachings of the *Spring and Autumn Annals* [on the five principal classics], we should use the Chinese way to change the way of the barbarians, not use the way of the barbarians to change the Chinese way. Therefore, if a concubine harbors the virtue of a wife, then we should make her a wife; if a courtesan performs the deed of a concubine, then we should make her a concubine. Those who entrust themselves to their lovers for the sake of *qing*, I hereby acknowledge their *qing*. Those who sacrifice their lives because of genuine *qing*, I would be the last to suspect that their motivation may be impure. This follows the motto, "a gentleman takes delight in praising those who perform good deeds." Otherwise, are we to say that menial laborers and offspring of concubines are not capable of bringing loyalty and filial piety in their nature to full play?[55]

Here Feng brings into play the distinction between Chinese and barbarian and connects it to the virtue of chastity, implying that chastity was a Chinese female virtue, and thus to deny a lowly Chinese woman the opportunity to perform that Chinese wifely duty was to reject her Chinese identity and to turn her into a barbarian. With ethics and culture so intricately linked together, not to cultivate the morality of the marginal members of society could be viewed as making this periphery uncivilized,

52. Hsü, "Courtesans and Scholars", p. 44.
53. *Ibid.*
54. Cited in *ibid.*, p. 59.
55. Hua-yuan Li Mowry, *Chinese Love Stories from the "Ch'ing-shih"* (Hamden, CT, 1983), pp. 38–39.

and that posed a threat to the integrity of Chinese culture. Courtesans, being at the bottom of gender and class hierarchies, symbolized the periphery of the periphery, and they therefore needed to be incorporated into mainstream Chinese culture.[56]

Besides this male reading of the cult of *qing*, there was also the female appraisal of this phenomenon. As Dorothy Ko suggests, the cult engendered for the woman writer a new, positive image. Now, women could aspire to create literature as an expression of true self. "The marginality of women's words, irrelevant to any claims of formal political power, became the very source of their salvation."[57] *Qing* opened new doors for both courtesans and upper-class women. Conventional morality prescribed a wife's role to be fertile, chaste, and reverential – but now, in the late Ming, a certain "romantic equalitarianism" crept into the discourse of orthodoxy, and even marriage could be romanticized. By watching plays such as those by Tang Xianzu (1550–1616), whose 1598 drama "Peony Pavilion" told the story of a girl who falls in love with a young man in a dream and subsequently dies of longing, but returns from the dead after she appears in his dream and he opens her grave, and they are reunited,[58] women from all status groups fell under the spell of *qing*, and were captivated by eroticism and passion.

As such, while wives became more romantic, courtesans grew more legitimate. In entertainment quarters all over the empire, the courtesan's aura and artistic talents became all the more valued. In the early seventeenth century more and more courtesans entered the homes and the estates of the powerful, both as concubines and as "first wives". Among the most celebrated unions of members of the male elite with brilliant courtesans were those of Qian Qianyi (1582–1664) and Liu Shi (1618–1684),[59] Mao Xiang (1611–1693) and Dong Xiaowan (1625–1651), and Gu Mei (?) and Gong Zhilu (1615–1673).[60]

Late Ming literatus–courtesan couples had a romantic idea that not only were they destined to marry each other but also that their life together would constitute an exemplary "wonderful tale that will last for a thousand autumns".[61] It is also important to realize that both in public and private, late Ming courtesans emphasized their moral qualities, rather than their talent, among their admirers. While the late Ming courtesans began to see

56. Hsü, "Courtesans and Scholars", p. 76.
57. Ko, *Teachers of the Inner Chambers*, pp. 50–51.
58. Idema and Grant, *The Red Brush*, pp. 500–504.
59. On this couple, see the important study by Kang-i Sun Chang, *The Late-Ming Poet Ch'en Tzu-lung: Crises of Love and Loyalism* (New Haven, CT, 1991).
60. On Gu Mei, see Victoria Cass, "Gu Mei, the Courtesan Ideal", in Georges Vigarello (ed.), *100,000 Years of Beauty: Classical Age/Confrontations* (Paris, 2009), pp. 100–102.
61. Richard Hessney, "Beyond Beauty and Talent: The Moral and Chivalric Self", in Robert Hegel and Richard Hessney (eds), *Expressions of Self in Chinese Literature* (New York, 1985), pp. 214–250, 239.

Figure 2. The well-known Ming courtesan, Gu Mei, depicted as an ascetic by the seventeenth-century painter, Zhang Putong.
Original in Nanjing Museum; reproduced from Cass, Dangerous Women, *colour plate 4. Used with permission.*

themselves as virtuous women, upper-class women tried to create a new self-image as "talented women" (*cainü*).[62] Within domestic spaces, courtesans

62. In contrast, those particular qualities in an upper-class woman's character that were most valued were purity, devotion to service, diligence, frugality, and resourcefulness. See Susan

and upper-class wives also now mingled in ways that were unprecedented: upper-class wives befriended courtesans by exchanging poems and paintings; wives invited "singing girls" to parties in private villas.[63]

In the works of the elite women Xu Yuan (1560–1620) and Lu Qingzi (fl.1590s), many instances of artistic and emotional exchanges between them and courtesans were noted.[64] Xu Yuan, for example, made no secret of the fact that she was a great admirer of one of the most famous courtesans of her day, Xue Susu (1575–1652?), and published Xue's poems in her printed collection.[65] By the early seventeenth century it was no longer uncommon for both categories of women to have their poetry published in the same anthologies that were edited by both men and women.[66] These compilations convey both the celebration of the beauty, glamour, and elegance of courtesans as well as the talents of upper-class wives, along with their occasional envy of each other. Wives might have resented the courtesans' relative freedom from domestic responsibilities and burdens.

THE END OF AN ERA

By the time Zhang Dai had compiled his Taoan "dream memories", he had already witnessed the cataclysmic fall of the Ming, which had originated in the combined turmoil of local rebellions and foreign invasion by the Manchus.

Mann and Cheng Yu-yin (eds), *Under Confucian Eyes: Writings on Gender in Chinese History* (Berkeley, CA, 2001). During the late Ming some men also became obsessed with the relationship between beauty and moral deportment. On this theme, see H. Zurndorfer, "Willowy as a Willow", in Vigarello, *100,000 Years of Beauty*, pp. 113–115.

63. Ko, *Teachers of the Inner Chambers*, p. 259.

64. *Ibid.*, pp. 266–274.

65. On Xue Susu, see Daria Berg, "Cultural Discourse on Xue Susu, A Courtesan in Late Ming China", *International Journal of Asian Studies*, 6 (2009), pp. 171–200. On relations between upper-class wives and courtesans, see *idem*, "Female Self-Fashioning in Late Imperial China: How the Gentlewoman and the Courtesan Edited *Her* Story and Rewrote *Hi*/story", in *idem* (ed.), *Reading China: Fiction, History and the Dynamics of Discourse: Essays in Honor of Professor Glen Dudbridge* (Leiden, 2007), pp. 238–289.

66. A pioneering study of these anthologies is Kang-i Sun Chang, "A Guide to Ming-Ch'ing Anthologies of Female Poetry and Their Selection Strategies", *The Gest Library Journal*, 5 (1992), pp. 119–160; see also *idem*, "Ming and Qing Anthologies of Women's Poetry and Their Selection Strategies", in Widmer and Sun Chang, *Writing Women in Late Imperial China*, pp. 147–170; Clara Wing-chung Ho, "Encouragement from the Opposite Gender: Male Scholars' Interests in Women's Publications in Ch'ing China", in H. Zurndorfer (ed.), *Chinese Women in the Imperial Past* (Leiden, 1999), pp. 308–353. Modern scholars are still very much in the process of recovering the *thousands* (emphasis added) of writings and collections authored and edited by women since earliest times. Recent work has focused not only on locating the texts written by women, but also on determining patterns of writing and publication. New discoveries are becoming accessible through databases and websites. See, for example, the Ming Qing Women's Writings website http://digital.library.mcgill.ca/mingqing, which makes available works in Canada's McGill University collection and Harvard University's Harvard-Yenching Library.

The Manchus went on to establish the Qing dynasty (1644–1911), but they did not complete the unification of their empire until 1683, and thus political breakdown, warfare, and dislocation lasted nearly four decades. Men and women were astonished by the sudden overthrow of the Ming, pondered the causes of the dynastic collapse, and began to search for an explanation in terms other than Manchu military prowess. As Chinese men like Zhang Dai, who lost most of his material possessions (including his home), agonized over the causes, they increasingly came to the conclusion that the liberalism and "loose morals" of the latter half of the Ming dynasty were the primary causes of the debacle.

But before then, during the hectic period of dynastic disorder and fighting between rival forces, the expression of Ming loyalism became widespread, and courtesans were important agents of loyalist resistance. According to Kang-i Sun Chang, "after the fall of the Ming, the courtesan became the metaphor for the loyalist poets' vision of themselves".[67] The predicaments of both loyalists and courtesans were similar, locked in the futility of recalling a world that had collapsed, and resuscitating meaning in their shattered public and private lives.[68] On a practical level, courtesans – with their wide social networks and their itinerant lifestyle – could serve as scouts, messengers, and fundraisers;[69] over time, they earned a reputation as "inspiring" for their principled stand against the invader. Committing suicide in public as protest, many courtesans ended their lives as martyrs and suffered the ultimate sacrifice for their loyalty.[70]

Gradually, however, the symbolic status of courtesans shifted – from representing the ideals of freedom, self-creation, and the possibility of heroic action – to that of a lost world of elegance, style, and grace.[71] The transformation in attitude towards courtesans, from one of culture and nostalgia to vulgarity and pity by the nineteenth century, may be attributed to several factors. First, in the years after the Ming downfall, a reversion to (Song dynasty) neo-Confucian orthodoxy on the part of Chinese scholars and male intellectuals set in, and adherence to ritual prescriptions became extremely important.[72] The revival of classicism in the Qing era hardened the line between orthodoxy and heterodoxy, making it more difficult for scholars to romanticize their relationships with courtesans. Secondly, the Qing takeover had destroyed many of the large fortunes of the Lower

67. Sun Chang, *The Late-Ming Poet Ch'en Tzu-lung*, p. 17.
68. Dorothy Ko, "The Written Word and the Bound Foot: A History of the Courtesan's Aura", in Widmer and Sun Chang, *Writing Women in Late Imperial China*, pp. 74–100, 86.
69. Ko, *Teachers of the Inner Chambers*, p. 281.
70. Frederic Wakeman, "Romantics, Stoics, and Martyrs in Seventeenth Century China", *Journal of Asian Studies*, 43 (1984), pp. 631–665.
71. Ropp, "Ambiguous Images of Courtesan Culture", p. 19.
72. Chow Kai-wing, *The Rise of Confucian Ritualism in Late Imperial China: Ethics, Classics, and Lineage Discourse* (Stanford, CA, 1994).

Yangzi region (where, for example, Zhang Dai had originated) and changes in the tax structure prevented the accumulation of the kinds of fortunes that had maintained the late Ming "good life".

This situation may explain why, from the 1680s, publishers no longer rushed to produce new titles for upper-class "leisure reading". The last major anthology of women's literature was printed in 1690, and the next one would not appear until 1773.[73] Also relevant is the new regime's growing control over printed materials, which led publishers to favour reprinting new editions of old, well-established texts rather than engage in new projects.

Another factor contributing to the downfall of the courtesan image was new government legislation with regard to palace entertainment. The Qing state banned female entertainers from official functions, which in the long run deprived courtesans of the security of their status and led to the expansion of private commercial entertainment giving new licence to pornographic sex markets.[74] At the same time, educated upper-class women appropriated the poetic genre, which had once been an integral part of courtesan literature. The wives and daughters of the scholar-elite distinguished their own erudition from the courtesan talents which they now trivialized.[75]

By the late eighteenth and early nineteenth centuries, courtesans came to be seen more and more as objects of pity and sorrow. Modern literary scholars have argued that Qing literatus and courtesan poems from that time place less emphasis on love, talent, glamour, or nostalgia, and more on the sufferings of courtesans from sexual exploitation, bondage, and shame. In the nineteenth century, the "vulgarization" of courtesan culture had become a fact. In 1818, Peng Huasheng, a chronicler of Nanjing's "flower houses", had printed a handbook (which he sold for profit) to those in need of advice about attending these quarters. Ko sums up the contents of the guide, and its purchasers: "Not only did the courtesan turn out to be the shadow of her glamorous past, the scholar (client) was at best an impersonator of a literatus."[76] Merchants and semi-literate traders had become the new patrons, while the women themselves were more likely to be illiterate and thus incapable of engaging in the arts and skills once expected of their Ming counterparts.[77]

73. Idema and Grant, *The Red Brush*, p. 357.
74. Susan Mann, *Precious Records: Women in China's Long Eighteenth Century* (Stanford, CA, 1997), pp. 127–128; Yan Ming, *Zhongguo mingji yishu shi* [A History of the Courtesan's Art in China] (Taipei, 1992), pp. 130–134.
75. Mann, *Precious Records*, pp. 127–128.
76. Ko, "The Written Word and the Bound Foot", p. 75.
77. A new phase in the history of prostitution begins in the mid-nineteenth century with the development of Shanghai into a metropolis. See Gail Hershatter, *Dangerous Pleasures: Prostitution and Modernity in Twentieth-Century Shanghai* (Berkeley, CA, 1997); Christian Henriot, *Prostitution and Sexuality in Shanghai* (Cambridge, 2001); Catherine Vance Yeh, *Shanghai Love: Courtesans, Intellectuals, and Entertainment Culture, 1850–1910* (Seattle, WA, 2006); and

CONCLUDING OBSERVATIONS

One of the most important impressions that this examination of Chinese prostitutes and courtesans conveys is the changing dynamics of work and ethics in the late Ming period. Confucianism, which underwent a certain transformation in the sixteenth century thanks to the influence of Wang Yangming's thinking, impacted the ethos of both men and women. Despite an explicit legal code that denigrated both prostitutes and courtesans, both types of entertainer became enmeshed in the changing values of late Ming society and culture. Formally, neither kind of woman was prevented from improving her social station through her profession (or "work"). But it was the courtesan, with her sophisticated training and talents, that provoked the blurring of social strata and raised the question of what was most desirable in a good (*liang*) woman. The ancient Chinese system of "four commoner status" groups did not impede the demonstration of her abilities or the appreciation by both men and women of her "work", i.e. the advancement of music, poetry, and painting. That the courtesan became the centre of a Confucian moral universe through the cult of *qing* was in itself an affirmation of the extent to which the values associated with Wang Yangming's philosophy had penetrated the lowest layer of the late Ming social order.

As we have indicated, however, the reign of the courtesan's golden aura was limited, to one brilliant period during the dazzling late Ming dynasty. Her magic did not endure, and eventually she became commoditized, like the Ming prostitute whose lifestyle and work reflected the ups and downs of market forces. The latter's path to liberation was usually concubinage, which provided at least the possibility of economic security and social mobility. The fall of the Ming and the institutionalization of the Qing did not change or affect her prospects in the long run. In contrast, for the courtesan, the Manchu conquest began the process of her vulgarization and aesthetic downfall.

The Ming defeat triggered political and identity crises for Chinese intellectuals, who sought salvation through their rehabilitation of the classical heritage and the cultivation of Confucian virtues based on the performance of ritual. By the end of the seventeenth century, they had created a social order broadly supported by a strict kinship organization that prized chastity and patriarchal values, and one that eliminated the role the prestigious courtesan had once held in Chinese society.

H. Zurndorfer, "Review of Catherine Yeh, *Shanghai Love*", *China Review International*, 15 (2008), pp. 438–441. For a general historiographical discussion of prostitution in modern history, see Timothy Gilfoyle, "Review Essay: Prostitutes in History: From Parables of Pornography to Metaphors of Modernity", *American Historical Review*, 104 (1999), pp. 117–141.

IRSH 56 (2011), Special Issue, pp. 217–243 doi:10.1017/S0020859011000502
© 2011 Internationaal Instituut voor Sociale Geschiedenis

Japan in the Seventeenth Century: Labour Relations and Work Ethics*

REGINE MATHIAS

Faculty of East Asian Studies, Ruhr-Universität Bochum

E-mail: regine.mathias@rub.de

SUMMARY: In Japan, the transformation of labour relations from medieval forms of serfdom, lifelong service, and *corvée* labour to short-term contracts and wage labour was already under way by the seventeenth century. In the second half of the seventeenth century short-term employment based on contracts became common. Indentured labour gradually changed into wage labour. Government policies included enabling greater mobility for the workers, while also trying to set limits to migration flow to the cities. Some Confucian scholars welcomed this new form of labour relations; others condemned them. The few sources about the work ethics of waged workers imply mockery about their loose morals and work attitudes, but also complaints about workloads and exploitation.

INTRODUCTION

Around 1500, Japan's elite was in the midst of prolonged warfare, the supremacy of the central government was fast declining, while many territorial lords (*daimyō*) were assuming unprecedented power. The whole country was in a process of political decentralization, which was accompanied by social upheaval on various levels. During this development many of the traditional structures, such as the landed estates, which had been the primary production units in medieval Japan, were finally destroyed, and the territorial lords gradually gained direct control of the people in their domains.

Sources on the life and work of the common people are scarce and scattered, and little is known about the work situation and the work ethics of those who performed manual labour. Confucianism or neo-Confucianism, which was to become the main ideology in the seventeenth century, was known, but not widespread. If there was any kind of work ethic, it would

---

* In this article east Asian names are given in the sequence family name – personal name. Exceptions are made in cases where authors have adopted Western personal names.

have been rooted in Buddhism. Although artisans with special skills, who could probably be regarded as semi-free, formed small guilds (*za*), and sought employment by local lords and temples in some places, the prevalent forms of labour were serfdom, lifelong service (semi-free indentured service), and *corvée* labour.

In the last three decades of the sixteenth century, efforts began to unify the country under a new central government. After a decisive battle in 1600, a new regime under the control of the supreme military governors (*shōgun*), the Tokugawa family, was set up and lasted for more than 250 years until the Meiji Restoration in 1868. Many historians regard the so-called Tokugawa (or Edo) period as comparable with the early modern period in European history. In the evolving political and administrative system, the central power of the shogunate coexisted with more than 200 feudal domains, whose lords were legally vassals of the shogun, but acted as rather independent rulers in their domains. To maintain this delicate balance of power, the Tokugawa shoguns established an administrative framework based on policies already introduced by their predecessors, by which they tried to control their vassals firmly and stabilize their own rule.

Among the measures to achieve that goal, two are of special importance for changes in labour relations: first, a strategy of urbanizing the warrior class by separating warriors and peasants and forcing the former to reside in the emerging castle towns; and second, a system of alternate attendance (*sankin kōtai*), by which the feudal lords were to live alternately in Edo and in their domains, building and maintaining castles and residences in both places. The result was an unprecedented boom in urban construction starting in the 1580s and extending far into the seventeenth century. Castle towns had to accommodate thousands of warriors and their entourages as well as artisans and merchants who provided the material basis for their living. This created a huge demand not only for goods and services, but also for manual labourers, which forced the shogunate to overlook the traditional ban on peasant migration and reluctantly concede the development of new forms of service and labour, especially in the cities, but also in some rural areas.

In the 1580s and 1590s Toyotomi Hideyoshi had explicitly forbidden the hiring of day labourers. In his "Edict on Change of Status" of 1591, which was part of his efforts to separate warriors from peasants, disarm the peasantry, and stabilize agricultural production after long years of war, Hideyoshi demanded that "if any farmer abandons his wet and dry fields and engages in trade or offers himself for hire for wages, not only is he to be punished, but also his fellow villagers".[1] During the following decades,

---

1. David J. Lu (ed.), *Japan: A Documentary History* (New York, 1997), p. 194.

however, this attitude on the part of the central administration was softened and adapted to the changing situation.

Studies on this transformation process which focus on work, the emergence of an urban workforce, ensuing changes in labour relations in rural and urban areas, or the spread of a work ethic and its actual impact on the thought and behaviour of the workforce are still few in number. There are, however, groundbreaking works by Thomas C. Smith, Saitō Osamu, Herman Ooms, Gary Leupp, Mary Louise Nagata, and others, whose findings have greatly helped in formulating the following outline of the transformation of labour relations in rural and urban areas, and the possible impacts of a work ethic.

THE SITUATION IN RURAL AREAS

Despite the sudden emergence and growth of castle towns and other urban centres at the turn of the sixteenth century, the majority of Japanese people continued to live and produce in the countryside throughout the early modern period (1600–1868). While we have a rich stock of sources concerning the seventeenth to the nineteenth centuries, the economic historian Hayami Akira has pointed out that "since there are few literary source materials in Japan much before 1600 that tell us about social conditions, such as how peasants lived and produced, no real contrast can be made between pre-1600 and post-1600 socio-economic conditions through primary historical sources".[2] Therefore the following remarks on traditional forms of labour in agriculture will focus mostly on the period after 1600.

The complete disintegration of the landed estates in the sixteenth century was accompanied by the expanding autonomy of newly emerging village communities on the one hand, and by the efforts of the *daimyō* to gain control over their territories and people on the other. In this process the *daimyō* developed a great variety of systems and regulations to cope with landholdings, tax collection, and recruitment for military service, but the unification process which started in the late sixteenth century established new principles of land possession. A nationwide cadastral survey (*taikō kenchi*) registered plots of land in the names of peasants, who could henceforth claim possession rights for these parcels, while proprietorship remained with the territorial lord. Even though the cadastral survey laid

---

2. Hayami Akira, "A Great Transformation: Social and Economic Change in Sixteenth and Seventeenth Century Japan", in Erich Pauer (ed.), *Silkworms, Oil and Chips* (Proceedings of the Economics and Economic History Section of the Fourth International Conference on Japanese Studies, Paris, September 1985), *Bonner Zeitschrift für Japanologie*, VIII (Bonn, 1986), pp. 3–13, 5; repr. in Hayami Akira, *Collected Papers of Akira Hayami: Population, Family and Society in Pre-Modern Japan* [The Collected Papers of Twentieth-Century Japanese Writers on Japan], IV (Folkestone, 2009), pp. 42–51, 43.

the ground for the emergence of a peasant economy, based on labour-intensive, small-scale family farming, it did not create one single class of small, independent cultivators. Instead, the social structure of the village communities comprised several strata, from wealthy and influential farmers to smaller independent cultivators, cultivators dependent on landowning patrons, landless peasants, and serfs.[3]

RECIPROCAL LABOUR IN THE COUNTRYSIDE

Although large landholdings did not completely disappear, the majority of the landowning peasants (*honbyakushō*) were registered for smaller plots of land of one *chō* (c.1 hectare) or less. It seems that often the plots became so small that they could no longer support even the nuclear family. According to a treatise on farming from 1685, the *Hōnen zeisho* [Writings on Taxes in Years of Abundance], "everywhere fields are divided and re-divided, until finally holdings of seven, five, and even one *tan* [c.1,000 square metres] or less appear. The holders of such small farms put their children out in the service of others."[4] This statement is supported by other sources. Smith mentions the example of a group of sixty-nine servants in one village in 1678, of whom "all but one came from families with fewer than five *koku* of arable and forty-one [...] from families with fewer than three *koku*",[5] which means that the income in rice did not suffice to feed more than two to four persons in the household.[6]

Service in the countryside could take on several forms, which can be roughly divided into hereditary servants (*fudai*) and indentured servants bound for exceedingly long terms (*genin*), but the lines between these categories are often blurred and the terms are used interchangeably. Besides those two categories, which could be labelled "agricultural servants", Smith distinguishes a third group, namely serfs, who would farm small plots of land allotted to them by the landholder, to whom they owed labour services in return. Smith calls them *nago*, but there are many other local names (*hikan* for instance) for these dependent cultivators of land.

Although it is extremely difficult to assess the numbers of *genin* and *nago*, Smith used scattered population registers to estimate that *genin* accounted for about 10 per cent of the peasant population in the seventeenth

---

3. Wakita Osamu, "The Social and Economic Consequences of Unification", in John Whitney Hall *et al.* (eds), *The Cambridge History of Japan*, IV: *Early Modern Japan* (Cambridge, 1991), pp. 96–127, 105–110.
4. Thomas C. Smith, *The Agrarian Origins of Modern Japan* (Stanford, CA, 1959), p. 12.
5. *Ibid.*
6. One *koku* is equivalent to 180 litres of rice, which is sufficient to feed one person for one year. But since peasants usually had to pay taxes in rice, the amount at their disposal was much less than the number of *koku* registered for their fields.

century, whereas the proportion of *nago* varied greatly. The results of a census in Buzen (northern Kyūshū) carried out between 1681 and 1684 show that 36 to 60 per cent of the village population were *nago*. In another example of 14 villages in Echigo (now Niigata prefecture) the *nago* made up between 4 and 70 per cent of the peasant population.[7]

Hereditary servants and long-time indentured servants, whose term ranged from ten years to a whole lifetime, lived with their master and worked for him in the fields as well as in the home or in the household business. They were considered part of the family. The master was responsible for their food and clothing, and, in the case of young servants, also for their upbringing. Such servants were usually registered in the population registers as family members, but with a notation that marked them as servants, not kin. They often seem to have been treated quite similarly to the younger children of the master's family.

According to Smith, hereditary servants could marry and form their own families, who would often move into a separate dwelling near the main house. Although servants or their children could be sold or given as servants to daughters of the master upon marriage, many of them seem to have lived with the master's family for generations.[8]

Hereditary servants were either offspring of such servants or acquired by purchase or as a "gift" from poor families. Selling surplus members of poor families as either hereditary or long-term servants to better-off families in need of labour was obviously very common. Smith cites the journal of a peasant family in the eighteenth century, in which statements on crop failures are often accompanied by reports of local families selling members as hereditary servants. He also gives the example of a single county in northern Honshū, where during the 7 years from 1622 to 1629 more than 6,000 people were sold as hereditary servants.[9]

That selling people into service was a very widespread phenomenon is also shown by the frequency of laws dealing with this topic in the seventeenth century. Although trade in human beings (*jinshin baibai*) had been periodically banned before, and although the *daimyō* Toyotomi Hideyoshi, the second of the three "great unifiers" of the country, had explicitly outlawed trade in persons (*hito no baibai*) in 1587, the selling of children by families in economic distress seems not to have been affected by these laws. Between 1616 and 1716 the Tokugawa shogunate issued numerous laws banning the sale of persons, while at the same time limiting service terms to three years in the early laws and ten years in the later ones.[10]

---

7. Smith, *Agrarian Origins of Modern Japan*, pp. 8–10.
8. *Ibid.*, pp. 13–14.
9. *Ibid.*, p. 15.
10. Gary P. Leupp, *Servants, Shophands and Laborers in the Cities of Tokugawa Japan* (Princeton, NJ, 1992), p. 20.

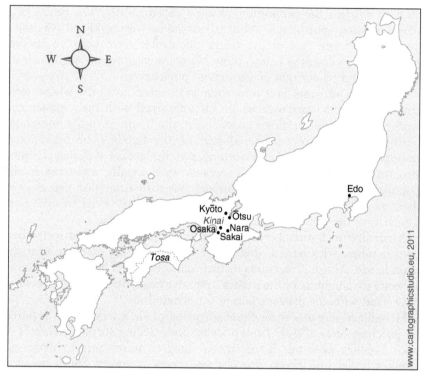

Figure 1. Map of Japan.

These laws were soon integrated into village regulations, as two examples of rules for the five-household neighbourhood units from 1640 and 1662 show. Both contain clauses prohibiting traffic in humans and limiting the terms of indentured servants.[11] Little is known about the implementation of these rules in the villages, but as stories of children sold into long-term or lifetime service by their families in times of distress continue to be told throughout the early modern period, this custom seems to have prevailed until far into the nineteenth century.

The perseverance of long-term or lifetime service is also apparent in the development of laws. Whereas laws in the first half of the seventeenth century tended to ban indefinite or lifetime service completely, later ones (1675, 1698) stipulated that service could be extended (unlimitedly) by mutual consent (*sōtai shidai*). The rationale behind this apparent retrogression is not clear, but one reason could have been the attempt to respond to a certain demand and to stabilize labour relations during a period of great change. As will be shown

11. Herman Ooms, *Tokugawa Village Practice: Class, Status, Power, Law* (Berkeley, CA [etc.], 1996), pp. 353ff.

in the second part of this article, short-service terms of six months or one year had already become quite common at the end of the seventeenth century in many areas, especially in the urban labour force, and therefore long-term service did not regain its former importance. It seems to have prevailed in some rural areas and in the realm of skilled labour in crafts and trade, while casual labour and unskilled work in urban areas tended towards a market-like relationship based on wages.

Another part of agricultural labour was provided by the *nago*, who cultivated land but were completely dependent on the landholder for housing, tools, animals, and other resources. In return they owed the landholder labour services upward of 30 or 40 days per year, which could be extended in some areas in certain years to as much as 200 days.[12]

FROM SUBSISTENCE FARMING TO COMMERCIALIZED AGRICULTURE AND SIDE WORK

With the expansion of commerce and industry in the late seventeenth and throughout the eighteenth century, some economically advanced areas saw a transformation of agricultural labour, which gradually spread to other parts of the country. These developments began to evolve first in Kyōto and the Kinai area, i.e. the provinces surrounding the cities of Kyōto, Nara, Ōsaka, and Ōtsu, as well as in the port town of Sakai (Figure 1).

Kyōto had been the hub of commercial activities for a long time. In the fourteenth century peasants in nearby villages apparently began to produce goods such as noodles, lamp oil, vinegar, and malt to sell in the cities. Some of these peasants even formed guilds (*inaka-za*) under the protection of powerful patrons, modelled after similar organizations of artisans and merchants in Kyōto and other cities.[13] At the same time, coins imported from China since the end of the twelfth century circulated not only in the central Kinai area but also in villages and markets along the great highways and became an additional incentive for peasants to produce for the market. In the fourteenth and fifteenth centuries the number of cities and towns as well as their population increased. Much of this growth was based on the growth of commerce, which expanded to regional markets. So, in the mid-sixteenth century, the Kinai area was economically already far advanced, and commercial transactions at markets and annual taxes were based mostly on coins. There were also other "scattered islands of commercial farming in Japan".[14]

12. Smith, *Agrarian Origins of Modern Japan*, p. 26.
13. Nagahara Keiji, "The Medieval Peasant", in Kozo Yamamura (ed.), *The Cambridge History of Japan*, III: *Medieval Japan* (Cambridge, 1990), pp. 301–343, 327–328; Wakita Haruko, "Towards a Wider Perspective on Medieval Commerce", *Journal of Japanese Studies*, 1 (1975), pp. 321–345, 336–337.
14. Smith, *Agrarian Origins of Modern Japan*, p. 67.

The reforms during the unification process greatly changed the framework for agricultural and commercial activities. New policies of registering land in the name of the cultivators since the 1580s, and the "return of the rice-using economy" through the introduction of the *kokudaka* system, in which land was measured in terms of rice output (*kokudaka*), and rice became again the main basis of taxation, put an end to the medieval economy.[15] However, these changes did not prevent the further spread of commerce and its growing importance for the economy as a whole, although they might have contributed to form its special structure, which differs from similar developments in Europe.

From the late 1630s the Tokugawa shogunate began to cast its own coins in large quantities, and the almost monetary role of rice was complemented by a tri-metallic currency system of gold, silver, and copper monies. Over time money became the common medium of exchange in the cities, but also at numerous rural markets, which sprang up everywhere. A list of commodities regularly sold at a village market in the Aizu domain (now Fukushima prefecture) in 1665 included cloth, harnesses, cotton, paper, rice, soya beans, firewood, hoes, hoe handles, sickle handles, winnowing baskets, looms, tobacco, grain, vegetables, mortars, straw hats, and straw matting.[16] The wide range of goods sold and purchased at that market shows that, already in the second half of the seventeenth century villagers relied on these markets for buying, but also for selling, many essentials.

With the spread of commerce and industry in the seventeenth century, cotton, one of the main cash crops, became prevalent in many areas, while others such as indigo, tobacco, and safflowers were produced as regional specialities. The production of raw cotton provided additional work for peasants and also entailed the emergence of a cottage industry gradually producing cotton thread and cloth far beyond the needs of the peasant families.

The growing importance of the domestic production of raw silk and silk cloth, which came to be substituted for expensive imports from China from the beginning of the eighteenth century, also created new opportunities for secondary employment for peasant families. Some other traditional side activities of peasants, such as hemp production, bleaching, and weaving, expanded considerably after the late seventeenth century.[17]

The commercialization of agriculture and the growth of rural industries as well as the growing demand for labour in the urban centres influenced the composition of the rural labour force in many parts of the country.

---

15. Concerning the background to this development see Kozo Yamamura, "From Coins to Rice: Hypotheses on the *Kandaka* and *Kokudaka* Systems", *Journal of Japanese Studies*, 14 (1988), pp. 341–367; Wakita Osamu, "The *Kokudaka* System: A Device for Unification", *Journal of Japanese Studies*, 1 (1975), pp. 297–320.
16. Smith, *Agrarian Origins of Modern Japan*, p. 73.
17. *Ibid.*, p. 77.

Smith relates the gradual disappearance of hereditary servants in economically advanced regions and their replacement by servants hired for a fixed period and payment (*hōkōnin*) to the spread of cash crops and other forms of commercialization in rural areas. Another phenomenon he mentions was the increase in tenant cultivation, which spread from the Kinai area, where it was already quite common in the seventeenth century, to other economically advanced regions during the eighteenth century. In these regions, *nago* often seem to have become tenants or to have been replaced by tenants during this gradual shift, while there were some rare cases in which *nago* purchased their land and personal freedom from their master.[18]

Although many of the changes starting in the mid-seventeenth century seem to suggest that patterns of rural industrialization in Japan were similar to those in western Europe, in his comparative studies on proto-industrialization Saitō Osamu stresses the structural differences, which also influenced the form of labour within that framework.

In Japan the development of rural industries had little impact on demography and the internal structure of the traditional peasant family economy. As the population density was three times higher than that of Flanders at the beginning of the eighteenth century and farm units were extremely small, the development of rural industries generally did not result in further fragmentation of the farms. Instead, farmers increased their land productivity by using new technologies, fertilizer, and improved irrigation as well as labour-intensive cultivation methods. At the same time, they took advantage of newly emerging opportunities for side work in crafts, commerce, and transport to supplement their incomes.

The strong intertwining of agriculture and rural industry, which Saitō regards as characteristic for most parts of Japan throughout the early modern period, makes it difficult to clearly differentiate between labour for subsistence and labour for a market. Both were usually conducted in the same household, though not necessarily by the same persons. The workforce available to the farm household had to be allotted to farming (food crops) and rural industries (including cash crops), and this was done, as Saitō points out, often along gender lines.[19]

THE ROLE OF WOMEN

Especially in textile production the division of labour between the sexes within peasant households was relatively clear. In contrast to traditional side work such as paper manufacturing, which was done by the whole family in the slack season, employment in textile production was limited

---

18. *Ibid.*, pp. 109–110, 131–137.
19. Saitō Osamu, "Population and the Peasant Family Economy in Proto-Industrial Japan", *Journal of Family History*, 8 (1983), pp. 30–54, 40–41.

mostly to the women in the household. The assignment of the work of
spinning and weaving to female members of a family can be traced back
far into Japanese history and can also be found in China and other parts of
the world. Shortly before the spread of rural industrialization, an edict,
said to have been issued by the shogunate in 1649 and addressing the
peasants directly, stated that "Both husband and wife should work for a
living: the husband in the fields, the wife at the loom and preparing the
evening meals".[20] In a well-known and widely read treatise on proper
behaviour *Onna Daigaku* [The Great Learning for Women], published in
1716, we find a similar statement:

> A woman must be ever on the alert, and keep a strict watch over her own
> conduct. In the morning she must rise early, and at night go late to rest. Instead
> of sleeping in the middle of the day, she must be intent on the duties of her
> household, and must not weary of weaving, sewing, and spinning.[21]

As this manual was addressed primarily to upper-class women, it shows
that this kind of work was seen as suitable for women of all classes.

Saitō argues that in the course of Japan's proto-industrialization, this
traditional division of labour in the peasant family was maintained even
when textile production grew and turned into a cottage industry producing for a market, which had to meet a rapidly increasing demand on a
national scale. Although there obviously existed a regional division in the
workflow between areas growing and ginning cotton and those processing it by reeling, spinning, and weaving, the latter tasks were nearly
always taken up by wives and daughters of peasant households who
worked at home. This holds true at least for the seventeenth and eighteenth centuries, as a document from 1803 shows, which states "as for by-
employments, the men cut firewood and fodder; the women spin and
weave cotton yarns for use by the family and for sale if any is left over".[22]

Rare exceptions to this pattern of labour division were the highly
professionalized traditional silk weavers of Nishijin in Kyōto, who were
mostly male. Their work was apparently seen as a craft and therefore
treated differently from the production of home-made cotton thread and
cloth. When silk spinning and weaving spread to rural areas, its situation
became similar to that of cotton production.

20. Based on the English translation by Ooms, *Tokugawa Village Practice*, pp. 363–373, 368.
The edict is commonly known as the Keian Edict, as it was issued in the second year of the
Keian era. In the 1990s its authenticity began to be disputed by some scholars. In his short
introduction to the translation Ooms briefly refers to the debate concerning the authenticity of
this edict.
21. The treatise is attributed to the Confucian scholar Kaibara Ekiken (1630–1714). The
English translation is by John Murray, *Women and Wisdom of Japan* (London, 1909), p. 40.
22. Cited in Smith, *Agrarian Origins of Modern Japan*, p. 78.

Figure 2. Threshing and husking rice. The picture from the *Nōgyō zensho* shows men and women working together in threshing rice (below) and husking it (above). Men's kimonos are shorter and they wear a towel twisted into a headband, while women wear a sort of headscarf. The woman in the middle is breastfeeding an older child.

Miyazaki Yasusada (Antei), Nōgyō zensho [The Farmer's Compendium] (1696), reprinted in Yamada Tatsuo et al. (eds), Nihon nōgyō zenshū, XII, Nōgyō zensho, Books 1–5 (Tokyo, 1978), p. 42.

Men usually worked in the fields, and if they took up side work it was mostly in crafts, transport, or petty trade. Based on figures from the nineteenth century, Saitō remarks that in areas with rural industries the proportion of men with side work (dual occupations) was generally lower than that of women.[23] This suggests the important role of women's contribution to Japan's rural industries, especially in the field of textiles.

This view is not undisputed. While some authors, including Murakami Nobuhiko, a writer and author of studies on women's history, emphasizing the subordinate position of women in the hierarchical "house system" (*ie-seido*) at that time, deny the possibility of men and women cooperating in productive labour, and declare that the contribution of female labour was negligible, others, such as the Marxist historian Inoue Kiyoshi, regard peasant women of the Tokugawa period as relatively powerful and claim they were engaged in productive work cooperatively with male family members.[24] Yet even though the rise of rural industry largely occurred through the expansion of by-production in peasant households without changing the existing social structures and thus the subordinate position of women in the family and in society, the rapid spread of these rural cottage industries shows that through their by-production the material contribution of women must have been very substantial.

Spinning and weaving were not the only female tasks. Unlike women in northern China, who were strongly discouraged from working in the fields, Japanese women also worked on the land. Except for some women from wealthy peasant families, women from peasant households usually took part in agricultural work, especially in the busy seasons of planting and harvesting. This is evident from several agricultural treatises (*nōsho*), which were published in growing numbers from the end of the seventeenth century onward. Based on Chinese models or on information collected in Japan, and sometimes even on personal work experience, the authors describe various aspects of agricultural activities in writing and in pictures, often with the intention of advancing commercialized farming.

For example, illustrations in the *Nōgyō zensho* [The Farmer's Companion] from the second half of the seventeenth century show women participating in rice planting, weeding, or threshing, in the latter case working side by side with men (Figure 2).[25] Planting the rice seedlings in the main field was obviously a typical, though not exclusive, job for women. An agricultural

23. Saitō, "Population and Peasant Family Economy", pp. 40–41.
24. A short outline of this dispute can be found in Wakita Haruko and Suzanne Gay, "Marriage and Property in Premodern Japan from the Perspective of Women's History", *Journal of Japanese Studies*, 10 (1984)), pp. 73–99, 96–97.
25. Drawings in Miyazaki Yasusada (Antei), *Nōgyō zensho* [The Farmer's Compendium] (1696), repr. in Yamada Tatsuo *et al.* (eds), *Nihon nōsho zenshū*, XII, *Nōgyō zensho*, Books 1–5 (Tokyo, 1978), pp. 38–39, 41–42.

Figure 3. Planting and weeding rice. *Saotome* (rice-planting women) are planting the seedlings (right), while a man with a hoe is standing behind them. Another woman offers tea or water (left). While men are drawing water, women are weeding the field. Another man with a hoe is passing by. *Miyazaki Yasusada (Antei)*, Nōgyō zensho *[The Farmer's Compendium] (1696), reprinted in* Yamada Tatsuo et al. (eds), Nihon nōgyō zenshū, XII, Nōgyō zensho, Books 1 to 5 *(Tokyo, 1978), pp. 38–39.*

treatise from 1707, the *Kōka shunjū* [Cultivating the Soil from Spring to Autumn], gives detailed instructions on how many *saotome* (rice-planting women) one needed to work a field of a certain size.[26] The appearance of the obviously young, good-looking *saotome* in the fields each May seems to have attracted great attention and is mentioned in several verses in the *Aizu uta nōsho* [Agricultural Treatise from the Aizu Region in Verses] (Figure 3).[27]

In the course of the eighteenth century, the demarcation between men's and women's work apparently became more and more blurred. While the

26. Tsuchiya Matasaburō, *Kōka shunjū* [Cultivating the Soil from Spring to Autumn] (1707), repr. in Yamada Tatsuo *et al.* (eds), *Nihon nōsho zenshū*, IV (Tokyo, 1980), pp. 17–18.
27. Sase Yojiuemon, *Aizu uta nōsho* [Agricultural Treatise from the Aizu Region in Verses] (1704), repr. in Yamada Tatsuo *et al.* (eds), *Nihon nōsho zenshū*, XX, *Aizu uta nōsho, Makunouchi nōgyō-ki* (Tokyo, 1982), pp. 74–75. The author (1630–1711) came from a wealthy family of village headmen and knew peasant life and agricultural work from his own practical experience – like many of the Japanese writers of agricultural treatises. So we can assume that, even though he was influenced by Chinese writings on agriculture, his writings reflect the reality in eastern Japan.

hoe is depicted as a typically male tool in the illustrations of the *Nōgyō zensho*, the *Aizu fūzoku chō* [Record of Customs from the Aizu Region], written 100 years later, mentions that "[w]ithin the last thirty years women gradually have taken hoes and dug in the fields [...], doing the same agricultural work as men [...] and a really strong woman can work harder than a man". There are similar stories in another source, the *Ryūryū shinku-roku* [Record of the Hard Work of Peasants] from 1805, about women in the mountains of Echigo province (now Niigata prefecture). They are said to have worked together with their husbands, using axes, forester's hatchets, and sickles, leading a horse or an ox and hauling heavy burdens, and "being not inferior to men [in their work]".

The apparent praise of strong women doing hard work like men in both examples might have contained a slightly critical undertone though: in the same text in the *Aizu fūzoku chō* the author deplores the disappearance of the beautifully dressed *saotome* of earlier times, who had given way to women working in the fields, unkempt and dressed like men, "so that sexes could no longer be told apart".[28] It is interesting to note that in these sources, aesthetic criteria are used to convey the impression of certain kinds of work in the fields as being appropriate for women, whereas others where women obviously cross the border into the realm of men's work lead to the loss of their womanliness.

Besides agriculture, women worked in a large number of jobs. In areas where mining was flourishing, women – usually the wives and daughters of the miners – worked in the mines above ground as sluice operators (*nekonagashi*) and hand pickers (*ishidori*) (Figure 4), as numerous examples in picture scrolls on mining illustrate. In urban centres women also worked outside the home.

It seems that certain ideas concerning the virtuousness of women and chastity, originating in China, which emphasized that women should stay at home, not work alongside their male relatives in the fields or outside the home, and not remarry after the death of their husbands, were known in Japan, but they had little influence among the lower classes of the rural and urban population.[29] In the seventeenth century the division of labour in peasant household chores and field work seems to have been even more pronounced than in later years, when women expanded their activities and joined men in their tasks.

28. *Aizu fūzoku chō* [Record of Customs from the Aizu Region, 1807] and *Ryūryū shinku-roku* [Record of the Hard Work of Peasants, 1805], both cited by Sugano Noriko, "Nōson josei no rōdō to seikatsu" [Work and Daily Life of Peasant Women], in Joseishi Sōgō Kenkyūkai (ed.), *Nihon joseishi*, III, *Kinsei* (Tokyo, 1982), pp. 63–94, 92–94; part of the English translation of the citations is based on Anne Walthall, "The Life Cycle of Farm Women", in Gail Bernstein (ed.), *Recreating Japanese Women, 1600–1945* (Berkeley, CA, 1991), pp. 42–70, 57.
29. Walthall, "Life Cycle of Farm Women", p. 57.

Figure 4. Women working in the mines. Women were employed in mines for many tasks relating to processing the ore, which was mined by men. This picture (from a picture scroll on mining) shows women dividing the ore into three categories by washing it and probing it with a hammer. *Picture scroll*, Kingin saisei zenzu [On the Mining of Gold and Silver in Sado]. *Property of the University of Freiberg, Germany. Used with permission.*

THE SITUATION IN URBAN AREAS

The Japan of the Tokugawa period was one of the most urbanized regions of the world. More than twenty major castle towns, including Edo and Ōsaka, were established or expanded in the three decades between 1580 and 1610. They quickly grew, and it is estimated that at the end of the seventeenth century 8 to 9 per cent of the population lived in cities and towns with more than 30,000 people, and in some cases with several hundreds of thousands of inhabitants.[30] If smaller market towns of 3,000 inhabitants are included, the share of the urban population rises to 16 or 17 per cent. The urban growth was led by Edo, the population of which increased from about 100,000 in 1610 to roughly 400,000 in the 1640s, to as many as 800,000 in the 1680s, and to over 1,000,000 inhabitants by the 1720s.[31] In the large cities, new patterns of consumption and new modes of social organization and labour relations evolved, and gradually spread to smaller towns.

30. John Whitney Hall, "The Castle Town and Japan's Modern Urbanization", *The Far Eastern Quarterly*, 15 (1955), pp. 37–56, 44, 51. Around 1700 about 10 per cent of the population lived in cities of over 10,000 inhabitants.
31. Gilbert Rozman, "Edo's Importance in the Changing Tokugawa Society", *Journal of Japanese Studies*, 1 (1974), pp. 91–112, 93, n. 7.

The traditional labour force of the sixteenth century in non-agricultural occupations consisted mostly of three groups: conscripted peasants, artisans, and hereditary domestic servants in samurai households. For larger projects, such as the construction of houses, castles, or roads, the feudal lords and their local retainers relied on *corvée* labour by the peasantry. Ever since the first legal code of the eighth century, *corvée* labour (*buyaku*) had been a kind of tax to be paid by the peasants.

The second group were the artisans (*shokunin*). While the term in the thirteenth and fourteenth centuries obviously described all kinds of skilled people working outside agriculture, artisans in the narrow sense of this term (*shūkōgyōsha*, literally "handworker") emerged during the fifteenth and sixteenth centuries. The social status of these artisans was characterized by a tendency towards increasing freedom to travel and to enter employment. However, the degree of this individual freedom is still disputed among scholars.[32] The range of occupations was already quite differentiated, and they were obviously paid for their work, though in kind (as unhulled rice). There were artisan organizations, mostly small local guilds (*za*, *kabu-nakama*) in the early sixteenth century, but they were dissolved in the process of unifying the country, because they were often seen as an obstacle to trade expansion. In the Tokugawa period, exclusive trade organizations (*nakama*, *kabu-nakama*) and artisan groups resurfaced in the cities.

The third group were servants. There were many terms for these, including *fudai* (hereditary), like the servants in the countryside, or *hikan* (in this context meaning servant of an urban family), and they were distinct from slaves. They could, for example, get married as they wished, but they and their descendants were considered members of their master's household and were not free to leave their employer.[33] If a family was split up, the girls would follow the mother and the boys the father. Jansen described the *fudai* in the samurai households in the fief of Tosa (Shikoku) as semi-free indentured servants.[34] There are few documents on servants in commoner households in the late sixteenth and early seventeenth century, but they also seem to have been *fudai* or in a similar position, and there is no evidence of a different form of non-hereditary, short-term service at that time.[35]

---

32. A thorough analysis of the term *shokunin* and its historical interpretations can be found in Klaus Vollmer, *Professionen und ihre "Wege" im mittelalterlichen Japan. Eine Einführung in ihre Sozialgeschichte und literarische Repräsentation am Beispiel des Tōhoku'in shokunin utaawase* (Hamburg, 1995), *passim*, and pp. 101–102.
33. Leupp, *Servants, Shophands and Laborers*, p. 13.
34. Marius B. Jansen, "Tosa in the Seventeenth Century: The Establishment of Yamauchi Rule", in John W. Hall and Marius B. Jansen (eds), *Studies in the Institutional History of Early Modern Japan* (Princeton, NJ, 1968), pp. 115–130, 106, 121.
35. Leupp, *Servants, Shophands and Laborers*, p. 15.

THE INTRODUCTION OF LABOUR CONTRACTS

The seventeenth century saw a major transformation in the organization and the character of service and labour. Initially, traditional forms of work still prevailed. A hundred years later several authors deplored the disappearance of lifetime servants and *corvée* labourers. These changes started in the early half of the century, but gathered momentum after 1650 and, according to Mary Louise Nagata, provided a coherent framework of labour relations that lasted for 200 years.[36]

In her comprehensive study of the development of labour contracts concerning service in merchant, artisan, and manufacturers' households, Nagata has traced the beginnings of such contracts to the seventeenth century, although they became common only a century later. According to her findings, summarized below, during the seventeenth century the repeated bans by the Tokugawa shogunate on selling people into service made it necessary for those engaged in craft, trade, and industries to look for other forms of employment. At the same time many businesses went through a period of rapid expansion, creating a demand for labour that could not be satisfied by employing only kin, children of friends, or other people well known to the employer. To secure a disciplined and stable labour force, employers started to use contracts, which in the late seventeenth century still tended to be verbal, but which were soon replaced by written contracts.

These contracts served first and foremost as "letters of guarantee", signed by a guarantor, who knew the applicant and took responsibility for his or her good conduct. Such contracts soon became standardized, and typical clauses would include: the relationship between guarantor and employee; hints concerning the religion of the employee to indicate that he was not a Christian and was registered at a certain temple; a pledge that the employee would obey the laws and rules of the employer's household; and the contract provisions and responsibilities of the guarantor. The involvement of such a guarantor had been required by the central government as early as 1665 in the face of widespread abuse, such as running away and not fulfilling contracts, and instability. Laws in the years 1666 to 1668 sharpened the regulations, indicating that the employers' worries and the government's efforts to retain (or gain) control over the new forms of employment had not yet been successful.[37] Nagata points out, that "[a]t the end of the seventeenth century wage labor was common and written contracts identifying one or more guarantors were the main mechanism for controlling abuses of the system".[38]

---

36. Mary Louise Nagata, *Labor Contracts and Labor Relations in Early Modern Central Japan* (London, 2005), p. 122.

37. *Ibid.*, pp. 15–16, 54–56, 72.

38. *Ibid.*, p. 16.

Service in merchant or artisan households was usually based on long-term contracts. Servants, male and female, lived on site, being provided with a bed, board, clothing, and other necessities by the employer. When these households started to hire more short-term labour for unskilled or semi-skilled tasks, two different modes of employment evolved during the eighteenth century: long-term contracts – often for periods of ten years – were used for apprentices, skilled labour, and management employees, while domestic servants often had short contracts ranging from six months to one year.[39]

As early as 1610 a "servant replacement day" (*dekawari-bi*) on which servants could be dismissed or hired was designated in Kyōto, and Edo introduced this custom three years later. During the seventeenth century the system became common in most cities and even in villages. During the Genroku period (1680–1704) a second replacement day was added, making it possible to hire and fire servants, and from the perspective of servants to leave their employer, every six months. Dazai Shundai (1680–1747), a Confucian scholar, complained in his writings about these new developments, which loosened the bond between master and servant. He wrote: "In China there is no class similar to that of the house servants of these times, who are called *dekawari* servants [...]. They change their masters each year and therefore their employers do not show them much kindness, and the employees show very little fidelity to their masters."[40]

Changes occurred too in the payment of wages. According to Nagata's findings,

> In the late seventeenth century wages for labour contracts still tended to be paid in advance to the employee's family, making wage labour an indentured relationship. By the early eighteenth century contracts began to specify that the wage would be paid directly to the employee either at the end of the contract or at periodic intervals during the contract.[41]

We can conclude therefore that, starting around the mid-seventeenth century, servants, who until then had been limited mostly to samurai households, became a widespread phenomenon in commoners' households and businesses in urban areas. This process was accompanied by significant changes, such as the emergence of written contracts, the transition from indentured service to wage labour, the increase in short-term employment, and wage standardization. At the same time, labour relations in services requiring intensive training and special skills tended to retain many features of the traditional long-term paternalistic employment system.

39. *Ibid.*, pp. 16–17.
40. Leupp, *Servants, Shophands and Laborers*, pp. 22–24.
41. Nagata, *Labor Contracts and Labor Relations*, p. 16.

THE DEVELOPMENT OF FREE AND CASUAL LABOUR

As mentioned before, the decades around the turn of the sixteenth century were a period of unprecedented urban growth. The Tokugawa regime and the feudal lords invested in infrastructure by building roads and waterworks, organized transport, and operated mines. Wakita Osamu suggests that for certain construction projects, such as Ōsaka Castle, the regime at times mobilized 10,000 workers per day. That figure was presumably the number of man-days and included construction workers, workers in quarries, lumberjacks, transport workers, and various kinds of artisans.[42] The simultaneous realization of many large-scale and even more small-scale projects must have created an enormous demand for labour, which could have never been met solely by peasant *corvée* labour, without seriously endangering agricultural production – and thereby also the tax income of the feudal elite, because taxes were paid in kind, mostly in rice.

In his detailed and comprehensive study on the rise of urban labour in Tokugawa Japan, Leupp concludes that from the mid-1630s a new type of hired casual labourer came to replace *corvée* workers in castle-town construction projects. While in the 1580s and 1590s Toyotomi Hideyoshi had still explicitly forbidden the hiring of day labourers, the attitude of the central administration changed during the following decades.

In 1636 a supervisor of construction works at Ōsaka Castle, the territorial lord of Higo, Hosokawa Tadatoshi, wrote a memorandum to the shōgun, stressing that it would be preferable to hire wage labourers rather than use *corvée* labour; the latter should better concentrate on rice production.[43] In 1653, an edict was issued in Edo stating "As it was formerly commanded, people working as day-laborers must receive a license (*fuda*) from the day-laborers' chiefs (*hiyatoi-gashira*). Anyone employing persons without such a license will be fined. This is a criminal offense."[44] This is said to be the first surviving edict mentioning day labourers in this context. Four years later a similar edict was issued in Ōsaka. Both edicts seem to indicate that around the middle of the century the shogunate had given up its general rejection of hired labour, and was trying instead to cope with the new kind of labour force by introducing new methods of control.

Most of these casual labourers came from impoverished rural areas and had flocked to the cities and towns in their thousands, searching for work and a way to make a living. According to Rozman, Edo's population may

---

42. Wakita Osamu, "Kinsei shoki no toshi keizai" [Urban Economy in the Early Years of the Early Modern Period], *Nihonshi kenkyū*, 200 (1979), pp. 52–75, 63. These figures are based on estimates by Wakita, who calculated the number of labourers by taking the overall costs of labour and dividing them by average wages. According to this, there would have been several millions of people (or possibly man-days) per year.
43. Leupp, *Servants, Shophands and Laborers*, p. 17.
44. *Ibid.*, p. 160.

have grown by 10,000 immigrants a year during the first half of the
seventeenth century, and by 15,000 immigrants a year during the second
half.[45] The casual labourers were employed on a daily, ten-day, twenty-
day, or monthly basis. As the free movement of people was still forbidden
and peasants were not supposed to leave their land, the government at
first repeatedly rounded up these rural immigrants in the cities, especially
in Edo, and returned them to their native villages. Around the middle of
the seventeenth century, as the above-mentioned edict shows, the shogunate seems to have changed its policy and started to recognize casual
labour as part of economic and social development. Around 1700 one-
fifth to one-third of the urban population in Japan consisted of hired
servants, shop hands, and manual labourers.[46]

A closer look at the composition of this labour force shows that it comprised both men and women. Although women were fewer in number than
men, they performed many jobs in the cities, such as shop hands, tailors,
laundresses, dyers, pedlars, and hawkers.[47] Leupp mentions one example of
thirty-two day labourers in the castle town of Kasama (Hitachi province,
now Ibaragi prefecture) in 1705, among them six women, who were all
widows. Other examples also suggest that women often had to work to
make a living or at least supplement their insufficient household income. For
them, the growing diversity of jobs in the cities offered alternatives to the
traditional resort in times of economic need, namely prostitution.

A rare example of female artisans is given in one of the writings by Ihara
Saikaku (1642–1693), who mentions female carpenters who worked at the
women's quarters in the Imperial Palace in Kyōto and "do this for a living".[48]

The age of day labourers varied greatly. Some labourers seem to have
begun working at the age of fourteen or fifteen but, as Leupp points out,
in several documents the recorded average age of day labourers is surprisingly high, sometimes even exceeding fifty years.[49]

In contrast to most of the *corvée* labourers, who were provided only with
room and board, the newly emerging group of casual labourers were
obviously paid wages. Conservative intellectuals noted and often deplored this
change. In 1730 the Confucian scholar Ogyū Sorai (1666–1728) wrote: "Until
seventy or eighty years ago the employment of day-laborers was unheard of".
Around the same time, his contemporary Dazai Shundai noted that:

> It is rare nowadays to use peasants as corvée labor. For such [tasks] as public
> work, workers in the capital are hired for wages [...]. Nowadays lords do not
> employ people of their provinces, but hire them for wages in Edo. Wage-work

45. Rozman, *Edo's Importance*, p. 100.
46. Leupp, *Servants, Shophands and Laborers*, p. 176.
47. *Ibid.*, p. 139.
48. Cited in *ibid.*, p. 138.
49. *Ibid.*, p. 139.

(*chinpu*) is, by the current custom, referred to as day labor (*hiyō*). For virtually every type of work, people are hired for money. So people do not suffer, but on the contrary, they prosper. This is different from the old practice.[50]

So, at the end of the seventeenth century wage labour was widespread in urban areas, and even in Dazai Shundai's statement this is depicted as a positive trend.

One question is whether wages were paid directly to the individual worker. A regulation dating from 1657 that tried to limit the wages to be paid to different groups of day labourers gave the respective amounts in "one unit of gold (*ryō*) per 45, 65 or 70 persons", depending among other things on whether they owned their tools or not. This seems to indicate that the whole sum was often given to some kind of labour boss, who would then in turn hand part of it to the workers he was in charge of, and keep the rest to pay for his expenses and a profit.[51]

Wage levels seem to have fluctuated widely depending on demand and supply, and the authorities repeatedly (though mostly unsuccessfully) tried to keep them down. The new economic developments, the emergence of wage labour, the rise and fall in prices and wages, and the growing impact of money on the economy were important topics in scholarly debates in Japan from the late seventeenth century onward. In the early phase, neo-Confucian scholars, including Arai Hakuseki (1657–1725) as well as Ogyū Sorai and Dazai Shundai, dominated the debate. They mostly deplored the new developments.

In contrast, the economist and philosopher Miura Baien (1723–1789), a contemporary of Adam Smith, although very critical about the money economy and the accumulation of wealth in the cities, did not plead for the complete abolition of money and wage labour. Instead he wrote a chapter on "the price of wage labour", in which he thoroughly analysed the connections between the situation in rural areas and wage labour in the cities. In his eyes, the shift of large numbers of poor peasants between agricultural work in years of abundance and wage labour in the cities in years of bad harvests was the main reason for wage instability. So he recommended improving the economic situation of small peasants to keep them on the land and separate them from urban wage labourers.[52] In his writings he acknowledges the existence of wage labour as an irrevocable fact, proving the consolidation of the new

---

50. Citations based on *ibid.*, pp. 16–17.
51. *Ibid.*, p. 161.
52. Based on the complete German translation of Miura's work *Kagen*; Miura Baien, *Kagen. Vom Ursprung des Wertes. Faksimile der zwischen 1773 und 1789 entstandenen Handschrift* (Düsseldorf, 2001), Günther Distelrath *et al.* (eds), *Kagen. Vademecum zu einem japanischen Klassiker des ökonomischen Denkens. Kommentarband* (including the complete German translation of *Kagen*) (Düsseldorf, 2001). Here I refer to the chapter "Der Preis der Lohnarbeit" in *Kommentarband*, pp. 187–191.

economic trends, but he advocated measures to reach a balance between rural and urban developments, rather than leaving them to market forces.

The emergence of new forms of urban labour with short-term contracts and a comparatively free labour force, along with increasing migration to the cities leading to a growing number of urban poor, alarmed the authorities. They reacted by setting up new measures and mechanisms of control.

One measure was to round up peasants and other people from the countryside in the cities and order them to return to their villages. This policy, called *hitogaeshi* (to return people), was sporadically applied throughout the Tokugawa period, but intensified in the late 1780s and the 1840s, when famine drove large numbers of peasants from the countryside into the cities. Repeated edicts by the central administration (*hitogaeshi-rei*), however, suggest that this policy did not succeed, probably due to the deteriorating situation in many villages, the sheer numbers of immigrants, and the lack of sanctions. These and other measures, and their consequences, show that the authorities could not and would not prevent the spread of wage labour in the cities and towns, even though this was clearly undermining the ideological basis of the political, social, and economic system. Nevertheless, the emerging labour market around 1650 had clear limits. The individual labourer may have been free in comparison with part of rural society, but this freedom was strictly regulated and became even more so in the course of the eighteenth century when administrative policies seem to have become more effective.

WORKERS' ATTITUDES TOWARDS WORK

After this exploration of both government policies towards work and mobility at the central and local levels and the opinions of scholars and thinkers, the question of the workers' own attitudes and self-image needs to be addressed. Moral indoctrination provided another option for control.

Contemporary sources give us little information about the moral ideas or the work ethic of servants and labourers. The spread of neo-Confucian ideas in the seventeenth century led to moral rules and prescriptions of correct behaviour for the "four status groups" (warrior, peasant, artisan, merchant), which became firmly entrenched in society after the turn of the century but whose origins can be traced to the reforms of Toyotomi Hideyoshi in the 1580s. The underlying theoretical construct, based on an ancient Chinese model, combined legal conceptions and a moral hierarchy with a social division of labour.[53] The interrelation of occupation and

---

53. In Japan the four status groups (*shimin*, also translated as four classes, four peoples, four orders, and in German *Vier-Stände-System*) were often reduced to three by merging the last two groups, artisans and merchants, into one, and labelling them "town dwellers" (*chōnin*). A comprehensive outline of questions related to the historiographical treatment of status, class,

morality resulting from this concept constituted the framework in which scholars in the Tokugawa period reflected upon work and social status.

In his study on the perception of work in Tokugawa Japan, Takemura Eiji shows that the terms used for work (*sugiwai*, *nariwai*) in a Japanese–Portuguese dictionary from 1603 implied a productive activity to gain the means of one's living. But other terms, such as *shokubun* or *tenshoku*, referred to "one's occupation or trade (*shoku*), fulfilling an allotted part (*bun*) in society". According to this neo-Confucian ideology, all status-related occupational groups were expected to "be diligent in fulfilling one's own *shokubun*". So the concept of work was strongly related to one's role and status in society.[54] As Takemura relies, among other sources, on one of the supplements written by Kaibara Rakuken (1625–1702) to the above-mentioned *Nōgyō zensho*, published in 1696, we can assume that this concept of *shokubun* was already part of the practical literature for peasants in the late seventeenth century.

One of the most influential schools in the dissemination of such a work ethic for the three lower-status groups was the *Shingaku* [The School of the Heart] by Ishida Baigan (1685–1744). Under the leadership of Ishida Baigan and his successors, the teachings of Shingaku spread from Kyōto and Ōsaka to other parts of the country during the second half of the eighteenth and the early nineteenth centuries. At its height there were more than 170 centres and Shingaku academies in various parts of the country, many of them in towns that were not castle towns, and in rural areas. So Ishida Baigan's ideas were disseminated among all status groups during the decades after his death.[55]

He propagated the pursuit of self-cultivation among all status groups, not only the elites, while at the same time linking it to practical action, namely the devotion to one's work and the acquisition of skills. He saw the *shokubun* as an assignment by Heaven and argued that "samurai are samurai, peasants are peasants, and merchants are merchants. [...] if one is loyal to Heaven's assignment, and is devoted to it, one shall certainly reach the state of fulfillment".[56] While adhering to status distinctions, Ishida Baigan apparently demanded respect for all who fulfilled their role in society. In one of his writings, "Tohi mondō" [A Dialogue between Town and Country] from 1739, a merchant's apprentice speaks with contempt about day labourers, to which Ishida Baigan replies: "How do we differ from day laborers? It is

---

and the social division of work is provided by Douglas R. Howland, "Samurai Status, Class, and Bureaucracy: A Historiographical Essay", *Journal of Asian Studies*, 60 (2001), pp. 353–380, 353–367.
54. Takemura Eiji, *The Perception of Work in Tokugawa Japan: A Study of Ishida Baigan and Ninomiya Sontoku* (Lanham, MD, 1997), pp. 24–27.
55. *Ibid.*, pp. 94–96.
56. *Ibid.*, pp. 55–56. English translation by Takemura Eiji.

narrow-minded to regard day laborers as lowly". Other examples stressing that artisans and other workmen are as important to society as samurai, peasants, and merchants also prove that there was no general disdain of physical labour displayed in the writings of the intellectual elite.[57]

The question remains how and to what degree Confucian values and ideas about hard work, diligence, and fulfilling one's role in society were internalized by the lower classes of society. They must have been exposed to and influenced by contemporary ideas about morals and appropriate behaviour.

First, in the first half of the seventeenth century, most of them came from rural areas. In the above-mentioned edict of 1649, peasants were admonished to rise early and go to sleep late, work with the greatest diligence, and not waste time and resources. Advice books such as the *Nōgyō zensho* contained not only practical advice but also moral ideas. Second, those who worked for longer periods in merchant houses or artisan workshops would have been exposed to similar ideas there. Third, such ideas could have been circulated by those members of the merchant or artisan status groups who controlled the labourers, such as the *hiyatoi-gashira* (merchants), officials of the registry, or even landlords. Last but not least, the poor houses or workhouses may also have served this purpose.

That they were not necessarily just punitive institutions but regarded by some authorities as an example of benevolent government and assigned an educational task is conveyed in the statement of a senior councillor in 1778, which expresses hope that "immoral and dissipated vagrants" committed to the workhouses at the Sado mines could be "rehabilitated", and after "mending their ways" return to society.[58] Work was obviously used as an instrument to discipline those who were seen as a threat to the social order of Edo and other cities, but potentially also as an instrument for improvement. These examples concern vagrants, but the lines of demarcation between vagrants and day labourers were blurred, and many of the "vagrants" might have been unlicensed casual labourers.

A final interesting point, mentioned by Leupp, is the fact that, at least as late as the early nineteenth century, inmates of the Edo *yoseba* (large workhouse) were exposed three times a month to a kind of rehabilitation programme, in which they had to attend lectures given by scholars of the Shingaku school, a moral doctrine amalgamating Confucian, Shinto and Buddhist elements with a strong work ethic, predominant in the merchant class.[59] This example is too late to use as evidence for the situation in 1650. It marks, however, the end of a development during which ideological concepts of work were spread among the status groups. It is doubtful that workers around 1650 had already internalized such ideas,

---

57. Leupp, *Servants, Shophands and Laborers*, pp. 150–151, 126.
58. Tanaka Keiichi, *Sado Kinzan* [Sado Gold Mines] (Tokyo, 1980), pp. 228–229.
59. Leupp, *Servants, Shophands and Laborers*, p. 174.

but the 1649 edict on peasants shows that the indoctrination of society's lower classes had already begun by then.

To what degree these moral ideas shaped their actions and attitudes and how they might have resisted them is hard to say. In popular fiction, especially in the novels of the seventeenth-century writer Ihara Saikaku, as well as in many *senryū* (short comical verses) and *kobanashi* (humorous anecdotes), servants are often depicted as lazy, pleasure loving, gossip-prone, and unreliable, sometimes clumsy and ignorant, sometimes very shrewd. Hired workers are similarly depicted drinking, gambling, and spending their earnings in the pleasure quarters.[60]

These stereotypes were obviously especially popular with the public, because they contravened the prevailing Confucian values. On the other hand they might also partly reflect the fact that the new kind of short-term employment might have loosened the bonds with employers and offered these groups opportunities to pursue their own ideas about a good life. They nevertheless hardly reproduced the authentic view of the groups concerned.

Work songs, which could reflect this view, exist, but it is nearly impossible to link them to a certain period of time. Some like rice-planting or weaving songs could probably be traced back to the seventeenth century, while others dealing with coal mining or female workers (*jokō*) can be linked at best to the late eighteenth and early nineteenth century because the work they describe did not exist in earlier times.

If the songs relate directly to the work, the most frequent topic is the hardship endured by workers. In the cotton beaters' song, work is characterized by words such as *tsurai* (harsh, severe) or *kurō* (trouble, hardship).[61] "Sing, sing they kept urging me, but a song wouldn't come out, only sweat", or "If you're suffering at work, instead of crying, sing. If the song is good, you'll cheer up".[62] In some songs related to peasants' work we find complaints about backs sore from planting rice or the expressions of loneliness by indentured servants, but rarely expressions of social or political protest or antagonism towards one's immediate superiors.[63] Hughes cites two examples of songs expressing critique. In one, a local entrepreneur is bedevilled by indigo workers: "the tycoon of Awa is a devil from hell; he does not extract indigo dye, he extracts blood". Another one focuses on the relationship between peasant and the local landlord: "the peasant is mouse, the squire is a cat, his eyes on the peasant

60. *Ibid.*, pp. 108–112, 151.
61. Machida Kashō *et al.* (eds), *Nihon minyō shū* [Collection of Japanese Folk Songs] (Tokyo, 1963), pp. 203–204.
62. David W. Hughes, *Traditional Folk Song in Modern Japan: Sources, Sentiment and Society* (Folkestone, 2008), pp. 73–74.
63. *Ibid.*, p. 56.

drowsily [thinking I'll catch him]",[64] but they could be from the eighteenth or nineteenth centuries. Other songs, such as the pottery song from Bizen, praise the master, "The Lord of Bizen is a great and noble man. Thanks to our lord the kiln flourishes. When the kiln flourishes so does the whole village".[65]

Indirect information about the work ethic of servants or employees in merchant and artisan households is likely to be found in sources dealing with conflicts between masters and servants. Nagata has pointed out that contracts usually contained provisions against absconding and disappearing after theft. According to her, swindling scams were apparently a problem in the seventeenth and eighteenth centuries, and guarantors were usually held responsible for bringing the fugitives back or compensating the employer for his losses. The few cases she presents in her study seem to indicate that such troubles occurred quite frequently, even with the same person being hired, fired, and re-hired.[66] So a broader analysis of this kind of source could surely provide us with a better insight into the attitudes of workers and servants towards their work.

CONCLUSION

So far Japanese economic historians have focused mostly on the eighteenth and early nineteenth centuries as periods in which certain new characteristics of the Tokugawa period, such as urbanism, commercial agriculture, and the growing importance of the money economy, fully developed. The years 1500 and 1650, which were fixed as cross sections in the framework of the comparative research project to which this article contributes, have no special meaning in Japanese history. A closer look, however, reveals that 1500 may be seen as symbolizing a period in which the old order of the landed estates was rapidly dissolving, and new forms of labour relations among artisans and other workmen were evolving.

The cross section of 1650 sets the focus on the seventeenth century. It turns out to have been of special importance for the formation of new forms of labour relations, the development of industry in rural areas, the increase in female labour, and for reflection on all these changes. One of the main trends in both urban and rural areas was the development of short-term employment. In the course of the seventeenth century, lifelong service in urban, and partly in rural, households was replaced by forms with a fixed span of years, which by the end of the century could be freely negotiated between employer and employee. For those aspiring to a career of service in the households of merchants and artisans, the form of

64. *Ibid.*, pp. 59–60.
65. *Ibid.*, p. 52.
66. Nagata, *Labor Contracts and Labor Relations*, pp. 101–118, *passim.*

long-term service was preserved, but as more and more strangers were employed, written contracts became quite common.

At the same time, casual labour remunerated with wages replaced *corvée* labour in the towns and larger cities. This led to the emergence of an urban stratum of day labourers, workmen, small artisans, and pedlars, who often came from the countryside. The shogunate tried to control the evolving market for this kind of urban labour by strict regulations, but the repeated issue of such regulations shows that its efforts were only partly successful. Finally, even Confucian scholars such as Dazai Shundai and also the shogunate itself had to concede that the new forms of labour also had advantages.

The prevailing ideology of neo-Confucianism was without doubt very influential in shaping the concepts of work and one's role in society based on status and occupation. While it is hard to grasp its direct impact on the daily life of the people, images of indolent servants with loose morals on the one hand and the complaints about exploitation on the other have been passed down to us in literary and historical documents. Reconstructing the work ethic as it was understood and practised by the lower classes of Tokugawa society remains a topic for further research.

IRSH 56 (2011), Special Issue, pp. 245–261 doi:10.1017/S0020859011000526
© 2011 Internationaal Instituut voor Sociale Geschiedenis

The World of Labour in Mughal India (c. 1500–1750)

Shireen Moosvi

Centre of Advanced Study in History, Aligarh Muslim University

E-mail: shireen.moosvi@gmail.com

Summary: This article addresses two separate but interlinked questions relating to India in Mughal times (sixteenth to early eighteenth century). First, the terms on which labour was rendered, taking perfect market conditions as standard; and, second, the perceptions of labour held by the higher classes and the labourers themselves. As to forms of labour, one may well describe conditions as those of an imperfect market. Slave labour was restricted largely to domestic service. Rural wage rates were depressed owing to the caste system and the "village community" mechanism. In the city, the monopoly of resources by the ruling class necessarily depressed wages through the market mechanism itself. While theories of hierarchy were dominant, there are indications sometimes of a tolerant attitude towards manual labour and the labouring poor among the dominant classes. What seems most striking is the defiant assertion of their status in relation to God and society made on behalf of peasants and workers in northern India in certain religious cults in the fifteenth to the seventeenth centuries.

The study of the labour history of pre-colonial India is still in its infancy. This is due partly to the fact that in many respects the evidence is scanty when compared with what is available for Europe and China in the same period. However, the information we do have, in Persian (then the official language), regional, or local languages, and in European languages (from missionaries, merchants, and travellers), enables us to explore the major forms of labour that prevailed in India during the late sixteenth century and the entire seventeenth century, and to trace the perceptions of the social status of the labourer that were held by the superior classes and by the labourers themselves.

FORMS OF LABOUR

During the period we are dealing with, India was known all over the world for its manufactures, which it exported notably to western Asia and Europe. These included various kinds of cotton textiles (calico, dyed and printed), silk fabrics, indigo, and damascened steel. In other words, it possessed a large craft sector that also catered to its own considerable domestic market. It is estimated that India's urban population had grown to about 15 per cent of the total population,[1] put at 145 million, which would mean an urban population of nearly 22 million. This may provide us with some idea of the size of the internal market formed by the towns alone. For its internal money use India absorbed a significant proportion of the huge quantities of silver that were then flowing into Europe from the Spanish-controlled silver mines of Mexico and Peru. My estimates of Mughal currency output show the following peak annual averages in tons of silver: 246.29 tons (1586–1595); 290.70 tons (1596–1605); 213.12 tons (1626–1635); and 188.39 tons (1696–1705).[2] We should also consider the copper coinage, which in the seventeenth century served as fractional money.

With money use on such an extensive scale, it is not surprising to find that in the towns money wages were universally in vogue for both skilled and unskilled labour and in domestic service. In the *A'in-i Akbari* (c.1595), an official account of the Mughal Empire, Abu'l-Fazl provides detailed rates for wages for all such categories, stated invariably in copper coins when daily rates are quoted.[3] Wages were apparently generally paid on a daily basis, and only regular employees, whether craftsmen or domestic servants, received their pay monthly. It is true that some employers paid their servants partly in kind (old clothing), and delayed salary payments were common; but the basic rates seem always to have been fixed in money.[4] This is borne out by all the incidental references to wages paid, whether in Indian records or in the accounts of European travellers and documents of the "factories" of the European East India Companies in the seventeenth century.[5] Money wage payments can thus be regarded as largely the rule in seventeenth-century Indian towns and markets, and in imperial and aristocratic establishments. "Commodified labour" was thus practically universal.

---

1. Irfan Habib, "Potentialities of Capitalistic Development in the Economy of Mughal India", in *idem, Essays in Indian History* (Delhi, 1995), p. 201. The estimate of India's total population, c.1600, is taken from Shireen Moosvi, *The Economy of the Mughal Emperor, c.1595: A Statistical Study* (Delhi, 1987), pp. 389–406.
2. Shireen Moosvi, "The Silver Influx, Money Supply and Prices in India during the 16th and 17th Centuries", *Journal of Economic and Social History of the Orient*, 30 (1987), p. 68.
3. Abu'l-Fazl, *A'in-i Akbari*, H. Blochmann (ed.) (Calcutta, 1867–1877), I, pp. 134–135, 143–144, 149–151.
4. For a detailed account and full references see Moosvi, *Economy of the Mughal Empire*, pp. 331–338.
5. W. Foster, *A Supplementary Calendar of Documents in the India Office Relating to India or to the Home Affairs of the East India Company 1600–1640* (London, 1928), p. 66; Pietro Dalla Valle, *Travels in India*, E. Grey (transl.) (London, 1892), p. 62; J. Ovington, *A Voyage to Surat in the Year 1689*, H.G. Rawlinson (ed.) (London, 1929).

The forms in which such wholly or partly "commodified labour" was found can be broadly categorized as follows.

Non-market institutions

Apart from domestic servants in the imperial household and in those of nobles (the latter to be included in the state apparatus for the present purpose), there were cavalrymen and clerks, employed in large numbers, usually on monthly salaries. Skilled artisans and labourers worked in imperial and aristocratic establishments, called *karkhanas* (workshops), which produced goods of various sorts for use in the employers' households, as well as for use as gifts. These workshops are described in detail in the *A'in-i Akbari* and by Francois Bernier (in India, 1658–1668).[6] The *A'in-i Akbari* furnishes us with details of wage rates for different kinds of work, invariably in terms of money, and on a daily basis. But in construction work carried out under imperial aegis, piece rates are also specified.

Market-governed, private employment

(a) Self-employed:
The self-employed population consisted largely of peasants, who, with their families, cultivated the land with the aid of their own cattle and tools, and paid tax and rent to the state or the local potentate.[7] Since the tax/rent was paid generally in money and only rarely in kind, a large part of the peasant's produce was put on the market, though naturally a part too was kept by him for direct consumption. Peasant labour could therefore be deemed to be only semi-commodified.

The labour of such artisans as weavers, ironsmiths, carpenters, and oil pressers, who worked at home and sold their products either from their homes, which served as their shops, or at fairs or markets,[8] was, on the other hand, almost wholly commodified. Their position as free-market operators was, it is true, often modified when they accepted advances (*dadani*) from merchants and committed themselves either to work for them alone, or to supply them their products at fixed prices and on a preferential basis.[9]

6. See, for example, Abu'l-Fazl, *A'in Akbari*, I, pp. 102–104; Francois Bernier, *Travels in the Mogul Empire 1656–68*, A. Constable (transl.) (London, 1916), pp. 258–259.
7. For a general view of the peasants' economic and legal position see Irfan Habib, *The Agrarian System of Mughal India (1556–1707)*, 2nd edn (New Delhi, 1999), ch. 4.
8. A very interesting passage on the relationship of self-employed weavers to the market can be found in a report from Patna in W. Foster (ed.), *The English Factories in India 1618–1621 [to] 1668–1669*, 13 vols (Oxford, 1906–1927), I, pp. 192–193.
9. *Ibid.*, for example *1624–1629*, p. 149; *1637–1641*, p. 137; *1646–1650*, p. 159; *1661–1664*, pp. 111–112.

Employers: This category includes a class of peasants (described in Marxian literature as "rich peasants") who in Mughal times cultivated large areas of land using their own ploughs and cattle, assisted by labourers. They were both self-employed and employers.[10] Among artisans, we learn of goldsmiths, who employed assistant workmen in their *karkhanas*,[11] but I have found no reference to other artisans employing paid assistants.

(b) Market wage earners:
One class of wage earners was formed by those who worked in merchants' *karkhanas* or workshops. These were workshops run by "rich merchants and tradesmen, who pay the workmen rather high wages" (Bernier).[12] In 1620 the English East India Company's factors set up a temporary "Cor Conna" (*karkhana*) at Patna employing nearly 100 persons to wind silk for them.[13] It was considered unethical to take work from a labourer and not pay the agreed wage for it.[14] But the practice of holding back wages was apparently quite common.

In rural localities, agricultural labourers worked on the lands of peasants at different tasks. Fixed share-cropping arrangements with such labourers are not reported. Usually wages were paid in cash or kind on a daily basis,[15] or partly daily and partly on a seasonal basis. It is possible, however, that here the caste system in the shape of the general repression of the "untouchables" (see below) influenced the level of wage rates and depressed them in relation to what they would have been if the "outcastes" had also been landholders or been allowed full freedom of choice and movement.

(c) Piece-rate wage earners:
Clear evidence for piece-rate payments in certain categories of work is found in the *A'in-i Akbari*, especially for construction work, as has already been noted.[16] In such work as that of cloth washers (who used an indigo wash to prepare the final form of woven cloth), ordinary washermen, silk winders, and spinners, it is inconceivable that any remuneration other than on a piecework basis could have been paid.

10. For this class see Habib, *Agrarian System of Mughal India*, pp. 135–137.
11. See the dictionary published by Tek Chand Bahar, *Bahar-i 'Ajam* (compiled 1739) (Lucknow, 1916), s.v. *karkhana*.
12. Bernier, *Travels in the Mogul Empire*, pp. 228–229.
13. Foster, *English Factories in India*, pp. 197–198.
14. Abdu'l Qadir Badauni, writing in 1598, quotes a saying of the Prophet to the effect that God holds as His enemy anyone who takes work but does not pay the wage for it; *Najatu'r Rashid*, S. Moinul Haq (ed.) (Lahore, 1972), p. 240.
15. Habib, *Agrarian System of Mughal India*, pp. 137, 141–144, for this entire paragraph.
16. Abu'l-Fazl, *A'in Akbari*, I, p. 170.

(d) Indentured labour:
It is true that the *Arthasastra*, the famous text on government and law, datable to c.100 AD at the latest, provides for persons to work for a creditor for a certain period to pay off a debt. Such practice, however, seems to have been very rare in most parts of Mughal India. Debt slavery obliging debtors to work in the fields of the creditor is known to have prevailed only in certain areas of Bihar in early colonial times.

(e) Chattel slaves used in production for the market:
Although slave artisans were known in the period of the Delhi Sultanate (the thirteenth and fourteenth centuries), by the time of the Mughal period such slaves are no longer mentioned. Agrestic slavery, however, existed in Malabar (Kerala) and Bihar around 1800, and is described in Buchanan's detailed local surveys.[17] But outside of these areas Irfan Habib has been able to cite only one instance, from Gujarat for 1637, where a peasant claimed to possess a slave, presumably for work in the field.[18]

(f) "Demiurgic" labour:
This is a category of semi-commodified productive labour which is, perhaps, largely confined to India: the particular term used here was given to it by Max Weber.[19] This was a system in which the occupational fixity of the caste system and a semi-hierarchical village organization (conventionally called "the village community") created a system of set obligations and rights under which the so-called "rural servants" (*balutas*), for instance, worked and obtained their livelihood. In general, in return for their services they were allowed to hold small pieces of land tax free (the tax which was usually borne by the village as a whole), and/or to claim modest shares in the grain harvest, given to them by each peasant at harvest time. Individuals such as hereditary barbers, potters, carpenters, blacksmiths, watchmen, shoemakers, carcass removers, and sweepers rendered certain recognized services to all (or the leading) villagers, with extra payments for work rendered outside of these customary services. Such arrangements, with certain variations, existed practically all over Mughal India.[20] Here customary entitlements to land and wages in cash and kind were inextricably linked; and these kept the families of the artisans and labourers practically tied down to their villages, though there was seemingly no legal bar to their movement, so far as we can see.

---

17. Francis Buchanan, *Account of Journey from Madras, & c.*, 3 vols (London, 1807); and district surveys of eastern India (1801–1812), abridged and printed in Montgomery Martin (ed.), *The History, Antiquities, Topography and Statistics of Eastern India*, 3 vols (London, 1838).
18. Habib, *Agrarian System of Mughal India*, p. 142.
19. For an interesting discussion of this term and the historicity of the form of labour it represents, see Hiroshi Fukazawa, *The Medieval Deccan* (Delhi, 1991), pp. 199–244.
20. Habib, *Agrarian System of Mughal India*, pp. 156–158.

(g) Domestic service:

The domestic service sector in Mughal India was exceedingly large. Not only did the aristocracy maintain a considerable number of servants, the employment of domestic servants by "middle-class" groups was also quite extensive. Pelsaert, writing around 1626 at Agra, noted that "Peons or servants are exceedingly numerous in this country, for everyone be he mounted soldier, merchant or king's officials – keeps as many as his position and circumstances permit".[21] Bernier, the French traveller, tells us that personal servants in the Mughal army were "indeed numerous",[22] and Fryer, writing of the period 1672–1681, remarked more specifically that "however badly off a [cavalry] soldier is, he must have three or four servants".[23]

In the aristocratic households servants were appointed for specific duties, so that, as Pelsaert tells us, "in the houses of the great lords each servant keeps himself strictly to his own duties".[24] On the other hand, the servants working for lower officials and ordinary people had to perform varied functions. *Khidmatgars* (personal attendants) of an officer of moderate rank, Anand Ram Mukhlis (c.1745), also worked as cooks.[25] The treatment meted out to servants often depended on the temper of the master. Some, like Abu'l-Fazl, did not like to scold them directly;[26] another noble was such a hard taskmaster that he even made his torch-bearers and musicians, normally working at night, work as building labourers so that they might not remain idle in daytime.[27] There was, however, some disapproval of physical ill-treatment. The historian Badauni tells us of the refusal of a mystic at Kalpi (UP) even to speak to a visiting commander who beat and abused his servants.[28]

Non-market, non-free labour (slavery and forced labour)

By c.1600 slave labour formed a small component of the labour force, being restricted largely to domestic service (where free servants normally predominated) and concubinage. Akbar made notable attempts to forbid the trade in slaves and forcible enslavement. He freed all the imperial

21. Francisco Pelsaert, *Remonstrantie* (c.1626), W.H. Moreland and P. Geyl (transl.), published as *Jahangir's India: The Remonstrantie of Francisco Pelsaert* (Cambridge, 1925), p. 61.
22. Bernier, *Travels in the Mogul Empire*, p. 380.
23. John Fryer, *A New Account of East India and Persia, Being Nine Years' Travels, 1672–1681*, 3 vols (London, 1909–1915), I, p. 341.
24. Pelsaert, *Remonstrantie*, p. 62.
25. Anand Ram Mukhlis, *Safarnama-i Mukhlis*, S. Azhar Ali (ed.) (Rampur, 1946), pp. 91, 96.
26. Shaikh Farid Bhakkari, *Zakhirat-ul Khawanin*, Syed Moinul Haq (ed.) (Karachi, 1970), II, pp. 376–377.
27. *Ibid.*, pp. 341–342.
28. Abdu'l Qadir Badauni, *Muntakhabu't Tawarikh* (Calcutta, 1864–1869), III, pp. 6–7.

slaves, who "exceeded hundreds and thousands".[29] But domestic slaves and concubines remained an essential feature not only of the aristocratic household but also of the homes of lower officials and even ordinary people. In his verses the satirist Jafar Zatalli (1710) suggested that a small household could still comprise the master, his wife, a male slave, and a slave girl.[30]

The practice of forced labour (*begar*) was generally considered unethical, though it was widely prevalent in relation to certain occasional tasks, such as baggage conveyance, imposed on specific lowly rural castes or communities. Akbar in 1597 and Shahjahan in 1641 issued orders abolishing the practice of *begar* (forced labour) extracted for various tasks in Kashmir, such as picking and cleaning saffron flowers and carrying timber and firewood.[31] It is interesting that an inscription at the gate of Akbar's Fort at Nagar in Srinagar (Kashmir), built in 1598, explicitly proclaims that no unpaid labour was used there, and 11,000,000 *dams* (copper coins) from the imperial treasury were spent on wages for labour.[32]

Women in the workforce

Even in fairly advanced market economies, women's labour is largely unremunerated in terms of money, and is often subsumed within family income, obtained by the men of the household. This was largely true of Mughal India as well. In agriculture women undertook weeding and transplanting, picked saffron flowers (in Kashmir), husked and ground grain, besides looking after cattle or working at textile crafts, ginning cotton, and spinning yarn. They assisted their artisanal menfolk in nearly all the work done at home. Clay was prepared by women while the men potters worked on the wheel. Here, as in corn milling, heavy work could be assigned to women without any qualms.

In some crafts women worked directly for wages too, and here again they could be given heavy work to do. In Mughal paintings depicting building construction, we see women pounding limestone to obtain lime mortar, sieving lime (Figure 1) and bearing (on their heads) bricks and lime to carry to bricklayers (as they still do). As far as we can judge, the division of labour by gender was practically all pervasive, even within the same occupation (women were spinners, men weavers; men were bricklayers, women brick carriers).[33] There appears to have been little competition between the two sexes for the same kind of job. In domestic service, where this could conceivably happen,

29. Abu'l-Fazl, *Akbarnama* (c.1600), Ahmad Ali and Abdur Rahim (eds), 3 vols (Calcutta, 1873–1887), III, pp. 379–380.
30. *Kulliyat-i Jafar Zatalli*, Naeem Ahamad (ed.) (Aligarh, 1979), p. 132.
31. Abu'l-Fazl, *Akbarnama*, III, pp. 727 and 734; Amin Qazwini, *Badshahnama* (c.1638) (transcript of Rampur MS, at Department of History Library, Aligarh), pp. 509–510.
32. Hasan, *Tarikh-i Hasan* (Srinagar, n.d.), III, note on p. 443.
33. For details and full references see Shireen Moosvi, *People, Taxation, and Trade in Mughal India* (Oxford, 2008), pp. 135–158.

Figure 1. Painting by Tulsi, with Akbar's figure by Madho the Younger (c.1595).
Abu'l-Fazl, Akbarnama *(Calcutta, 1984). Reproduced from Moosvi*, People, Taxation, and Trade
in Mughal India. *Used with permission.*

the presence of male and female slaves introduced a complicating factor in the wage market that was not present in non-domestic lines of work.

THE PLACE OF LABOURING CLASSES IN SOCIETY: REALITY AND PERCEPTION

The foregoing survey of labour relationships discloses an advanced state of differentiation in society, based on factors that can be regarded as historically universal: forcible expropriation of one class by another; property inheritance; and the growth of money relationships. In India, however, there was an additional factor, namely the caste system. The caste system is not easy to define, since it has enormous complexities and has undergone variations across regions and over time. Broadly, however, it implies the presence of communities, or *jatis*, that are endogamous and have fixed occupations traditionally assigned to them. They are theoretically arranged in a hierarchical order, each *jati* being either assigned to one of the larger orders (*varnas*), namely Brahmans (priests; though theoretically there should be no *jatis* among Brahmans), Kshatriyas (rulers and warriors), Vaishyas (traders), and Shudras (manual workers), or, put among the out-castes, the so-called Untouchables or menial workers (Chandals).

The caste system thus limits not only vertical social mobility, but also horizontal mobility; it is the latter which makes it so unique, and which often explains the apparently innumerable social divisions among Indian labouring classes. In practice, of course, the caste system has had its own elements of flexibility. Certain communities move up (when economic circumstances improve) in the hierarchical ladder by adopting the customs and rituals of higher castes – a process now called "Sanskritization" by sociologists. New castes are spawned to take up new occupations. The presence of non-Hindu communities, notably Muslims, which are not incorporated into the caste system (though they themselves do not remain uninfluenced by its customs and prejudices), introduces another element allowing adjustment to economic change. Theoretically, Muslim communities are more open to horizontal mobility, and this, with certain limitations, has been observable in practice as well.[34]

In his account of Hinduism in the *A'in-i Akbari*, Abu'l-Fazl reproduces the classical conceptions of the caste hierarchy.[35] We have here the four

---

34. Louis Dumont, *Homo Hierarchicus: The Caste System and its Implications* (London, 1972), p. 257; Mirza Qatil, *Haft Tamasha* (Lucknow, 1875), pp. 88–89. Qatil says that among the Hindus caste remained unaltered even if a Khatri (Kshatriya) took service as a lowly water carrier. On the other hand, a low-caste man such as a *kahar* (palanquin carrier) could never rise in status whatever profession he actually pursued. It was otherwise among the Muslims however: here occupations actually undertaken determined status.

35. Abu'l-Fazl, *A'in Akbari*, II, pp. 153–156.

orders, Brahmans, Kshatriyas, Vaishyas, and Shudras, and the occupations assigned to them. Painters, goldsmiths, blacksmiths, and carpenters are explicitly classed among Shudras. Abu'l-Fazl also follows the classical law books, such as the *Manusmriti* (first century AD), in tracing the origins of the various outcaste communities to the offspring of particular breaches of the law of endogamy. Curiously enough, what he omits to stress here is the idea of purity and pollution (doubtless exaggerated out of all proportion by Louis Dumont and his followers), under whose influence certain kinds of manual work, such as sweeping or leather dressing, were regarded as impure and fit only for the outcaste or the lowly.

But Abu'l-Fazl also offers other perceptions of class ranking. Invoking traditional Iranian wisdom, Abu'l-Fazl states that mankind is divisible into four groups: first, warriors, who are like fire; second, artisans and merchants, who correspond to air; third, men of letters, such as philosophers, physicians, accountants, architects, and astronomers, who together resemble water; and fourth, peasants and cultivators, who are comparable to earth.[36] In this arrangement artisans and merchants are given precedence not only over peasants but even over men of letters. Quite striking surely is the fact that men of religion are not even considered.

Elsewhere, Abu'l-Fazl ranks all professions into just two classes, placing that of warriors again at the higher level, and that of peasants and other professionals next. He then goes on to state that the Greeks had classified professions into three types: noble, ignoble, and middling. The noble professions are: (1) those based on the use of reason, contributing to farsightedness and administrative competence; (2) those based on knowledge, such as those of persons engaged in writing or oral eloquence; and (3) those based on strength of heart, such as the military profession. The three types of ignoble profession are those that (1) are against the interest of the people, like hoarding; (2) are contrary to sobriety, such as buffoonery; and (3) are detestable, such as the professions of barber, tanner, and sweeper. (The latter might reflect a distinct influence of the Indian concept of "impure" work.) The middling professions are divided into (1) essential, such as agriculture; (2) those that one can live without, such as cloth dyeing; (3) basic (*basit*) crafts, such as carpentry and iron or metal work; and (4) secondary (*murakkab*) crafts, such as weighing and tailoring.[37]

Such ranking systems were largely theoretical. There could be other official or quasi-official conventions. In censuses of certain towns of the region of Marwar (western Rajasthan) given in the singularly interesting statistical work, Munhta Nainsi's *Marwar ra Parganan ri Vigat*, compiled in 1664, the total number of houses is recorded. These are categorized

36. *Ibid.*, pp. 3–4.
37. *Ibid.*, p. 291.

according to the castes or professions of their occupants.[38] The lists of castes in five of the six towns are not given in any identifiable order, but bankers are mentioned first. In Merta, the sixth and largest town, there seems to be a hierarchical arrangement. We have, first, the Brahmans (priests), Kayasths (clerks), Rajputs and soldiers (*sipahi*), followed by a category designated *pavan jati* ("working castes"), where the houses of fifty other castes, artisanal, menial, and mercantile, are enumerated.[39] The peasants are not listed, presumably because they were not found among townsmen. In this list a clear preference is given to the intellectual classes (Brahmans and Kayasths), followed by soldiers, and only below them come the artisans, menial workers, and merchants, the last three groups being mixed up without any seeming care for hierarchy.

The attitude towards artisans, peasants, and labourers among those speaking for the state, such as Abu'l-Fazl and Nainsi, thus seems mixed, with a recognition of their necessity tempered with a sense of the authors' own superiority and distance from them. In this context, the exaltation of manual labour by the famous Mughal Emperor Akbar (reigned 1556–1605), both in words and action, seems notably singular. One of his recorded statements is that "an artisan who rises to eminence in his profession has the grace of God with him. Holding him in honour amounts to worship of God."[40]

His own treatment of an expert dyer as revealed by the chance survival of three documents seems to be well in line with these sentiments. Three *farmans* (imperial orders) of his relate to a certain *Ustad* Ramdas *rangrez* (dyer), the prefix *ustad* indicating that he was a "master" dyer. The first *farman*, dated 7 April 1561, assigns Ramdas the revenues of a village near Agra in lieu of his salary. When he probably retired the next year, he was granted 21.73 hectares of land in the same locality as an *in'am* (pension grant). Though no longer in imperial service, he still retained direct access to the Emperor; and on his personal petition against a certain Darayya for not repaying a loan and instead accusing Ramdas of insanity, the third *farman* was issued in 1569. It directed the local revenue collector to make Darayya repay the loan and to take him to the local *qazi* (judge) to extract an undertaking not to harass Ramdas again.[41]

Though there is no explicit rejection of the caste system or untouchability in any statement attributed to Akbar,[42] one finds him appointing

38. Munhta Nainsi, *Marwar ra Parganan ri Vigat* (c.1664), Narain Singh Bhati (ed.), 2 vols (Jodhpur, 1968–1969).

39. *Ibid.*, I, pp. 496–497; II, pp. 9, 83–86, 223–224, 310.

40. Abu'l-Fazl, *A'in Akbari*, II, p. 229.

41. See Irfan Habib, "Three Early Farmans of Akbar, in Favour of Ramdas, the Master Dyer", in *idem* (ed.), *Akbar and His India* (Delhi, 1997), pp. 270–293.

42. On the contrary, Abu'l-Fazl ascribes a statement to Akbar that "the superintendents should be vigilant that no one abandon his profession at his own will"; *A'in Akbari*, II, p. 244.

the untouchable Chandals as members of his palace guard and giving to their leader the fairly high title of *rai* (literally "chief", "prince"). The official chronicler tells us that the Chandals, who were considered outcastes, and described as thieves and highway robbers, began to be employed by many nobles as watchmen after such a display of imperial patronage for them.[43] Abu'l-Fazl also informs us that sweepers, who were called *kannas* or "menials", were redesignated by Akbar as *halalkhor* (earners of legitimate wages),[44] clearly in order to eliminate a pejorative characterization.

Akbar's own habit of performing manual labour aroused the astonishment of Jesuit missionaries visiting his court. Father Monserrate, who saw him in 1581, tells us: "Zelaldinus [Akbar] is so devoted to building that he sometimes quarries stone himself, along with the other workmen. Nor does he shrink from watching and even himself practising, for the sake of amusement, the craft of an ordinary artisan."[45] In his account based on Jesuit letters from the Mughal court, Father Pierre du Jarric has this description of Akbar: "At one time he would be deeply immersed in state affairs, or giving audience to his subjects, and the next moment he would be seen shearing camels, hewing stones, cutting wood, or hammering iron, and doing all with as much diligence as though engaged in his own particular vocation."[46]

In many ways, such as his attitude towards women's rights and slavery, not to speak of his hostility to religious bigotry, Akbar remained unique.[47] His successors as well as the aristocratic classes in general by no means shared this interest in and respect for artisanal labour. Yet Akbar's own conduct shows that it would be a mistake to assume that the attitude towards manual labour in Mughal India universally conformed to a particular stereotype.

SELF-PERCEPTION OF ARTISANS AND LABOURERS

It is not easy to set boundaries between the social ideas of the higher or elite classes and those of the lower orders. It is obvious that the caste system would not have established itself and functioned so successfully had the lower castes and the outcastes to a large extent not accepted it as representing a divinely ordained institution. It is therefore particularly noteworthy that from the late fifteenth century we begin to witness artisans and labourers who assumed the garb of religious preachers and asserted the dignity of their profession in the eyes of God.

---

43. *Idem, Akbarnama*, III, p. 604; *idem, A'in Akbari*, I, p. 189.
44. *Idem, A'in Akbari*, I, p. 144.
45. Anthony Monserrate, *The Commentary of Father Monserrate, SJ, on his Journey to the Court of Akbar*, J.S. Hoyland and S.N. Banerjee (transl.) (Cuttack, 1922), p. 201.
46. Pierre du Jarric, *Akbar and the Jesuits*, C.H. Payne (transl.) (London, 1926), p. 28.
47. See Irfan Habib, "Akbar and Social Inequities", *Proceedings of the Indian History Congress* (Warangal, 1993), pp. 300–310.

A notable representative of Brahmanical orthodoxy, Tulsidas (fl.1570), author of a very popular version of the religious epic *Ramcharitmanas*, noted as an astonishing phenomenon of his day that "low-caste people such as oilmen, potters, untouchables (*svapachas*), fishermen, watchmen, and distillers simply shave their heads and turn into mendicants, at the loss of their wife or household goods".[48] Their one act of defiance led to others. They tended to form part of a religious movement, now often called Popular Monotheism, which, rejecting both Hinduism and Islam, India's two major religions, preached an unalloyed faith in one God, abjuring all ritual and the constraints of the caste system. Apart from the cloth printer, Namdev (c.1400) of Maharashtra, a major figure in this movement was Kabir, a weaver from the city of Banaras (Varanasi) in Uttar Pradesh, who lived around 1500.

Some time before 1603, the fifth Sikh Guru (Master) composed a set of verses in the name of the peasant saint Dhanna, which he included in the *Guru Granth Sahib*, the Sikh scripture, assembled by him in that year.[49] These verses bring out so well the defiant perception of the artisans' own proximity to God that they deserve to be given in full.

> In Gobind [God], Gobind, Gobind was Namdev's heart absorbed;
> A calico-printer worth half a *dam* [petty copper coin] became worth a *lakh* [=100,000].
> Abandoning weaving and stretching thread, Kabir devoted his love to God's feet;
> Though a weaver of low family he obtained untold virtues.
> Rav Das who used to remove dead cattle, abandoned worldly affairs,
> Became distinguished, and in the company of the saints obtained a sight of God.
> Sain, barber and village drudge, well known in every house,
> In whose heart the Supreme God dwelt, is numbered among the saints.
> Having heard all this, I, a Jat [peasant], applied myself to God's service;
> I have [now] met God in person and great is the good fortune of Dhanna.[50]

Of the four premier artisanal religious leaders mentioned in these verses, we have compositions included in two massive collections compiled in the late sixteenth and early seventeenth centuries, namely the *Guru Granth Sahib*, the Sikh scripture, and the *Sarbangi* of Rajabdas, of the Dadupanthi sect.[51] Owing to their early date, they enable us to capture

---

48. *The Ramayana of Tulsi Das*, F.S. Growse (transl.) (Delhi, 1978), p. 690. I owe this reference to Professor Ramesh Rawat.
49. It is best to use the text published by the Shiromani Gurdwara Prabandhak Committee, Amritsar, in Gurmukhi (the original script). I have used the text transcribed in Nagari script (with word separation), published by the same authority in Amritsar in 1951.
50. *Guru Granth Sahib*, original text transcribed in Nagari script (Amritsar, 1951), I, pp. 487–488. The translation of the passage in M.A. Macauliff, *The Sikh Religion* (Oxford, 1909), p. 109, has been modified by reference to the text.
51. The Dadupanthis were followers of Dadu (c.1575), a cotton carder, and one of the notable monotheistic teachers of the time. On the Dadupanthi compilation, see Charlotte Vaudeville, *Kabir* (Oxford, 1974), I, pp. 58–60.

Figure 2. Mughal School, mid-seventeenth century.
Miniature in the Leningrad Branch of the Institute of the Peoples of Asia. Reproduced from Habib, *Agrarian System.* Used with permission.

the original compositions as they circulated in their earliest form among the common people in the various spoken languages, including Marathi, Awadhi, Braj, and Panjabi. One can see from a Mughal painting by the famous artist Bichitr (fl.1630) how they must have been sung out to the poorest of the poor (Figure 3).

There, verses are addressed largely to persons of the same class as that of their authors. And while the message is strongly monotheistic, the pride in their hereditary mundane callings is frequently manifest – note for instance their bold presumption in seeing God as a skilled artisan. Thus Kabir: "None knows the secret of the Weaver. He hath woven the warp of the whole world."[52] To the earlier Namdev, the cloth printer, God could be a carpenter: "My Carpenter pervadeth all things; My Carpenter is the support of the soul."[53] He also sees Him as a potter who has fashioned the world.[54]

God also appears to Kabir in the garb of persons who had influence on the artisan by way of trade. In one of his verses, God is the just merchant, while in another He is a strict moneylender. Elsewhere, by implication, man is the artisan who sells his wares to Him, or has borrowed money (his life) from Him.

There was no sense of shame felt for their own lowly professions. Ravidas owned that members of his family still went around Banaras removing dead cattle.[55] He is explicit in pronouncing his indifference to caste and claimed that "belonging to caste and being out-caste matters not for God's love, the path being open equally to all, Brahman, Bais (Vaishya), Sud (Shudra) and Khatri (Kshatriya), as well as Dom, Chandar (Chandal, outcaste), and Malechh (Muslims)".[56]

These preachers thus asserted that for the very reason of their lowly position as artisans and workers, they were the more favoured by God. They did not challenge the existing social restrictions, such as caste endogamy, or fixed hereditary occupations. What they did challenge was the status assigned to the artisans and workers on the basis of the pervading concept of caste and social hierarchy.

The popularity that the artisanal preachers' compositions gained caused bitter hostility from a section of the educated classes. For Tulsidas (c.1570) such claims of the lowly (Shudras) were those of false pretenders and their appearance the sure sign of the Kali (Evil) Age.[57] This opinion was probably widely held, since Tulsidas's *Ramcharitmanas* is one of the

---

52. *Guru Granth Sahib*, I, p. 484.
53. *Ibid.*, p. 656.
54. *Ibid.*, p. 1292.
55. *Ibid.*, p. 1293.
56. *Ibid.*, p. 858.
57. *Ramayana of Tulsi Das*, p. 687.

Figure 3. Painting by Bichitr (c.1635).
Victoria and Albert Museum, I.M.27-1925. Reproduced from Habib, Agrarian System. *Used with permission.*

most popular versions of India's sacred epic. But some of the educated nevertheless held a different view. The notable Muslim theologian, Abdu'l Haqq Muhaddis (fl.1600), records a conversation that took place between his father and grandfather as early as 1522, its message being that Kabir deserved respect as a "monotheist", being neither a Muslim nor a Hindu.[58] Abu'l-Fazl (c.1595) finds in Kabir "a broadness of path and an elevatedness of vision", and says: "[t]he door of spiritual truth became open to him somewhat and he abandoned the obsolete customs of the age. He has left behind many Hindi verses containing the truths he preached."[59] Such praise of Kabir suggests a curious indifference in the higher circles of the Mughal elite to Kabir's lowly artisanal affiliations, and a willingness to exalt and share common truths with him, although he himself rejected their religion (indeed, all religions) *in toto*.

It is tempting to suppose that among both the labouring poor themselves and the elite, a breach in the faith in the old established order was being brought about largely owing to changes in the position of the artisans caused by the development of money relations and the broader market framework. This hypothesis can, however, be juxtaposed with another hypothesis, equally speculative. Islam, as understood in pre-modern times, was almost as sympathetic to concepts of hierarchy as traditional Hinduism. Yet the fact that the beliefs of these two religions were in constant contention, in circumstances of largely peaceable coexistence, opened the doors to ideas and assertions for which neither provided any room. And so, for the first time, the artisan had a choice in matters religious that he had never enjoyed before. With such choice available he could at least see both God and himself in a new light, his own.

---

58. Abdu'l Haqq, *Akhbaru'l Akhyar* (Deoband, 1913–1914), p. 306.
59. Abu'l-Fazl, *A'in Akbari*, I, pp. 393–433.

IRSH 56 (2011), Special Issue, pp. 263–274 doi:10.1017/S0020859011000447
© 2011 Internationaal Instituut voor Sociale Geschiedenis

Norms of Professional Excellence and Good Conduct in Accountancy Manuals of the Mughal Empire

NAJAF HAIDER

Centre for Historical Studies, Jawaharlal Nehru University

E-mail: snajafhaider@yahoo.co.in

SUMMARY: In Mughal India, accounts were kept by individuals and institutions for purposes of reference and planning. Accountancy required a set of objectives and techniques for collecting, organizing, and presenting information so that it could then be put to use. It also fostered learning. Subsisting on formal or informal training, professional accountants equipped themselves with linguistic and mathematical skills, the art of notation, mnemonic devices, and the ability to translate loosely defined units into precise terms and numbers. Accountants were an important component of the state apparatus, village administration, and elite household management. In the seventeenth century manuals were produced in Persian by private individuals for the guidance of persons seeking to acquire proficiency in accountancy (*siyaq*) and clerical work. No study has been made so far of the manuals themselves nor of the people who compiled or used them. This introductory essay examines the manuals (generally titled *Dasturu-l Amal*) and the information they contain about the system of accountancy as well as about the professional ethics and norms of ideal behaviour of the secretarial class.

We know little about the attitudes of ordinary workers to their work in medieval India. As a rule they neither reflected upon nor organized their thoughts to set them down in books. It is from the writings of the literate elite that we may get some understanding of how work in general and professions in particular were perceived, through remarks framed usually either within a religious or a dominant intellectual tradition.

This short essay is about norms of work and good conduct among a group of professionals in Mughal India who remain too little studied even though they were responsible for producing and managing huge numbers of records; they also wrote manuals about themselves and their work. They were members of a secretarial class, notably accountants and record-keepers, who flourished in the sixteenth and seventeenth centuries under the Mughal and later the British Empire.

In Mughal India individuals and institutions kept records and accounts to gather and preserve information for reference and planning. Record-keeping and accountancy required clear objectives and reliable techniques to collect, organize, and then present information so that it would be useful. The art of learning was developed too as professional record-keepers and accountants equipped themselves with linguistic and mathematical skills, the skills of notation, mnemonic devices, and the ability to translate loosely defined units into precise terms and numbers. Record-keepers and accountants were an important component of the state apparatus, elite household management, and village administration. We cannot put a number on their population but, given the size of the Mughal lower bureaucracy, it must have been quite large.

The two institutions which generated and preserved sizeable records of their transactions were the state and the market. Much like merchants, the state possessed goals which implied costs. Warfare, administration, and taxation placed sustained demands on officials to work out suitable proportions of power, efficiency, and resources and to draw up balance sheets of their goals and achievements, income and expenditure, investments and returns. Records of information needed during such evaluations helped the state better to rehearse conceptually its policies and actions. Tangible evidence of the association between curiosity and statecraft was the impetus given to secretarial work, record-keeping, statistics, and accountancy.

In the seventeenth century manuals, or model textbooks, were written which were known as *Dasturu-l Amal* (literally Book of Rules), and they were copied and circulated for the guidance of persons seeking to acquire proficiency in accountancy, clerical work, administrative procedures, and the duties of government officials. The manuals were written in Persian, the language of administration throughout the Mughal Empire, except for village accounts, for which local languages were used. With the exception of one work published in the nineteenth century, all the manuals exist only as manuscripts and they have been used by scholars for the information they contain about economic history or state administration.[1] However, neither the texts themselves nor their authors have ever been studied.

STRUCTURE AND CONTENT

The manuals are mostly anonymous, but they appear to have been written by professionals rather than scholars and may have been used by individuals at home and in colleges and workplaces as learning aids. The contents are organized and everything is stated clearly and precisely. The

1. Anonymous, *Dasturu-l amal i Alamgiri* [*Manual of Alamgir*] (Bihar, c.1659,), MS, British Library, Add. 6599, ff. 1a–133a; Jagat Rai "Shujai" Kayath Saksena, *Farhang i Kardani* (Dhaka, 1679,), MS, Maulana Azad Library, Aligarh, Abdus Salam, Farsiya 85/315; Anonymous, *Dasturu-l amal i Ilm i Navisindagi* [*Manual of the Science of Accountancy*] (Bengal or Orissa, last quarter of the seventeenth century), MS, British Library, Add. 6599, ff. 133b–185a; Munshi Nandram, *Siyaqnama* [*Book of Accountancy*] (Allahabad, 1694–1696, Lucknow, 1879); Anonymous, *Khulasatu-s Siyaq* [*Essence of Accountancy*] (Punjab, 1703), MS, British Library, Add. 6588.

approach is practical, and information is given to the extent that the writer thought was necessary for those learning record-keeping and accountancy with little or no knowledge of these arts, and who wanted to obtain a government job or a private job with an aristocrat.

The manuals are structured more or less uniformly. The subject matter is divided into several parts offering technical information relevant to the job, and, at least in one manual, there is a section on norms of professional excellence and ethics.[2] The technical part usually discusses six themes, namely numbers, notions of time and calendars, accountancy, record-keeping, the duties of government officials, and statistical information about the Mughal Empire. An interesting aspect of one of the manuals is that it reproduces real documents and statistics as illustrations rather than preparing fresh model ones. Those particular documents, of an extremely important nature, have survived only in that manual.

The first part is usually on arithmetic and computation, which required a knowledge of Indian, Persian, and Arabic numerals, decimal values, modes of computation, multiplication tables, calculation of crop-yields, salaries, wages, and rates of interest, surface areas suitable for land, cloth, stone, wood, and so on, and tables to calculate agricultural land, units of weights and measures such as those for jewellers, goldsmiths, and grocers, currency exchange rates, and tables for calculating fractions of money. The second part deals with the reckoning of time and eras. The Mughal chancery employed various eras for dating documents, coins, and chronicles: the lunar Islamic or *hijri*, luni-solar Indian, and purely solar (*Ilahi*) eras, and the Turkish cycle of twelve years.

In the last quarter of the sixteenth century currencies, exchange rates, weights, and calendars were standardized. In 1584 a solar calendar was introduced (*Ilahi* era) in all government offices and almanacs and henceforth documents, seals, and coins carried the solar *Ilahi* year of 365 days and twelve months that began on the day of the vernal equinox. Each month had a fixed number of days calculated on the basis of the sun's entry into the zodiac station. The preference of the Mughal emperor Aurangzeb for orthodox Islamic practice brought the Islamic calendar back.

The third theme in the manuals is the principle and technique of accountancy. The information is of immense value to understanding the major transition in the language and techniques of accountancy that had wide-ranging implications for the secretarial class. According to the manuals, before 1584 all accounts were kept in the Indian style and based on the principle of chronology in a single account book (*bahi*). The Iranian style of accountancy, based on Arabic strokes, words, and numerals, was introduced in government offices in 1584. New clerks, accountants, and

---

2. *Dasturu-l amal i Alamgiri*, ff. 23b–24a, 39a–40a.

finance officers were appointed and new regulations for maintaining fiscal records were framed and put into practice.

The Iranian style of accounting required the use of a special technique of writing and organizing words and figures known as *siyaq*. In *siyaq*, the account was organized into lines, heads, and characters of fixed length, number, and terms. The lines, points, and surfaces had properties for organizing space. The system of notation used in accounting for administration and commerce was called *raqam*, in which numbers were written as monograms. The largest number of documents containing *siyaq* numerals to be found in archives anywhere in the world are the accounting records of Mughal India.

The fourth part of the manuals covers records. All medieval governments were capable of measuring and dividing everything from farm produce to patronage. However, from the last quarter of the sixteenth century, Akbar's administration implemented a series of measures to impart precision to the work of government, and increased the tendency to work with numbers, such as the division of the empire into manageable territorial units, and the control of them through multiple chains of command. The bureaucracy was organized into ranks with dual numbers; there was an obligation to maintain fixed quotas of soldiers and horses corresponding with numerical ranks, and the right to draw matching salaries from territories yielding predetermined cash revenues which were tabulated in a specially devised money of account. Mughal monetary policy was itself based on complex quantitative calculations.

A leading book on state regulations devotes a whole chapter to the duties of the state accountant and suggests that he should be righteous in his conduct, accurate in writing, and skilful in handling numbers. According to the standards set by a finance minister in the last quarter of the sixteenth century, accountants should observe state regulations and render clear statements. According to him, their business rested upon inquiry and investigation rather than conjecture and approximation.[3]

THE SOCIAL IDENTITY OF THE SECRETARIAL CLASS

For centuries in northern India scribes and accountants were Indians belonging to the three castes: Kayasths (clerks), Khatris (traders), and Brahmans (scholars and teachers). Among the three, Kayasths were the most prominent and are described in our sources generally as accountants. Even after the establishment of Muslim rule there was no change either in the language of administration at the provincial level or in the social composition of the secretarial class, since very few senior state officials,

---

3. Abu'l-Fazl, *A'in-i Akbari* [*Regulations of Akbar*], H. Blochmann (ed.) (Calcutta, 1867–1877), I, p. 288.

Figure 1. Image of a Mughal scriptorium (*kitabkhana*) showing the arts of writing, painting and paper-making. In the main frame, a teacher dictates a text to a pupil (possibly a prince), while on the platform below a scribe works on a scroll even as he exchanges glances with a painter. The painting illustrates the text of *Akhlaq i Nasiri*, a thirteenth-century Persian work on ethics and politics that was kept in Akbar's library and read out to him. The inscription at the bottom of the painting reads "Amal S[ur] Jiv" [work of Sur Jiv].
Aga Khan Trust for Culture, Geneva. Used with permission.

who were mostly Turks, Afghans, Iranians, or Central Asians, were familiar with the Hindwi language and script.

In the second half of the sixteenth century, there was a concerted attempt to make Persian the sole language of state records at all levels except for the village, and the man credited with bringing in the change was an Indian minister appointed by Akbar, Raja Todar Mal (d. 1589), who had himself excelled in both the Indian and Persian traditions of record-keeping and accountancy. The change must have had implications for the existing secretarial class insofar as huge numbers must have lost their jobs. They came back to great effect by learning Persian and the new system of accountancy so that they could compete among themselves and with Muslims for administrative positions. Members of the Hindu "intellectual" class, whose occupation was writing, and the secretarial and accountant castes were promoted in the bureaucracy of Akbar's time, a famous example being Raja Todar Mal.

If the traditional account of the sixteenth-century changes in the language of administration is correct, then the systematization of the state apparatus might have created opportunities for the secretarial class to learn Persian and acquire the new techniques of accountancy to get into the lower bureaucracy. Even though the older class of accountants and record-keepers came back, the Indian system of accountancy and record-keeping was replaced by a new Perso-Islamic system.[4]

ACCOUNTANTS AND THEIR EDUCATION

In Mughal India there were many places where one could be educated to take up a profession: home, school, at the house of a teacher-scholar, and in the workplace. The children of merchants were equipped with elementary mathematical skills, probably at home. A French jeweller who made frequent visits to India over a span of two decades and who was quite familiar with the customs and traditions of the mercantile class made the following observation:

> They [merchants] accustom their children at an early age to shun slothfulness, and instead of letting them go into the streets to lose their time at play, as we generally allow ours, teach them arithmetic, which they learn perfectly, using for it neither pen nor counters, but the memory alone so that in a moment they will do a sum, however difficult it may be. [They use the same] figures in their books, both in the Empire of the Great Mogull [Mughal], as well as in other parts of India, although the languages may vary.[5]

We know from the autobiography of a Jain merchant, Banarasidas, who flourished in the first half of the seventeenth century, that he went to

---

4. *Khulasatu-s Siyaq*, ff. 64b–65a.
5. J.B. Tavernier, *Travels in India*, V. Ball (trans.), 2nd edn, revd W. Crooke, 2 vols (London, 1925), II, pp. 143–144.

Figure 2. Scene from a school (*madrasa*); painting by Dharamdas.
MS, Khamsa of Amir Khusrau, Walters Art Gallery, Baltimore, no. 10,624, f. 98. Used with permission.

school when he was eight. After finishing school, he learnt money testing (evaluation of the weight, fineness, and exchange rate of coins) and account-keeping at home and in the market.[6] The restructured school syllabus of Akbar's reign had a special focus on the science of numbers – computation (*hisab*), arithmetic (*hindisa*), mathematics (*riyazi*), and *mubahat*, which was something akin to civil engineering or the "construction and repair of buildings" – and included accountancy (*siyaq*) as a subject.[7]

Training in accountancy could be acquired from a professional working in an office. In another autobiographical account, a Brahman petty official named Balkrishan tells us that accountancy was his family profession, and he too was sent to the elementary school run by a Muslim teacher to read Persian books and acquire proficiency in all the rules of the language and letter composition. When he was older he was taken out of the school and attached to the department of a city official to learn arithmetic and accountancy.

> I found the task dull and uninviting but did not give it up out of respect for my brother. My heart was still in literature and often in place of figures I saw verses [...]. But my brothers counselled me and told me that it is easy to earn money (*naqd*) in accountancy from the start whereas in letter writing one has to wait far too long to get a job. I would be unwise, I was told, to forego cash for credit.[8]

Balkrishan had a passion for learning. In his own words, he burnt the midnight oil and did not rest for a moment. It served him well in his career. Despite his brothers' gloomy predictions he managed to get employment as a revenue official, and was once even promoted too.

NORMS PRESCRIBED FOR THE SECRETARIAL CLASS

The recommendations (*nasihat*) given to prospective professionals appear in only one manual.[9] The author mentions that he has collected them in one place from the dispersed writings of Iranian masters drawn from several sources. The section on recommendations has two components: the first relates to the general and special qualifications necessary for them, and can be classified as professional norms. The second component is about ethical standards and good conduct.

In the first part five essential qualifications are laid out for anyone to become a member of the secretarial class as well as to aspire to higher positions. The first is the art of writing, known as *insha*, notably the art of

---

6. Banarasidas, *Ardhakathanaka* [*Half a Tale*], Mukund Lath (ed. and trans.) (Jaipur, 1981), p. 227.
7. Abu'l-Fazl, *A'in-i Akbari*, I, p. 202.
8. *Maktubat i Balkrishan Brahman* [*Letters of Balkrishan Brahman*], MS, British Library Add. 16859, ff. 97a–b; Irfan Habib, *Medieval India: The Study of a Civilization* (Delhi, 2007), pp. 251–252.
9. *Dasturu-l amal i Alamgiri*, ff. 23b–24a, 39a–40a.

composing letters and drafting documents. Letters, documents, and accounts each followed a more or less fixed format which by the seventeenth century had acquired consistency in different departments or regions of the empire. Knowledge of written Persian and its phraseology was therefore considered to be the basic requirement for secretarial jobs. We have seen in the case of Balkrishan Brahman that he was first sent to a teacher of Persian language and literature to acquire that basic knowledge and training.

The second quality the manual lays out is the knowledge of special techniques of accountancy (*siyak*), and the third a good knowledge of arithmetic (*hisab*). We have already discussed those two branches.

The fourth quality listed is fluency in spoken Persian. There were professionals in Mughal India who could understand but could not speak Persian. That was a definite handicap because in government departments high-ranking nobles usually held the superior posts while the lower bureaucracy was staffed with clerks, accountants, and petty officials. The high officials mostly spoke Persian with felicity, either because they were ethnic Iranians, Central Asians, or even Afghans, or because they had learnt the language to conduct administration. Since secretarial tasks involved paperwork as well as taking instructions and dictation from superiors, fluency in the spoken language was considered essential.

The fifth qualification mentioned is full knowledge of all types of record kept in the various departments (tax, mint, market, for instance) and all thirty-six workshops or *ateliers* (*karkhana*). Much like the modern Indian bureaucracy, the Mughal state generated immense amounts of paperwork. We know from the manuals themselves, as well as from surviving documents, that the numbers were huge and in many cases a single record was kept in many variations and recensions.

The manuals emphasize that proficiency and experience in the art of writing *insha*, accountancy, and record-keeping guaranteed excellence and upward professional mobility. It is said that skill is like a tree and performance its fruits. Performance was measured in terms of the ability to withstand the scrutiny of strict auditors (*musatufi*). The combination of the art of letter composition and accountancy was the ideal, but difficult to achieve. Chandrabhan Barhaman, letter writer to the Mughal emperor Shahjahan, advised his son Tej Bhan to learn, if he could, both letter composition and accountancy: "There are very few letter-composers (*munshis*) who know accountancy, and fewer among accountants who are letter-composers. One can outshine others by combining the two skills."[10] In the testimony of the royal letter writer we have further evidence that the manuals did indeed reflect the reality of the profession.

---

10. Chandrabhan Barhaman, *Chahar Chaman* [*Four Gardens*], Seyed Mohammad Yunus Jafery (ed.) (Delhi, 2007), p. 175.

The section of the manual dealing with the conduct of life is interesting insofar as it has practically no direct connection with the profession itself except for its opening remark, which could perhaps be considered to be general. In fact, if we did not know the context it would be almost impossible to guess which professional group it is addressed to. It begins by prescribing that once a person had attained the age of twenty-one and acquired the five basic qualifications mentioned earlier he is ready to seek employment in the imperial administration or in the offices of the nobles. Once employed, he is required to serve his department with the utmost integrity and efficiency and retain the goodwill and cooperation of all his colleagues and subordinates.

A personal element is introduced into the professional norms with the advice that whenever he wishes a task to be satisfactorily carried out by his subordinates and servants he should issue instructions in the same way as he issues them to his children, politely and affectionately rather than authoritatively or harshly. At the same time he should not be totally dependent on his subordinates. He should verify whether the job had been well done and if not he should make amends.

The accountant and record-keeper was expected to follow a strict and organized routine. During the last quarter of the night, just before the twilight brightened into dawn, he was expected to get up, bathe, and perform his religious rituals, *puja*, or any other form of worshipping God. The reference especially to the Hindu form of worship (*puja*) suggests the religious identity of the core audience of the manuals. Once the sun was up, he was advised to eat something and get on with his day's work. Work was important but the day was not devoid of leisure (*fursat*), the time spent with his friends and family after finishing work. In the first quarter of the night, before he went to sleep, he was reminded to pray once again. It was strongly advised not to sleep in the first and last quarters of the night. These were the times when angels roamed the earth and blessed those found in the act of worship and protected them from calamities and adversities. The angels condemned all those who were found whiling their time away.

That is once again an interesting piece of advice, since the concept of angels is Islamic and alien to Hinduism. The manner in which Islamic norms became assimilated into the religious-ethical world of a largely Hindu professional group signified the transition that took place from a purely Indic system of accountancy and record-keeping to the Perso-Islamic one now practised predominantly by Hindu caste groups.

The contents of the section on recommendations becomes progressively more ethical and formulaic. Advice related to personal conduct and norms of social behaviour among professionals appeared in one manual as the virtue of the right sort of speech ("Do not speak more than is necessary and unless spoken to"); signs of good fortune (*nek bakhti*), such as the desire to seek knowledge (*talib i ilmi*), generosity (*sakhawat*), a pleasing countenance (literally a smiling face), truthfulness, good deeds, making an effort to gain employment (*koshish i kasb*), and generosity towards family members ("Do not accumulate but consume wealth"); and signs of misfortune (*bad bakhti*), such as sloth (*kahili*), harshness (*sakht rui*), and pride (*takabbur*). The list of recommendations then goes on as follows:

(1) Treat your parents and guardians with kindness and gratitude. Do not curse your children. If you find your friends and acquaintances in trouble, try to help them rather than make excuses.
(2) Do not put (too much) trust in the good will of the king, governor, and employer.
(3) The things one should desire or seek in this world are consultations with the wise (*mashwarat ba aqilan*), avoidance of the company of women, keeping company with mendicants (*darweshan*).
(4) (a) Never accept or give out anything in trust deposit without a receipt (*be sanad*).
   (b) Do not lend money to friends or borrow from them. It can destroy friendship.
   (c) Treat your guests with warmth. Talk to them, offer them food and when they leave walk a few steps with them.
   (d) Do good deeds all your life. Good and bad deeds influence the outcome of your actions in this world.
   (e) Treat everyone with respect.
(5) (a) Do not travel alone or with strangers.
   (b) Pay full attention to whatever you hear.
   (c) Eat only *halal* food. While eating always give something from it in charity.
   (d) Never bathe naked (*barahna ghusl makun*).
   (e) Comb your moustache everyday (*har roz mui ra shana kard*).
   (f) Look at your face in the mirror during the day but not at night.
   (g) Do not stand guarantor to anyone. If you do, thoroughly examine the matter.
   (h) Beware of three things: enmity (*dushman*), fire (*atish*), and debt (*qarz*).

I have reproduced a few norms as they appear in one manual without attempting to streamline or synthesize them. It is quite clear that they are fragmentary and lack systematization or organization of any kind, bordering on thought. Put together the whole section on ethics stands on its own. It seems as if our protagonists were living in two separate worlds, one professional and the other personal or social with no overlap. The professional world was defined by knowledge, skill, accuracy, and righteousness. The private social world was dominated by norms of good behaviour and various "dos and don'ts" drawn apparently from diverse sources. That appears to be the unique and characteristic feature of literature produced by a professional group, and such literature can be contrasted with the organized and orderly statements framed within certain well-established traditions about work and work ethics made by theologians and intellectuals and intended for the aristocracy.[11]

CONCLUSION

It can be argued from a study of the manuals that there was a large market for professional accountants and record-keepers in the state sector. The bureaucracy of the state created regular employment for skilled professionals to work in various departments, as the Mughal bureaucracy and chancery followed a uniform procedure for creating and keeping accounts throughout its empire. Given the practice of transferring high officials from one department to another it was necessary for the state to have a uniform set of procedures and techniques that could be understood and followed by everyone everywhere. The procedures and techniques were predominantly Perso-Islamic methods adapted to the Indian situation.

In a certain sense it was a free labour market in which all adult males – there is no evidence of women's participation in the profession – who were proficient in the Persian language and the art of accounting and record-keeping were able to be recruited and promoted. The professionals were mostly Hindus drawn from the secretarial and intellectual classes which had been serving the various imperial and regional administrations for centuries. Their willingness and ability to adapt to the new tradition symbolized the dynamic nature of the secretarial class, although the class itself seemed to have been limited to specific castes.

The manuals generally throw light upon themselves and the purpose for which they were written rather than upon the practitioners or how others perceived them. From internal evidence it seems that those practitioners perceived themselves as subordinate officials devoted to the task they were required to perform and to making their way up the occupational ladder by displaying professional excellence and adhering to a set of moral values to satisfy and please their patrons and superiors.

11. Baqar Najm i Sani, *Muiza i Jahangiri* [*Advice on Statecraft*], Sajida Sultana Alvi (ed. and trans.) (Albany, NY, 1989); Aziz Ahmad, "The British Museum Mirzanama and the Seventeenth Century Mirza in India", *Iran*, 13 (1975), pp. 99–110; see also Rosalind O'Hanlon, "Manliness and Imperial Service in Mughal North India", *Journal of Economic and Social History of the Orient*, 42 (1999), pp. 47–92.

IRSH 56 (2011), Special Issue, pp. 275–296 doi:10.1017/S0020859011000435
© 2011 Internationaal Instituut voor Sociale Geschiedenis

Labour Ideologies and Labour Relations in Colonial Portuguese America, 1500–1700*

TARCISIO R. BOTELHO

Department of History, Universidade Federal de Minas Gerais

E-mail: tbotelho@fafich.ufmg.br

SUMMARY: During the two first centuries of Portuguese colonization in America there was an intense debate about the legitimacy of enslaving Africans and Indians. In Portuguese America, the mission to spread the Christian faith was connected with the subjection of populations on both sides of the Atlantic Ocean to an ideology that considered labour as God's punishment for Adam's sin. In that sense, the justification of the unfree labour inflicted upon Indians and Africans in Portuguese America was a product of the same ideology, one that condemned manual work as rendering a man dishonourable. The purpose of this article is to review the debate from its medieval origins in Portugal, and to examine what effect the arrival of the Jesuits in America had on that debate, until the final prohibition of Indian enslavement in the mid-eighteenth century, documented by letters, reports, and sermons.

INTRODUCTION

This article aims to discuss labour ideologies in Portuguese America during the sixteenth and seventeenth centuries in connection with changes to labour relations. It adopts the definitions of the Global Collaboratory on the History of Labour Relations, which divides the workforce into three major groups: "commodified labour" (working for the market or for non-market institutions, self-employed, employers, chattel slaves); "reciprocal labour" (housewives, dependants); and "tributary labour" (forced labour, serfs). Looking at the transformations in labour relations during the initial two centuries of Portuguese colonization in America, we can see two major changes: first, the widespread use of commodified labour, and second, the

* I should like to acknowledge the financial support of CNPq (National Council for Scientific and Technological Development, Brazil, grant number #310248/2007-8) and FAPEMIG (Research Support Foundation of Minas Gerais State, Brazil, grant number #PPM-00334/2008), and also to thank Christine Moll-Murata, Karin Hofmeester, and Douglas Cole Libby for their comments on earlier versions of this article, David Lopez for his help with the map, and Litany Ribeiro Pires for help in translating from the Portuguese.

predominance of chattel slavery at a time when, in Europe, free labour was becoming the most important labour relation.

The widespread use of slavery in connection with production for the market defined the history of Portuguese America. During the sixteenth century, the establishment of sugar mills polarized colonial society into masters and slaves. Between those two poles other forms of labour relation could be found; though less important and subordinate, they were present to a varying extent in the workforce. First, there was an increasing proportion of self-employed and independent producers such as farmers and peasants, craftsmen, specialized workers, and the like, who were free workers dedicated to commodified labour for the market. Second, the Indians were organized into small villages (*aldeamentos*) controlled by religious orders, especially the Jesuits; they may be regarded as workers subject to reciprocal labour within their communities. From the second half of the seventeenth century until the eighteenth, *aldeamentos* declined in number and importance while free labour increased along with the expansion of sugar mills, farms, and cattle ranches.

Labour ideologies were profoundly influenced by that process. Medieval ideologies of social organization were very important in the establishment of a social orientation to the master's ideal of honour. On the other hand, we can find some discourses on Indians and slaves that reinforced the disqualification of manual work – "to work with one's own hands" – as God's punishment for sin. To discuss all these topics, I shall start by describing the formation of colonial Portuguese America, with a discussion about the colonization process and how the population submitted to the Portuguese colonists. After that, I shall discuss ideological views of the work of masters ("the nobility of the land") and slaves ("the hands and feet of the sugar-mill master").

THE FORMATION OF COLONIAL PORTUGUESE AMERICA

The initial Portuguese colonization of America included a period of exploitation and the establishment of *feitoria* houses that extended from 1500, when the first Portuguese fleet arrived in Porto Seguro, to the 1530s. The presence of an autochthonous population and the greater interest of the Portuguese in trading with Asia justified their adoption of an unstable form of occupation, which resulted in the settlement of a small number of Europeans, mainly men. It followed naturally that families were formed with indigenous women, given that such was the only opportunity for "domestic" life that the Portuguese men had at the time.

Colonization of a permanent nature started in 1530 with the arrival of expeditions which brought the first people willing to settle on the land. The institution of an inheritable captaincy system was intended to encourage permanent settlement, with the Portuguese Crown's current interest in Asia as the predominant factor. Before 1550, only the captaincies of São Vicente and Pernambuco could be regarded as successful, while in Santo Amaro, Espírito Santo, Porto Seguro, Ilhéus, and Itamaracá success was marginal. São Tomé, Bahia, and Maranhão had failed dismally, while the other five captaincies remained unexplored.

The 1540s saw a crisis unleashed by the reaction of the indigenous population to permanent occupation. Along with threats of invasion by other European maritime powers, the recently founded colony was on the brink of collapse. Given the steady loss of its monopoly over Asian commerce, the Portuguese government decided to adopt a stricter policy for America, and so in 1549 a general government was established, led by Tomé de Sousa from 1549 to 1553, which spared no effort to overcome the pervasive instability that the colony was experiencing. The first three general governments managed to reverse the situation, and by about 1570, at the end of Mem de Sá's government, it is possible to conclude that Portuguese colonization in America had been consolidated.

From that point on, the colony saw the expansion of sugar-cane plantations, which began to cover larger areas in the Zona da Mata in the north-east, from Bahia to Rio Grande do Norte. Later, activity expanded to the south, finding in Campos, Rio de Janeiro, a particularly suitable area for the cultivation of sugar cane. During the seventeenth century regions such as Maranhão and Pará were occupied, as were Santa Catarina and Rio Grande closer to the turn of the eighteenth century. In the last decade of the seventeenth century and the first decades of the eighteenth century, the discovery of gold and diamonds brought exploration and the definitive incorporation of the interior of the American continent.

It is, however, important to note that the sugar industry was the basis of Portuguese settlement in Brazil, and that the *engenho*, which means sugar mill but, by extension, sugar plantation too, embodied much more than just agricultural exploitation. In fact, it constituted the nucleus of Brazilian colonial society at least until the end of the seventeenth century, and the crucial role of the *engenho* in Brazilian society is a central theme of Brazilian historiography. From the colonial chronicles until the arrival of traditional historiography at the beginning of the twentieth century and the modern historiography of the last few decades there has been a long tradition of studying the Brazilian sugar industry.[1] Even after the development of a gold-mining society in Minas Gerais, and the progressive diversification

---

1. See, for example, Pero de Magalhães Gândavo, *Tratado da terra do Brasil: Historia da província Santa Cruz* (Belo Horizonte, 1980); Gabriel Soares de Sousa, *Noticia do Brasil* (São Paulo, 1974); Gilberto Freyre, *Casa-grande e senzala* (Rio de Janeiro, 1933); Stuart Schwartz, *Sugar Plantations in the Formation of Brazilian Society: Bahia, 1550–1835* (Cambridge, 1985); and Luiz Felipe de Alencastro, *O trato dos viventes: formação do Brasil no Atlântico Sul, séculos XVI e XVII* (São Paulo, 2001).

of the colonial economy at the end of eighteenth century, colonial social organization was continuously influenced by the relationship between masters and slaves that had initially been built up in the *engenho*.

In this process of establishing a stable colonial society in Brazil, the crucial problem to be solved was that of the labour force. As Stuart Schwartz emphasized, since its Mediterranean experience the sugar-cane economy had been characterized by relatively large land units, well-developed long-range commerce, and enslaved or coerced labour.[2] Use of the Indian population was the first option tried by the *senhores de engenho* (sugar planters). When the Portuguese arrived in this part of America, they found none of the complex pre-Colombian state organizations, such as those which confronted the Spanish, first in Meso-America and later in the central Andes. There was also a much lower demographic density and attendant scattering throughout the territory. What followed the arrival of the Portuguese was a process of acculturation of these people, achieved by means of the villages organized by the Jesuits and a few other religious groups, and enslavement.

The clustering of Indians in villages first started on the coast, after the adoption by Portugal of a more effective colonization policy. In 1549, the first Governor-General, Tomé de Sousa, brought Jesuits with him, whom he put in charge of contacting and organizing the indigenous population in what would become one of the vectors of the process of their incorporation into the Portuguese colonization project. The villages saw stagnation, success, and failure until the 1570s, in the midst of a decline in the indigenous population, when they were dispersed throughout more extensive territories. By the end of the seventeenth century, the various religious orders were administering villages in places as far apart as the Amazon and the extreme south of the Portuguese colony in America. In the second half of eighteenth century, the villages were the subject of a dispute due to the new policies adopted by Marquês de Pombal, the main minister of the Portuguese Crown, in his administration of the Portuguese overseas empire.

The other tactic for incorporating the indigenous population into Portuguese America was enslavement. Added to the cultural conflicts, the initial attempts of early colonizers were complicated by the demographic crisis of the 1540s, which resulted from the sum of a number of factors, including wars, epidemics, and famine. From 1560 and the Caetés War, the numbers of Indians living on the coast and in neighbouring areas diminished. From then on, the supply of indigenous slaves dwindled steadily too, and there was more incentive to send expeditions further and further inland.

The advance of Portuguese colonization based on the expansion of sugar production and the steady decrease in the indigenous populations

2. Schwartz, *Sugar Plantations*, p. 3.

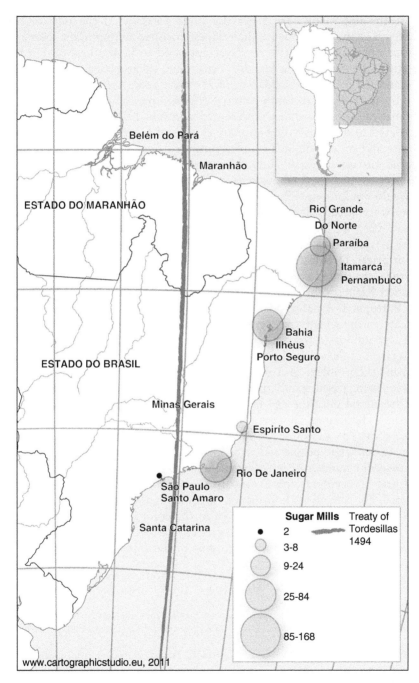

Figure 1. Sugar mills in Brazil in 1629.
Frédéric Mauro, Portugal, o Brasil e o Atlântico, 1570–1670 *(Lisbon, 1997), p. 255.*

made the option of African slavery quite feasible. At the turn of the sixteenth century, although Indian slaves remained an important source of labour on plantations African slaves appeared to be the best option for meeting the needs of a rapidly expanding sugar economy. Growing demand led to the consolidation of the slave trade across the Atlantic,[3] and by the mid-seventeenth century Africans predominated in the slave population, while Indians represented a residual segment and became restricted to the economic periphery of the colony. At the same time, the Jesuits and other religious orders continued to organize the indigenous people into newly established *aldeamentos* under a labour relation I will describe as reciprocal labour within their communities.

We do not know precisely when the first Africans arrived in Brazil, but there were already substantial numbers of them at the beginning of the 1540s. Pero de Magalhães Gândavo, a colonial chronicler, calculated a total of 2,000 to 3,000 black people in Brazil in 1570, and in 1587 the Jesuit priest, José de Anchieta, mentioned 14,000 in his letters.[4] Estimates for the slave trade have been relatively well studied by several researchers. Herbert Klein synthesized the data to show a total of 50,000 slaves arriving on Portuguese-American shores in the sixteenth century (1530–1600), 560,000 in the seventeenth century, 1.68 million in the eighteenth century, and 1.72 million in the nineteenth century up to 1852.[5]

In terms of the stock of slaves at different times during colonization, there remains the problem of a simple lack of information, with estimates less precise, being based mainly on informed guesswork. More reliable estimates for the period until the end of the seventeenth century were produced by Contrera Rodrigues, in 1935.[6] He mentions a total population of over 100,000 in 1600 and of 184,000 in 1660. Of that 100,000, there might have been 30,000 white people and 70,000 mixed race, black, and Indian in 1600; by 1660, the number of white people and free Indians had reached 74,000, and that of slaves 110,000. In 1690, the population might have been over 242,000, but there is no information on its composition.

The sugar mill took a central role in the colonial economy, becoming the nucleus upon which colonial society was organized. It retained its indisputable position until the beginning of the eighteenth century, when

3. An excellent description of the "African option" can be found in Schwartz, *Sugar Plantations*, Part 1.

4. H.B. Johnson, "A colonização portuguesa no Brasil, 1500–1580", in Leslie Bethell (ed.), *História da América Latina, Volume 1: América Latina colonial* (São Paulo, 1998), pp. 241–281, 268.

5. Herbert Klein, "Tráfico de escravos", in FIBGE, *Estatísticas históricas do Brasil* (Rio de Janeiro, 1990), pp. 53–61, 60.

6. These estimates were synthesized in Clotilde Andrade Paiva, José Alberto Magno de Carvalho, and Valéria da Motta Leite, "Demografia", in FIBGE, *Estatísticas históricas do Brasil*, pp. 19–52, 30.

gold deposits discovered in the interior of Portuguese America started competing for primacy. It is estimated that by 1630 inhabitants of sugar-producing areas amounted to more than three-quarters of the total population of Portuguese America. In those areas more than two-thirds of the population was enslaved, and although there was a significant proportion of free people working in sugar mills (I estimate it at less than 20 per cent of the total labour force) slavery was the predominant labour relation.[7]

Although there were other important social categories within colonial society, the central role played by the sugar-based economy gave rise to the basic polarity between masters and slaves. Therefore, in order to understand the work ethics prevailing throughout the Brazilian colonial period it is necessary to understand the values and norms orientating those two poles: the sugar-mill masters, on the one hand, and the slaves on the other. In the case of the slaves, it is important to highlight the division between Indians and Africans in the sixteenth and seventeenth centuries, a division that came to an end only in the eighteenth century.

THE SUGAR-MILL MASTERS, OR THE NOBILITY OF THE LAND

In their transplantation to America, the Portuguese brought with them notions of social hierarchy firmly rooted in the ideas of a society that had inherited medieval principles. Because of that, the work-related values and norms that prevailed throughout the Brazilian colonial period are best approached by first looking at their medieval Iberian heritage.

At the end of the eleventh century, social stability was considered the absolute organizing principle of Portuguese society. In Portugal, as in the rest of medieval western Europe, the representation of society was regarded as the prime social ordering system, within the tradition of Indo-European society in general. At the beginning of the eleventh century Adalberón de Laon developed the classic tripartite division of society: *oratores*, *bellatores*, and *laboratores*.[8] In other words, the organization of society was based on its division into the clergy, the nobility, and the people, each of which were conscious of their duties and performed their functions in harmony.

In Portugal, until the end of the thirteenth century the terms used to refer to the nobility or the class of masters expressed the idea of "the one that holds power" rather than "the warrior". In that sense it came down to

---

7. These estimates are included in an unpublished paper presented to the Fifth Workshop of the Global Collaboratory on the History of Labour Relations, 1500–2000, Düsseldorf, 12–14 November 2009.
8. Jacques Le Goff, *Time, Work, and Culture in the Middle Ages* (Chicago, IL, 1981), p. 53; see also Georges Duby, *The Three Orders: Feudal Society Imagined* (Chicago, IL, 1981).

"the capacity to manage, administer, and command".⁹ Therefore the privileges of the nobility included not only the appropriation of assets, but also ways of exerting power over men: "exerting public authority, judging, commanding warriors, collecting taxes, enforcing the law".¹⁰ Those deprived of such privileges were dependent on the nobility and had no alternative but to subject themselves to it. They were the dependants whose prerogatives were limited to the possession of their own bodies and land, and that is why they dedicated themselves to productive activities. Thus, they were the *laboratores*. At that time, dependants were divided into distinct categories of worker: inheritors, settlers, commission agents (butlers, judges, and leaseholders), wage-earners, and other fringe categories such as hunters or fishermen. Work was a mark of those on the lowest rungs of society.

In the fourteenth and fifteenth centuries, Portuguese society was still conceived within that model, but political, economic, and social transformations started to appear in social interactions, both within the existing orders and between them. According to José Mattoso, "the prerequisite of this hierarchical social-political inequality, co-natural to the image of the society of orders, expanded within each one of them. In other words, it encroached upon the inner parts of the third [order] and strengthened itself in the second [order]."¹¹ The influence of mobile wealth, in other words money, started to be felt in all states. In the fifteenth century, "the rule of the quantitative, the appeal of the century, allures all: kings, noblemen, clergymen, bourgeoisie, and artisans. They all rely on money to be and to go up, but all of them dismiss it as tarnishing. Divided minds, ambivalent attitudes."¹²

In that series of transformations, the townspeople started to form a cluster of occupations and professions. The criteria of wealth, prestige, and power set them apart as "good men" (or bourgeoisie), artisans, manual workers, and servants. Their segment invaded the fringes of the clergy and the nobility, especially the king's vassals, the usurping noblemen, shield-men, and bourgeois knights. But people still defined themselves by their work. Work was equated with suffering, the result of the punishment of Adam, who, because of his sin, had to toil to get his sustenance. Only farming had some value, since it provided people with their food. However, as businesses, services, and handicrafts developed, cities began producing wealth, which was increasingly becoming the key to power. Steadily, the concept that divided society into three orders ebbed away.

At the end of the Middle Ages, it makes more sense to say that Portuguese society was organized into "estates". Although it still thought of itself as a

9. José Mattoso, *História de Portugal*, II (Lisbon, 1993), p. 176.
10. *Ibid*, p. 197.
11. *Ibid.*, p. 396.
12. *Ibid.*, p. 421.

society of orders (which implied a much more rigid conception of society), in this new society of "estates" occupations, codes, and professions now defined social status. In that sense, "knowledge and wealth, or personal and familial success, become more relevant as the real propellers of social mobility, supplanting attributes that had customarily been exclusively inherited".[13] The colonists of Portuguese America therefore brought with them these concepts of society.

As society was based on agriculture, it inherited social principles that tended to value that type of work. Sugar planting, in turn, favoured the consolidation of a pattern of behaviour compatible with the ideal of the nobility, especially when it came to creating a long roll of dependants. Social hierarchization played an essential role in the order of social life. Stuart Schwartz mentions a letter by Duarte Coelho, donatary of the captaincy of Pernambuco, in which the occupations of his settlers were described.[14] At the top of the list came the sugar-mill masters. They were in charge of directing operations, and were made even nobler as they controlled the work of freemen as well as of slaves, who were their dependants. Then came the sugar-cane farmers, dependants to varying degrees on the owners of the sugar plantations, which was where their cane was milled. Cane farmers aspired to become sugar-mill owners too, and that motivated a small degree of social mobility, especially among whites. The men dedicated to the production of food for local consumption were regarded as being similar to European peasants, and for that reason they were respected since they were essential to everyone. After them were mentioned the merchants and artisans. Slaves did not feature in the description, despite the fact that they formed the majority of the inhabitants.

In that social order then, sugar-mill masters were at the apex of a pyramid. In 1629 there were 346 sugar mills in Brazil, some of which were owned by religious orders.[15] If it is assumed that each mill-owning family had 6 members, about 2,000 people were at the top of the pyramid, of a total population estimated at 156,800 inhabitants.

The ideal of nobility would dictate performance and behavioural patterns. In the absence of noble blood, a nobleman was defined in the colony by what it was not fitting for him to do: he should never do manual work, own a shop, make crafts, nor perform any less noble occupation. Ideally, his income would come from rents or public office. Everyone aspired to the titles, status, and privileges of the aristocracy. Climbing up the rungs of the social ladder meant a person would first be elevated to the status of a nobleman, which was granted to the first-born, to those able to boast

13. *Ibid.*, p. 474.
14. Schwartz, *Sugar Plantations*, p. 26.
15. Mauro, *Portugal, o Brasil e o Atlântico*, p. 255.

some military rank, and those holding attitudes and values cultivated by
the sugar-plantation masters. In their society, the first conquerors and
their descendants occupied a special place, calling themselves the "noble
families" or the "nobility of the Republic".[16]

Such noblemen would spend their lives without doing any manual work,
as that would have been considered demeaning. The presence of Indians and
Africans made every European into a potential "good man". As a result, new
social distinctions were created which were based on culture and skin colour.
According to Schwartz, the connections established between origin and/or
colour, on the one hand, and the internal structure of property and the labour
force, on the other, "reinforced the social hierarchy and reaffirmed the gra-
dations in a practical and demonstrable way. The *engenho* [sugar mill] was
both mirror and metaphor of Brazilian society."[17]

The quest for wealth in the colony allowed migrant groups to embrace
profitable activities, which also provided them with attributes belonging
to the status of nobility, at least in the colonial context. *Cristãos Novos* (or
New Christians, converted Jews and their descendants) and some members of the commercial bourgeoisie, two groups considered inferior by
Portuguese society, were commonly found among the sugar-mill masters,
but that did not prevent them, as a class, from seeing themselves as the
nobility of the land. Later on, people born in Brazil joined such immigrants and their children. Throughout Brazilian colonial history, however,
the sugar-mill masters sought to consolidate themselves as a colonial
nobility by means of functions, actions, and lifestyle. The process proved
contradictory because, according to Schwartz, "the successful pursuit of
wealth in the context of this tropical colony upset Portuguese hierarchies
of status, race, and wealth and created a series of negative images that
denied the residents of Brazil the social recognition they prized".[18]

THE SLAVE OR "THE HANDS AND FEET
OF THE SUGAR-MILL MASTER"

As discussed before, Portuguese colonial society in the Americas was
organized around the division between freemen and slaves. In looking at
the two extremes of the sugar-mill masters and their slaves it is possible to
discern the ethical logic related to work that permeated social relations in
the colony. Therefore, in view of what we already know about the sugar-
mill masters, it is necessary to compare the two forms of slavery present
during the colonial period: the enslavement of Indians and that of Africans.

16. João Luis Fragoso, "A nobreza da República: notas sobre a formação da primeira elite
senhorial do Rio de Janeiro (séculos XVI e XVII)", *Topoi*, 1 (2000), pp. 45–122.
17. Schwartz, *Sugar Plantations*, p. 251.
18. *Ibid.*, p. 272.

To approach the theme, it is important to go back to its original Iberian roots. Among the *laboratores*, defined as dependants who dedicated themselves to production activities, the servant class stood out as the old slaves who had not been freed but placed in the domain and given land.[19] The advance of the *Reconquista*, the "reconquest" of Muslim-dominated land in the Iberian peninsula, boosted the number of Moorish slaves in the hands of Christians, especially in Portugal. Domestic slaves remained important until the mid-thirteenth century; later they became the property of the king. It is necessary to point out, in our case, that in Portugal slavery remained an important labour relation and, as the Portuguese advanced across the southern Atlantic in the fifteenth and sixteenth centuries, it underwent a period of intensification.

The implantation and growth of the sugar-based economy in the Atlantic islands (Madeira and São Tomé) led to the strengthening of slavery as an institution and its steady redefinition as the prevailing labour relation in an activity geared to the market. When sugar production was introduced into Portuguese America, slavery naturally emerged as the ideal labour relation, already tested and approved in previous experiments carried out by the Portuguese themselves. The establishment of this labour relation as the structure at the basis of the colonial reality brought about the consolidation of a fundamental principle that permeates its entire history: the distinction between slavery and freedom. However, the racial element that permeated slavery in the New World created a new status criterion that dictated social life and ideology in the colony. Schwartz states that Brazilian society was the result of integration between the large plantations and the social principles that already existed in Europe, with slavery bringing about new principles of hierarchy, based on race, acculturation, and social condition.[20]

Initially, slavery in Portuguese America was based on the capture of Indians living on the Brazilian coast or in the hinterland. Eventually, the difficulties of maintaining the supply of such labour at the level demanded by the sugar industry, the demographic and social limits to the adaptation of the Indian population to the kind of work imposed by the sugar mills and plantations, and the progressively improved structure of the Atlantic slave trade led to a reduction in the number of Indians employed as slaves in Brazil and to an increasingly significant presence of Africans. Conflicts with the Jesuits and other religious orders who had taken on the task of converting the Indians also played a part here, and over time and with the advance of colonization, indigenous slavery was pushed to the fringes of the colonial system.[21]

---

19. Mattoso, *História de Portugal*, p. 200.

20. Schwartz, *Sugar Plantations*, p. 251.

21. A detailed study of indigenous slavery in Brazil can be found in John M. Monteiro, *Negros da terra: índios e bandeirantes nas origens de São Paulo* (São Paulo, 1994).

It is necessary to understand the disputes sparked by the enslaving of Indians and Africans. The debate that divided colonists and the regular clergy, especially the Jesuits, reveals other facets of the ideology of work that accompanied the establishment of Portuguese colonial society in America. Among the main points in the debate, I should like first to examine how the Jesuits viewed indigenous and African slavery in Brazil. The central role played by the Jesuits in the debate, and the importance of the Jesuits to different aspects of colonial life, not only religious life but the economy, education, and culture, justify the decision to concentrate on written records left by priests as they sought to spell out the work ethics that orientated their political actions.

JESUIT VIEWS OF INDIGENOUS LABOUR

As already mentioned, the Indians were the first option for the supply of compulsory labour in the first sugar plantations in Portuguese America. However, the debate that had been going on since the early advances of the Spanish among the Amerindian societies led the Catholic Church to take a stand, recognizing the human condition of the people and there-fore definitively forbidding their enslavement.[22] In 1537 Pope Paul III promulgated the papal bull *Sublimus Dei*, consolidating the Church's position and declaring that:

> [...] the said Indians and all other people who may later be discovered by Christians, are by no means to be deprived of their liberty or the possession of their property, even though they be outside the faith of Jesus Christ; and that they may and should, freely and legitimately, enjoy their liberty and the possession of their property.

As a consequence, "nor should they be in any way enslaved; should the contrary happen, it shall be null and have no effect".[23]

The Jesuits arrived in Portuguese America in 1549, brought by the first Governor-General, Tomé de Sousa. Having been charged with the reli-gious indoctrination of the Indians, the Jesuits soon saw themselves engaged in a dispute with the settlers, because, in observance of *Sublimus Dei*, the Jesuits were opposed to the enslavement of the Indians. They set up a system of settlements by which they organized the Indians in compliance with principles that sought to combine the way of life of the Indians with their acculturation, resulting from their evangelization.

22. A good discussion about the time Spaniards first arrived in America and found a completely different society can be found in Tzvetan Todorov, *The Conquest of America: The Question of the Other* (New York, 1984); and David Brading, *The First America: The Spanish Monarchy, Creole Patriots and the Liberal State, 1492–1867* (Cambridge, 1991), chs 3 and 4.
23. Quoted by Paulo Suess (ed.), *A conquista espiritual da América Espanhola* (Petrópolis, Rio de Janeiro, 1992), pp. 273–275.

In these settlements work played a central role in the process of adaptation of the Indians to the European way of life. However, the Jesuits were accused by the settlers of monopolizing the indigenous labour, and the Jesuits in turn responded by putting pressure on the Portuguese government to enforce the prohibition of Indian slavery.

As a result, in 1570 the Portuguese Crown issued a law banning Indian slavery, except in the cases known as "the fair war" (*guerra justa*). According to that principle, only Indians hostile to Portuguese colonization could be made slaves after being captured. Alternatively, Indians who were made prisoners of other tribes and were rescued by expeditions of white settlers (*resgate*) could also be made slaves; after all, they had been rescued from death by white people. In 1595 and in 1609 other laws of similar content were enacted, but the "fair war" and "rescue" principles remained as legitimate reasons for Indian slavery. It was only in the second half of the eighteenth century that Indian slavery was effectively banned, having survived in a few economically less dynamic parts of the colony.

According to Schwartz, three expedient measures were used by the Portuguese to make the Indians useful to the economy of the colony.[24] The first was direct coercion by means of enslavement, transforming them into chattel slaves who produced goods for the market. If, on the one hand, the Portuguese Crown accepted the requests of the Jesuits to ban Indian slavery, on the other, their understanding of the economic needs of the settlers led them to maintain some loopholes in the law, allowing Indian slavery to go on by means of the fair war and rescue practices. The second measure was the settlements established by the Jesuits and other religious orders aimed at creating an indigenous peasantry, thus making the Indians fit in with European demands for their acculturation and de-tribalization, and that I regard as reciprocal labour within communities. As the creation of a peasantry came to nothing, the Jesuits then started to justify the continuation of their actions by emphasizing the supply of a military and labour force for the colonization enterprise. The third measure was the progressive integration of the Indians, who were individually incorporated as waged workers into an incipient labour market; in that case, Indians were transformed into market wage-earners.

During the time that they were in the Portuguese colony (1549–1759), the Jesuits became deeply involved in the debate over captive labour, especially in relation to the Indians, and were instrumental in challenging the claims made by settlers to the Portuguese government. These disputes brought to the surface very important aspects of the way the Jesuits looked at the matter of work.

24. Schwartz, *Sugar Plantations*, pp. 42-43.

From the first years of the colonization of Portuguese America, the clergy, especially the Jesuits, sought to emphasize the precedence of evangelization over mere economic interests. Serafim Leite mentions the first provincial superior of the Society of Jesus in Brazil, Father Manoel da Nóbrega, writing to the Governor General Tomé de Sousa in 1559:

> These settlers fail to understand that the intention of our Holy King [D. John III], in his glory, was not so much to obtain gold or silver, or to people the land or build mills, or still bring wealth to the Portuguese in Portugal, as it was to glorify the Catholic faith and save souls.[25]

Work nevertheless played a central role in the routine of Jesuit settlements, for as we have seen their objective was to create a peasantry along the lines of European models, by way of the conversion and acculturation of the Indians. That resulted in a mixture of conversion and work.

The emphasis placed on work instigated conflicts with the settlers, who were equally interested in the low cost of the labour provided by Indian slavery. The conflict unleashed an acrimonious debate between representatives of the settlers and members of the clergy. The main argument of the settlers was that, since the Jesuits kept Indians working in the settlements, they were monopolizing their work and preventing the settlers from enjoying the economic advantages of so abundant and cheap a source of labour. This is how the Jesuits responded to the objections of the settlers, represented by Gabriel Soares de Sousa, that they were using the work of the Indians for their own benefit:

> The only solution to this state is to have a lot of peaceful people in the settlements around the mills and farms because in this way there will be someone to fight the enemies, like the French, the English, and the Aimorés, who have done and are still doing so much evil, and someone to keep a tight rein on the black people from Guinea, who are so many and who fear no one else but the Indians. The only way to have this is by doing as His Majesty has ordered, although this order is not obeyed, that there should be no slaves in the same way as there are none in Peru.[26]

Starting in the sixteenth century, the debate over the nature of labour relationships to which the Indians could be subjected extended throughout the seventeenth century. The great intellectual figure among the Jesuits during that period was Father Antônio Vieira. He was born in Portugal in 1608 and died in Bahia in 1697 after a long and adventurous life during which he was recognized as the most prominent intellectual in the Portuguese empire. As highlighted by Alfredo Bosi, Vieira was an adviser to kings, confessor to queens, preceptor of princes, a diplomat in European courts, an advocate of the New Christians, a missionary in Maranhão and Pará, and

---

25. Quoted by Serafim Leite, *Historia da Companhia de Jesus no Brasil* (Rio de Janeiro, 1938), II, p. 4.
26. *Ibid.*, p. 92.

finally the provincial superior of the Jesuits in Bahia.[27] He was an important advocate of the work of the Jesuits in Portuguese America and was a strong opponent of the claims made by the colonists.

Chased out and expelled from Belém do Pará together with other Jesuits because of their opposition to the enslavement of the Indians, Father Vieira delivered a sermon in Portugal in 1662, before the queen: the "Sermon of the Epiphany", in which he stated his opposition to the settlers and defended the necessity of the presence of the clergy in converting and protecting the Indians. According to Vieira, without the priests "[W]hat would become of the poor, helpless Indians, the prey and scrap of all this war? What would become of the Christians? What would become of the *catechumens* [newly converted Christians]? What would become of the populace?"[28] The work of the Jesuits made possible the conversion of these animal-like beings.

> Those were the very barbarians or brutes who, deprived of the use of reason or sense of humanity, would relish human flesh, and from their skulls make cups to drink their blood, and from their bones flutes to celebrate with their guests. And these today are the beasts that, instead of taking our lives, welcome us and worship us, like the lions worshipped Daniel; these birds of prey that, instead of eating us, provide for us, in the same way as the crows provided for Elijah.[29]

Father Vieira pointed out the abject material poverty the Indians lived in to justify the efforts made by the Jesuits to convert them and discipline them for work:

> [...] our stars perform their missions among poverty and helplessness, among disgust and misery and the helpless of the most uncultured of peoples, the most vile of peoples, the basest human beings of all that are born in this world. These people, who received so little from nature, for whom art and fortune made no effort at all, for whom a tree provides clothing, food, weapon, shelter, and a boat.[30]

Then, Vieira pointed to the racial component backing up the intentions of the settlers to enslave Indians: "But nothing is enough to curb the greed and tyranny of our defamers, as they claim [the Indians] are black, and therefore will have to be slaves."[31] This statement reveals a surprising anti-racist discourse that also serves the purpose of highlighting the combination of social position and racial condition so characteristic of Brazilian colonial society:

> If you despise me because you are white and I am black, do not think about colours; think about cause. Think that the cause of this colour is the sun, and you

27. Alfredo Bosi, *Dialética da colonização* (São Paulo, 1992).
28. Antônio Vieira, *Sermões* (Porto, 1950), II, p. 36.
29. *Ibid.*, p. 40.
30. *Ibid.*, p. 42.
31. *Ibid.*, p. 43.

will soon see how unfair your judgement is. The nations, some are whiter, others are blacker, because some are closer and other are farther away from the sun. And can there be worse inconsideration of understanding, or a most dreadful mistake of judgement among men than that I should be your master because I was born farther from the sun and you be my slave because you were born closer to it?[32]

However, the condemnation of those racial aspects of Indian slavery did not result in the condemnation of slavery as a labour relation. Vieira concluded his arguments by saying:

It is not my intention to ban slavery, What I want from this court, as is obvious and can be seen from my proposal, is that a committee of experts on the subject be formed, as was done before, and that the members declare, as it is declared by law – which is already registered – the reasons for "legal captivity".[33]

For Vieira, slavery was not the issue, given that it was the labour relation that sustained the economy and society and had been widely known since the beginning of Portuguese history. However, it would be up to the Portuguese government to draft and enforce clear principles governing licit and illicit captivity of the Amerindians.

As we shall see, it is important to emphasize that this definition of principles did not pertain to Africans, who were considered legitimate slaves. Anti-racism for Vieira was connected with the principles made explicit in *Sublimus Dei*. Indians were recognized as human beings with souls, and their enslavement was an obstacle to an efficient conversion. The enslavement of Africans was accepted as a natural way to save their souls to rescue them from that continent where conversion was impossible. In Vieira's view, race did not justify enslavement; conversion was the central aim that would be obtained through religious protection of the Indians and enslavement of Africans. In that sense, Vieira was not being contradictory, although his ideas were not shared by all the clergy.

That sermon exemplifies some of the ideas Vieira and the Jesuits had about the Indians; however, the place labour occupied in the project for society conceived by the Jesuits is not made very clear. That appears in a more explicit way in their sermons to black people, where it took the form of an ideological justification for the captivity of blacks.

THE AFRICAN SLAVES: JESUIT VIEWS FROM
VIEIRA TO ANTONIL

The transition from the predominance of the Indians over the Africans in the composition of the slave workforce lasted half a century, starting

32. *Ibid.*, p. 44.
33. *Ibid.*

from 1570. During that time the Jesuits took a stand in relation to African slavery too. Their view was pragmatic, as the Jesuit order, little by little, became one of the leading masters if not the greatest owners of mills and farms in the Portuguese colony in America, and consequently of African slaves. They defended the principle that the enslavement of Africans was necessary in order to free both the blacks and the Indians. It would free the blacks because it would release them from physical death caused by war, and from spiritual death caused by paganism back home in Africa. Slavery would free the Indians because, with African captivity, it was possible to release the Indians from slavery and then complete their conversion.

Apart from that, it was generally understood that without African slaves it would not have been possible to provide efficient and reliable labour in Brazil, workers capable of leaving the Jesuits free to carry out their real mission, which was the catechization of the Indians and Africans and the education of the settlers. In 1561, for example, Father Manoel da Nóbrega declared:

> Because we all admit that it is not possible to live without some [slaves] who will fetch wood and water for us and daily make the bread we eat, and do other chores that we cannot do for our brothers, especially because we are so few that we would no longer be able to take confessions and everything else [...] it seems that the Company must have [slaves] and acquire [them] exactly by the means allowed by the Constitutions, whenever possible, for our Schools and boys' homes.[34]

Moving in the same direction, in 1574 the attorney of the Portuguese Jesuit missions in Lisbon, Father Vale-Regio, informed Rome that the intention of avoiding slavery in Jesuit schools was possible only in Europe because "in India and in Brazil, where there are no other services but those performed by the slaves, there is no alternative but to use them".[35]

Once the moral dilemma over African slavery had been overcome within the Society of Jesus, throughout the seventeenth century the ideological role of the Jesuits became clear. Once again, Father Antônio Vieira was the leading figure in the construction of a discourse justifying African slave labour. Among a set of sermons delivered by him at different times during the seventeenth century, there were several dedicated to Our Lady of the Rosary, the patron saint of blacks. Generally addressed to the brotherhoods of the blacks, who organized themselves around the cult of the saint, the sermons were addressed to captive and freed Africans alike. They were, therefore, messages addressed directly to those who were the object of the preaching, so that they differed from the sermons for the Indians, since sermons to them were already addressed to a congregation of settlers or people in government. In other words, the

34. Quoted by Leite, *Historia da Companhia de Jesus no Brasil*, p. 349.
35. *Ibid.*, p. 345.

sermons by Father Vieira acknowledged the Africans and their descendants as direct interlocutors, while the Indians received no such
acknowledgement, since they were under the guardianship of the government or of religious orders.

Among the different sermons with Africans and their descendants as
interlocutors, I would initially highlight Sermon XIV in particular, which
was delivered in 1633. The emphasis is placed initially on the argument
that enslavement in Africa and exile to Brazil must be seen as an
opportunity for conversion to the Christian faith, and hence a route to the
door to paradise after death. It might have seemed like bad fortune at first,
but it was really a miracle: "Oh, if the black people taken from the depths
of their Ethiopia, and brought to Brazil, knew how much they owe to
God and His Holy Mother; for this that might look like uprooting,
captivity, and misery, but is in fact a miracle, and a great miracle."[36]
This miracle was expressed in the similarity between the fate of the
slave working in the mill and Jesus Christ's fate, his crucifixion:

> In the mill you are imitating crucified Christ [...] because you suffer in a very
> similar way to his suffering on the cross and all of His Passion. His cross was
> made of two logs, and yours in the mill is made of three [a reference to a new type
> of mill introduced in the seventeenth century]. In that place there was no shortage
> of sugar cane either, because it featured in the Passion twice: once serving as the
> sceptre of mockery and then as a source of the bile [*sic*] into which the sponge was
> dipped. Part of Christ's Passion was at night without sleep, and part in daylight
> without rest, and such are your nights and your days [a direct reference to the
> uninterrupted workload in the sugar mill during the cane harvest]. Christ naked
> and you naked; Christ with no food and you hungry; Christ abused in every way
> and you abused in every way. The manacles, the prisons, the whipping, the wounds,
> the offensive words, all this is part of your imitation that, if combined with
> patience, will gain you the right to martyrdom.[37]

According to Alfredo Bosi, in that sermon Father Vieira invoked an
argument that reinforced both

> [...] the discourse of sensitivity, which saw and expressed the agony of the
> slaves, and the discourse of understanding, capable of pointing to the iniquitous
> character of a society where men created by the same God the Father and
> redeemed by the same God the Son were set apart as masters and servants.[38]

The inequality so created appeared as the fall of humanity from an initial state
in which there would be no masters and servants. The connection between
work, in this case extremely painful and amounting to a great sacrifice, and
the punishment of Adam and Eve's original sin was thus remade.

36. Antônio Vieira, *Sermões* (Porto, 1951), XI, p. 305.
37. *Ibid.*, pp. 309–310.
38. Bosi, *Dialética da colonização*, p. 144.

In Sermon XXVII, Father Vieira again took up the idea of worthy sacrifice by elevating the condition of slavery to a divine level. Captivity would be only partial because while the body would be in agony the soul remained free:

> So that, my black brethren, this captivity in which you suffer agony, however hard and rough it may be, or seem to be, is not total captivity, or for everything you are, is but half captivity. You are captive in that outer half, the vilest part of your beings, which is the body; in the other part, however, the inner and most noble part, the soul and all that belongs to it, you are not captive, you are free.[39]

The core of his argument consisted of enticing the minds of bondsmen with the prospect of freedom in the other world, in the world of God, that would come to them after death:

> Because this great change of scene I am talking about will not be between you and them but, rather, between you and God, it will not be your masters who will serve you in Heaven, as it may well be that they will not get there, but God himself. It is God that will serve you in Heaven because you served Him on earth.[40]

Vieira took the paradigm of passion as a justification for captivity. However, as Alfredo Bosi pointed out, while the crucifixion of God appears in the gospels as an example of injustice and a farce, in Vieira the sacrifice of slavery was propitious, valid in its own right.[41] Therefore, the sermon assumed an ideological character, highlighting the inequality, suffering, and expropriation the slaves were subjected to, and at the same time advocating the need for them to suffer their fate as the only path leading to eternal glory.

What did those to whom Vieira directed his sermons think about them? We have little direct evidence about that. Literacy in colonial Brazil was very low, and few written sources have survived from the period. Indirect proof pointing to the acceptance of Vieira's arguments is the fact that he was continuously invited to speak by brotherhoods dedicated to Our Lady of the Rosary. Those brotherhoods were maintained by slaves and freed Africans and Afro-Americans, suggesting a widespread acceptance of Vieira's ideas among the most Catholicized part of the population.

This strand, followed by the discourse of the Jesuits about slavery, which solved the moral dilemma posed for them when slavery began in the sixteenth century in the Americas, paved the way for submission to a pragmatic discourse, orientated by the economic logic of the colonial enterprise. According to Bosi, the moral conscience expressed in Vieira was smothered by colonial mercantilism.[42]

---

39. Antônio Vieira, *Sermões* (Porto, 1951), XIII, p. 340.
40. *Ibid.*, XII, p. 362.
41. Bosi, *Dialética da colonização*, pp. 147–148.
42. *Ibid.*, p. 154.

That discourse is clearly expressed in a treatise published in Portugal in 1711, the pamphlet *Cultura e opulência do Brasil* [Culture and Opulence in Brazil], signed by a certain André João Antonil.[43] Just after publication, the work was banned by the Portuguese government as it contained details about the colony that were not supposed to fall into the hands of other European colonial states. The work was finally republished in the nineteenth century, and in the twentieth century it was discovered that the author was João Antônio Andreoni. Andreoni was an Italian Jesuit who had been invited to work with Father Vieira in Bahia at the end of the seventeenth century but disagreed with him about the conduct of the Jesuit enterprises in Brazil. At the end of his life, Vieira felt that he had been betrayed by his former pupil.

The work contains a very detailed account of the colony's economic activities. It refers to sugar and tobacco production, gold mines, and cattle raising and described the routes leading into the interior of the colony. It is a singular document about Brazil's past, as it contains, among other things, a detailed description of the workings of the sugar-cane mills. And it is precisely when it comes to sugar production that an ideological strand appears. According to Antonil, slavery appeared to be a given for sugar production. All the moral dilemmas about compulsory labour relations in the colony, which haunted the Jesuits during the previous centuries, disappeared in the light of efforts to objectify the slaves. Chapter 9, which deals with the slaves in the sugar mills, opens with the following concise statement: "The slaves are the hands and feet of the sugar-mill master, because without them in Brazil it is impossible to make, preserve, or expand the farms, of have a mill operating at all."[44]

That conception can be associated with an attitude to work that emphasized the legitimacy of the direct exploitation of the worker by the owner of the means of production. So, when the sugar-production process is synthesized in chapter 12 ("What sugar suffers from its birth to the moment it leaves Brazil") the author makes use of a discourse which associates the workers directly with the goods they produce. As Bosi points out, the chapter is distinguished for the use of passive verbs and metonymies, by which the tool replaces the worker, thus giving away how little the workers were valued in the result of their work.[45] The sugar cane takes on the status of subject: it suffers and aches in order to be transformed into sweet sugar. It is interesting to compare this discourse with that of Father Vieira, in which the slave was the subject of suffering and his work compared to Christ's Passion. For Antonil, sugar cane played

43. I have used a recent Brazilian edition: André João Antonil, *Cultura e opulência do Brasil* (São Paulo, 1976).
44. *Ibid.*, p. 159.
45. Bosi, *Dialética da colonização*, p. 174.

the role of leading actor in the crucifixion scene, a clear denigration of the hands-on worker. Then, by the beginning of the eighteenth century, manual labour had been totally devalued and not even the suffering associated with slavery was considered a sure path to Heaven.

FINAL CONSIDERATIONS

Slavery survived in Brazil until 1888, when Brazil became the last country in the Western world to abolish it. Slave labour relations during the period of its use were fully ingrained in society, from the export sector to the urban domestic and service sector, as well as in small-scale production. The trade in slaves across the Atlantic remained active until 1850, and its continuity was what guaranteed the deep penetration of the institution of slave labour. It was only towards the end that slavery started to lose strength, as reproduction rates among Brazilian slaves were rather low and the remaining contingents of bondsmen were concentrated in very few economic sectors.

The end of slavery meant that slaves were neglected and left to fend for themselves, there being no public policies to provide for those who were emancipated. Indeed, the main public policy on labour relations involved incentives to large-scale European immigration, which began in the 1870s and peaked in the 1890s. The policy had a racial component, since the immigration of white people was conceived of as a way to minimize miscegenation, and by reducing inter-racial mixing in Brazil to help minimize dependency on a "lazy population". Mass immigration brought about new free labour relations, needed for work in the quickly growing coffee industry in the state of São Paulo and, on a smaller scale, in the state of Minas Gerais. It was important too for the occupation of the south of the country. In fact, the free European worker was associated, in more economically dynamic regions, with the physical replacement of black or *mestizo* workers with white workers.

The other side of the coin of Brazilian slavery was the preservation of a work ethic identified with the so-called nobility of the land, the Portuguese style of colonization in Brazil. Until at least the first half of the nineteenth century, the Brazilian elite followed a pattern of behaviour by which their earnings from economic activities were compulsively converted into sterile investments, completely marginal to the logic of expanded capital reproduction. In a study on the behaviour of the mercantile elite of Rio de Janeiro for the fifty years between 1790 and 1840, João Luis Fragoso and Manolo Florentino showed how income from agricultural exports was converted into urban real estate, or into means of generating revenues other than production industry.[46] In other words,

46. João Luis Fragoso and Manolo Florentino, *O arcaísmo como projeto: mercado atlântico, sociedade agrária e elite mercantil no Rio de Janeiro, c.1790–c.1840* (Rio de Janeiro, 1993).

the sterilization of productive capital – or the pursuit of other ways of generating revenues outside the production sphere – reinforced the non-capitalist character of the production process.

That logic of reproduction of the mercantile elites calls to mind what was previously identified as the distinctive character of the "nobility of the land" who had settled the Portuguese colony in the Americas when sugar-cane planting was first adopted. The distinctive symbols of that social group, especially as they were deprived of noble lineage, were, first and foremost, the need not to work, especially not doing manual work, the ability to live within their means, and the capacity to occupy positions in public organizations, which guaranteed the exercise of political power. It is interesting, incidentally, to see how the undercurrents of work relationships still set the guidelines for the behaviour of important elements of the Brazilian elite even in times of great transformation, such as the beginning of the nineteenth century. The pattern of their behaviour can be seen as the complement to a work ethic that preserved slave labour and at the same time devalued the direct worker, encouraging the "ennobling" behaviour of the elites while promoting a workless lifestyle, the ultimate aim of those who longed to ascend the social ladder.

IRSH 56 (2011), Special Issue, pp. 297–318 doi:10.1017/S0020859011000472
© 2011 Internationaal Instituut voor Sociale Geschiedenis

Free and Unfree Labour in the Colonial Andes in the Sixteenth and Seventeenth Centuries

RAQUEL GIL MONTERO

*Instituto Superior de Estudios Sociales (CONICET-UNT),
Tucumán*

E-mail: raquelgilmontero@gmail.com

SUMMARY: This article analyses free and unfree labour in mining centres in the Andes during early Spanish colonial times. It focuses on two themes: the condition of indigenous or "native" people as "free labourers", and the *mita* system of unfree labour. For that purpose I shall consider the cases of Potosí, the most important mining centre in the Andes, and San Antonio del Nuevo Mundo in southern Bolivia, a large mine unaffected by the *mita* system of labour obligations.

In 1977 I observed a ceremony during the San Bartolomé fiesta (24 August) when people remembered how the mitayos had joined the day after going to Potosí. One mounted "mitayo" brought "documents" in his hat, and the people told me that they were remembering how their ancestors had gone away to earn the rights to their land, "eating earth in the processing mills" of Potosí.[1]

The conquest of the Americas coincided with a period of European demographic expansion and changes in the technology of warfare that demanded – among other things – an increase in the production of metals.[2] Mining was one of the most important activities in the New World, and it began, as did the history of indigenous labour in the Andes, almost immediately after the arrival of the Spaniards and their conquests in the early 1530s, when they started to exploit old mining centres belonging to the former rulers, the Incas, and to look for new ones.

In the Andes, the indigenous populations were the principal labour force because of their numbers and because silver mining, the most significant economic activity in the region during colonial times, took place in

---

1. Tristan Platt, "Tributo y ciudadanía en Potosí, Bolivia. Consentimiento y libertad entre los ayllus de la Provincia de Porco, 1830–1840", *Anuario de Estudios Bolivianos, Archivísticos y Bibliográficos*, 12 (2008), pp. 331–395, 385, n. 57 (my translation).
2. Hans-Joachim Kraschewski, *Betriebsablauf und Arbeitsverfassung des Goslarer Bergbaus am Rammelsberg vom 16. bis zum 18. Jahrhundert* (Bochum, 2002), pp. 13–14; Julio Sánchez Gómez, *De minería, metalúrgica y comercio de metales*, 2 vols (Salamanca, 1989), I, p. 91.

298 Raquel Gil Montero

the arid upland territories they inhabited. Silver mining required a complex organization, and supplies of food, wood, salt, clothes, and other goods had to be brought in over vast distances. Some old traditional mines such as Porco or Carabaya were surrendered to the Spaniards in the early years; others were kept secret, at a time considered by many historians as turbulent and violent.

The principal event that changed the history of mining in the Andes in colonial times was the "discovery" of Potosí in 1545. During its silver boom, Potosí accounted for 90 per cent of the silver output of the Peruvian Vice-royalty.[3] Three steps were important in making Potosí such a centre: the organization of labour, improvements in technology, and the supply of mercury.

The main coordinator of the mining system was Francisco de Toledo (1515–1582), the Viceroy of Peru from 1569 to 1581. In order to provide a stable allocation of labour for the mines every year, he created the so-called *mita* system. The Potosí *mita* was a state-coordinated form of draft labour, organized in the 1570s, whereby communities belonging to sixteen provinces throughout the region were obliged to send a designated number of workers (men aged between eighteen and fifty) to work for specific mining concerns. The *mita* system was originally devised by the Incas, but the Spanish, particularly under Viceroy Francisco de Toledo in the 1570s, adapted and expanded it to serve the needs of the mining economy. There were also other *mitas*, not concerned with mining, but they were less important than the system under discussion here.[4]

Mines in the Andes were located mostly in territories where mining activity had been present before the Spaniards came and where there were significant populations, important differences from the case of most of the mines in Mexico, which was the other important mining centre during colonial times.[5] The Spanish, however, considered the high regions to be isolated deserts, mostly because of the absence of trees and agriculture. In 1585, Capoche wrote about Potosí: "It is situated in cold, snow-covered, sterile, fruitless and almost uninhabitable high lands. Because of its bad temperament [i.e. climate] [...] no sustenance grows there but some potatoes."[6]

3. Enrique Tandeter, "Los ciclos de la minería de metales preciosos: Hispanoamérica", in *idem* and Jorge Hidalgo Lehuedé (eds), *Historia general de América Latina*, IV: *Procesos americanos hacia la redefinición colonial* (Madrid, 2000), pp. 127–148.
4. The three most important books on the Potosí *mita*, which explain its characteristics and evolution, are Peter Bakewell, *Miners of the Red Mountain: Indian Labour in Potosí, 1545–1650* (Albuquerque, NM, 1984); Jeffrey A. Cole, *The Potosí Mita, 1573–1700: Compulsory Indian Labor in the Andes* (Stanford, CA, 1985); and Enrique Tandeter, *Coacción y mercado. La minería de la plata en el Potosí colonial, 1692–1826* (Buenos Aires, 1992).
5. Peter Bakewell, *Minería y sociedad en el México colonial. Zacatecas (1546–1700)* (Mexico City, 1976); Carmen Salazar-Soler, "'Quilcar los indios': a propósito del vocabulario minero andino de los siglos XVI y XVII", in Ana María Lorandi *et al.* (eds), *Los Andes, cincuenta años después (1953–2003). Homenaje a John Murra* (Lima, 2003), pp. 281–315.
6. Luis Capoche, *Relación general de la Villa Imperial de Potosí* [Biblioteca de Autores Españoles] (Madrid, 1959 [1585]), p. 75 (my translation).

Potosí grew rapidly as a result of mining and other commercial activities. The majority of its population were indigenous people who worked in the mines and processing mills, although, in spite of the importance of the *mita* system, the majority of the indigenous inhabitants were, if we can believe the sources, "free wage labourers". All indigenous men aged between eighteen and fifty had to pay tribute as vassals, sometimes to the Crown, sometimes to an individual Spaniard. What they paid as tribute changed over time, and the total amount included not only money, but also labour and goods.

Some communities too were obliged by Viceroy Toledo to adopt *mita* as a system of forced labour to help fund the initial investments in the new amalgam technology. Some Indians went to the mines to fulfil their *mita* obligation by working there, and their wages were assessed at a figure below market value, but others went there as free labourers. Most tribute was valued in silver or money, and therefore working in the mines at market-rate wages to earn the money to pay the tribute was more advantageous than rendering the service directly in the form of labour.

Because of the *mita* system, forced labour in Potosí was, and is, at the centre of the discussion among historians about mining activity in the Andes, and *mita* has been considered the worst example of forced labour ever since the struggle for independence. However, in a recent article, Tristan Platt qualified it as a system of "voluntary unfree labour". Although *mitayos* were obliged to go to mining sites, some historians, including Platt, argue that the natives had an opportunity to negotiate because the Spaniards required the approval of the local native authorities. Platt adds that fulfilling the terms of *mita* meant receiving benefits, in a kind of reciprocity pact between the Spanish and the natives. In the epigraph to his article, Platt describes a contemporary representation of the "colonial pact" that existed in what is now northern Potosí, a reference to the past origins of the institution of the *mita* system. In many of his studies Platt stresses the fact that the indigenous people had a changing capacity for making deals based on their autonomy and relative power, even in the most coercive colonial situations. Tandeter found other examples of the "colonial pact" from the beginning of the nineteenth century in Oruro (see Figure 1).[7]

COLONIAL MINING AND POPULATION IN MODERN-DAY BOLIVIA

Throughout the early colonial period it was the mining economy that fuelled population growth in territories regarded by the Spanish as infertile and dry. Such growth was possible because of large-scale immigration to mining

7. Tandeter, *Coacción y mercado*, p. 32.

Figure 1. Andes cities and mines during the seventeenth century.
Natural Earth (www.naturalearthdata.com), August 2010

centres by labourers from all corners of the Peruvian viceroyalty. The labouring population needed to be fed and kept supplied, and the people who brought the provisions – often from very distant places – also added to the population. In his *Natural and Moral History of the Indies*, Father Acosta noted:

> In very harsh lands, dry, and infertile, with very high mountains, sharp crevasses, and very inhospitable, gold and mercury mines were established, and there also took place the washing and processing of gold. All this wealth was destined to go to Spain. After the discovery of the West Indies, other similar harsh, laborious, infertile, and barren places were occupied for such purposes. It was the love of money that made such places liveable, rich, and populous.[8]

In Bolivia today, this dry highland is called the *altiplano* and was conquered by the Incas before the Spaniards went there. In 1535 a small group of Spaniards, followed by some native authorities (Incas and other ethnic groups), together with many indigenous warriors, crossed the

8. José Acosta, *Historia Natural y moral de las indias* (Mexico City, 2006 [1589]), p. 161 (my translation).

highlands in the direction of Chile. The traditional historiography relates that everything was accomplished by only a small group of Spaniards. Everything about them is recorded: their names, numbers, weapons, and what finally became of them. In recent years, however, the role of indigenous allies and authorities has been emphasized more and more, and so have their different strategies. Diego de Almagro, for example, went to Chile with very important Inca authorities. They mobilized thousands of warriors, and on their way south concluded peace agreements with other authorities. The locals were also able to reveal, or not to reveal, to the Spaniards the sites of mines and other riches.[9]

The name of the province Almagro crossed was Charcas, the major part of what is now Bolivia and the most important mining district during Inca and pre-Inca times, but his group turned south, not knowing that they were leaving such wealth behind. It was not until 1538 that Paullu Inca and a number of other indigenous authorities decided to reveal to the Spaniards the Inca mine in Porco (see Figure 1).[10]

Potosí on the other hand was "discovered" only in 1545. The official Spanish history tells that it was a desert and that the find was made by Diego Guallpa, a "servant". He lost a llama and had to stay overnight in Potosí, where he happened upon the silver quite by chance.[11] Recent studies show that the location was known to the Incas and to the pre-Inca population and that the region was inhabited. By September 1545 there were 170 Spaniards and 3,000 Indians settled at the foot of the Potosí mountain, writes Cook.[12] Within just two years, there were around 2,500 houses and 14,000 inhabitants. In the beginning, the exploitation of the mines was based on native technology, but adapted to the colonial scale of production. The refining process, too, was carried out using native practices, with wind furnaces (*huayras*) placed at the top of the mountain.

As already mentioned, the early colonial years were turbulent: the Spanish arrived in the midst of a civil war between two Inca descendants vying with one another to rule the empire and started a merciless war of conquest which was itself followed by a Spanish civil war. There is an important and still ongoing discussion about the demographic transformation

9. Medinaceli Ximena and Arze Silvia, "Los mallkus de Charkas. Redes de poder en el norte de Potosí (siglos XVI y XVII)", *Estudios Bolivianos*, 2 (1996), pp. 283–319.
10. Tristan Platt and Pablo Quisbert, "Tras las huellas del silencio. Potosí, los Incas y el Virrey Toledo", *Anuario de Estudios Bolivianos, Archivísticos y Bibliográficos*, 12 (2008), pp. 389–428.
11. There are at least two versions of the discovery, and the bibliography is very large. See, for example, Julio Lucas Jaimes, *La Villa imperial de Potosí, su historia anecdótica, sus tradiciones y leyendas fantásticas. Su grandeza y opulencia fabulosas* (Buenos Aires, 1905), pp. 1–6; and Pedro Vicente Cañete, *Historia Física y Política de la Provincia de Potosí*, with an introduction and notes by Gunnar Mendoza (La Paz, 1952 [1797]), I, pp. 49–51.
12. Noble David Cook, *Demographic Collapse: Indian Peru, 1520–1620* (Cambridge, 1981), p. 236.

in the Andes, referring to factors such as civil war, violence, conquest, and epidemics.[13] Although information is scarce for the first few decades, specialists agree on the rhythm of the dramatic decrease in population.

The Spaniards began their domination in Cuzco – the Inca's capital city – where they settled in 1535, and two years later they moved to Lima. In the 1540s they organized the first royal inspection (*visita*) in order to collect information about the Andean population and resources; such inspections were repeated from time to time. Based on those sources, scholars believe that the worst period of the demographic downturn was after the Toledo reforms of the late 1570s.[14] In spite of the devastating effects of the wars and epidemics, the most important factors affecting the native population seem to have been the forced recruitment of labour and the organization of indigenous villages, called *repartimientos*. The latter were new towns where the native population were forced to live, established in order to control, indoctrinate, and tax them more efficiently. According to Cook, the first "universal plague" arrived in Cuzco in 1585 (measles and smallpox).[15] The forced concentration and migration favoured the spread of such epidemics.

What happened in Charcas is important for the discussion of the demographic decline because Potosí, the main gathering place for all migrants, lay in that province. The recorded diminution of the tribute-paying population does not mean that the native population necessarily shrank at the same pace, as was assumed by earlier research. During the reforms implemented by Viceroy Toledo, many tributaries (in the Latin American historiography, tributaries were indigenous people obliged to pay tribute) began to migrate and their tributary status changed. Another fundamental process for the history of the Americas, the mixing of ethnic groups in the so-called *mestizaje*, started at the same time. Of course, such new considerations do not mean that demographic decline did not take place. What is at the centre of the discussion nowadays is its intensity and geographical setting.

Summing up the main facts affecting the native population in what is now Bolivia, we should mention migration, a significant increase in mortality rates, changes in tributary status, urbanization around mining

13. *Ibid.*, p. 247, speaks about collapse as a process taking place along the Pacific desert strip and in the low-lying areas of the northern highlands; according to him, the highlands proper experienced a less pronounced downward spiral.
14. Franklin Pease and Frank Moya Pons (eds), *Historia General de América Latina*, II: *El primer contacto y la formación de nuevas sociedades*, p. 162. This is not, however, the opinion of other scholars, such as Assadourian. See Carlos Sempat Assadourian, "'La gran vejación y destruición de la tierra': las guerras de sucesión y conquista en el derrumbe de la población indígena del Perú", in *idem, Transiciones hacia el sistema colonial andino* (Lima, 1994), pp. 19–62.
15. Noble David Cook, "Epidemias y dinámica demográfica", in Pease and Moya Pons, *El primer contacto*, pp. 301–318.

centres, and the mixing of ethnic groups. The principal causes of all of that can be found in the organization of tribute and labour.

COLONIAL TRIBUTES AND LABOUR

Tribute received from indigenous people were considered to be "personal tribute" payable by all "free vassals" of the Crown of Castile, men between the ages of eighteen and fifty.[16] At first, the Crown ceded the right to collect this tribute to a number of individual Spaniards, the so-called *encomenderos*, in recompense for their services. The Spanish obliged Indians to pay them in goods, silver, or personal services.

Did tribute exist during pre-Hispanic times? John Murra – probably the best-known specialist in central Andean history – believes that it did not. According to him, people owed the Incas principally "energy" for work and only some "crude" goods, in the sense meant by Claude Lévi-Strauss, that is: honey, feathers, fish, and eggs gathered from wild birds.[17] In the early royal inspections, however, the natives asserted that they gave the Incas "crude" and also "processed" goods, including textiles, llamas, and wool, and, most importantly, that they provided labour for agriculture, mining, warfare, and herding; they might also provide persons, women, servants, and local individuals for sacrifice. The Incas assumed the power to demand such services, and the Spanish too later began to ask for labour in line with their own needs, namely for cultivation, transport, and working in the mines. There was continuity with the Inca system, but some data suggest that the Spanish asked for a wider range of goods as well, and almost all testimonies agree that there was practically no limit to their demands.

Under the rule of Viceroy Pedro de la Gasca (1546–1550), the colonial authorities began to regulate the tribute imposed on the natives. It is interesting to note that, in many cases during that period of government, tribute was the result of negotiation, because tribute is stable and profitable only if tributaries are able to pay it. As far as we know from Spanish texts, the native inhabitants told the authorities that they had not been consulted during the inspection carried out by the Spanish official, Ortiz de Zúñiga.[18] Some of the indigenous authorities claimed that "they were visited and counted and the tributes valued, but without their opinion or

---

16. Ronald Escobedo Mansilla, *El tributo indígena en el Perú (siglos XVI–XVII)* (Pamplona, 1979), p. 22. In some periods and regions, all married men or men between the age of fifteen and fifty were liable.

17. John Murra, "¿Existieron el tributo y los mercados en los Andes antes de la invasión europea?", in *idem, El mundo andino. Población, medio ambiente y economía* (Lima, 2002), pp. 237–247. "Crude" products were natural products usually gathered by young people. Murra also proposed that there were different norms that ruled natural and processed goods.

18. Carlos Sempat Assadourian, "La renta de la encomienda en la década de 1550: piedad cristiana y desconstrucción", in *idem, Transiciones hacia el sistema colonial andino*, pp. 171–208.

approval having been requested".[19] The complaints also stressed the difference between paying in labour and paying in goods, demanding that the latter be reduced.

One can see a transition from one kind of payment to the other and, in the second category, a shift to payments of money, which obliged the locals to work to obtain the money to fulfil their obligations. Moreover, such protests show that the indigenous people expected that they should have the option to negotiate, and that they resented having their bargaining position weakened. According to the value of the tribute assigned by La Gasca, the natives of the Andes had to pay the highest rate in the Spanish overseas territories, amounting to 5–6 pesos, while in New Spain (Mexico) the natives paid the equivalent of 2 silver pesos, and in the Philippines less than 1 peso.

In his negotiations with private Spanish entrepreneurs, La Gasca was unable to discuss the mining labour organized by the first generation of entrepreneurs,[20] for his mission was to reconcile the needs of private mining speculators with those of the Crown, rather than to protect the indigenous population. The native people of Charcas wanted to contribute using silver and not other goods, and they wanted to go to Potosí to work in the mines there, rather than in "mines" in general. In the early days of Potosí, where processing was dependent on native furnaces, the indigenous people had some degree of control over silver production and could earn more money.

A royal inspection organized a few years after this first assessment and before the introduction of the *mita* system allows us to describe the labour provided by the native people for the conquerors. The natives living in Chucuito, the Lupaqa, were in a singular position within the Peruvian context because they were one of the few groups who managed to pay tribute directly to the Crown and not to Spanish individuals (the *encomenderos*). The witnesses interviewed for the royal inspection affirmed that under the Incas, who had conquered them some years before the Spaniards came, the Lupaqa had to provide tribute in the form of men for military service, women as concubines and mistresses, boys and girls for sacrifice, artisans to work in Cuzco, a workforce for the gold and silver mines, tribute in the form of clothes and food (such as potatoes, *quinua* grain, and llamas), "crude" goods such as feathers and fish, as well as to maintain local places of refuge, where travellers could obtain food, shelter, and rest for themselves and their animals.[21]

---

19. Iñigo Ortiz de Zúñiga, *Visita de la provincia de Huánuco en 1562* (Lima, 1967–1972), p. 43; quoted in Assadourian, "La renta de la encomienda", p. 171.
20. Conquest and mining were private initiatives. The Crown gave private entrepreneurs labour, land, and tributes to encourage them to engage in conquest and invest in technology.
21. *Visita hecha a la provincia de Chucuito por Garci Diez de San Miguel en el año 1567*, palaeographic version by Waldemar Espinoza Soriano (Lima, 1964).

Tribute demands under the Spanish amounted to an annual payment of 18,000 pesos and 1,000 items of clothing, plus various kinds of labour service. The Lupaqa organized themselves to collect the money and clothes. Part of the money was acquired through an allotment of mine-workers for Potosí (in 1567, for example, 500 workers were sent to the silver mine and, in 1578 – that is, after Toledo's reforms – 2,000 from almost 15,000 domestic units). They also rented themselves and their animals for transport, sold llamas or wood, and worked as journeymen. Workers were paid for their labour in silver, with which they could pay all, or almost all, of the tribute to the Spanish.

They owed labour service to Spanish officials, including local gover-nors, Church officials, and other local and regional elites. Labour was required for service in hostels for travellers, and building and maintenance of churches, providing the money and goods for religious festivals and holidays, and the workers carried out domestic work in the houses of the Spanish elite and tended their animals. According to witnesses of the royal inspection in Chucuito, during Inca times the subject indigenous people had to pay tribute mostly in labour and a few goods, though women and children were also in demand.

What then was the difference with the Spanish? As some indigenous authorities told the royal officers, the Spanish had no limits to their demands, although they had to negotiate with ethnic authorities, and they centred their desire on silver and textiles. The natives were also obliged to provide personal services, and not only to the royal authorities but to other Spaniards as well, for example to travellers.

At the time of the royal inspection in the late 1560s, the concept of the New World as a territory based on its economic utility to the Crown became concrete policy. It identified the usefulness to Castile with what was fair for the indigenous people. The policy was put into action by the following two viceroys for Peru and New Spain: Francisco de Toledo and Martín Enriquez.[22] The Crown asked for money ("money, money, coins, coins", said Enriquez)[23] and that implied an emphasis on the production of silver and the greatest possible extension of forced labour systems.

The process took place simultaneously with the degradation of the power of religious orders. Toledo made a new assessment of the tribute, but the most important reforms were the reorganization of the indigenous population into *repartimiento* towns to facilitate a better administration of labour and tribute, and the organization of the *mita* system. In the early 1570s the Church started to complain, but the necessity to the Crown of

22. Carlos Sempat Assadourian, "Acerca del cambio en la naturaleza del dominio sobre las Indias: la mita minera del Virrey Toledo, documentos de 1568–1571", *Anuario de Estudios Americanos*, 46 (1989), pp. 3–70.
23. *Ibid.*, p. 6.

the miners drowned out the clergy's voices. At the same time, the *enco-menderos* began to lose their power, and after the reforms tributes were payable to the Crown. The *encomienda* system weakened in the Andes, and after several decades only other kinds of tribute remained.

FREE AND UNFREE LABOUR IN POTOSÍ

At the beginning of the exploitation of Potosí, the Spanish miners took advantage of native technology and knowledge, which was of course adapted to the extreme conditions of mining in the Andes. Almost all the mines were at high altitude, where there is very little, if any, combustible material. The native ovens used to smelt the ores used different kinds of local grasses, such as *ichu*, a native form of hay that can be harvested every two years, or other vegetation, and during the first few decades Potosí was crowded with such ovens. The Spaniards also used the locals to look for mines, to extract and transport ores, and to carry out all the steps needed in processing the metals.

Until Toledo, labour organization was based on two kinds of worker: *indios de encomienda* and *yanaconas*. The first were subject to individual Spaniards, were obliged to pay them tribute in the form of services or goods, and worked at unskilled tasks in the mines; the latter also worked for the Spaniards as a kind of servant, working as specialized artisans in Potosí. Almost all processes, from the extraction of the minerals to the smelting of the metals, were performed by indigenous people.

In the early 1570s production decreased at Potosí. The rich ores that had permitted traditional indigenous techniques to be used had already become scarcer by the 1560s, but over the following decades a combined change in technology and better organization of the workforce led to a unique boom in silver production. On the technological side, the adaptation of a method of cold amalgam suitable for the quality of ores found in Potosí, the discovery of the Huancavelica mercury mine in Peru (Figure 1), and the solving of various problems concerning those innovations, such as water management and the construction of mills for a different scale of production, allowed the mining centre to increase production to its highest level during colonial times (see Figure 3 below). The new technology did not completely replace the old methods, but it became dominant. The boom augmented the demand for workers, and it was against that background that Viceroy Francisco de Toledo organized the renewed *mita* system, based on an earlier indigenous institution.[24]

According to Murra, the *mita* during the Inca period entailed that a proportion of the domestic units in a community had to provide their labour for a fixed period, during which they had to carry out a range of

---

24. Cook, *Demographic Collapse*, especially ch. 12, "Mining and Population in the Central Sierra".

tasks such as repairing and building roads or bridges, tending the animals destined for public or religious use, working in the mines or in agriculture, and participating in military campaigns.[25] Some local authorities too had the right to use labour from their own communities.

Viceroy Toledo adapted the idea of the *mita* system and organized an annual forced migration to Potosí during the 1570s. In 1578 it was decided that more than 14,000 natives and their families would be required to work in the mines for a wage set below the market rate. Under the system, every year a proportion of the adult male native population from designated towns had to go to Potosí. They took their families with them and used the "wages" earned by all of them mostly to pay their adult male tribute obligations. The system served too as a method for Toledo to encourage Spanish entrepreneurs to invest in new technology in the course of the construction of the mills. They were given the *mita* workers, unskilled forced labourers who received a lower wage than free labourers, and in return the Spanish entrepreneurs had to build the mills, artificial lakes for water management, and the rest of the necessary infrastructure. The system was thought of as a temporary solution, but it lasted until independence (1825).[26]

The new mining and metallurgical processes were rather complex and increased the necessity for the division of labour. Ore was extracted from mine galleries and taken to a location where labourers broke it up to facilitate its removal from the mine. Other workers were on hand to separate useful material from waste.[27] All tasks except portering were performed by free workers. Llamas or mules were used to transport ore to the mills, where another gang of *mitayos* loaded it into the machinery. The next process, amalgamation, was then tackled by free labourers.

A description of Potosí from 1603 details part of the labour system.[28] There were around 58,800 Indians working in Potosí (almost 20 per cent of the total indigenous population from Charcas and La Paz included in the Toledo inspection). Only 5,100 of the total Indian labour force were *mitayos*, 10,500 were *mingas* (contracted workers), and 43,200 free wage earners. Although the *mitayos* numbered fewer than 10 per cent, they were important to the mining economy: they had to perform tasks that others did not want to do, and for a lower wage.[29]

---

25. Murra, "¿Existieron el tributo y los mercados?", pp. 237–247.
26. Cole, *The Potosí Mita*, ch. 1.
27. The description in Tandeter, *Coacción y mercado*, p. 16.
28. "Descripción de Potosí", in Silvio Zavala, *El servicio personal de los indios en el Perú. Extractos del siglo XVII* (Mexico City, 1979), II, pp. 16–25.
29. The number of *mita* labourers is still being debated by scholars because there are few concrete sources, but also because many of the *mitayos* worked as free labourers during the weeks they had for rest. The figures taken from the 1603 description of Potosí are for discussion purposes only.

Table 1. *Description of Potosí and its mines, 1603.*[30]

Indigenous people	Task	Numbers
Repartimientos	Working in mines	4,000
Mingas	Being "rented"	600
Boys	Cleaning metal	400
	Looking for metal on the surface	1,000
Repartimientos	In processing mills	600
Mingas	In processing mills	4,000
Indigenous (men and women)	Working with llamas	3,000
	Transporting metals on llamas	320
Repartimientos	Looking for salt and bringing it to Potosí	180
Mingas	Bringing salt	1,000
Merchants	Selling wood	1,000
Indigenous (men and women)	Carrying fuel	1,000
	Carrying *cocha* (llama excrement)	500
Indigenous (men and women)	Gathering llama excrement, also used as a fuel	200
	Making and carrying coal	1,000
	Making candles	200
	Carrying food and other goods	10,000
Total		29,000

Source: "Descripción de Potosí", in Zavala, *El servicio personal de los indios en el Perú*, II, pp. 16–25.

One of the worst jobs in the mines was removing the ore. The *mitayos* had to climb up and down in the mines using ladders, transporting 45 kilograms in each sack of ore at a quota rate of 25 sacks a day. Rodrigo de Loaisa, a Spanish cleric living in Potosí, noted in 1586: "If twenty healthy Indians enter on Monday, half may emerge crippled on Sunday".[31] Some of the tasks fulfilled by the labourers were related in the above description of Potosí. This description included other workers in Potosí, apart from those working directly in mines or processing mills.

Table 1 shows the proportion of free and unfree labourers working in the mines and mills, and the general tasks performed by all the workers there. As we can see in Tables 1 and 2, workers comprised not only tributaries (men aged between eighteen and fifty) but also women and children, whose presence reinforces the idea that the indigenous people were working to earn the money to pay tribute and not only as "free labourers". That whole families worked in the mine implies, first, that tribute was not considered an individual obligation and, second, that it was difficult to fulfil, which meant that tributaries needed assistance.

30. In constructing this table I have retained the terminology of the original text.
31. Cook, *Demographic Collapse*, p. 238.

Table 2. *Other workers, Potosí 1603.*

Workers	Task	Numbers
Women (indigenous)	Prostitution	"A large number"
Women (of a higher social status)	Prostitution	120
Women	Washing clothes	100 "houses"
Men	Miners	"More than 100"
Indigenous	Herding llamas	312

Source: "Descripción de Potosí", in Zavala, *El servicio personal de los indios en el Perú*, II, p. 26.

Working in the mines of Potosí was just one component of the labour provided by the indigenous population. The journey started in their settlements, where all *mitayos* joined up to go to the mines. In 1603 Alfonso Messia, a Spaniard who encountered such a group on his way to Potosí, described the impact of the Potosí *mita* on the inhabitants of Chucuito, where approximately 2,200 *mitayos* left each year, taking their wives and children with them. They had to travel 480 kilometres from the coast of Lake Titicaca to Potosí, which took them about two months:

> I have twice seen them and can report that there must be 7,000 souls. Each Indian takes at least eight or ten llamas and a few alpacas to eat. On these they transport their food, maize and chuño [dried potatoes], sleeping rugs and straw pallets to protect them from the cold, which is severe, for they always sleep on the ground. All this cattle normally exceeds 30,000 head. [...] Only some two thousand people return: of the other five thousand some die and others stay at Potosí or the nearby valleys because they have no cattle for the return journey.[32]

Potosí was the unrivalled centre of the Spanish Empire in South America. Yet, there were a great many smaller mines, and one can suppose that the labour systems varied according to circumstances. How was the work organized in those mines where the *mita* did not exist? The case of San Antonio del Nuevo Mundo in the province of Lípez allows us to expand our view and to analyse free labour.

SAN ANTONIO DEL NUEVO MUNDO: "FREE LABOUR"

Lípez is situated in the southernmost Bolivian highlands, bordering the international frontier with Chile and Argentina to the west and south. South-east Lípez, which in the seventeenth century had a mining centre

---

32. Alfonso Messia, "Memorial sobre las cédulas de servicio personal de los indios (c.1600)", in *Colección de documentos inéditos relativos al descubrimiento, conquista y colonización de las posesiones españolas en América y Oceanía*, VI (Madrid, 1886), pp. 140–142, quoted in Cook, *Demographic Collapse*, pp. 242–243.

called San Antonio del Nuevo Mundo (Figure 1), is too cold and dry
for the development of any economically significant agriculture. This led
to pastoral specialization and a strong tendency among its inhabitants to
link up with farming communities from other regions, mainly but not
exclusively through caravan traffic. Emphasis on herding results in
smaller populations with dispersed settlement patterns and high seasonal
mobility.

San Antonio del Nuevo Mundo is situated in the most hostile part of
López, the south-east, at 4,500 metres above sea level. In 1602–1603, at the
time of the first royal inspection, there was just a small population of
herders living there, but eighty years later, during a new and important
colonial inspection, almost all the population from López, both north and
south, were living in San Antonio. When asked why they had come to live
there, those interviewed unfailingly answered that it was because their
native towns were "sterile" and because this new place offered them better
opportunities for work.

The mines of San Antonio were exploited only for a century, and
occasionally later on, but on a smaller scale, and after its silver boom
almost everybody went to live elsewhere. Historical research on this
mining centre is still in progress and there is still very little known about
its early days in the 1640s.[33] However, we can be certain that in 1683 more
than 2,000 indigenous people were working there at the time of the
inspection.

There are at least two different kinds of source for the analysis of labour
relations in the mine: the royal inspections, and legal records. There were
two royal inspections related to San Antonio which inform us about the
indigenous labour world, one in 1683 and the other in 1689. Based on
their data, we can assert that many of the indigenous workers in the mines
came from other regions, mostly from the Bolivian highlands (the *"mita*
area" – see Figure 2). They transported salt, firewood, and ore. Almost all
of them maintained links with their communities of origin and with the
governor there, to whom they were still paying taxes. As an example, the
following is one answer given by the Indians of Paria during the
inspection of 1683:

> I asked them why they had left their provinces to come to this town, and how
> long they had been living here, and they answered that because their land was
> very sterile, providing no possibility to grow food to live on, nor pastures for
> their animals, and that is the reason why they have moved to this settlement to
> work in the mines and mineral refinery of this area and to others to carry metals,
> firewood, and salt to refine the metals, and it has been for twenty years that

33. Peter Bakewell, *Plata y empresa en el Potosí del siglo XVII. La vida y época de Antonio López de Quiroga* (Pontevedra, 1988).

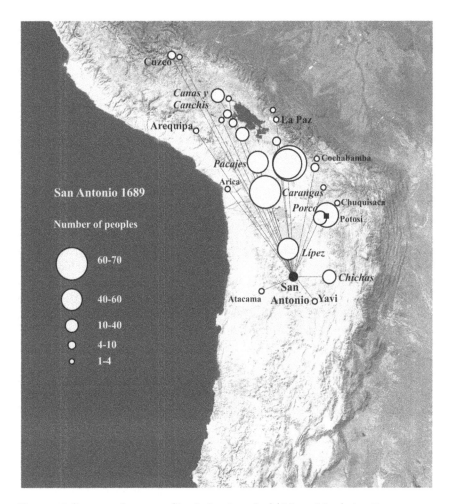

Figure 2. Indigenous migrants working in San Antonio del Nuevo Mundo in 1689.
NASA. Population source: AGN 13-23-10-2

some of them live in this province, and others for the last eight years, and that they pay taxes to their *curacas* [ethnic authorities] and that they all belong to the Potosí *mita* where they pay in cash or in labour.[34]

The royal inspection shows that an important part of the indigenous mining population came from different places, some of them very distant. They were not *mitayos*: in theory they went to work there voluntarily.

34. Archivo General de la Nación Argentina [hereafter, AGN], Sala 13-18-6-5, Padrones de Potosí 1602–1683.

The inspection of 1683 focused on the mines; the second one, of 1689, provides us with a more complete picture of the region, since it takes into account the many other herders living nearby.[35] Both inspections point to a variegated indigenous population working the mines, stemming from different communities and trying to earn money.

Through the information provided by those sources we can grasp some aspects of the mining setting. The migrants went to San Antonio mostly with their families, and they stayed there many years. The majority were herders, since animals were used daily in all stages of the production process and to supply the town and mines. A few of them were muleteers from the Atacama Desert who came with goods and stayed there, or continued to work in transport. Mules were very expensive to feed in San Antonio, because of the poor grass and the extra food needed. The majority of the pack animals were llamas, and their herders were natives from many places in the highlands, including north Lípez. Llama herders were crucially important to this very high mine, with no agriculture and no vehicles.

In those years, the population of Lípez was living around the mining complex in the south-east and had virtually abandoned its old settlements to the north. Indigenous labourers were used directly in the mines as miners, and for transporting ore from the mines to the mills; then, more of them began actually to work in the mills. More still acted as porters, carrying food and everything else needed to survive and work at so great an altitude.

Legal records show a more heterogeneous population living in San Antonio. During the century when the mine was functioning, a town was constructed, and later a township closer to the mines, inhabited by people who wanted to take advantage of its location. In the township one might have encountered both Spaniards and *mestizos* trading in stolen silver, and others running illegal mills. There were general stores where indigenous people sold stolen tools in exchange for wine or other goods.[36] Slaves from Angola and the Congo were sold, owners being Spanish or Indian.[37] A flourishing economic life developed around the mines, and it attracted all sorts of labourers, and not only natives.

In a schematic synthesis we can conclude that many of the owners of mines and mills were Spanish, and so were some of the specialists, such as carpenters from Potosí who came to build the galleries, mercury traders, colonial authorities, and merchants. The natives on the other hand worked mostly in mines, mills, transport, in providing food to the miners,

35. Raquel Gil Montero, "Los pastores frente a la minería colonial temprana: Lípez en el siglo XVII", in Lautaro Nuñez and Axel Nielsen (eds), *Viajeros en ruta: arqueología, historia y etnografía del tráfico Surandino* (forthcoming).
36. Archivo y Bibliotecas Nacionales de Bolivia [hereafter, ABNB], Minas 59, San Antonio del Nuevo Mundo, 1686/1687.
37. ABNB, Escrituras Públicas, Tomo 137, fo. 104.

and in herding animals. Slaves were not really important in terms of numbers, and I have been unable to find any description of their duties.

For about a century, San Antonio was a mining centre created around important silver veins. During that time, in a territory 4,500 metres above sea level that had scarcely been inhabited before, thousands of labourers arrived and settled. Some came from very distant places, with their animals, and lived around the mines, in or near the town of San Antonio. There was no *mita* system in Lípez. Many of the migrants declared that they were *mitayos*, that they had previously worked under the Potosí *mita* system, or had worked for payment in silver. The silver they earned was necessary to pay tribute and other colonial obligations.

DISCUSSION

Enrique Tandeter shares Platt's view, cited at the beginning of this essay, that the *mita* was a colonial pact in which indigenous people played a significant role and had some scope to negotiate. However, this analysis focuses on a period during which the *mita* was different from that organized by Toledo. Although the number of *mitayos* decreased during that time, their proportion in relation to the total number of labourers rose. At the end of the colonial period, nearly half the labourers in Potosí were *mitayos* and the rest were free. As noted earlier, at the beginning of the seventeenth century about 10 per cent of workers were *mitayos*.[38] The *mita* system was much more important at times when production at Potosí was less profitable.

In many respects, the *mita* system changed over time, and the differences are important for analysing labour relations during the sixteenth and seventeenth centuries. Initially, Toledo granted mining entrepreneurs an allocation of a "labour rent".[39] Other than in the case of the Lupaqa people mentioned before, the individual colonialist entrepreneurs, not the representatives of the Spanish state, collected that rent as money or in kind. From the very beginning it was possible for the *mitayo* to fulfil his obligation in silver.

At first, Toledo allotted mining entrepreneurs a number of labourers for unskilled tasks and at low wages. They were a stimulus to the important investments needed for the changes required by the new amalgam technology. In time, and with the departure of so many *mitayos*, the possibility of fulfilling obligations in silver became more common, enabling an entrepreneur to pay other workers and replace the ever-increasing number of absentees. In the course of the second half of the seventeenth century, many

---

38. This proportion is difficult to determine exactly; it is more a case of what the documents suggest. There are no statistics.
39. Tandeter, *Coacción y mercado*, p. 18.

mining entrepreneurs made use of that possibility, which was sometimes considered more profitable than actually running the mines. Nonetheless, it did not become a general phenomenon and remained merely another way to oblige indigenous people to earn money.

The *mita* system has a further implication: in comparison with the old indigenous methods, the new system of amalgam-forming increased the need for a division of labour. Under the new system the *mitayos* performed the hardest and least specialized tasks for less money. So what was the difference between working in a mine to fulfil an obligation and working as a *mitayo*? Simply this: a free labourer could earn more money than a *mitayo*, and could obtain better paid work down the mines.

The *mita* system changed in quantitative terms too. In 1578, the fixed total of migrants was 14,181; in 1633, 12,354; in 1688, 5,658; and in 1692, 4,101. It is safe to assume that the reduction was a direct consequence of demographic decline. Between the two royal inspections, the first ordered by Viceroy Francisco de Toledo (1573) and the second by Viceroy Duke De La Palata (1683), the indigenous population of the highlands diminished by 45 per cent and migration increased. However, production at Potosí and the demand for labour also decreased strongly during the seventeenth century, while the *mita* allocation kept pace with production (see Figure 3 below).

The royal inspections and the collection of tributes in Potosí showed changes over time between different categories of tributary. The best known is the increase in migrants. Moreover, the number of *indios de encomiendas* decreased and that of *yanaconas* (that is, labourers separated from their communities and considered by many authors as servants of a kind) increased. A number of *yanaconas* had worked in Potosí right from the very beginning, as specialized artisans.

One finding of the royal inspection ordered by La Palata in 1683 is that in the province of Charcas almost half the indigenous people present were migrants.[40] The traditional explanation for the increase was that many left their communities to try to avoid the *mita*.[41] However, recent research

---

40. Nicolás Sanchez de Albornoz, *Indios y tributos en el Alto Perú* (Lima, 1978), p. 49.
41. The bibliography on these migrants is large. The first general study was that by Sanchez de Albornoz, *Indios y tributos en el Alto Perú*. During the next decade, several new interpretations contributed to a better understanding of the *forasteros*: Carlos Sempat Assadourian, "La organización económica espacial del sistema colonial", in *idem, El sistema de la economía colonial. El mercado interior, regiones y espacio económico* (Mexico City, 1983), pp. 255–306; Thierry Saignes, "Ayllus, mercado y coacción colonial: el reto de las migraciones internas en Charcas (siglo XVII)", in Olivia Harris, Brooke Larson, and Enrique Tandeter (eds), *La participación indigena en los Mercados Surandinos. Estrategias y reproducción social. Siglos XVI al XX* (La Paz, 1987), pp. 111–158; and Thierry Saignes, "Políticas étnicas en la Bolivia colonial. Siglos XVI–XIX", in *Indianidad, etnocidio e indigenismo en América Latina* (Mexico City, 1988), pp. 41–77. During the royal inspection of La Palata the authorities and the Viceroy himself thought that the *forasteros* wanted to avoid *mita* and tributes.

Figure 3. Silver production in Potosí (in pesos), 1545–1823, and *mita* allocations.
Silver production dataset in Richard Garner, Economic History Data Desk: Economic History of Latin America, United State and New World, 1500–1900, *downloaded from https:// home.comcast.net/~richardgarner05/tepaske.html. The* mita *allocation is taken from Tandeter,* Coacción y mercado, *pp. 39 and 40.*

shows that many migrants were working in different mines (following their discovery, and the silver boom), and that they were paying tribute and paying for the cost of their replacement under the *mita*, at least during the seventeenth century.[42] *Mitayos* and *yanaconas* were migrants, but there were also "free" indigenous migrants.

The term "migrant" included anyone who moved in search of work or to trade in the camps, but *mitayos* and *yanaconas* theoretically moved with the knowledge and on the orders of the Spanish Crown or of individual mining entrepreneurs, although other workers could migrate without official permission. During the seventeenth century people migrated chiefly because of colonial obligations, and most of them moved to the mines. Migration decreased in the eighteenth century.

After the Toledo reforms, the tribute of the *yanacona* was valued and they, or their landlords, were then obliged to pay it. The series of records of their payments, however, is incomplete: we have information for the periods 1574–1604 and 1660–1690. Taking into account only those years for which data exist, the *yanacona* were fewer than 10 per cent of all those obliged to pay tribute in the second half of the sixteenth century and

42. Ann Zulawsky, "Forasteros y yanaconas: la mano de obra de un centro minero en el siglo XVII", in Harris, Larson, and Tandeter, *La participación indigena*, pp. 159é192; Gil Montero, "Los pastores frente a la minería colonial temprana".

around 40 per cent in the second half of the seventeenth century. We can also regard the *yanaconas* who worked in the mining cities and paid tribute to the Crown after the Toledo reforms as "free labourers", similar to other tributaries who migrated to Potosí.

What can be proposed then on the basis of this information? According to the scholars previously quoted, during the early decades of the colonial period we observe an important change: *encomenderos* and other conquerors made people work for them without limits in almost all productive tasks – agriculture, construction, mining, and transport. The natives had to give them their labour "tribute" as part of an *encomienda*, and in Potosí specifically they worked mostly at unskilled tasks. There were also other labourers, the *yanaconas*, specialized servants who, while they worked for the Spanish, did so as skilled artisans at Potosí. The discussion of the nature of this tribute is still open: did the natives also have to give goods to the Spaniards? For Murra, that signifies an important difference: during Inca times the natives had to work for the conquerors, or to deliver both men and women to them, which was later interpreted as reciprocal labour, and not as tribute.[43]

An important change in relations between conquerors and subjects was the assignment of value to the tribute, which implied that the natives had to pay certain allocations of silver, or pesos, and some goods. They had other obligations too, such as personal services, to the Church, to civil authorities, and to Spanish travellers, to which can be added the *mita*, which was more complex than its Potosí counterpart. The "conversion" of tribute and *mita* into money induced the indigenous people to embark upon commercial activity in their attempts to obtain the means to pay tribute. The information contained in the royal inspection of San Antonio is very clear in this respect: all migrants went there to work, because there they could find a job to pay for their clothes, food, and their obligations.[44] Their statements show that working in the mines was not really voluntary. People from northern Lípez claimed that:

> [...] almost all men and women, and boys and girls, from this village of San Agustín de Chuica are working in San Antonio de Lípez, and in other places of this province, under the charge of different persons, some Spanish, some indigenous, and although they [native local authorities] insisted [to the owners of the mines] that those workers [indigenous tributaries] be allowed to come to the village during the inspection, they do not even come to the religious feasts that are in this month, and the *curacas* [native authorities] were offended when they tried to bring them out of San Antonio.[45]

There were also two important differences in mining tasks and organization in the period before and after Toledo's reforms. On the one hand,

43. Murra, "¿Existieron el tributo y los mercados?"
44. AGN, 13-18-6-5.
45. AGN, 13-23-10-2.

in Potosí the use of traditional technology allowed the natives to participate in all mining processes, whereas later, the amalgam method put the organization of the processes into the hands of the entrepreneurs, so that native people lost their agency. On the other hand, the organization of the *mita* system coincided with the end of the *encomiendas*. Although mining was a private enterprise, with the organization of the *mita* the Spanish Crown had the power to organize and distribute forced labour among the mines.

Moreover, it is essential to take the differing contexts into account. During the Toledo reforms, but especially afterwards, the indigenous population diminished significantly for many reasons, including conquest, wars, epidemics, the demands of the work, and migration. A relatively small number of Spaniards managed to conquer a huge territory, often with the support of indigenous authorities as important allies. Those authorities negotiated with the conquerors and were in a way the beneficiaries of many of the changes, and responsible for procuring tribute. Some indigenous societies participating in the *mita* system were stratified, such as the Lupaqa, and their authorities exerted considerable influence on their people. The links between many authorities and their subjects were strong and explain why the tribute system and the *mita* were honoured even when the subjects were far from their communities.

CONCLUSION

Although it is still difficult to state it with certainty, it seems that the changes to the labour system implied a rupture of community links, hence the increased numbers of *yanacona* servants, but also of migrants who changed their tributary status. There was an increased proportion of forced workers in the mines, because of the drop in production, a shift from personal services to tribute, and a better situation for indigenous negotiation, for by then people had more knowledge about the colonial system, and the Crown was more heavily dependent on tribute. That was the historical context that the people of Potosí were referring to when they recalled their past as *mitayos* in the late twentieth century – and which Platt described so vividly in the lines cited at the beginning of this essay.

During early colonial times, and principally in the first few decades, many indigenous people, not only the *mitayos*, were obliged to work in the mines. The need for labourers, especially after the Toledo reforms and the silver boom, implied that the colonial authorities were concerned with the organization of the labour market, but after the silver crisis fewer labourers were needed. All the changes occurred in a context of a steep decrease in the size of the population during the sixteenth and seventeenth centuries, and its recovery after the last epidemic in 1720.

Mining was also an opportunity for individuals to earn more money to fulfil their colonial obligations. For the *mitayos* it was more rewarding to pay for a replacement than to work in the mines. Contrary to the opinions of some viceroys, the majority of the indigenous people usually migrated precisely because of their obligations and not because they wished to avoid them. Speaking about "free labour" in a context of tribute, then, means only the possibility of choosing the place and the tasks to perform there, but is not really equivalent to any modern concept of a labour market.

The institution of the *mita* changed over the years and the concept varied with respect to unfree labour and tribute relations. A closer analysis of historical labour relations allows us to distinguish such faint traces. Considered in the long run, the era of the Toledo reforms in the 1570s, and the subsequent century, were the worst periods in terms of pressure on, and extraction from, the native population.

International Review of Social History
Published for the Internationaal Instituut voor Sociale Geschiedenis, Amsterdam

SUBSCRIPTIONS

International Review of Social History (ISSN 0020–8590) is published in three parts in April, August and December plus one special issue in December. Three parts plus one special issue form a volume. The subscription price (excluding VAT) of volume 56 (2011) which includes electronic access and delivery by air where appropriate is £160 net (US$273 in the USA, Canada and Mexico) for institutions; £48 net (US$78 in the USA, Canada and Mexico) for individuals ordering direct from the publisher and certifying that the journal is for their own personal use. Single parts and the special issue are £42.50 (US$72.50 in the USA, Canada and Mexico) plus postage. An electronic only price available to institutional subscribers is £136 (US$235 in USA, Canada and Mexico). EU subscribers (outside the UK) who are not registered for VAT should add VAT at their country's rate. VAT registered subscribers should provide their VAT registration number. Japanese prices for institutions are available from Kinokuniya Company Ltd, P.O. Box 55, Chitose, Tokyo 156, Japan.

Orders, which must be accompanied by payment, may be sent to a bookseller, subscription agent or direct to the publisher: Cambridge University Press, The Edinburgh Building, Shaftesbury Road, Cambridge CB2 8RU; or in the USA, Canada and Mexico: Cambridge University Press, Journals Fulfillment Department, 100 Brook Hill Drive, West Nyack, New York 10994–2133. Periodicals postage paid at New York, NY and at additional mailing offices. Postmaster: send address changes in USA, Canada and Mexico to International Review of Social History, Cambridge University Press, 100 Brook Hill Drive, West Nyack, New York 10994–2133.

Information on International Review of Social History and all other Cambridge journals can be accessed via journals.cambridge.org

GUIDELINES FOR CONTRIBUTORS

Manuscripts are considered for publication on the understanding that they are not currently under consideration elsewhere and that the material – in substance as well as form – has not been previously published. Two copies of the manuscript should be submitted. Each article should be accompanied by a summary, not exceeding 100 words, outlining the principal conclusions and methods in the context of currently accepted views on the subject. All material – including quotations and notes – must be double-spaced with generous margins. Use of dot-matrix printers is discouraged. Notes should be numbered consecutively and placed at the end of the text. Spelling should be consistent throughout (e.g. Labour and Labor are both acceptable, but only one of these forms should be used in an article). Turns of phrase using masculine forms as universals are not acceptable.

Sample citation forms

Book: E.P. Thompson, *The Making of the English Working Class* (London, 1963), pp. 320–322. Journal: Walter Galenson, "The Unionization of the American Steel Industry", *International Review of Social History*, 1 (1956), pp. 8–40. Detailed instructions for contributors are available from http://www.iisg.nl/irsh/irshstyl.php. Twenty-five free offprints of each article are provided, and authors may purchase additional copies provided these are ordered at proof stage.

For EU product safety concerns, contact us at Calle de José Abascal, 56–1°, 28003 Madrid, Spain or eugpsr@cambridge.org.

www.ingramcontent.com/pod-product-compliance
Ingram Content Group UK Ltd.
Pitfield, Milton Keynes, MK11 3LW, UK
UKHW020339140625
459647UK00018B/2227